Dynamics of Language Contact

English and Immigrant Languages

W9-AEU-256

The past decade has seen an unprecedented growth in the study of language contact, associated partly with the linguistic effects of globalization and increased migration all over the world. Written by a leading expert in the field, this new and much-needed account brings together disparate findings to examine the dynamics of contact between languages in an immigrant context.

Using data from a wide range of languages, including German, Dutch, Hungarian, Italian, Spanish, Croatian and Vietnamese, Michael Clyne discusses the dynamics of their contact with English. Clyne analyzes how and why these languages change in an immigration country like Australia, and asks why some languages survive longer than others. The book contains useful comparisons between immigrant vintages, generations, and between bilinguals and trilinguals.

An outstanding contribution to the study of language contact, this book will be welcomed by students and researchers in linguistics, bilingualism, the sociology of language and education.

MICHAEL CLYNE is Professorial Fellow in Linguistics and Director of the Research Unit for Multilingualism and Cross-Cultural Communication at the University of Melbourne. His books include *Language and Society in German-Speaking Countries* (Cambridge, 1984), *Community Languages: the Australian Experience* (Cambridge, 1991), *Pluricentric Languages* (1992), *The German Language in a Changing Europe* (Cambridge, 1995) and *Intercultural Communication at Work* (Cambridge, 1995).

Cambridge Approaches to Language Contact

General editor
SALIKOKO S. MUFWENE
University of Chicago

Editorial board
Robert Chaudenson, *Université d'Aix-en-Provence*
Braj Kachru, *University of Illinois at Urbana*
Lesley Milroy, *University of Michigan*
Shana Poplack, *University of Ottawa*
Michael Silverstein, *University of Chicago*

Cambridge Approaches to Language Contact is an interdisciplinary series
bringing together work on language contact from a diverse range of research
areas. The series focuses on key topics in the study of contact between
languages or dialects, including the development of pidgins and creoles,
language evolution and change, world Englishes, code-switching and
code-mixing, bilingualism and second language acquisition, borrowing,
interference, and convergence phenomena.

Published titles
Salikoko Mufwene, *The Ecology of Language Evolution*
Michael Clyne, *Dynamics of Language Contact*

Further titles planned for the series
Guy Bailey and Patricia Cukor-Avila, *The Development of
African-American English*
Maarten Mous, *Controlling Language*
Edgar Schneider, *Post-colonial Englishes*
Clancy Clements, *The Linguistic Legacy of Spanish and Portuguese*

Dynamics of Language Contact

English and Immigrant Languages

Michael Clyne

University of Melbourne

CAMBRIDGE
UNIVERSITY PRESS

PUBLISHED BY THE PRESS SYNDICATE OF THE UNIVERSITY OF CAMBRIDGE
The Pitt Building, Trumpington Street, Cambridge CB2 1RP, United Kingdom

CAMBRIDGE UNIVERSITY PRESS
The Edinburgh Building, Cambridge, CB2 2RU, UK
40 West 20th Street, New York, NY 10011-4211, USA
477 Williamstown Road, Port Melbourne, VIC 3207, Australia
Ruiz de Alarcón 13, 28014 Madrid, Spain
Dock House, The Waterfront, Cape Town 8001, South Africa

http://www.cambridge.org

© Michael Clyne 2003

This book is in copyright. Subject to statutory exception
and to the provisions of relevant collective licensing agreements,
no reproduction of any part may take place without
the written permission of Cambridge University Press.

First published 2003

Printed in the United Kingdom at the University Press, Cambridge

Typeface Times 10/12 pt   *System* LATEX 2$_\varepsilon$ [TB]

A catalogue record for this book is available from the British Library

ISBN 0 521 78136 1 hardback
ISBN 0 521 78648 7 paperback

Contents

Map and figures

Tables

Series editor's foreword

The series Approaches to Language Contact was set up to publish outstanding monographs on language contact, especially by authors who approach their specific subject matter from a diachronic or developmental perspective. Our goal is to integrate the ever-growing scholarship on language diversification (including the development of creoles, pidgins and indigenized varieties of colonial European languages), bilingual language development, code-switching and language endangerment. We hope to provide a select forum to scholars who contribute insightfully to understanding language evolution from an interdisciplinary perspective. We favour approaches that highlight the role of ecology and draw inspiration both from the authors' own fields of specialization and from related research areas in linguistics or other disciplines. Eclecticism is one of our mottos, as we endeavour to comprehend the complexity of evolutionary processes associated with contact.

We are very proud to add Michael Clyne's *Dynamics of Language Contact* to the ALC series. Focusing on Australia, and yet relating his findings to those of numerous other scholars on similar phenomena elsewhere, the author provides a most authoritative study on the impact of the dominant language (English in the present case) on other languages. This book is a meticulous documentation of language change under conditions of language shift, spanning several generations of immigrants from Europe, Asia and Latin America. It is a detailed analysis of historical, social and structural factors that bear differentially on how a language is affected by a dominant one, even when the systems are as closely related as are Dutch and German, and when, from the point of view of ethnicity and culture, their speakers can (for all practical purposes) be lumped in the same stock, as opposed to, for instance, the Vietnamese or the Chinese. The facilitating role of typological similarities and differences in both bilinguals and trilinguals are explored very insightfully, showing in a fascinating way that the role of language-internal factors during change under conditions of shift need not be subordinated to that of language-external ones. Yet, genetic linguistic differences do not account for structural erosion in ways that encourage easy, across-the-board predictions, thus corroborating the view that theories of evolution are more about explaining the past than predicting the future. In addition,

Michael Clyne makes a genuine effort to clarify concepts and terms that have become more and more confusing over the past few decades.

It would not be overly optimistic of me to predict that *Dynamics of Language Contact* will be seminal over the next few decades. The book is likely to spur comparisons of Australia and North America as Anglophone former settlement colonies, as well as studies intended to test several relevant hypotheses on other territories. This is another must-read for students of language contact in general, quite consistent with the ALC's ambition.

University of Chicago   SALIKOKO S. MUFWENE

Acknowledgments

As the data employed for this monograph was collected, transcribed and analyzed by and with the help of many others over several decades, it would be impossible to thank all those who deserve thanks, and I would like to express my gratitude to them collectively. My thanks also to the many colleagues whose writings and personal input have stimulated my ideas or caused me to modify them.

I would like to mention specifically a number of people who have helped with this project: those who have reanalyzed some of their data for me with certain issues in mind – Tuc Ho-Dac, Jim Hlavac and Lin Zheng; those who have assisted with the analysis of particular data – Marguerite Boland, Tibor Endrody, Paola Cassia, Sue Fernandez and especially Sandra Kipp; Alexandra Aikhenvald, Salikoko Mufwene and Sandra Kipp, who have generously given up their time to read and comment on the manuscript; those who have kindly read and advised me on sections of the manuscript – Kees de Bot, Pim Levelt, Salikoko Mufwene, Leslie and Marianne Bodi, Irene Donohoue Clyne, Jim Hlavac and Petek Kurtböke; those who have helped with the production of this book – Andrew Winnard, the patient Linguistics editor, and his colleagues at Cambridge University Press, Kylie Martin, Felicity Grey who compiled the indexes and especially Anya Woods for her technical and editorial assistance. My thanks are also due to Salikoko Mufwene, the series editor, for his kind and helpful advice. Any imperfections remaining are the result of mine, and many of the above will be delighted that this task is finally completed.

I am also grateful to the Australian Research Council for financial assistance for this and earlier research projects.

Map 1.1 is reprinted from Willem Levelt, *Speaking: from Intention to Articulation*, © The MIT Press, by kind permission.

Abbreviations

ACC	accusative
ADESS	adessive
ADJ	adjective
AUX	auxiliary
CLA	classifier
COMP	complementizer
CP	complementizer of projection
DAT	dative
DIMIN	diminutive
DM	discourse marker
FEM	feminine
GEN	genitive
IMPER	imperative
INDIR	indirect
INF	infinitive
INFL	inflection
IP	inflection phrase
LOC	locative
MASC	masculine
MOD.PRT, MP	modal particle
N	noun
NEUT	neuter
NOM	nominative
O, OBJ	object
PASS	passive
PAST.PT	past participle
pl	plural
PP	prepositional phrase
PRES.PT	present participle
PRT	particle
REFL	reflexive

REL.P	relative pronoun
S, SUBJ	subject
sg	singular
SM	system morpheme
V	verb

Conventions used in the examples

..	a hesitation of two seconds or more
...	a hesitation of three seconds or more
(A)	a filled pause
(H)	a nervous laugh
italics	trigger-words
SMALL CAPITALS	transversions

1 Introduction

1.1 Interrelationships

The past decade or so has seen an unprecedented growth in the study of language contact from a number of theoretical perspectives. Much of this has been the result of the European Science Foundation's Network on Code-Switching in the late 1980s and early 1990s, coordinated by Georges Lüdi. Some of the fruits of this work can be seen in Milroy and Muysken (1995) which brings together in one edited volume many approaches to language contact research. The arena of language contact research is now much wider, including what were previously emigrant rather than immigrant nations in Europe (e.g. Sweden, Germany, Italy) as well as former colonies in Africa, resulting in less usually studied pairs or groups of languages in contact. The linguistic effects of globalization and increased migration have also boosted the research activity in languages in contact. Preoccupation with universals and theoretical models has mainstreamed the field within so-called 'core linguistics' as well as in sociolinguistics and psycholinguistics. (It should be remembered that the development of sociolinguistics owes much to early language contact research, e.g. Haugen 1953; Weinreich, Labov and Herzog 1968). As I hope to show throughout this volume, language contact is a multidimensional, multidisciplinary field in which interrelationships hold the key to the understanding of how and why people use language/s the way they do. This includes interrelations between the structural linguistic, sociolinguistic and psycholinguistic; between typology and language use; between macro- and microdimensions; between variation and change; between synchrony and diachrony; between the linguistic, sociological, demographic and political. Languages in contact are, after all, the result of people in contact and of communities of people of different language backgrounds in contact. The analysis of language contact data can also throw light on how language is processed as well as on how language changes. It is not surprising that both the new specialist journals on language contact founded recently, the *International Journal of Bilingualism* and *Bilingualism: Language and Cognition*, are dedicated to (different) interdisciplinary approaches as have been the largescale conferences in Britain and the Netherlands on bilingualism and on language shift and loss respectively.

The interaction of approaches to language contact encompasses four major functions of language (Clyne 1991: 3–4):

1. The most important medium of human communication.
2. A means by which people can identify themselves and others.
3. A medium of cognitive and conceptual development.
4. An instrument of action.

Linguistic behaviour in relation to languages in contact is both an expression of multiple identity and a response to multiple identity. It also constitutes the satisfaction of a need to communicate and act in particular situations and follows an understanding of language as a resource. In our discussion of language change, maintenance and shift, we will demonstrate how these are the fulfilment of a dichotomy of need and will.

1.2   Aims

This monograph considers aspects of language contact on the basis of the comparison of data across language dyads and triads in the same environment, extending and reappraising paradigms; it also utilizes work from adjacent fields. This, the first chapter, will introduce the field, present some basic definitions, and some brief background information on the immigrant history and linguistic situation in Australia, where the data was gathered. In chapter 2, which focuses on the life changes of immigrant languages in contact with English, mainly following a macrosociological approach, it is possible to proceed from the data to a consideration of different models, as this can be done through 'ordinary language'. Chapter 3 will discuss some issues concerning theoretical and terminological frameworks for the structural aspects of language contact. The next two chapters are concerned with how people use the resources of more than one language, and introduce a predominantly linguistic approach. Chapter 4 focuses on the actual structures of the languages in contact, and on language change. Chapter 5 explores how typological factors facilitate switching between languages. Chapter 6 attempts to account for these linguistic issues psycholinguistically. With chapter 7, we enter not very well chartered waters – pragmatic/discursive language contact phenomena and the relation between cultural values and language change and shift. Chapter 8 is an attempt to integrate some of the dynamics discussed in previous chapters. In a sense, this monograph is a sequel to *Community Languages: the Australian Experience* (Cambridge, 1991), but focused more on linguistic issues and directed to a more international readership.

1.3   The field

The field of language contact has changed considerably in recent years. Over the past decade or two, much thought and discussion has gone into the formulation of constraints and the development of theoretical frameworks and processing models. The advent of electronic communication has facilitated feedback and collaborative thinking between researchers in this field.

The new developments in the four large areas of the field are reflected in four edited volumes – on grammatical aspects of 'code-switching' (Jacobson 1998[1]), processing models of bilinguals (De Groot and Kroll 1997; Nicol 2001), code-switching in conversations (Auer 1998) and reversing language shift (Fishman 2001a). The past decade has seen a continuing development of the Matrix Language Frame Model (Myers-Scotton 1993a, 1997a; Myers-Scotton and Jake 1995, 2000) and the refinement of Poplack and Sankoff's model based on a borrowing – code-switching dichotomy and universal constraints (Poplack and Meechan 1988; Sankoff 1998). Monographs by Treffers-Daller (1994), Backus (1996), Halmari (1997) and others not only discuss contact between particular languages in specific situations but also contribute to theoretical model building. In particular, Muysken (2000) has argued that there are three types of 'code-mixing' as he calls it and each requires a different kind of treatment. A discussion of these models will be found in section 3.4.4. The work on conversation analysis presents another way of understanding what happens when people alternate between languages and why they do it. Moreover, it encourages a reappraisal of the entire concept of 'code-switching' (see section 3.2). At the same time, language contact continues to enjoy a rather separate life within historical linguistics (with Thomason and Kaufman 1988 as a landmark) as well as in creole studies. The two-volume handbook of contact linguistics (Goebl et al. 1997) is an international, European-oriented state-of-the-art coverage of the field of language contact at the time.

The relation between internal and external motivations of change has been the subject of much discussion in historical linguistics, sometimes with some scepticism regarding contact influences (e.g. Harris and Campbell 1995). Silva-Corvalán (1994) and others (e.g. Clyne 1991: 176–86) have shown the duality of internal and external influences. Hawkins (1986) provides a framework for contrastive typology in establishing underlying generalizations about a language following Sapir's notion of drift – the way a language keeps changing in the same direction. This will be drawn on occasionally to show the complementarity of internal and external influences. Gonzo and Saltarelli (1983), Thomason and Kaufman (1988), Dorian (1999) and others have shown that through the reduction of communicative functions of the community language with every generation in the immigrant country, the grammatical structures are reduced (being adaptations of a 'fading' grammar), normative monitoring is progressively weakened, and the lexical component is reduced, requiring increasing amounts of transference. What evolves is a restructured and simplified system. However, increasing transference can result in enrichment of grammatical structure (Dal Negro n.d.; Dorian 1999).

The field of language maintenance and shift as a separate research area was developed largely by Fishman in major publications commencing in 1966. He has been responsible for qualitative as well as quantitative paradigms and models linking language with nationism and nationalism (Fishman et al. 1985; Fishman 1989, 1991; see chapter 2). Studies on language maintenance and shift in this field are now taking place in many immigrant countries (e.g. Extra and Verhoeven 1993a, b; Broeder and Extra 1999; De Vries 1999; Boyd et al. 1994; Clyne 1982, 1991; Clyne and Kipp 1997).

An emergent and partly overlapping field is intercultural communication within linguistics. Most of the progress has been in contrastive and intercultural pragmatics (e.g. Blum-Kulka, House and Kasper 1989; Wierzbicka 1991; Kasper and Blum-Kulka 1994), but there is also an increasing literature in cross-cultural discourse (see, for example, Connor and Kaplan 1987; Clyne 1994b; Duszak 1997). Variation in pragmatic and discourse patterns is based on cultural values, as is variation in language shift patterns, and it will be assessed (chapter 6) to what extent these overlap.

In the 1950s and 1960s, there was a tendency for dynamic situations (such as language contact) to be described with tools created for mainly stable ones (dialectology of closed, homogeneous communities), insofar as such stable situations actually existed. Recently the tendency has been to create finite universal rules to cover constantly changing, varying situations (see section 3.4). This monograph endeavours to capture the dynamics of the variability while at the same time drawing on the theoretical advances of recent years.

1.3.1   Plurilingualism

In this monograph I will consider bilinguals to be people employing two languages, who recognize themselves and are recognized by others as using two languages (see Pauwels 1986: 7) and to be bilinguals. Trilingualism/multilingualism has been traditionally subsumed under bilingualism (e.g. Haugen 1956: 9). There is a rapidly growing literature in the field of trilingualism, especially in the context of third-language acquisition (see, for example, Cenoz and Jessner 2000; Cenoz, Hufeisen and Jessner 2001; also Clyne 1997b), and in this study, bi- and trilingualism will be seen as subsets of plurilingualism.

The assertion that bilinguals are not double monolinguals and should not be studied from monolingual perspectives has been echoed by many others, notably Grosjean (1982), Romaine (1995) and Gardner-Chloros (1995). Some plurilinguals come from diglossic situations with a functional specialization between two languages or varieties (one vernacular and one superposed) (Ferguson 1959; Fishman 1967; see section 2.3).[2]

I will take over Haugen's (1953: 334) differentiation between two types of first-generation bilinguals, which he terms Generation 1b and 1a.

Generation 1b share some characteristics with the second generation – native-like pronunciation in both languages, childhood experience in both languages because of early migration, all or most schooling in the majority language, and early acquisition of the national language.

Generation 1a do not usually exhibit native-like pronunciation in the majority language, nor have they had early childhood experience or all or most schooling in it.

We will draw the line between the two groups at age twelve although there is no hard and fast boundary. On the basis of analysis of and native-speaker listener tests on the speech of German immigrants in South Australia, Stock (1979) reports a grey area between eight and twelve, where there is much variation between speakers. Those who migrated after the age of twelve, however, are invariably recognizable as non-native speakers of English. They are past Piaget's concrete operation stage which is relevant to the mode of second language acquisition.

1.3.2   Language attrition

'Language attrition' is basically a psycholinguistic term, relating to the language skills of an individual. De Bot (2001) defines 'attrition' as 'language knowledge loss over time', making it a subset of his 'language loss' – 'decline of language skills in individuals and groups'. The term 'language attrition' is sometimes employed for those changes in usage resulting from language contact situations, which are described as 'L1 attrition in an L2 environment' (van Els 1985). Also relevant to the present monograph is 'L2 attrition in an L2 environment', especially among elderly migrants who have changed their lifestyle and substantially reduced their use of L2. A methodological problem lies in the relative dearth of longitudinal studies, i.e. if we don't know what someone knew before, how do we know what they have forgotten? Language attrition is generally postulated on the basis of comparisons between cross-sectional data (different people in different age groups), between generations (second and first), and between immigrants and those who stayed in the country or region of origin (cf. also Jaspaert and Kroon 1988). One longitudinal study is De Bot and Clyne (1989, 1994; see section 5.5).

I see the following difficulties with a language attrition approach employing surrogates for longitudinal data:

1. Cross-sectional comparison between older and younger informants does not necessarily produce the same results as longitudinal comparison of the same informants.
2. We do not know how to calculate how much of the first generation's competence in a language is available as input to the second generation.
3. The language of people who did not emigrate is also likely to change, but in a different way to those who entered a language contact situation (cf. Sasse 1992).

Nevertheless, attrition is one possible cause of language contact phenomena (see below, section 3.4). The distinction between attrition and availability (De Bot 2001) and the significance of Green's (1986) categories, 'active', 'selected' and 'dormant' languages will be discussed in section 6.3.4.

Often it is transference from L2 that is seen to indicate attrition. Studies of attrition are basically studies of language contact phenomena. For instance, Waas (1996) examined the German of sixteen informants in Sydney and found that, ten to twenty years after their immigration, they could not use L1 'without L2'. This is basically what we found across all our corpora. Waas was also able to ascertain a correlation between level of proficiency in German and retention of German citizenship and active affiliation with ethnic organizations.

1.4   The corpus

The language data on which this monograph is based has all been collected in Australia, a country of immigrants in which a wide and ever increasing range of typologically different languages are in contact with one overarching language, English (and, to a lesser extent, with one another). The contact is due to interaction between different individuals, families, communities and cultures in Australia. Through the Australian situation, I hope to consider processes and mechanisms of language change and shift, types of language contact phenomena, and universal and typological motivations in language contact.

The linguistic 'core data' which was collected over nearly four decades is from plurilinguals whose language other than English – German or Dutch – is related to it. It includes bilinguals and trilinguals so that it can be ascertained whether one group with all three languages demonstrates the same phenomena as groups with two of the languages. The German bilingual corpus includes data from different generations, vintages and bilingual situations. Two more sets of trilingual data, Hungarian–German–English and Italian–Spanish–English, provide the opportunity for comparison with the other corpora (notably Dutch–German–English)[3] because of variation in typological distance (section 3.6). The monograph is also informed by data from Croatian–English and Vietnamese–English bilinguals, kindly made available for reanalysis by Hlavac (2000) and Ho-Dac (1996, 2001)[4] respectively from their doctoral theses. In a more peripheral way, I am also citing some findings and examples from Australian-based research by Zheng (2000, Mandarin), Bettoni (1981a, 1985, Italian), Tamis (1986, 1988, Greek), Kaminskas (1972, Spanish), Endrody (1971, Hungarian) and Kurtböke (1998a, Turkish), the latter based on Turkish–Australian newspaper texts rather than spontaneous speech. Unfortunately Kovács's (2001) book on Finnish–English and Hungarian–English code-switching appeared too late to be worked into the manuscript. Table 1.1 summarizes details of the data. Most of it comprises recorded conversations between the informant and a field worker, but in recent corpora this is supplemented by self-recorded conversations between the informant and friends. The informants were specifically asked to speak a particular language and to speak the way they normally would speak. Generally, people were asked to talk about their work, family, leisure activities, a book they had read or a film they had seen, and (where appropriate) their first impressions of Australia or changes in their district since they were children. A number of pictures, such as an Australian country scene, a beach scene and a more neutral city scene, provided further stimulus. Typically the recording was about twenty minutes per informant. Some English was also elicited from the informants. In the case of the trilinguals, different segments of the interview were conducted in each of the languages (Clyne 1997b), about twenty minutes per language, and some of the informants also responded to a request for self-taped conversations in each of the languages with people with whom they normally used the language.

Specific points of grammar (e.g. gender, plurals – Clyne 1970c; Monheit 1975) were elicited from German–English bilingual children attending Saturday schools to complement spontaneous data (see section 4.4.3, section 4.4.4).

In addition, four sets of periodic census data on language use are analyzed and complemented by small-scale community studies of language maintenance (e.g. Arabic, Chinese, Dutch, German, Greek, Italian, Spanish, Macedonian – see chapter 2). There is also data from ethnolects of Australian English (e.g. Greek-, Yiddish-, German-based) and communication in English as a lingua franca (see chapter 6).

1.5   The Australian immigrant situation and the corpus

Societal plurilingualism in an immigrant situation such as in present-day Australia can be differentiated in a number of ways from other language contact situations (stable minorities such as in enclaves (*Sprachinseln*), colonialism, border bilingualism, temporary migration and the addition of a language of wider communication) by the number of 'minority' languages in the community, (in most cases) the permanence of residence, and the extent of integration into the 'mainstream' community. There is, in Australia, no territorial principle on which languages are officially distributed or recognized. Australia is an

Table 1.1 *Data summary*[a]

Language	Number	Vintage	Generation	When recorded
German/English	200	Postwar	1a,b/2	1963–4
	50	Prewar	1a,b/2	1968
	20	Pre/Postwar	3	1994
	61 sample (total 182)	Former enclaves Wimmera, Western District	2/3	1966–73
Dutch/English	200	Postwar	1a,b/2	1970–1 (some re-recorded 1987, 1991)
Cro/Eng (Hlavac 2000)	100	Postwar	2	1995–6
Viet/Eng (Ho-Dac 1996)	14 sample (total 50)	Recent	1b/1a	1993–4
Ger/Hung/Eng	36	Prewar/Postwar	1a (2)[b]	1996–7
Ger/Dut/Eng	36	Postwar	1a	1996–7
Ital/Spa/Eng Supplementary	36	Postwar	1	1997–8
Mandarin/Eng (Zheng 2000)	30	Recent	1b/2	1993–4
German morphosyntactic elicitation (Clyne 1970)	74	Postwar	1b/2	late 1960s
(Monheit 1995)	76	Postwar	2	mid 1970s

[a] All the data used is from Melbourne, except for the German corpus from former enclaves, also in the state of Victoria.
[b] Four second-generation speakers.

island continent. To leave it requires a long plane journey. It is not possible to cross a border into, or take a train or car trip to, a country using another language as a *de iure* or *de facto* official language. The immigration experience constitutes a new beginning. This is reflected in the ways in which a new way of life, a new environment is talked about. It can even mean choosing not to speak one's old language. Immigrant languages are distinguished from indigenous languages insofar as they are usually available from the country of origin and not completely lost when language shift occurs.[5] For that reason I consider that the use of the term 'language death' employed for the immigrant languages considered here is of questionable value. In other ways the immigrant situation offers similar evidence of language change, 'switching' and convergence to other contact situations, including indigenous ones (cf. e.g. McConvell 1985, 1988; Bavin and Shopen 1985).

The following brief sketch focuses on the groups whose language data forms the basis of this study.

When the first European settlers – British convicts and their masters and some free settlers – arrived in Australia in 1788, there were about 250 languages spoken on the continent, indigenous languages with a symmetrical relationship between them (see Dixon 1980). This is slightly more than the number of languages (mainly immigrant languages) recorded in the 1996 Census. Now English is very much the dominant language. There has been a continuous history of multilingualism, with some interruptions due to xenophobic policies during and after the world wars. But the languages have not been the same. Of the original 250 indigenous languages, only forty-eight were recorded in the 1996 Census and many of these will not survive another generation. This issue is beyond the scope of this monograph. (For information on this, see Dixon 1980.) Throughout the history of Australia and the six British colonies that preceded the federated nation, there has been an open-ended tension between English monolingualism as a symbol of a British tradition, English monolingualism as a marker of Australia's independent national identity, and multilingualism as a reflection of a social and demographic reality and of an ideology of an independent multicultural and outreaching Australian nation. (For details of this historical development, see Clyne 1991: 2–31.)

1.5.1   German

Some of the data utilized here was gathered in rural areas of western and north-western Victoria (see map 1.1 below),[6] which were originally settled mainly from Silesia, Prussia and Saxony between the 1850s (Western District) and the 1870s (Wimmera). Some of these settlers had remigrated, from enclaves in South Australia to other places or from western to northwestern Victoria. These enclaves (*Sprachinseln*) developed a bilingualism in which German was

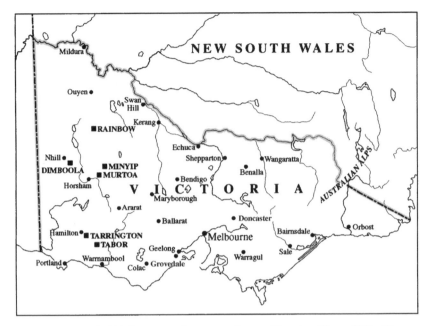

Map 1.1 Old German settlements under consideration (Clyne 1972: 55)

the language of everyday communication in home and community, the language of farm, orchard and vineyard. It was the language of the church and one of the languages of the bilingual church primary school in each settlement. Church and school had a homogenizing effect on German with no distinct dialect being used. The fact that the domains (e.g. home/work/neighbourhood, church/school) overlapped to a large extent strengthened language maintenance. English was the language of administration and was the medium of communication with the 'outside world'. The Western District settlements were more enclosed than those in the Wimmera which had surrounding ethnically mixed settlements as well as the predominantly English-speaking main town (Hamilton or Horsham respectively). Educational and religious literature as well as fiction were produced by German publishing houses in South Australia and Victoria. Secular and religious German newspapers published in Australia and also some from America were read in the German settlements. The German press of the 1860s indicates that it was possible to undertake all one's business transactions in German in Melbourne and Adelaide at the time. However, language shift occurred rapidly in the cities and large towns and the settlements close to them. That applied to most of the immigrant languages. The homogenizing effects of the Education Acts of the 1870s and 1880s, establishing free, compulsory and secular state schools with a basic common curriculum, caused a decline in linguistic pluralism except in the actual enclaves, and this was exacerbated by the increasing international conflict. During and immediately after World War I, strong anti-German sentiments affected the status and function of German in Australia, with place name changes, a ban on German publications and the prohibition of bilingual education. After 1918, German religious services continued in some settlements, often alternating with English ones, but German became largely a family and social community language, increasingly limited to communication with or in the presence of the older (and in some families, the middle) generations. In some settlements, such as Tarrington (formerly Hochkirch), there were a small number of German immigrants between the wars, who married local inhabitants and revitalized the use of German to some extent. The Second World War generally led to a more rapid decline in the use of German in former *Sprachinseln*. Except in the more retentive settlements in South Australia, German church services ceased altogether and German lost its last public function.

When our data in the former enclaves was collected in the late 1960s and 1970s, German was not employed as an active medium by the vast majority of the informants in Victoria and New South Wales, although a few had maintained contact with the language through postwar immigrants in a nearby provincial town or with immigrants in Melbourne through partnerships with an immigrant Lutheran parish there. However, those in more secluded places had been less affected by shift. The fact remains that by the time of the recording, there was in the former enclaves no real function for German and it was used mainly 'zum Spaß' (for a joke).

The aggressive monolingualism generated by the First World War and its aftermath set the tone in Australia for the next half century. It hit the 1930s refugees from Nazi Germany and occupied lands very hard with the imminence of war. In spite of being refugees, generally of Jewish descent, or married to someone of Jewish descent, they were classed as enemy aliens and their language was the aggressor language. At the same time, they were fleeing from a native land in which a racist regime had deprived them of their 'Germanness'. This applied less to those from Austria for it was German and not Austrian culture that was propagated by the Nazis. Postwar Austria developed the myth of Austria as the 'first victim' of Nazi Germany.

Different people reacted differently to the role of the German language in their identity. Some maintained German and asserted their position as bearers of German-language culture, similarly to other refugee groups. Others wanted to break with the past by shifting rapidly and completely to English. Still others, interpreting Nazi atrocities as an indication of the failure of assimilation, emphasized their Jewish identity, shifting to English (integrating some Yiddish words in in-group communication). Still others used a mixture of English and a Jewish ethnolect of German or Austrian German (cf. Jacobs 1996), despite some hostility to German Jews in a Jewish community made up increasingly of descendants of Yiddish communities in eastern Europe. Some of the refugees were from Austro-Hungarian families or were from urban middle-class Hungarian backgrounds characterized by Hungarian–German bilingualism. After the war, many of the refugees who had maintained German formed the basis of a cultural elite which was joined by some postwar migrants. They shared some cultural and welfare societies, read the same community-language newspapers, and frequented the same shops, restaurants and holiday guest houses.

While we are not including a corpus from the Templars, they have contributed to the German-speaking environment by their strong retention of (a Swabian variety of) German for at least two generations in Australia. Descendants of a pietist sect from Württemberg (southwest Germany) who had formed closed settlements in Palestine in the 1860s and 1870s, they were deported and interned in Australia during the Second World War. The Templars re-established their communities in several Melbourne suburbs, with dense networks (cf. Milroy 1980) based on in-marriage and a strong institutional infrastructure (churches, Saturday schools, cultural and social networks, and an old people's home).

The 'displaced persons' from refugee camps in Germany constituted the first phase of the postwar mass immigration program. As many had little or no English on arrival but varying degrees of competence in German due to bilingual upbringing (especially in central Europe), schooling or exposure in German labour and refugee camps, German was used initially as a lingua franca among the migrants (Hungarians as well as Poles, Croats, Czechs, Ukrainians, Latvians, Lithuanians and others) and to them by the Australian authorities. English gradually replaced German in most cases except for those families where one parent had German as L1, but for many, German symbolized an ongoing high cultural relationship.

The German-speaking postwar migrants came from Germany, Austria and Switzerland. Some of the German migrants were originally from the German Democratic Republic (GDR), from former German territories in the east from which Germans had been expelled, or from ethnic minorities in central and eastern Europe. The majority came in the mid to late 1950s or early 1960s, but German-speaking migration has continued to a lesser extent even to the present day. As this period was still the assimilationist era in Australian history, and there was still antagonism to things German, the postwar migrants kept a low profile and language shift proceeded rapidly. While each vintage of German-speaking immigrants had their areas of settlement, often co-settling with other immigrant groups of the same vintage, German is now the least concentrated of the major immigrant languages in Melbourne, Sydney and Adelaide (Clyne and Kipp 1998).

1.5.2   Dutch

The Dutch speakers were a compact immigrant group, almost all arriving in the 1950s. They were the model immigrants of the time as they tried to emphasize their similarity to the dominant group, assimilated outwardly and did not remain visible as a minority. Many of them used English to their children and eventually to their spouses as well. Even their community infrastructure was not developed until two decades after immigration. They were more concentrated in their settlement patterns than the German speakers partly because of the role of centralized church-based emigration societies in much of the immigration. However, the churches themselves propagated the use of English (see below, section 2.5.1). There are some Dutch–German–English trilinguals, who generally had Dutch or German as L1 but acquired the other language through migration or first through study and then through marriage or work in the respective country before emigrating to Australia.

1.5.3   Italian

Italian speakers have been coming to Australia since early in the nineteenth century. There have been numerous vintages of migration and much chain migration, though most of the immigrants came in the 1950s. For several decades, Italian has been the most widely used community language in Australia. However, the language actually spoken most often was a dialect, usually from diglossic areas in Calabria, Sicily or Veneto. But as the first generation started dying out, in the absence of new Italian immigration language maintenance declined and so did the regional (and village) community base. Helped by the largescale teaching of Italian, there was a gravitation towards a more standard Italian or at least *italiano popolare* (common colloquial Italian) as the symbol of Italo-Australian identity.

1.5.4   Spanish

The Spanish immigrants came mainly in the 1950s and early 1960s, the Latin Americans in the 1970s and 1980s. Some of the Latin American migration (of Chileans and Salvadoreans) is the result of political upheavals in the home country. There is evidence of convergence between Italian and Spanish among the Italian–Spanish–English trilinguals and of increased use of Italian in Australia due to the large Italian-speaking community.

Spanish speakers have come from both Spain and Latin America (notably Chile, Argentina and El Salvador). Many of the Argentinian and Chilean migrants were from originally non-Spanish-speaking, especially Italian, families. There were among the Latin Americans two types of Italian–Spanish bilinguals – those who were born in Latin America of Italian parents, and those who came as adolescents and young adults from Italy and were now remigrating to Australia with their own families.

1.5.5   Vietnamese and Chinese

Up to the early 1970s, Australia exercised immigration restrictions on people of 'non-European' descent. Since then, some of the largest groups from Asia have been those speaking Chinese varieties, especially Cantonese, Mandarin, sometimes alongside Taiwanese, Hakka and Hokkien. The period since the early 1990s has brought large numbers of Hong Kong Chinese to Australia, some anxious as to the effects of the return of Hong Kong to China, most of them skilled or business migrants and subsequently people who came within the category of family reunion. Many of them retained business links with Hong Kong and regularly commuted between their new and old countries. The numbers of Taiwanese, also largely skilled and business migrants, were small at first but have increased substantially. Students from the People's Republic of China (PRC) who were in Australia at the time of the Tiananmen Square revolt in 1989 were granted asylum, and they have been joined by family and by other migrants from the PRC. There are also Chinese speakers from Indo-China. Apart from speakers of Chinese varieties, the Vietnamese – first refugees, then economic migrants and family of the earlier arrivals (chain migration) – are the largest group from Asia.

1.5.6   Some other groups

There was also an established community of Greek speakers in Australia by the time of largescale Greek migration in the 1960s. Some of the earlier arrivals were immigrants of the interwar period. Some were immediate postwar immigrants from Egypt and Cyprus. Mass immigration from Greece in the late 1950s and 1960s made Melbourne one of the largest Greek-speaking cities of the world. Initially Greek speakers were one of the most concentrated groups; they are now the second most dispersed of the larger language communities in Melbourne.[7] Another large group from the late 1940s and early 1950s were the Maltese. They came with British passports and maintained a low profile as a 'non-English group' until their representatives joined in the changes of the 1970s, then establishing a welfare umbrella organization, Saturday schools and radio programs, and instigating language programs at primary, secondary and tertiary levels. This followed the independence of Malta (1964) and the development of Maltese, previously the L language of a diglossic relationship with English (Fishman 1967; Ferguson 1959) into an H language. The Greeks were followed by Turks in the 1970s and then various groups from Yugoslavia, notably Croats,

Serbs and Macedonians. These joined earlier communities of speakers of their languages (in the case of Macedonian speakers, from northern Greece).

1.5.7 Multi-vintage groups

As with German (see above), Hungarian (1938, 1949, 1957, later), Czech (1938, 1949, 1968), Croatian (1949, 1960s, 1980s and 1990s) and Polish speakers (1949, 1980s), the vintages do not always have enough in common to want to communicate with each other. All these migrations were the result of political events in the homeland. The earlier groups were all refugees; the latest ones came following political liberalization. The same applies to some Arabic, Mandarin and Cantonese speakers. With Mandarin and Cantonese speakers, differences include not only vintage and country of origin but also socioeconomic status and therefore settlement concentrations and networks, the recent Mandarin speakers from Taiwan and Cantonese speakers from Hong Kong being predominantly in the category of wealthy 'business migrants'. Earlier vintages of speakers of Chinese varieties included Cantonese and Hakka speakers from Vietnam and Cambodia and Hakka speakers from East Timor. (Earlier) Christian and (later) Muslim Lebanese form distinct communities with different language attitudes (see section 2.5.7).

1.5.8 The more general environment

Melbourne, the city of our research, now has a population of 3.28 million. The metropolitan area stretches over 7703.5 square kilometres. Socioeconomic mobility has traditionally been a feature of Australian society and one of the motives for immigration. Many of the suburbs inhabited by recent immigrant groups have been first areas of settlement of successive ethnolinguistic groups. It is a characteristic of Melbourne that there is cosettlement of diverse language communities. In 1996, 42 per cent of municipalities had more than 1,000 home users of three languages other than English, one of them as many as fourteen. It is time of immigration rather than cultural similarity that has generally led to cosettlement (exceptions are areas of concentrated Jewish or Muslim settlement). The change from Greek as a concentrated language community to a dispersed one within a generation and its complete movement out of some areas demonstrates the rapidity of dispersion patterns, sometimes as a result of socioeconomic mobility.

As a new group arrived and entered at the bottom of the escalator, everyone else moved up. The postwar immigration scheme was founded on the perceived need for an increased population to 'protect' Australia from invasion and to provide manual labour for expanding secondary industry. Even those groups, mainly refugees, who were declassed from professionals and business people to manual workers in the immigration process held hopes for the future of their children. However, the combination of longterm structural unemployment and the entry of 'business migrants' near the top of the escalator (following the decreasing need for unskilled workers) has disrupted the process of socioeconomic mobility somewhat.

The data on which our corpora are based was gathered in Victoria, and (apart from the data from former German enclaves) especially in Melbourne. Up to the 1996 Census, all postwar censuses showed that Melbourne had attracted the largest proportion of home users of languages other than English. In 1996, Sydney overtook Melbourne because most of the newest groups have settled predominantly in Sydney. It was in Melbourne that many of the multicultural policies were developed. It also had a multilingual population in the nineteenth century.

1.6   Policy

Australia does not have an official language although, in practice, English, the lingua franca, fulfils most of the functions of an official language. The Constitution and the laws are in English. Consequently, pre-naturalization interviews assessing the prospective citizen's understanding of rights and obligations are conducted in English (Piller 2001). On rare occasions legislation is passed simultaneously in English and other languages. For instance, the (Galbally) *Report on Post-Arrival Services and Programs for Migrants* (1978) was passed by Parliament symbolically in ten languages. Many public notices are translated into a multiplicity of community languages. The unofficial standing of English distinguishes Australia from, say, Canada, which has French and English as official languages despite a language diversity similar to Australia, and those states of the US which have declared English to be their official language. There are no official barriers to community language use in public; nor is there any language other than English which officially has preferential treatment over the others.[8] Unlike in various European countries, Australian educational institutions offer community languages as subjects for anyone to take and do not restrict them to students of the appropriate ethnic background. Some community languages are taught at school as part of the regular curriculum, and some of the same languages and others are taught at regular state schools on Saturdays. Some are offered by part-time ethnic schools conducted by community organizations.

Language attitudes keep changing (Clyne 1991: 6–25). As has been mentioned above, for most of the twentieth century, Australia exercised an assimilation policy. This encouraged language shift. For most of the period of the postwar mass immigration scheme, there were still laws prohibiting bilingual education and limiting the amount of broadcasting in 'foreign languages', there was little mainstream school teaching of the languages of the immigrants and little provision of services in such languages (Clyne 1991: 15–18). Any facilities in immigrant languages (e.g. language classes, libraries, ethnospecific social welfare, broadcasting) had to be provided by the ethnic communities themselves.

Since the early 1970s, Australia's self-concept has changed from that of a British outpost to that of an independent multicultural nation in which people, languages and cultures from all over the world have a legitimate place. However, policy has been one of interactive multiculturalism and not ethnic separatism. In the 1970s and early 1980s, a number of new developments brought into the public domain what came to be called 'community languages' (languages other than English, resulting from immigration, used in the Australian community; Clyne 1991: 19–22, 2001; Ozolins 1993), for example:

• the lifting of restrictions on broadcasting in languages other than English;
• a government-funded national TV network, beaming films in languages other than English (LOTEs) with English subtitles and also daily or weekly half-hour news broadcasts;
• financial subsidies and other assistance for part-time ethnic schools and community welfare programs, including ethnospecific care for the aged;
• the establishment of government-funded multilingual public radio stations in which community members present the programs, giving people opportunities for active as well as passive maintenance;
• the widening of the range of languages offered at school and university, the availability of most community languages as subjects in the final secondary school examination (currently forty-three), and the establishment of school centres at which a range of community languages are taught on Saturdays to those whose day schools do not offer them;
• public library resources in community languages;
• a telephone interpreter service functioning in about ninety languages, in addition to interpreters in hospitals and courts, with police and the like.

Only community language newspapers (section 2.5.6) remain completely private. Such indicators of linguistic pluralism do not necessarily prevent language shift but they do give status to community languages and input opportunities to those seeking them. It should be noted that the second generation is generally not interested in the ethnic press or community language radio (see Clyne and Kipp 1999).

Many of these initiatives were made possible through grass-roots lobbying on the part of a coalition comprising ethnic groups, teachers and academics, teacher organizations and trade unions.

As decisions on language(s) tended to be ad hoc and piecemeal, there was also a push for a coherent, comprehensive national languages policy. In 1982, a bipartisan committee of parliamentarians was commissioned to inquire into the need for a policy on all aspects of language(s) in Australia. The guiding principles developed by the committee – competence in English for all; maintenance and development of languages other than English (LOTEs), both indigenous and community languages; provision of services in LOTEs; and opportunities for learning LOTEs – were taken up in most subsequent language policies.

The National Policy on Languages (Lo Bianco 1987) presented a rationale and implementational strategies for maintaining and/or developing bilingualism in all Australians, based on a balance of social equity, cultural enrichment and economic strategies, drawing on local and international research. It also included funding proposals, which were approved. Moreover, it established a complementarity between (Australian) English, the national language and other languages used in Australia. In accordance with more general government policies, the balance has since shifted towards the economic benefits of multilingualism and an emphasis on English literacy for labour market needs (see, for example, Lo Bianco 2000), and this is reflected in more recent policy documents such as the *Australian Language and Literacy Policy* (Dawkins 1991a) and *Asian Languages and Australia's Economic Future* (Rudd 1994). The Productive Diversity campaign, spearheaded in 1992 by the then Prime Minister, Paul Keating, and similar state initiatives, emphasized the value of cultural and linguistic diversity to the economy. Funding for language programs has been cut, in common with most other government activities. Most of the initiatives have, however, become part of Australian reality today. However, the periodic success of the xenophobic One Nation Party in some rural areas, especially in Queensland, indicates that support for multiculturalism cannot be taken for granted in those districts where there is little presence of non-English speakers, whether indigenous or immigrant.[9]

Much of the language policy implementation in education is now occurring at the state level, as states have constitutional responsibility for primary and secondary schooling and there is much variation between state policies (see Ozolins 1993; Clyne 1991: chapter 5; Kipp, Clyne and Pauwels 1995: 1–20). In Victoria, for instance, at the time of writing, the policy is for all children to take a LOTE throughout primary school and in at least the first four years of secondary school. Program models and quality and time allotment differ greatly. In New South Wales, the minimum requirement is for 100 hours of LOTE study in junior secondary school. Languages taught vary between the states due to the demographic situation and the importance attached to community languages in the state. The main languages taught in Victorian schools are French, German, Indonesian, Italian, Japanese, Mandarin Chinese, Modern Greek and Vietnamese. Other languages offered in mainstream schools include Arabic, Korean, Macedonian, Russian, Spanish, Turkish, Aboriginal languages and Australian Sign Language. However, it can be said that, in general terms, throughout Australia, languages of economic significance have been taking precedence over those of importance only within Australia's cultural diversity. In this respect, globalization may be harming Australia's multiculturalism. Nevertheless, in international terms, the nation's commitment to multiculturalism and multilingualism is still relatively strong.

Fishman (2001c), who was very enthusiastic about Australian language policy in the late 1980s (Fishman 1988), offering it as a model to the United States, has recently expressed the view that it has gone in the direction of the United States:

> The comfort that minority languages could take a decade ago from Australian language policy . . . has largely vanished in the interim. Instead of Australia being the forerunner of a sea change in the valuation of aboriginal or immigrant languages, on the part of English-dominant host-countries, the direction of influence has run in the opposite direction. The traditional American negativeness toward such languages . . . has crossed the Pacific and invaded Australia. (Fishman 2001c: 479)

However, I do not believe that there is any American influence in this Australian development. Positive changes in language policy have always rested on other enabling changes while deterioration has usually accompanied other negative developments. It is government policies and budgets which marginalize all social and cultural aspects of the nation, such as schools, universities, hospitals, social welfare, development aid, public broadcasting and the arts, and emphasize user pays, asset sales and profit making, that will automatically treat community languages less favourably than those of a previous era. All things considered, much of the agenda of the 1980s has been preserved even if pluralistic language policy is not high on the federal government agenda.

It is hoped that the above brief overview will provide some context for the following chapters.

2   Dynamics of language shift

2.1   Introduction

In this chapter, we are dealing with the macrolevel of language. In order to discuss the structural changes that occur in an immigrant language, we need to see the changes as part of a process of gradual, slower or more rapid shift from one language to another. In the present chapter, Australian data will be used to illustrate the dynamics of language shift from immigrant languages to English.[1] Some of the data that I will be studying is based on responses to the same census question at the same time (though not at the same time of people's migration history) in the same places. An attempt will also be made to view similar sets of data diachronically. In particular, this chapter will consider some of the factors promoting or impeding language shift and influencing the differential shift rates in different ethnolinguistic communities.[2] This data will be supplemented by studies of language use patterns. Various models will be considered to explain processes and mechanisms of language shift in the context of place, time and community. This is the field that owes much of its development to the innovative work of Joshua Fishman.

First let us elucidate the meanings that are given to 'language shift'.

i. It can refer to the language behaviour of a whole community, a sub-group within it, or an individual.

ii. It can mean a gradual process, a 'shifting', as has been described for the replacement of Hungarian by German in Oberwart in the Austrian state of Burgenland (Gal 1979). However, it can also mean that a language previously employed by an individual or group is no longer used at all by them.

iii. It can designate a change in:

    a. the main language;

    b. the dominant language of an individual or a group;

    c. the language of one or more domains – contextualized spheres of communication – such as home, work, school, church;

    d. the exclusive language for between one and three of the four language skills (listening, speaking, reading, writing).

It can designate the completion of the process. Thus it can be described on a continuum. Martín (1996) conceptualizes intermediate stages between language maintenance and shift, which he regards as a combined variable. For the purpose of this study, I will regard all aspects of language shift as the focus, with different types and degrees. However, the availability of census data on home language use offers comparability restricted to that domain. Language maintenance (LM) efforts and institutions, which are discussed briefly in chapter 1, prevent, arrest and reverse language shift.

While intragenerational language shift (LS) constitutes a change of behaviour, the difference between first- and second-generation use of the language can be attributed either to LS in that generation or to non-transmission to the next generation.

No instrument powerful enough to assess language shift adequately on a large scale has yet been devised. At the individual level, it would involve first establishing through a time log what kind of communication the individual engaged in for what amount of time and in what language and to compare that with the same assessment at some previous time. Unless a true longitudinal study is conducted, this involves memory and personal interpretation of one's reminiscences. Such an investigation is a very arduous process but has been undertaken – for instance, Gilbert (1970) did this, based on a questionnaire devised by Mackey (1966), for a single informant in Fredericksburg, Texas.

On a large scale, censuses in many countries elicit information on language. The information requested may be on general language use, home use, proficiency or 'mother tongue'/ first language acquired. All these questions yield quite different data, involving different degrees of subjective interpretation. Proficiency questions produce largescale individual variation of interpretation and therefore inconsistencies. The 1976 Australian census question: 'List all languages used regularly' was not repeated in subsequent censuses mainly because the numbers of speakers of some languages were inflated due to the inclusion of information on children learning a language at school but not using it in other domains. (This could have been avoided by an explanation of what should not be included.) The question employed in the 1986, 1991 and 1996 censuses read: 'Does the person use a language other than English at home?'[3]

Those responding in the affirmative were asked to indicate the language other than English spoken most often. The names of a number of languages were printed on the form and could be ticked, the others should be written in by the respondent. In 1996, the languages whose names were printed on the form were: Italian, Greek, Cantonese, Mandarin, German and Arabic. 'If more than one language other than English is used in the home, the one used most frequently has to be indicated.'

The restriction to the home domain is responsible for an underestimation of the numbers employing more established community languages, which younger and middle-aged speakers might use not in their own homes but in those of their parents or other older relatives or in community groups. Also, it means that any negative response is interpreted as meaning English only, e.g. widows, widowers or others living on their own who do not speak any language at home are deemed to speak (and therefore have shifted to) English only. The limitation to the home domain also results in an underestimation of numbers of speakers of community languages in areas where some of the older established languages are spoken. Although there is no recent overall statistical evidence on this, the 1983 Survey of two-thirds of 1% of the population found large discrepancies between home use and other regular use. For instance, 83.57% of first-language German speakers claimed to use German with friends and relatives but only 48.25% to employ it at home; for French the statistics were 66% (home), 87.02% (friends/ relatives), for Italian they were 95.28% (friends/ relatives), 81.85% (home).

The advantage of the home language question, however, is that it is a good predictor of future use and maintenance. If a language is not transmitted in the home, it is not likely to survive another generation. Although the question as to whether a language other than English is used in the home would appear to be objective, it requires interpretation. Some respondents consider that the amount or the 'quality' of the language used do not warrant claiming it. Conversely, even though it is used rarely and only with a minority of interlocutors, it may be considered something one would want to indicate and thereby boost the numbers of speakers of the language. There are anecdotal accounts that an ethnolect of Australian English (see section 4.6) with a small amount of transference from the community language such as Italian has been deemed to be that community language. In comparing responses to the mother tongue question in the 1960 and 1970 US censuses, Fishman (1985: 139) found that the numbers for some old-established languages such as Finnish and Swedish had risen by 1353.1% and 565.41% respectively. This Fishman attributes to the ethnic revival accompanying commitment to cultural pluralism. Similarly, increased claiming or exaggeration can be seen as a *barometer* of attitudes towards community languages.

Language use in the home may be affected by a number of events, including entry into the workforce, marriage, birth of a new child, the child(ren)'s entry into different stages of schooling, child(ren)'s departure from the parental home and the death of the spouse. For instance, marriage could lead to a shift in the home language for one or both the partners, the birth of a child to a shift to English only or to a reversal of shift to facilitate community language transmission, and the departure of the child from the parental home twenty or twenty-five years later could usher in reversal of shift.

In order to assess language shift, it is necessary to know what the speaker's first language and the current language use are. The former information is not elicited in Australian censuses so country of birth has to be employed as a surrogate – not a very reliable one as it does not work for minority groups, such as Italian speakers from Chile, Polish speakers from Germany, Yiddish speakers from Poland. For multilingual countries, such as Vietnam,[4] Sri Lanka, India and former Yugoslavia, it is impossible to deduce language shift this way, and they have been excluded from consideration. Although we are dealing with far from 'perfect data', I am confident that it is valuable enough to persevere with it.

What the statistics do not tell us is:

a. How much a speaker uses the language at home.

b. Who speaks what language to whom and when (Fishman 1967).

The census data will be supplemented by the results of small-scale surveys.

2.2   Language demography

The 1996 Census records 240 languages used in the homes of Australians. 14.6% of the Australian population (26.4% of people in Sydney, 25.4% in Melbourne) claimed using a language other than English in their homes. The most widely used languages are shown in table 2.1.

Table 2.1 *Fourteen most widely used community languages, Australia and Melbourne, 1996*[a]

Language	Australia	Melbourne
Arabic	177,599	38,775
Cantonese	202,270	52,373
Croatian	69,152	21,468
Dutch	40,766	13,935
German	98,808	21,772
Greek	269,770	120,470
Italian	375,752	143,406
Macedonian	71,347	31,016
Maltese	45,242	22,558
Mandarin	91,911	24,864
Polish	62,769	18,817
Spanish	91,254	21,632
Tagalog	70,444	14,929
Turkish	49,196	24,215
Vietnamese	146,265	53,524

[a] The list processed by the Australian Bureau of Statistics is limited by computer space and is therefore not sensitive to dialectal variation. For instance, 'Sicilian' is included under 'Italian' and 'Lebanese' under 'Arabic'.

The fastest growing language communities in Australia in the period 1991–96 were: Mandarin (+68.4%), Vietnamese (+32.7%), Cantonese (+24.2%), Macedonian (+10.3%), Arabic (+9%). The languages with significant decreases have been: Maltese (−13.5%), French (−13.3%), German (−12.8%), Italian (−10.5%). Greek, which had a continuous history of strong language maintenance, experienced a decrease in numbers of home users (5.6%) for the first time in 1996. The older languages, such as Greek, Macedonian, Maltese, Turkish and Italian, are heavily concentrated in Melbourne, while the languages of more recent immigrants from outside Europe, such as Arabic, Korean, Spanish, Hindi/Urdu and Tagalog, are strongly concentrated in Sydney. Fluctuation in the number of users may be attributed to new immigration; the birth of another generation of speakers in Australia; death; to a more limited extent, remigration; and new decisions to claim or disclaim the language as a home language.

2.2.1   Shift – first generation (overseas-born)

Taking all the speakers or potential speakers of a language in Australia, the rate of shift in home language will vary vastly between language communities and subgroups between them. It should be stressed that, while the statistics refer to the entire community of speakers of the respective language in Australia or some part of it, the responses were actually recorded for individuals, employing language in a home (family) context.

The 1996 Census, like its predecessors, demonstrated much variation across ethnolinguistic groups in the proportion of people recording that English was the only language used in their homes. There is a continuum which extends from people born in the (former Yugoslav) Republic of Macedonia (3% shift) to Netherlands-born (61.9% shift). Other birthplace groups with high language-shift rates are German/Austrian (48.2/48.3% respectively), French (37.2%), Maltese (36.5%) and Hungarian (31.8%). Other groups with low shift rates are those born in: Taiwan (3.4%), the PRC (4.6%), the Lebanon (5.5%), Turkey (5.8%), Greece (6.4%), Hong Kong (9%), Chile (9.8%) and Korea (11.6%). In the middle range of the continuum are those born in Italy (14.7%), Japan (15.4%), Spanish-speaking Latin America other than Chile (17.2%), Poland (19.6%) and Spain (22.4%). It has previously been suggested (Clyne 1982, 1991) that this represents a cultural–regional continuum, with LS increasing the further north and west in Europe the speaker's country of origin was, and decreasing the further south and east it was. (But see comment on Maltese below.) Statistics on east and southeast Asian groups do not indicate lower shift than for southern European/Middle Eastern groups of Islamic or Eastern Orthodox/Eastern rite Catholic backgrounds. This will be discussed further below, under section 2.2.2, but it should be remembered that the order in which immigrant groups came to Australia in the period since the Second World War

Table 2.2 *Language shift in the first
generation, 1996 (from Clyne and
Kipp 1997: 459)*

Birthplace	% shift 1996
Austria	48.3
Chile	9.8
France	37.2
Germany	48.2
Greece	6.4
Hong Kong	9.0
Hungary	31.8
Italy	14.7
Japan	15.4
Korea, Republic of	11.6
Lebanon	5.5
Macedonia, Republic of	3.0
Malta	36.5
Netherlands	61.9
Other South America	17.2
Poland	19.6
PRC	4.6
Spain	22.4
Taiwan	3.4
Turkey	5.8

represents a sequence of relative cultural distance from the most similar to
the most distant. In section 2.2.2.4 we will relate language shift in a number of
groups to period of residence. There is not much evidence that it is a differential
in language distance that is responsible for the variation in language shift. This
is testified in the vast differences in shift rate among speakers of languages
that are related and structurally and/or typologically approximately the same
distance from English:

Maltese 36.5%, Arabic (Lebanese) 5.5%
Hungarian 31.8%, Turkish 5.8%
Spanish (Chilean) 9.8%, Italian 14.7%, French 37.2%

Even in the same language, Spanish, those from Chile record a 9.8% shift
rate, those from Spain 22.4%. Incidentally, the high first-generation shift for
Japanese, Hong Kong Chinese and Koreans is probably attributable to the large
number of foreign students in these groups (living in ethnolinguistically mixed
households) together with an overproportionate number of single young adults
in earlier vintage migration, obvious candidates for exogamous marriages.

The central European nature of Hungarian and northern Italian culture and
the cosmopolitan, western European nature of French culture give them cultural

similarities with English speakers. Maltese culture has been strongly influenced by British culture due to colonization and by Italian culture through the Roman Catholic Church, to which almost all Maltese belong; through earlier contacts; geographical proximity; and the presence of Italian media. At the time when most of the Maltese immigrants left Malta, English and Maltese were in a diglossic relation in the island, with English as the H language and especially the language of higher secondary and post-secondary education. The literate read and wrote mainly English while there were many who were functionally illiterate. Maltese genetically is a Semitic language, enriched by Italian and English lexicon. (Unlike other Semitic languages, Maltese uses Latin script.) It would be interesting to consider whether the linguistic behaviour of people from other former British or American colonies (Fiji, Sri Lanka, the Philippines) is similar.

2.2.2   Shift – second generation (Australian-born)

The language 'shift' in the second generation is much higher than in the first generation but the continuum is very similar. As has been noted, the data does not enable us to differentiate between actual shift and non-acquisition. The lowest 'shift' is recorded for those born in Australia with at least one parent born in the (former Yugoslav) Republic of Macedonia (14.8%), Turkey (16.1%), Korea (18%) and the Lebanon (20.1%). The highest 'shift' was among the second generation of Dutch (95%), German/Austrian (89.7%), Maltese (82.1%), Hungarian (82.1%), French (77.7%) and Polish (75.7%) backgrounds. In the middle group were those from Greek (28%), Hong Kong (35.7%), PRC (37.4%), Italian (57.9%) or Spanish (63%) background. The second generation of Taiwanese parentage are so small in numbers that their 21% shift cannot be regarded as representative. It should be noted that the PRC and Hong Kong-descended second generation shift considerably more than their counterparts of Macedonian, Turkish and Lebanese origin.

What can be commented on is the remarkably high second-generation shift for those of Chinese and, to a lesser extent, Mandarin, Greek and Polish background, as compared to the first generation. This represents a 813% intergenerational language discontinuity (difference between second and first generation use of the community language in the home) for PRC families, 437.5% for the Greek families, 396.67% for Hong Kong families and 386.22% for Polish families, which moved each of these groups into a higher category of LS in the second generation. Intergeneration language discontinuity is calculated as the ratio of second- to first-generation shift expressed as a percentage. The much lower discontinuity in Hong Kong families than in those from the PRC can be attributed to continuing links with the homeland in the former case through frequent family and family business trips, facilitated by a high income level.

Table 2.3 *Intergenerational language discontinuity (second: first-generation shift ratio)*

Country of origin	%
Germany	186.1
Hong Kong	396.67
Hungary	258.18
Italy	393.88
Lebanon	365.47
Macedonia	493.33
Malta	223.1
Netherlands	153.47
Poland	386.22
PRC	813.0
Taiwan	617.6
Turkey	277.59

Many of the Hong Kong group transferred part of their business operations to Australia in anticipation of Hong Kong's return to China while many of those who originated in the PRC came to, or stayed in, Australia for purely political reasons.

The intergenerational language discontinuity of Greek was surprisingly high. Greek-Australians had previously been distinguished by their high retention rate. In the case of Italian-Australians, the 393.88% intergenerational discontinuity is also quite substantial. This needs to be seen in the dimension of time. Italian and especially Greek take longer to lose altogether than, say, German, due to greater cultural distance, lower levels of English proficiency, greater reliance on community language networks, and other factors discussed below. However, a home language shift from Italian and Greek is a product of time, with a substantial increase in community language use once the majority of the community has moved into the second and third generations. Papademetre and Routoulas (2001) argue that second-generation Greek-Australians do not perceive an advantage in their children learning Greek, reflecting the shifting ideology around biculturalism and bilingualism. Some groups, notably Dutch, German, French and Maltese, already have such a high LS that there cannot be further substantial intergenerational discontinuity.

The Polish statistics cannot be interpreted without careful cross-tabulation because of the differences between the groups of Polish speakers (immediate postwar and 1980s vintages).

The intergenerational shift for Spanish and French is relatively low. This may be due to the perceived international and high-culture status of the language. However, the high intergenerational discontinuity among families of Hong

Kong and Taiwan background bodes ill for the future of Cantonese and Mandarin languages in Australia. I refer again to the above discussion showing that home language does not constitute all regular use.

While it may appear that LS is often complete within three generations in many ethnolinguistic groups in the urban immigrant situation, this certainly did not apply in the German language enclaves dating back to the mid-nineteenth century. Here the language was frequently maintained for three, four or even five generations.

The above statistics are cross-tabulated in the following sections with a number of individual and group factors.

2.2.2.1   Exogamy (individual)

The second-generation statistics are aggregated, i.e. they include those with one or two parents from a particular background. The advantage of the aggregation is that the LS rate indicates the extent of parental exogamy and endogamy, i.e. the German statistic shows that there is a very high exogamy rate and the Turkish statistic demonstrates a high endogamy rate. Table 2.5 indicates that, for all groups, there is a considerably higher shift for those descended from exogamous marriages than those from endogamous ones. This applies less to those groups with a generally high shift, such as Dutch (80% endogamous, 91.1% exogamous), than to those where the shift is usually very small, such as Turkish (5% endogamous, 46.6% exogamous), or varied such as Japanese (5.4% endogamous, 68.9% exogamous). Attention is drawn to the very marked differences in LS between the Korean, Japanese and Hong Kong second generation of endogamous and exogamous parents (Korean 5.4%: 61.5%, Japanese 5.4%: 68.9%, Hong Kong 8.7%: 48.7%).

Those groups of Islamic or Eastern Orthodox background with low LS rates are, in fact, ones with high endogamy rates. For example, in the second generation, 88.7% of Turkish-Australians, 76.3% of Macedonian-Australians, 73% of Lebanese-Australians, 66.7% of Greek-Australians, but also 47% of Maltese-Australians, are from endogamous families. The same applies to 8% of those of French background, 12.7% of those with an Austrian background, 16.1% of German background but also 27.4% of Dutch background. Second-generation Australians of PRC (43.2%) and Hong Kong (32.6%) background fall into an intermediate position. Cultural and especially religious distance from the 'mainstream' may, through the encouragement of endogamy, be a protection against integration and LS.

2.2.3   Age (individual)

Language often functions as a marker of age-group identity. In the former German enclaves, at the time of our data collection, people were identified as

Table 2.4 *Language shift in the second generation (endogamous, exogamous, aggregated) (adapted from Clyne and Kipp 1997: 463)*

	Language shift (%)				
Birthplace of parent(s)	Endog.	Mother *x*	Father *x*	Exog.	Second generation (aggregated)
Austria	80	89.4	92.2	91.1	89.7
Chile	12.7	55.8	68.9	62.3	38
France	46.5	77	83.3	80.4	77.7
Germany	77.6	90	93.6	92	89.7
Greece	16.1	44.6	55.1	51.9	28
Hong Kong	8.7	43.9	53.9	48.7	35.7
Hungary	64.2	85.9	90.7	89.4	82.1
Italy	42.6	73.1	80.9	79.1	57.9
Japan	5.4	65	79.2	68.9	57.6
Korea	5.4	59	65.7	61.5	18
Lebanon	11.4	34.2	49	43.6	20.1
Macedonia, Rep. of	7.4	33.2	41.3	38.6	14.8
Malta	70	92	94	92.9	82.1
Netherlands	91.1	95.5	97.2	96.5	95
Other South American	15.7	61.3	74.2	67.1	50.5
Poland	58.4	81	89.8	86.9	75.7
PRC	17.1	46.1	58.1	52.8	37.4
Spain	38.3	69.6	78.3	75	63
Taiwan	5	28.7	30.7	29.2	21
Turkey	5	34.7	52.3	46.6	16.1

having proficiency in German largely on the basis of their age. For at least a generation, communication with older people was an important factor in language maintenance. Exactly the same has occurred in successive immigrant groups from all over the world. Often this is because the grandparent generation has little or no proficiency in English or much of their limited proficiency has been lost (De Bot and Clyne 1989, 1994). The older generation feels freer to move more exclusively in ethnospecific social networks once they are retired and once the children, frequently agents of LS, move out of the parental home (see, for example, Clyne 1977b for Dutch). On the other hand, in most groups, whatever language children may speak to their parents, they tend to communicate with each other in English. This has been observed in studies of German, Italian, Polish, Spanish, Turkish and Yiddish speakers (Clyne 1967, 1977a; Harvey 1974; Klarberg 1976; Smolicz and Harris 1976; Bettoni 1981a; Yağmur 1997; Clyne and Kipp 1999: chapter 2) A variant is where they speak the community language to each other in the presence of their elders. LS in early German settlements was actually attributed by Hebart (1938: 474) to children bringing English into the home.

Table 2.5 *Language shift in the first generation by age, 1996*

Birthplace	0–4	5–14	15–24	25–34	35–44	45–54	55–64	65+
Austria	22.3	24.5	33.4	53.1	63.0	61.9	43.4	33.6
Chile	15.2	9.8	8.1	17.5	9.1	6.4	5.4	6.8
France	24.5	30.3	31.9	41.0	38.2	41.3	30.7	34.7
Germany	21.5	31.5	37.7	50.5	59.9	62.9	38.1	31.7
Greece	11.6	10.8	9.9	14.4	13.6	6.2	2.9	3.4
Hong Kong	19.8	9.1	6.5	10.6	7.1	8.4	18.6	20.9
Hungary	16.7	6.2	16.3	23.6	36.5	43.5	37.5	23.5
Italy	16.4	22.8	19.2	29.3	30.6	20.8	8.3	6.5
Japan	13.1	13.4	13.7	13.8	13.6	18.5	22.1	32.1
Korea	41.8	41.9	9.1	7.2	4.1	2.4	3.2	5.2
Lebanon	3.9	3.6	3.3	6.5	5.6	6.3	4.3	6.2
Macedonia, Rep. of	1.5	1.0	2.9	6.9	3.7	2.1	1.1	1.3
Malta	27.4	39.7	40.2	51.4	48.0	40.8	28.3	19.2
Netherlands	39.0	54.4	49.6	61.5	77.3	76.4	58.8	40.5
Other South American	32.4	16.7	13.9	23.9	17.9	14.5	11.3	16.7
Poland	3.9	4.4	11.1	14.2	15.1	22.7	27.6	22.6
PRC	2.1	1.7	1.9	2.8	3.2	8.1	8.2	6.8
Spain	21.3	29.7	23.9	36.1	36.6	16.2	12.5	12.0
Taiwan	14.4	3.6	3.1	5.7	2.4	2.1	1.7	3.1
Turkey	2.6	3.2	4.6	7.4	5.8	4.9	4.6	7.2

Traditionally the oldest age group is the one that maintains their community language most in the first generation (Clyne 1991: 79). This still applies to some communities, e.g. Italian, Maltese, Spanish and Turkish. The shift is highest among the 25–34-year-olds, e.g. for French-, Greek-, Latin American-, Macedonian-, Maltese- and Turkish-Australians, who have now moved out of the parental home. In some of the older communities, however, the shift is even higher in the groups now aged 35–44 (Austrian, Dutch, Italian) or 55–64 (German, Polish), who formed nuclear families with people of other backgrounds or, having come to Australia as children, developed a relationship with a same-ethnicity partner through English, the language of the younger peer group. Such trends are more difficult to establish for more recently arrived groups because there is not yet a broad cross-section of the community.

2.2.4   Time (individual and group)

Over time, the rate of language shift of a group increases. This is due to (a) shift as a product of period of residence (see below), and (b) the increase in the number of people over the age at which they are likely to leave the parental home and shift to English as their only home language.

Of the groups with high LS (see table 2.2 above), the Maltese, French and Hungarians have increased their LS most. These early postwar groups have lost much of their first generation and many of those left arrived in Australia as young children and are comparable with the second generation. Among the groups now with a medium LS, the Spaniards and Italians have increased their shifts very substantially for much the same reasons. The Polish group have not increased their shift to quite the same extent due to new immigration in the 1980s, resulting in increased numbers and some new opportunities to use the language (see table 2.6). As with intergenerational shift, the Greek-born have increased their hitherto small LS substantially (by 45.45%) and there is a considerable increase even in the Turkish group. The data on those groups where there was comparable information in 1986 gives the impression that fluctuations in LS are generally demographically driven and that LS itself is inevitable in the Australian immigrant context.

Table 2.6 *Shift by Polish vintage –*
Polish-born

Pre-1981 arrivals:	28.3% shift
1981–5:	9.2%
1986–90:	6.2%
1991–6:	5%

Time coincides with vintage. In those groups with several distinct migration waves, commitment to language maintenance varies between these subgroups. Time also indicates the kind of Australia the immigrant came into – assimilationist or multicultural – so that their language use or shift reacts to the dominant community attitudes and government policies on language other than English. A study of Arabic, Chinese and Spanish language maintenance (Clyne and Kipp 1999), comparing two origin groups for each language, identifies distinctive attitudes on the part of predominantly 'newer' groups (e.g. Lebanese as compared to Egyptians, Arabic-speaking Muslims as compared to Arabic-speaking Christians, Chileans as compared to Spanish, Taiwanese as compared to Hong Kong Chinese). These groups developed their lifestyle and patterns of expectations of community attitudes and government policies at the time of immigration of the group. The 'older' groups display less assertive attitudes and rely less on institutional and financial support for language and cultural maintenance (e.g. radio, libraries) than the 'newer' ones. The former also use new technologies (including videos) less. They have less contact with the homeland (Clyne and Kipp 1999: 319–22).

Table 2.7 *First-generation language shift 1986–96 comparison (Clyne and Kipp 1997: 459)*

Birthplace	1986	1996	% change in LS
Netherlands	48.4	61.9	+78.29
Austria	39.5	48.3	+22.78
Germany	40.8	48.2	+18.13
France	27.5	37.2	+35.27
Malta	26.0	36.5	+40.38
Hungary	24.4	31.8	+30.32
Spain	13.1	22.4	+70.99
Poland	16.0	19.6	+22.50
Italy	10.5	14.7	+40.00
Greece	4.4	6.4	+45.45
Turkey	4.2	5.8	+38.00
Lebanon	5.2	5.5	+5.77

On the basis of 1986 statistics, a number of cut-off points in LS were postulated (Clyne 1991: 76–9):

1. After four or five years in Australia, probably due to pressure from the children;
2. After ten years, reflecting changes in attitudes and policies in Australia as well as the beginning of new initiatives in media, education and libraries. In some cases this also marked the arrival of a new vintage, e.g. a new group of Poles, providing opportunities for networking and language maintenance or new groups of more affluent and/or educated German or Chinese speakers, able to utilize improved communications with Europe – frequent trips, visits from relatives and material sent by relatives and friends;
3. After twenty to twenty-nine years – marking a new vintage in the case of Hungarian refugees post-1956 only;
4. After more than forty years, related to the symbolic function of community languages. A marked language shift is a reaction to political and/or racial oppression and wartime xenophobia in Australia. This applies mainly to German-born refugees who had their German identity taken away from them. Czech-born and Austrian-born refugees shifted only marginally more than Czech displaced persons of the late 1940s and Austrian economic migrants of the 1950s. This is due to their language or variety being identified as different to that of the aggressor.

Table 2.7 shows the variation in shift between the 1986 and 1996 censuses. (For the actual data, see Clyne and Kipp 1997: 459.) For most groups the shift became steeper after 1991. The Turkish-born experienced a decrease in shift in 1991, perhaps due to new immigration.

Table 2.8 *Second-generation language shift*
(aggregated) (from Clyne and Kipp 1997: 454)

Birthplace of parent/s	1986	1996	% difference in LS
Germany	88.2	89.7	1.7+
Greece	18.9	28.0	48.15+
Italy	46.6	57.9	24.25+
Malta	75.1	82.1	9.32+
Netherlands	93.4	95.0	1.71+

Table 2.9 *Language shift by period of residence*

Country		After 10–15 years in Australia	After 5–9 years in Australia
Austria	(86)	34.0	24.3
Chile	(96)	6.5	4.5
France	(86)	22.7	19.1
Germany	(86)	35.9	26.0
Greece	(86)	3.2	3.7
Hong Kong	(96)	8.1	4.0
Hungary	(86)	18.1	11.2
Italy	(86)	6.7	6.1
Lebanon	(86)	2.8	2.2
	(96)	3.2	2.0
Macedonia, Rep. of	(96)	1.9	1.1
Malta	(86)	16.1	12.0
Netherlands	(86)	41.8	26.1
Poland	(86)	13.1	5.2
PRC	(96)	1.5	2.1
Turkey	(86)	3.0	2.4
	(96)	3.8	3.3

Again, the proportional increase is particularly high for the more retentive groups. There is a gradual increase in language shift with the Italian and
Greek communities reflecting earlier trends in the Dutch, German and Maltese
communities.[5]

If we compare speakers who have been in Australia for about the same time,
the variation in LS across the groups is clearest. In table 2.9 we see that, while
LS increases over time, the rate over time is not constant across communities.
For this comparison we will need to use some 1996 and some 1986 statistics.
What is then not constant are the situation and policies in Australia (see sections
1.5, 1.6).

Table 2.10 *Language shift in second generation*
(from exogamous families)

Country	1986	1996	Difference in LS
Germany	96.16	92.0	−4.16
Greece	68.40	51.8	−16.60
Italy	78.51	79.1	−0.59
Malta	94.58	92.9	−1.68
Netherlands	99.09	96.5	−2.59

To a large extent, the same regional–cultural continuum mentioned above in relation to LS in general applies for those who had been in Australia for between five and fifteen years, indicating speedy shift for northeastern European groups, slow shift for southern European, South American and Middle Eastern groups, and very slow shift for people from the PRC and Macedonia. The unpredictability of shift for Poles can be attributed to a large migration from Poland in the 1980s (cf. section 2.2.2).

While language shift in the first generation and in the aggregated second generation has increased in all groups from 1986 to 1996, there has been a decrease in the LS in the second generation from exogamous marriages in that period for most of the groups for whom such comparable statistics are available. This is shown in table 2.10.

There are three main reasons for this:

i. the reintroduction of the community language through marriage between first- and second-generation Australians from the same ethnolinguistic background;
ii. children being raised on the one parent, one language principle;
iii. grandparents acting as main caregivers of young children.

In (ii), the importance of school entry as a factor in LS is reduced because of the significance of the community language in the child's relationship with one of the parents. In (iii), however, entry into primary school could have a dramatic effect, with the institution and the peer group and their English replacing the grandparents and their language.

2.2.5   Gender (individual)

Language shift tends to be higher among males than females in the first generation. The gender variation tends to be smaller, however, among newer groups such as Lebanese, Turks and South Americans than among more established groups such as German speakers, Hungarians and Dutch.

Table 2.11 *Language shift in the home by gender (first generation), 1996 variation between the LS of males and females*

Birthplace	Male (% shift)	Female (% shift)	Difference (male – female)
Austria	51.4	44.7	6.7
Chile	10.6	9.1	1.5
France	38.1	36.3	1.8
Germany	52.0	44.6	7.4
Greece	8.0	4.7	3.3
Hong Kong	9.2	8.8	0.4
Hungary	38	24.4	13.6
Italy	18.4	10.5	7.9
Japan	12.5	17.2	–4.7
Korea, Rep. of	8.5	14.5	–6
Lebanon	6.5	4.4	2.1
Macedonia, Rep. of	3.7	2.4	1.3
Malta	39.5	33.2	6.3
Netherlands	66.4	57.0	9.4
Other South America	18.6	16.0	2.6
Philippines	18.5	28.2	–9.7
Poland	23.1	16.3	6.8
PRC	4.5	4.8	0.3
Spain	24.5	20	4.5
Taiwan	2.5	4.1	–1.6
Turkey	7.2	4.5	2.7

This can be attributed to the high degree of exogamy in the latter groups, especially on the part of the men, and the low degree of exogamy in the former groups since exogamy is a factor in LS in the home (see section 2.2.2.1). The groups with markedly different patterns (higher shift for females or very little difference) are those from the Philippines, Korea, Japan, and, to a lesser extent, Taiwan and the PRC. Immigrants from the Philippines are predominantly females in exogamous marriages. Among those born in Korea, Japan and Taiwan too, the proportion of women in exogamous marriages in the early migration vintages greatly exceeds that of males. Gender variation in language shift is much smaller in the second generation, possibly because the exogamy rates do not vary so much between the genders, and gender roles approximate those of the mainstream population. Also, traditional gender roles are less marked in the second generation.

Pauwels (1995), in a comparative study of language maintenance and shift among German, Greek and Vietnamese speakers in Melbourne, is able to offer explanations for both cross-community and cross-gender variation in

LS. Women use their community language more than men in the Greek- and German-speaking communities but the situation is reversed in the Vietnamese community. Pauwels suggests that this may be related to the younger profile of the Vietnamese community, encouraging bilingualism. Vietnamese males identify the neighbourhood domain more with Vietnamese than do females. Greek speakers have the highest percentage of community language usage of the three groups. This is related to the fact that they (and particularly the women) also have the highest proportion of informants rating their English as poor. Greek speakers are the group more likely to use their community language in a full range of domains than the other two groups. In the transactional domain, second-generation German and Vietnamese women use the community language more than men, while the reverse applies to the Greek group. Winter and Pauwels (2000) show that genders and domains are complementary rather than in conflict when actual discourse on language use is taken into account.

2.2.6   English proficiency (individual)

In addition to the home language use question, there has been, since 1981, a question on self-rating of English proficiency:

> Does this person speak English:
> Very well / Well / Not well / Not at all?

While such self-rating questions have limited validity, especially since different people with the same proficiency level could respond quite differently, the responses do give some indication of confidence level in English. A comparison with language shift rates could indicate if lack of confidence in one's English could be a significant factor in language maintenance.

Although there is no complete correlation between low English language proficiency and low community language shift, the groups with a large proportion of speakers in the 'no English' and 'speak English not well' categories are, on the whole, those with a low LS.

From this it can be deduced that lack of confidence in English is an important factor in the low shift rate from Turkish and Macedonian, and it plays a part in Greek language maintenance (this is borne out in Jaspaert and Kroon's (1988) study of LS among Italian immigrants in the Netherlands and Flanders; and van Avermaet and Klatter-Folmer's (1998) study among Turkish and Italian immigrants in the Netherlands and Flanders respectively; and in Pauwels (1995); see section 2.2.5 above). In the case of Italian in Australia, the relatively high rate of non-confidence in English proficiency along with a fairly high language shift rate contradicts the above trend. For Dutch, German and French speakers, a high English confidence rate is associated with a high language shift. As we have seen earlier in this chapter, other factors such as period of residence and

Table 2.12 *English spoken 'not well' or 'not at all' self-rating according to home language*

Language groups	Percentage
Arabic	17.6
Cantonese	29.9
Dutch	3.0
French	6.1
German	4.2
Greek	17.8
Italian	16.4
Macedonian	20.5
Maltese	9.1
Mandarin	29.5
Spanish	18.1
Turkish	26.5
Vietnamese	43.0

cultural similarity also play a part in LS. In the case of Vietnamese, we do not have the language shift from Vietnamese with which to compare English proficiency. In comparing English proficiency with second-generation home language shift, the correlation is less strong. For Macedonian, Turkish and Arabic, the low English proficiency of the parental generation necessitates the use of the community language in the home for family communication. However, in one of the groups with a very high percentage of members with little or no English speakers – Cantonese speakers – the second-generation shift is substantially higher than for Macedonian, Turkish, Arabic and Greek. There are earlier indications that the same negative correlation may occur for Mandarin speakers. The Taiwan-descended second generation is still too small to confirm this with any confidence. In some groups with only a slightly smaller proportion of people with low English proficiency – Spanish, Greek, and especially Italian and Polish – the second-generation LS is quite high. In view of the immigration history of the groups, many of those with low proficiency would be in the grandparent generation.

In families where the parental generation has a limited knowledge of English, home use of the language in the second generation is a matter of *need*. Where the parents have a high competence in English, it is a matter of *will*. However, this applies less to the speakers of Chinese varieties who shift to a considerable extent in spite of a low proficiency rate in English.

In table 2.14, the figures in bold indicate the population proportion in the state with the lowest first-generation LS for that language. With very few exceptions

Table 2.13 *Second-generation language shift by English proficiency self-rated as 'not well' and 'not at all'*

Language	English proficiency within group	2nd generation LS
Arabic	17.6	20.1
Cantonese	29.9	35.7
Dutch	3.0	95.0
French	6.1	77.7
German	4.2	89.7
Greek	17.6	28.0
Hungarian	12.6	82.1
Italian	18.1	57.9
Macedonian	20.5	14.8
Maltese	9.1	82.1
Mandarin	29.5	3.4[a]
Polish	17.8	75.7
Spanish	15.4	Spain 63.0
		Chile 38.0
Turkish	26.5	16.1

[a] Taiwan-born.

Table 2.14 *Language shift in the first generation by state, 1996*

Birthplace	NSW	VIC	QLD	SA	WA	TAS	NT	ACT	AUS
Austria	49.8	46.1	48.2	46.6	49.1	53.7	55.4	49.1	48.3
Chile	9.9	7.6	14.4	13.8	12.1	16.8	18.8	12.6	9.8
France	37.1	38.7	36.2	38.6	35.1	43.4	30.7	38.6	37.2
Germany	49.1	47.1	48.1	**45.7**	50.7	50.8	50.1	51.3	48.2
Greece	6.2	**5.4**	15.6	6.1	13.6	11.0	4.8	8.8	6.4
Hong Kong	**6.8**	7.8	15.3	14.0	19.4	24.8	19.7	17.9	9.0
Hungary	32.0	28.2	36.2	32.0	32.7	52.3	48.9	33.5	31.8
Italy	15.5	**12.5**	22.1	13.8	16.0	28.3	24.3	21.3	14.7
Japan	14.7	17.0	13.0	20.0	17.3	17.0	17.5	26.1	15.4
Korea	7.2	19.1	13.7	48.4	29.9	56.0	67.6	22.3	11.6
Lebanon	**4.9**	5.4	19.7	9.4	14.8	30.4	37.5	10.3	5.5
Macedonia, Rep. of	3.1	**2.6**	9.1	6.6	2.9	16.7	0.0	6.3	3.0
Malta	36.7	*31.3*	57.3	46.5	67.1	73.8	66.7	56.0	36.5
Netherlands	62.8	62.1	62.6	61.0	**58.9**	60.7	66.9	65.3	61.9
Other South American	14.3	16.7	28.3	27.9	28.9	37.3	35.1	25.2	17.2
Poland	21.4	19.4	24.4	**14.5**	17.0	21.9	48.9	19.5	19.6
PRC	4.0	3.8	10.0	7.4	5.9	15.0	11.4	7.1	4.6
Spain	20	22.3	24.2	33.5	25.0	42.0	28.8	**18.7**	22.4
Taiwan	3.5	4.5	2.2	4.5	4.3	8.1	15.4	10.4	3.4
Turkey	5.2	**4.4**	15.3	9.8	12.0	6.7	12.5	14.3	5.8

(Taiwan-, French-born), the highest population proportion and lowest first-generation shift correspond.

2.2.7   Place (group)

In the post-Second World War period, speakers of community languages have been concentrated in urban centres, even more so than the rest of the population of what is the most urbanized country of the world. Whereas 14.6% of the population used a language other than English at home in 1996, the percentage was 26.4 in Sydney and 25.4 in Melbourne. Each of the metropolitan areas comprises a series of local government areas (LGAs). Community languages are more evenly distributed in Melbourne than in Sydney, which has stronger concentrations of individual languages, including English only (Clyne and Kipp 1998). The relative density of particular language communities was calculated on the formula:

$$\frac{A}{B} \times \frac{Bx}{Ax}$$

where A represents the number of speakers of a language in a LGA, Ax the number of speakers of that community language in the entire metropolitan area, B the total population of the LGA, and Bx the total population of the metropolitan area. The norm is 1.0. The composite concentration factors are calculated on a total of the three LGAs in Melbourne with the highest concentration of the relevant community language, the site of most of our studies. (For more details, including Sydney and Adelaide, see Clyne and Kipp 1998.)

Thus, Macedonian speakers have both the lowest LS (see above, sections 2.2.1 and 2.2.2) and the highest concentration, but Maltese speakers, with the second highest concentration, have experienced a relatively high LS; a low LS and a relatively high concentration do coincide for Turkish. The shifts from the languages with a medium concentration – Arabic and Italian – vary (low for Arabic, medium first generation, relatively high second generation for Italian). The languages that are widely dispersed also differ in shifts – ranging from very high for Dutch, high for German, medium for Spanish and Polish, and low in the first generation and medium in the second for Cantonese and Mandarin. Italian-Australians have shifted to English considerably more than Greek-Australians but Greek speakers are more dispersed. Dutch-Australians are more concentrated than German speakers but shift more. In the case of Greek, however, it could be argued that the language community was strongly concentrated twenty years ago (Clyne 1982: 17) and that that provided an impetus for language maintenance. In the case of Maltese and, to a lesser extent, Dutch, the presence in close proximity of a community of the same language background could even have stimulated shift because no attempt needed to be made to maintain contacts with some people with similar origins who would provide some

Table 2.15 *Concentration factors
for languages (from Clyne and
Kipp 1998: 51)*

Language	Melbourne
Macedonian	4.1
Maltese	4.0
Vietnamese	3.6
Turkish	3.4
Arabic	2.6
Tagalog	2.6
Italian	2.2
Serbian	2.1
Dutch	1.9
Polish	1.8
Spanish	1.8
Cantonese	1.7
Mandarin	1.6
Greek	1.5
German	1.1

functions for the community language. From the above it will be evident that
the relation between concentration and shift will vary according to the sociolinguistic characteristics and history of the language group. We do not have
the capacity to demonstrate the effects of concentration on LS variation *within*
a group. Martín's (1996) study of Spanish in Sydney has, however, provided
evidence for this, with an interactive relation between low English proficiency,
concentration and low shift.

2.2.8   Studies in other countries

Veltman (1983) uses US census data to compare the anglicization rate of different ethnic groups and particularly to establish differentials between language
and educational attainment/socioeconomic status. He found ongoing bilingual
patterns mainly among Navajo and Chinese speakers, slightly less among Greek
and Portuguese speakers and still less among Spanish speakers. Beyond that,
there is a high degree of anglicization. Second-generation decrease in language
maintenance is linked to parental language behaviour. Two fundamental differences between the US and Australia need to be emphasized: the much more
recent vintage of most ethnic groups in Australia and the majority minority
language position of Spanish speakers in most parts of the US as well as their
proximity to Spanish-speaking countries. It is a characteristic of Spanish speakers in the US that their monolingualism is related to educational attainment more

than any other language group. French and Polish speakers, however, record the lowest occupational attainment. Veltman rightly attributes the low occupational attainment of second-generation children who do not use their parents' language to possible white racism. Since the 1980s, large numbers of Asians have migrated to the US. The 2000 Census recorded a 41% increase in community language use from 1990 (Crawford 2001).

A study by Boyd et al. (1994) comparing the maintenance of English, Finnish, Turkish and Vietnamese, each in at least two Nordic countries, points to different outcomes according to a range of factors. For instance, she suggests that Americans maintain English more in Helsinki than in Copenhagen or Göteborg because Finnish is a far more difficult language for English speakers to acquire than Danish or Swedish and because of the value placed on multilingualism in Finland. Finns in Denmark use more of the majority language and in more situations than those in Göteborg because of Göteborg's regional and cultural proximity to the Finmark, the tradition of language shift among Finns there, and the smaller and denser networks than in Göteborg. The Turks in Sweden want their children to be proficient in the majority language more than those in Denmark, and the young people in Sweden achieve a higher degree of bilingualism.

In the Netherlands, there is no census. However, Broeder and Extra (1999) conducted surveys through primary school children (both first and second generation of immigrants) in 's Hertogenbosch on language dominance and proficiency and family language use. From this it can be deduced that Romany is the best-maintained community language and that others such as Turkish, Chinese, Berber and Arabic follow, in that order. The languages of the former colonies, Papiamentu (from the Antilles), Sranan and Hindustani (from Surinam) and Malay (from Indonesia) are chosen by less than half of the children at home, as are Spanish and English. The immigrant parents have a strong preference for the use of the community language.[6]

In his analysis of the 1991 Canadian census language data, De Vries (1999) finds Europeans, with the exception of Portuguese and Italians, shifting rapidly to one of the official languages, and East Asians shifting slowly. The first-generation shift appears, on the whole, to proceed faster than in Australia. Education (high level), place of birth (mostly European countries) and period of residence (recent arrivals), correlate positively with LS.

Roberts (1999) compares language maintenance/shift patterns and underlying attitudes in three communities in Wellington, New Zealand, differentiating between the New Zealand-born and the overseas-born generations. (She locates the communities in Stage 5 of Fishman's graded intergenerational disruption scale; see section 2.5.5.) Gujarati speakers are affected more by negative attitudes of New Zealanders than Dutch speakers, due to the latter's cultural similarity, earlier immigration and tendency to 'assimilate', and the Samoan speakers are affected less due to their homeland's close political ties with New

Zealand. Language maintenance patterns and attitudes can be found on a sliding scale – Samoan speakers are most favourable to language maintenance and Dutch speakers least. Samoan speakers favour ethnic schools most as well. Attitudes towards language maintenance become more positive in the second generation across communities, reflecting changes in New Zealand society.

2.3   Who 'speaks' what language to whom, when and for what purpose?[7]

The construction of language use in the home is a snapshot taken from a subjective (sometimes biased) position by one or more of the participants in the family speech situation. There are a considerable number of other facts about that speech situation that impinge on language choice – the participants/interlocutors in interaction, the range of communications in the home, the communicative functions and intentions, the symbolic significance of language choice in the home.

One possible framework for considering issues of language choice is Myers-Scotton's (1993b, 1998b) 'markedness' framework. Though it is basically about the social motivations for 'code-switching' rather than language shift, it does provide a model for the intentionality of language choice, especially where there is a departure from the expected. She develops the notion of the 'rights and obligations set', where speakers, who are 'rational actors', have a sense of markedness regarding the available linguistic codes for any interaction but choose codes according to interlocutor and situation, and according to the advantages and disadvantages of the choice in relation to the interlocutor and situation. The situational features for the RO set will vary between and within communities. Flouting of rules (i.e. code-switching in marked situations) will mark special intimacy, distance, irony and hostility, for example (for an application, see section 7.2.3.2). The framework rests on an inherent markedness evaluator which assigns evaluations of markedness to the language choice.

Meeuwis and Blommaert (1998) criticize Myers-Scotton's model on the grounds that the assumption should be variability not universality, that it does not account for empirical facts and that it rests on the universality of intentionality. Myers-Scotton (1998b), on the other hand, argues that models based on social identity or conversation analysis downplay the importance of rationally based choices. While agreeing with Myers-Scotton's articulation of factors making code-choices marked or unmarked, Mufwene (1994) raises the issue of conflicting factors (e.g. frequency, cultural significance of code-choice, participants) leading to different unmarked choices for different speech events. For an application of the markedness model, see section 7.2.3.2.

As our census data does not provide us with a detailed picture, I will employ some recent and earlier depth studies of language contact in Australia,

Table 2.16 *Family communication patterns*

Family language situation	German	Dutch
Parents speak English to each other	2 (5.88%)	14 (35%)
Parents CL[a] to each other, English to the children	–	10 (25%)
Parents CL to children who answer in English	17 (50%)	7 (17.5%)
Parents and children speak CL	15 (44.12%)	6 (15%)
Parents and children CL and English to each other, answered in English	–	3 (7.5%)
Total number of families	34	40

[a] CL = community language.

especially ones relating to German-, Dutch-, Arabic-, Cantonese-, Mandarin-
and Spanish-speaking bilinguals, to discuss the above question, based on
Fishman (1967). The *participants* in a plurilingual setting tend to be identified according to age/generation (see above, section 2.2.3). Any deviation in
this will be due to the period of residence and its covariant, English proficiency
of the older generation. Hulsen's (2000) finding that the networks of the first-
generation Dutch speakers in New Zealand are more multiplex (in the sense
of Milroy 1980) and more connected than those of the second and third generations probably has fairly universal validity. There is variation between the
communities in the general pattern of family discourse:

parents speak English to each other and to the children;
parents speak the community language to each other but English to
   the children;
parents speak the community language to the children who answer in
   English;
parents and children speak to each other in the community language.

Comparing the patterns in German- and Dutch-speaking postwar immigrant
families from whom linguistic data was recorded (Clyne 1967, 1977a; see table
2.16), it appeared that the presence of English was due to different reasons. It
should be noted that the Dutch families were interviewed eight to ten years later
and had had more time in Australia to take on the use of English in the home.

Thus, the dominant patterns among the Dutch-Australians were already
English only and using English to the children. Among the German speakers,
either the whole family spoke German or the children spoke to each other and
were addressed in English. It seems that the shift to English in German-speaking
families was instigated by the children while the shift in Dutch-speaking families was instigated at least in part by the parents. It is possible that this is due
to the Dutch speakers being recorded some years after the German speakers,
but my impression that there is a major difference in community language use

Table 2.17 *Home language use by birthplace group (Clyne and Kipp 1999: 301)*

Group	Adult to adult	Mother to child[a]	Child to mother	Child to child
Egyptian	CL: 77.8%	CL: 40%	CL: 37.5%	CL: 7.8%
	E: 16.7%	E: 26.7%	E: 25%	E: 80.8%
	CL/E: 5.6%	CL/E: 33.3%	CL/E: 31.3%	CL/E: 11.5%
Lebanese	CL: 83.3%	CL: 57.1%	C: 54%	CL: 26.9%
	E: 3.3%	E: 5.7%	E: 5%	E: 53.8%
	CL/E: 13.3%	CL/E: 37.1%	CL/E: 35%	CL/E: 19.2%
Hong Kong	CL: 76.9%	CL: 55.9%	C: 53%	CL: 30%
	E: 0%	E: 0%	E: –	E: 50%
	CL/E: 23.1%	CL/E: 44.1%	CL/E: 42%	CL/E: 20%
Taiwanese	CL: 100%	CL: 89.2%	C: 90%	CL: 33.3%
	E: 0%	E: 0%	E: –	E: 20.8%
	CL/E: 0%	CL/E: 10.8%	CL/E: 11%	CL/E: 45.8%
Chilean	CL: 80%	CL: 25.8%	C: 24%	CL: 0%
	E: 8%	E: 0%	E: –	E: 84.6%
	CL/E: 12%	CL/E: 74.2%	CL/E: 70%	CL/E: 15.4%
Spanish	CL: 96.9%	CL: 51.4%	C: 49%	CL: 0%
	E: 0%	E: 0%	E: –	E: 82%
	CL/E: 3.1%	CL/E: 48.6%	CL/E: 46%	CL/E: 18%

[a] 'Mother to child' was chosen in preference to 'father to child', for example, because of the more general applicability of this variable to our survey sample (a greater proportion of fathers were absent from the family).

between the two communities was confirmed by similar German responses to background questions in a study of the German of bilingual children at Saturday schools (Clyne 1970c) as well as by census statistics.

In exogamous families across communities, English is either used throughout or it is the language of family discourse, and each parent interacts with the child in their own language. In many other groups, there is bilingual discourse, with parents speaking the community language and children responding in English. The role of participants in language shift is related to the nature of social networks.

Tsokalidou (1994: 220) quotes a conversation in which second-generation Greek-Australians agree that people of their background would always use Greek to the first generation. A comparative study of Chinese, Spanish and Arabic (Clyne and Kipp 1999) shows a predominance of English as the medium of communication among the children and the community language as the medium in which the adults communicate. Thus, strong maintenance among parents does not necessarily translate into a similar pattern among the children.

This applies especially to the Spanish and Egyptian groups and least to the Taiwanese, who are the most recently arrived of the families, in which the parents have the lowest English proficiency.

However, none of the groups shows the same tendency for the children to respond to their parents in English as in the earlier Dutch- and German-speaking communities. In all groups except the Spain-originated, there were only small differences between mothers' and fathers' use of community language (CL) with the children. Fathers of Spanish origin used considerably more CL with their children than did mothers.

The Chinese and Spanish groups in the study by Clyne and Kipp (1999) showed a marked drop in 'same group' *social networks* between the first and second generation (42% to 5%, Spanish, 70% to 10%, Chilean, 88% to 14%, Hong Kong, 74% to 28%, Taiwan). Spanish-born (55%) and Hong Kong-born informants (52%) displayed the highest 'other' social networks in the first generation and they are the groups in the study whose children shifted the most.

In yet other groups or families (e.g. postwar German-speaking), it is the *range of communications*, and therefore the topic and domain, that determines language choice, often with much 'code-switching', especially where there is an intermingling of domains (when people are talking about school or work or 'mainstream' institutions in the context of the home domain). This is subject to change, e.g. with children extending their experience outside the family or proceeding through school, they will increasingly be unwilling or unable to make the effort to express their experiences and needs in a monolingual mode in the community language (see chapter 4).

Communicative functions and intentions may be subject to functional specialization according to language, e.g. complaints only in one language, letters or telephone calls only in English in the second generation.

The symbolic significance of language choice also varies. It may express solidarity with non-English-speaking relatives (e.g. in the Taiwan Chinese and Lebanese communities) or exclude others (e.g. English-speaking monolinguals).

In general terms, our trilinguals are particularly conscious of a clear functional differentiation between their languages and also of the relative material value of their languages, e.g. Hungarian with spouse/ German with friends/ English with their children and work colleagues; Hungarian or German as a private language/ German as a professional language/ English as a social language; Italian to express personal identity/ Spanish for family identity/ English for everyday wider communication; Hungarian as an ethnic language/ German as a supranational cultural language/ English for pragmatic functions. (For details, see Clyne 2000.) They are building on existing bilingual functional specialization due to earlier migration patterns or the status of German in Hungary.

Bettoni and Rubino's (1996) study of Sicilian–Italian–English and Venetian–Italian–English trilinguals in Sydney demonstrates the functions of the three codes in the context of a shift from dialect-Italian diglossia to English. Italian is the interregional language employed in the more public and formal domains. Dialect is bound to communication with people of the same regional background and especially with the first generation. The choice between dialect and English is often domain-specific. The use of dialect to address younger relatives is more common among Venetians, especially among the women, than among Sicilians.

Pauwels's (1986) research contrasted the language maintenance patterns of Swabians (from southwestern Germany) and Limburgers (from the southeast of the Netherlands). Limburgers are less likely to maintain Dutch because the identification of Limburgs as 'their' language and the rigid diglossia separates them from the rest of the Dutch-Australian community. Swabian is part of a continuum of German varieties which enables its speakers to accommodate to the wider German-speaking community.

2.4   Reading and writing

So far we have employed the term 'use' more or less synonymously with 'speaking' and our data is almost entirely spoken. In literate communities this is, of course, inadequate. Part of the shifting process entails the loss of literacy functions and/or the non-acquisition of literacy by the next generation. This is demonstrated in the only data on the reading and writing of community languages from the Australian Bureau of Statistics 1983 small sample of two-thirds of 1% of the population.

As will be evident from table 2.18, the community language speaking and reading rates are similar for Vietnamese speakers and, to a lesser extent, Spanish, Dutch and Greek speakers. High reading-to-speaking ratios can be due to:
(a) recency of migration (Vietnamese);
(b) high levels of language maintenance (Greek);
(c) a language of wider communication, with much available reading material (Spanish; but French does not have such a high ratio).
Maltese, Italian, Arabic and Chinese are examples of languages with a low reading-to-speaking ratios. This may be attributed to:
(d) low premigration status of the community language in the country of origin (Maltese);
(e) large numbers of non-standard speakers (Italian);
(f) writing systems very different to that of English (Arabic, Chinese);
(g) diglossia, hence limited exposure to the written standard (Arabic, Italian).

Table 2.18 *Reading and writing in community languages (based on ABS 1983)*

Language	% of readers to speakers	% of writers to speakers
Arabic	68.05	67.12
Chinese	66.99	65.25
Dutch	82.14	74.27
French	66.05	66.10
German	74.50	70.81
Greek	81.13	72.72
Italian	66.67	62.24
Maltese	48.39	45.20
Spanish	84.67	84.67
Vietnamese	97.04	100.84 (sic)

Illiteracy in a community language can be a motivating factor in LS as it leads to low self-esteem and estimation of the language, and decreases its market value. It also denies access to information in the community language.

2.5 Models

Let us now consider a number of models of language maintenance/shift to assess to what extent they can act as explanatory or even predictive frameworks for the situation I have described above. We have seen that LS is determined by a range of partly related group and individual dynamics.

2.5.1 Kloss: ambivalent factors

Kloss (1966) is a taxonomic model informed by the American immigrant situation. It identifies (group and individual) factors promoting language maintenance or shift and ones that are ambivalent in that they can promote either language maintenance or shift. It is therefore measurable, enables the identification of factors operative in a particular community and lends itself to comparison between communities and societies. The model is context dependent.

Those of Kloss's clearcut factors that could have relevance to Australia are:
(i) early period of immigration;
(ii) *Sprachinseln* (linguistic enclaves);
(iii) membership of a denomination with parochial schools;
(iv) pre-emigration experience with language maintenance.

'Former use of a community language as the only official language' does not apply in Australia. If the remaining clearcut factor, 'religio-societal insulation' is relevant in Australia, it probably applies only to some Hasidic (Ultra-Orthodox Jewish) denominations (Klarberg 1983).

The ambivalent factors are:

1. Educational level of the immigrant.[8] This is the only individual factor considered by Kloss. A higher educational level facilitates a high culture around the community language and additional opportunities to use it; a lower one promotes isolation from the dominant culture and therefore language maintenance. On the other hand, a higher level of education brings the immigrant closer to the dominant group's cultural life, while less education may lead to a more limited range of cultural activities within the ethnolinguistic group. Both of the latter promote language shift.

2. Numerical strength. Large groups can afford extensive language maintenance institutions (promoting maintenance) but cannot avoid multiple contacts with the dominant group (promoting language shift) as much as smaller groups can.

3. Linguistic and cultural similarity with dominant group. Smaller language and cultural distance makes it more difficult to protect the minority language from shift. However, because the dominant language and culture can be acquired more easily, this can also enable groups and individuals to devote more attention to language maintenance.

4. Attitude of majority to language or group. Hostility from the mainstream to a language or a culture can lead to assimilation or to a more defensive attitude to maintain them. Positive attitudes on the part of the majority can create a favourable environment for language maintenance or it can lead to apathy.

5. Interethnic differences/sociocultural characteristics have been discussed exhaustively above.

Early time of immigration coincided with *Sprachinseln* in many rural parts of Australia and was responsible for the maintenance of German over three to five generations in some districts (see section 1.5.1). In urban areas, language shift occurred at the time in much the same way as it does now. In fact, it could be argued that 'time of immigration' is an ambiguous factor since the dominant policies and attitudes (see ambivalent factor 4, also section 2.2.4 above) will change and affect LM or LS accordingly. From table 2.2 it will be evident that those groups who came in the early postwar period (Dutch, Germans, Austrians, Maltese, early vintage Poles and Hungarians) did not, on the whole, maintain their languages as much as the later groups. There was a major policy shift soon after most of the Italians and some of the Greeks arrived. Both ethnic groups, especially the latter, played an important part in bringing about this change through political lobbying and initiatives. But early time of immigration for some other groups (e.g. Latvians, Lithuanians, Croats) coincided with a refugee mentality in which people dedicated a great deal of effort to developing community language maintenance institutions to prepare for the time when they would return to their liberated fatherlands. This attitude was not characteristic of the later generations of mainly economic immigrants from Croatia, for instance.

As was discussed under section 2.2.4, groups that are predominantly of longer standing in Australia (Egyptians, Spaniards) are less likely to feel 'hard done by' in relation to support for their language and culture than the newer groups whose main vintage was after the policy change towards multiculturalism (Clyne and Kipp 1999).

Membership of a denomination with parochial schools promotes language maintenance only if the schools are conducted bilingually. Kipp (1980) shows that, whereas the United Evangelical Lutheran Church of Australia was far more intent on German language and cultural maintenance, members of the Evangelical Lutheran Church of Australia maintained the language better in Victorian rural areas. This could be attributed to the fact that, for religious reasons, ELCA ran bilingual day schools at a time when UELCA used German for religious instruction classes and Saturday language classes. The nineteenth-century Italian enclave New Italy in northern New South Wales did not maintain Italian the way Lutheran and Apostolic German settlements maintained German because New Italy had Catholic schools in which the Irish teachers insisted on the use of English as the only medium of instruction. Hardly any of the post-Second World War Christian day schools based on the Dutch Calvinist 'Reformed Church of Australia' teach Dutch, none of them teach bilingually, and nearly all the Reformed Church services are in English. This has both reflected and helped to promote the rapid shift from Dutch.

Premigration language maintenance experience is actually an ambivalent factor. Ethnic minorities from Egypt – French, Greeks, Italians, Maltese and others – have kept up high levels of multilingualism in Australia, and ethnic Germans from the Middle East and Eastern Europe have tended to maintain German better than German and Austrian immigrants (Clyne 1967: 119). Macedonians, who shift to English least, have had a long history of competition from other languages, especially Greek and Serbian, suppression of their language and denial of its existence, assaults on linguistic human rights in the terms discussed by Skutnabb-Kangas and Phillipson with Rannut (1994). The tendency for a language in a competition situation in its heartland to survive relatively well in Australia, however, is not evident in Frisian–Dutch bilinguals who generally shift to English only. Of a considerable but unknown number of large families from Friesland, there are only sixty-nine people in the whole of Australia who, according to the 1996 Census, speak Frisian at home. Also, Sorbian–German bilinguals who tended to co-settle with Germans in nineteenth-century rural settlements, generally shifted to German and English within a generation. In the late 1960s and early 1970s, the descendants of Sorbian settlers of the nineteenth century remembered only a few idioms in the language or could count up to five or ten in it. It was not until the 1980s that a Sorbian heritage movement started in Australia.

It is not possible to assess the factor *'educational level'* from the data we have available to us.

People of Greek birth or parentage have shifted to English less than many other language groups regardless of whether they are *numerically stronger* than those communities. (For instance, the numbers using Italian exceed those of Greek in all states and territories of Australia except the Northern Territory, and so do those speaking German at home in Queensland, Western Australia and Tasmania.) People from the Republic of Macedonia shift to English considerably less than those from Greece, except in South Australia, although the Greek community is much larger everywhere but in Western Australia. The Dutch were one of the largest postwar ethnic communities but only a small proportion of those of Dutch background use Dutch at home now. Thus, absolute numerical strength has little positive impact on language maintenance. However, if we compare the language shift from particular languages across states (table 2.14), we find that the state in which the birthplace group forms the *relatively* highest proportion of the total population is the one in which the shift from that language is least. This applies, for example, to the following groups: Greek, Italian, Macedonian, Maltese and Turkish in Victoria; Lebanese, Hong Kong Chinese and Korean in New South Wales; German and Polish in South Australia. As to the relation between numerical strength and the possibility of language maintenance institutions, even small groups can initiate institutional support organizations. For instance, the tiny Romany community in Perth is able to run both an hour's weekly radio program in the language as well as a Romany Saturday school.

An attempt was made above to differentiate between *cultural and language distance* as a variable (see above, section 2.2.1) and it was suggested that it is cultural distance that affects language shift differential.

The reaction to attitudes of the 'mainstream' community to the minority group(s) bears out its staus as an ambivalent factor on Kloss's scale. So a popular group of the 1950s such as the Dutch displays the highest LS. During the Second World War, some German-speaking families (including refugees) maintained the language privately, at home, in spite of their enemy alien status (see above, section 1.5.1). It is difficult to ascertain whether some more recent vintages of some ethnolinguistic groups are shifting less because of recency of arrival or because they arrived in Australia during a favourable 'attitude-policy era', i.e. since the 1970s. The latter would cast doubt on the myth of the third-generation revival (second generation shifts, third generation revives) (Hansen 1962). Such a revival would not be likely in times of international conflict and xenophobia. On the other hand, if the second generation has shifted completely, there is nothing to maintain, while if the second generation does maintain the language, there is no need for revival.

Sociocultural characteristics is too broad a category to be useful as it includes both cultural values systems and social characteristics resulting from migration, though there are ways in which the two may relate (e.g. cultural values and reasons for migration, and settlement patterns).

Elsewhere (Clyne 1982: 32–3) I have suggested two other ambivalent factors: ethnic denominations and the situation in the homeland. There are different positions that religious denominations may have to the relation between religion and language which will influence the maintenance of or shift from the language. For example, they may regard a specific language or variety as God's language or they may consider that the most appropriate language for the religious domain to be the one that is closest to the speaker, whether this is the original community language or the language to which they have shifted. Assimilation has been accelerated by some churches' policies on language and slowed down by others'. The policies fall broadly in the following categories (Clyne 1991: 132–7):

1. Rapid assimilation (example: Reformed Church, formed by Dutch Calvinists in the 1950s). There are no community language parishes. Periodic services in such languages for the benefit of recent arrivals are soon phased out and immigrants integrated into monolingual English-speaking parishes.
2. Transitional assimilation (examples: Australian Lutheran, Roman Catholic in the 1950s and 1960s). Language and religion are perceived as separate entities. Ethnic parishes or community language services are intended as a transition to full integration to monolingual English-speaking parishes.
3. Structural bi- or multilingualism (examples: ethnic congregations of Baptist, Uniting and some Anglican churches; Roman Catholic Church in the wake of Vatican II). Language and religion are regarded as linked in relation to identity and religious socialization. Self-contained ethnic congregations conducting services and other activities in a community language or bilingually exist within the framework of the wider church.
4. Pluralist separatism (most Eastern Orthodox churches and, to a large extent, Uniate Catholic Churches, e.g. Maronite, Ukrainian Catholic, also some German and Swedish Lutheran). Language is perceived as having a close link with religion. The community language, or in the case of most Orthodox Churches, an archaic liturgical variety, remains the language of religious observances, with varying concessions or lack of concessions to the younger generation who may desire bilingual services.

Woods (2000) demonstrates that each religious denomination has its own language culture which impacts on its policy and attitude towards the maintenance of religious and ethnic languages and shift to English in religion. It will be evident that, because of its predominantly Dutch-origin membership, the Reformed Church is an institution that furthers shift, while the Greek and Serbian Orthodox Churches slow it down. In some cases, a minister of religion will be seen in the community as the role model for 'correct language'. (Woods (2000) found this to be the case in the Slovak Lutheran Church, for example. Also, she refers to complaints concerning the language of some other clergy in other churches.) Eventually, religion and language may occupy different values compartments, neither complementary nor conflicting, in the individual or family.

The *situation in the homeland* of refugees can lead to a complete break with the language and culture of the oppressive regime from which they are fleeing (as with some German and Austrian refugees in the 1930s) or a preoccupation with the language and culture which has been 'corrupted' in the country of origin, as with Latvians, Lithuanians and some Croatians who came to Australia in the late 1940s and early 1950s, who were looking forward to returning to their homeland after its liberation.

We can see from the above that some of Kloss's clearcut factors can be ambivalent, that it is cultural rather than linguistic similarity that clearly affects language shift, and that relative numbers could be more important than absolute ones. Kloss's factors, which were developed on the basis of the former German enclaves in the US, are also generally relevant to LS in a contemporary immigrant situation. Most of them are, however, not as crucial as other factors which he has not considered, such as exogamy, age, time of arrival/ period of residence, English proficiency, or, in the first generation, gender.

What Kloss's model also does not do is to show which *combinations of factors* lead to language maintenance or shift. This has been considered statistically by Martín (1996) in a survey of Spanish in Sydney. Martín sees language maintenance and language shift as independent variables with intermediate variables between them and the factors influencing them as values. In section 2.2.1, we have described LS as a continuum. Martín conducts a correspondence analysis of a large number of factors influencing language use in his informants, e.g. country of origin, year of arrival, birthplace, parents' and children's birthplace, nationality, English proficiency, geographical concentration, employment status, ethnicity of parents-in-law, religion and language of services, attendance at soccer matches. This enables Martín to observe the extent to which a particular value differs from the sample norm rather than the relationship between the factors themselves. For instance, living in a suburb with a strong Spanish concentration, having overseas-born children, arrival aged forty-five to fifty-five, after the birth of the children, poor English proficiency, unemployment and attending Spanish Catholic services are factors that do not accompany shift. Martín warns against giving equal weighting to each variable.

2.5.2 Conklin and Lourie

Based on the American immigrant situation, Conklin and Lourie (1983) extend factors such as Kloss's to include those particularly relevant to the contemporary urban situation. They differentiate between factors promoting language maintenance and those promoting language shift. Their factors are generally clearcut ones, such as:

Political, social and demographic factors
1. Concentration (high concentration leads to LM, low concentration to LS; but see section 2.2.7 above).
2. Recency of arrival and/or continuing immigration (promoting LM).
3. Geographical proximity to homeland and ease of travel to homeland (low, LS factor; high, LM factor).
4. Permanence of residence (low, LM; high, LS).
5. Occupational continuity (high, LM; low, LS).
6. Concentration in particular occupations (high, LM; low, LS).
7. Social and economic mobility (high, LS; low, LM).
8. Educational level (high, LS; low, LM; Conklin and Lourie do accept that educated community leaders with good English remain 'loyal' to the community language, so that this is really an ambivalent factor).
9. Ethnic group identity as opposed to identity through nativism, racism and ethnic discrimination (if so, LM; if not, LS).

Cultural factors
1. CL institutions (if prevalent, LM; if not, LS; but see section 2.5.5 below).
2. Whether religious and/or cultural ceremonies require command of the CL or use another language/do not require an active language.
3. Whether ethnic identity is tied to the language and the CL is the homeland's language.
4. Emotional attachment to the CL as a defining characteristic of ethnicity.
5. (Where cultural factors 2–4 are positive, LM; see section 2.5.7)

Linguistic factors
1. Whether the CL is the standard written variety (LM) or a minor, non-standard and/or unwritten variety (LS).
2. Whether it uses Latin script (if yes, LM; if not, LS).
3. The international status of the CL (high, LM; low, LS).
4. Whether the speakers are literate in the CL and if CL literacy is used for communication in the community and with the homeland (LM).
5. Some tolerance and flexibility for loanwords (LM; too much or too little, leading to excessive mixing and LS, or problems expressing new experience and LS).

Many of these factors are dealt with in other sections of this chapter. While our data does not make possible comments on permanence of residence, occupational and vocational continuity, the following points illustrate the problematic nature of proposing factors in isolation in the context of LM and LS. For example, geographical proximity and ease of travel are often distorted by other factors, such as the use of English in the homeland (e.g. the Philippines, Malaysia). Recent immigrants have a greater expectation of visits 'home' than did earlier vintages (Clyne and Kipp 1999: 320–1). Non-continuing migration is sometimes associated with political events, and refugee groups are sometimes especially motivated to maintain their CL (see section 2.5.1). Some of the best-maintained languages in Australia do indeed use a script other than Latin (Macedonian, Arabic, Greek), while some of the least maintained languages (Dutch, German, Maltese, French) use Latin script (see section 2.4). Greek speakers continue a high level of CL literacy, while Macedonian has benefited from a strong oral tradition. The international status of German and French has not prevented a substantial shift from those languages. The Chinese writing system is probably a factor in second-generation LS. Thus it is important to see the factors as intersecting and contributing *in combination* to LM and LS.

2.5.3   Edwards

Another taxonomic–typological model is provided by Edwards (1992). It differs from Kloss's insofar as it is more exploratory and less experimental, i.e. it seeks distinctions rather than concentrating on those issues that present themselves as factors of LS in the situation being researched. It may thus be more useful across a wider range of linguistic minority situations, not just specifically immigrant ones. For instance, among categories described are: a language being unique to one state; non-unique but always a minority language; a minority and a majority language; language spoken in adjacent areas; being a cohesive language community or not (e.g. Basque vs. Saami); the location of the minorities. Thirty-three issues inform categorization. These include: attitudes of the majority to the minority; type of self-support for the language; type and strength of association between language and religion; economic health of the region. They also include very vague categories such as language–identity relationship and history of the language.

The answers to the questions enable Edwards to develop three variables – speaker, language and setting (with overlapping) – and a series of perspectives (based on the disciplines: demography, sociology, linguistics, psychology, history, politics/law/government, geography, education, religion, economics, and the media).

Some of the categories suggested by Edwards are also covered in the analysis of the Australian data in this chapter. In its entirety, the taxonomy is too complex for the purposes of this study. But many of the categories would be particularly useful to compare the same ethnolinguistic communities across immigrant countries, where the impact of the original homeland language situation and the differential treatment by the respective 'host country' can be assessed.

2.5.4   Giles, Bourhis and Taylor: ethnolinguistic vitality/intergroup relations

The issues of attitudes and identity have already come up in our discussion. These are crucial in Giles, Bourhis and Taylor's (1977) ethnolinguistic vitality model. (An extension of this (Bourhis 2001) includes orientations of the majority and minorities towards each other and the effects of state language policies on separatist, exclusionist or integrative orientations.) The model explains LS in terms of the relative value of accommodating to the mainstream group as opposed to preserving the integrity of one's own group. It is derived from Tajfel's (1974) theory of intergroup relations and Giles's speech accommodation model. An important question is – to what extent does the individual wish to keep identifying with the group or emphasize their own individuality and pass into the other group (convergence in terms of Giles and Powesland 1975)? Individuals unable to be socially mobile can either change the interpretation of the group attributes to make them desirable or facilitate an improvement in their situation through social action (Tajfel 1974). The future of the group's existence depends on its vitality and ability to 'behave as a distinctive and active collective entity in intergroup situations' (Giles et al. 1977: 308–9). This ethnolinguistic vitality is manifested in a number of components: economic status, self-perceived social status, sociohistorical factors such as historically acquired ability to cope with minority status,[9] the status of the language, and demographic aspects, such as numbers, group distribution and institutional support. Before we test a number of the suggested variables against the Australian situation, it should be mentioned that the majority–minority dichotomy works better for bilingual situations than for multilingual ones. In immigrant societies such as Australia, there are a large number of groups which are minorities to a different extent and in different ways. Some of the older established groups originating in northern and eastern Europe did not want to be associated with the more recently arrived southern European groups and later Asian groups and saw themselves – and are perceived by others – to be closer to Anglo-Australians. The same applied originally to the Maltese who later aligned themselves with the southern Europeans when multiculturalism became the accepted policy. Some of the northern and eastern European groups also eventually changed their position on this.

Our analysis of factors relating to language shift (see above) throws some doubt on the constituent parts of ethnolinguistic vitality:

(a) *Economic status.* This general category is determined by such factors as age (number of pensioners and children), unemployment rate and type of employment (professional, business, skilled trades, manual work). These are roughly concomitant with period of residence, English proficiency and educational level. Among the language communities with the highest proportions of labourers are those using low-shift languages (e.g. Macedonian, Korean, Turkish), a medium-shift language (Spanish from Spain) and a high-shift language (Maltese). The languages of skilled tradesmen are high-shift (German, Dutch) and medium-shift (Italian, Polish). Many communities are stratified socioeconomically – notably Mandarin and Cantonese. An absence of positive correlation between income and language shift has been found, for instance, among Spanish speakers in New York (García et al. 2001: 61).

(b) *Perceived status*. The classic case of a group with a high perceived ethnolinguistic vitality is Greek-Australians. They are a high-profile group noted for longstanding language maintenance. Giles, Rosenthal and Young (1985) report on a survey of perceived ethnolinguistic vitality among Anglo- and Greek-Australians of their own group and the other group. They showed the two groups agreeing on the higher status of Anglos and on certain demographic characteristics of Greek-Australians (e.g. birthrate, concentration), and each group exaggerating some aspects of their in-group vitality (e.g. Greeks' business status, Anglos' institutional support).

But the status of groups with high and medium shift (Dutch, Germans, Italians, Poles among others) has also increased as is witnessed by comparisons of public opinion polls eliciting attitudes on minority groups (Morgan 1951; OMA 1989). The myth of Melbourne being the third largest Greek city in the world is matched by the not so widely known one proclaiming it to be the world's largest Maltese city, which has not added much to the standing of the group or the maintenance of the language.

Yağmur (1997), using a vitality questionnaire devised by Bourhis, Giles and Rosenthal (1981), found Turkish migrants in Sydney to perceive that they have a low ethnolinguistic vitality (especially in comparison with earlier studies of Greeks and Italians) and the English-speaking dominant group a high one, yet Turkish-Australians record one of the lowest language-shift rates.

(c) *Sociohistorical factors*. We have already indicated that pre-migration experience with language maintenance can be an ambivalent factor although it often favours maintenance. It also needs to be stressed (see above, section 2.1; cf. Fishman et al. 1985) that attitudes do not always translate into actual language maintenance. This factor will be picked up again below, in section 2.5.7.

(d) *Language status*. Table 2.2 (first-generation LS) does not show evidence for a relation between international status of a language and its maintenance in the immigrant context. Languages of wider communication, German and French, have undergone a high shift, and Spanish is a low- or medium-shift language depending on the community (Spanish or Chilean). Japanese is also not very well maintained, and the intergenerational transmission rate of Italian has declined substantially. All these languages are taught in schools and universities. On the other hand, Macedonian, Turkish and Greek, which are taught much less widely, together with the more widely taught Arabic and Chinese, record low shift rates. The position of Greek needs to be monitored carefully since there has been an increase in LS and a concomitant decline in participation rates in primary, secondary and university Greek programs as well as in their availability.

However, when it comes to a comparison of the ethnolinguistic vitality of the same language in contact situations with different other languages, the model becomes very useful. While Dutch speakers have undergone substantial and rapid shift to English in the US, Canada and New Zealand (Klatter-Folmer and Kroon 1995; Klatter-Folmer 1995; Hulsen 2000) as well as in Australia, and to French in Canada (Primeau 1983), they maintained Dutch successfully in competition with various languages, including English, in parts of South Africa and with Malay in the Dutch East Indies, where Dutch was the language of the rulers. Dutch has also survived well in Dutch settlements in Brazil (Schoenmakers-Klein Gunnewiek 1995, 1998), in contact with Portuguese, which is not considered of the same importance as English in the above-mentioned immigrant countries.

(e) *Demographic factors.* The limitations and relativity of the numbers factor in language maintenance have been discussed above (section 2.2.7). The birthrate does not necessarily play a role since children tend to speak English to their siblings (see above, section 2.2.3). Institutional support (e.g. service delivery in the language, language programs in schools and on the public media) varies according to need, sometimes encouraged by a political lobby from the group itself or an interethnic alliance of committed Australians in general arguing on behalf of the group's interests. Thus in Australia, a group with very low status may receive resources and have an ethnolinguistic vitality promoted on the basis of that low status and the perceived needs.

While the above discussion draws attention to some of the difficulties in establishing ethnolinguistic variables, it should not detract from the quest for such an attitudinal umbrella to explain aspects of language shift. Bourhis (2001) argues that the ethnolinguistic model assists the reversing language shift model (Fishman 2001a; see below, section 2.5.6) by establishing a social ascendancy order of languages, though a low ethnolinguistic vitality may coincide with high maintenance as was the case in Quebec for many years.

The ethnolinguistic vitality model is particularly suited for binary systems with a choice between two dominant languages or ones with a stable minority. The multicultural situation as we encounter it in an immigrant nation such as Australia constitutes a highly dynamic and volatile context where there are many languages simultaneously in contact with the dominant high-status language.

2.5.5   Fishman et al.: quantitative model (1985)

Fishman et al. (1985) present, with caution, a model based on a combination of demographic and cultural/ethnic factors and language maintenance institutions to predict as well as explain changes in language use patterns and relative survival rates of immigrant languages. The predictive measures are:

(a) the number of immigrant language claimants *per se*, adjusted for average age;

(b) the institutional resources for language maintenance and other factors, such as religious and racial distance from the mainstream, in addition to period of major immigration;

(c) a compromise between the two.

In (b), Fishman et al.'s major groupings according to religious distance from the mainstream are: (1) Mainstream Protestants; (2) Western Catholics; (3) Other participant Christians; (4) Non-Christians; (5) Non-participants.

According to the three measures (a, b and c above respectively), the top 'surviving' languages are:

(a) Spanish, Italian, French and German;

(b) Hebrew, Korean, Albanian and Thai/Lao;

(c) Spanish, Hebrew, German and Polish.

Although the model is highly applicable and easy to work with, there are some difficulties in applying it to our data:

i. The assumed linear relationship between the number of institutions and language maintenance, even though such institutions may not be successful in promoting language maintenance. (See the reference to the media and part-time ethnic schools under section 2.5.6.) The prevalence of language maintenance institutions may be dependent on language maintenance patterns themselves.

ii. Groups with speakers of different religious affiliations, e.g. Lebanese speakers of Arabic (in Fishman et al.'s classification: Eastern Catholic/ Orthodox 3, Muslim 4), speakers of Albanian (Catholic 2, Orthodox 3, Muslim 4), German (Protestant 1, Catholic 2, Jewish 4), Hungarian (Protestant 1, Catholic 2, Jewish 4, Hasidic 5), Russian (Protestant 1, Orthodox/ Eastern Catholic 3, Jewish 4).

iii. The number of newspapers rather than the readership as a criterion. (However, it is very difficult to obtain reliable statistics on circulation as such figures tend to be inflated. Moreover, it is not easy to estimate how many people will read each copy of a newspaper in an ethnic community.)

iv. The exclusion of public library resources in the languages as they offer opportunities for both language and literacy maintenance.

v. The inclusion under language maintenance institutions of religious institutions using ancient languages for religious observances (e.g. Hebrew and Arabic which are in many cases not the community language of the speaker).

vi. For Australia, the location of Western Catholics as a no. 2 group when they are the largest religious denomination.

vii. The assumption that people with physical features visibly different from the mainstream ('features and/or pigmentation') will maintain their language better than those who do not. Our data shows that the shift among Macedonian- and Turkish-Australians and in the second generation among Greek-Australians is lower than that for those of the corresponding groups of Hong Kong and PRC backgrounds. Arabic and Chinese speakers have reacted quite differently to outbursts of racism in Australia, with Chinese speakers opting more for the use of English in order to avoid exacerbating differences and Arabic speakers running a campaign stressing the importance of Arabic language and culture for all Australians (Clyne and Kipp 1999).

Fishman et al. provide fascinating comparative data on a wide range of languages according to the many variables. They state clearly the hypothetical nature of the exercise of predicting the future from the present. This I certainly agree with, for immigration and settlement depend on a multitude of economic and political factors.

2.5.6   Fishman: reversing language shift (1991)

This model is concerned with intergenerational discontinuity and how it can be arrested and reversed. Fishman sees the 'destruction of a language' as stemming from dislocation and the destruction of a rooted identity. Language shift is located in social space and in relation to societal dynamics. At the centre of the model are eight stages of what he presents as a graded intergenerational disruption scale which he describes (Fishman 1991: 87) as 'quasi-implicational'. Each of these stages is a step towards reversing language shift. Let us consider the stages in relation to the Australian community language situation.

Stage 8. Reassembling the language is characteristic of languages in an advanced state of language shift or death such as some Australian indigenous languages. Stage 8 does not apply to immigrant languages because they are not in complete disrepair, and because their heartland lies outside Australia.

Stage 7. Elderly among themselves: learning, relearning without use and without intergenerational family or integrated community factors.

This is also becoming common where people are selecting their 'heritage' language in classes for the elderly.

Stages 5 to 8 are all concerned with the creation of special functions for the community language. They provide the minimum need to guarantee natural intergenerational language transmission and ensure the reversal of language shift (Fishman 1991, 2001c). Fishman has long (e.g. 1977) been advocating the position that, for minority languages to survive in the longer term, they must assume such distinctive functions, akin to those in diglossic situations.

Stage 6. Family–neighbourhood–community-based link with the younger generation is considered by Fishman to be crucial to reversing language shift insofar as it 'leaves behind an already ongoing sociolinguistic *modus vivendi* and create(s) another that is demographically concentrated and intergenerationally continuous' (1991: 92). Stage 6 is the one which Fishman asserts cannot be jumped across or dispensed with as it is crucial for intergenerational transmission.

The family–neighbourhood–community-based links are facilitated by extended families, which are not always available. This was one of the main factors responsible for the maintenance of German over three generations or more in the old German rural settlements. However, as we have seen in section 2.2.7 in relation to several languages in the contemporary urban situation in Melbourne, greater concentration does not necessarily coincide with lower shift. Also, the very strong concentration of Yiddish and of virtually all Yiddish-language maintenance institutions in two adjacent suburbs of Melbourne, as well as a concomitant concentration of the entire Jewish community in the same area, has not prevented the use of Yiddish in the home from falling to a very low level.[10] On the other hand, there are two positive developments which are occurring across ethnolinguistic communities, irrespective of family–neighbourhood–community links – raising children bilingually on the one parent–one language principle and the marriage of second-generation speakers to first-generation ones (section 2.2.4). Coming back to the former rural enclaves, the family–neighbourhood–community links remained intact when outside pressures led to a shift to English (Kipp 2002).

Stage 5. Formal linguistic socialization through agencies or institutions under Xish control that do not need to satisfy Yish[11] standards regarding compulsory education.

In 1997, almost 90,000 pupils in Australia attended ethnic supplementary schools held after school or on a weekend day in a total of seventy-three languages. At primary level, such schools have freedom over their curriculum.

The largest numbers were Chinese (22,000), Arabic (12,000), and Greek (12,000), previously by far the most common language in ethnic schools. In some of the longer established languages (e.g. German), the parents often have a limited knowledge of the language and do not use the language at home, placing unrealistic expectations on the school, which operates one morning per week. Fishman (1989: 30–1) stresses that schools must be an integral part of the 'family–neighbourhood' axis of child socialization and identity formation to make a real commitment to reversing language shift (RLS). Geographical dispersion of many communities in Melbourne restricts such links and even limits the opportunities of non-members of communities to develop sufficient language competence in the community language to be accepted within the community.[12]

Stages 4 to 1 involve 'increased power-sharing' rather than diglossia (Fishman 1991: 401).

Stage 4a. Xish-sponsored and controlled schools that are attended in lieu of meeting compulsory education requirements.

The full-time ethnic schools build on a tradition of non-government schools, most of them of religious foundation (e.g. Anglican, Presbyterian, Methodist). The seven Jewish day schools in Melbourne all represent a different ideological or theological direction. All teach Hebrew (with varieties ranging from Biblical Hebrew to Ivrit (Modern Israeli Hebrew), Klarberg 1983), two of them offering bilingual education with Hebrew as a medium of instruction. Two – a Yiddishist secular school and an Ultra-Orthodox school – afford Yiddish a place on the curriculum, the former because of an ideological commitment to the language, the latter in line with the Ultra-Orthodox tradition of not using Hebrew for secular purposes.

Two Greek Orthodox and one Greek community school in Melbourne teach Modern Greek for more hours per day than state schools and 'mainstream' non-government schools that offer it, but only one school has (recently) introduced bilingual education. Nearly all of the children at the Greek Orthodox schools are of Greek background whether they speak Greek at home or not. The Greek community school describes itself as multicultural and non-denominational and has a significant minority of children of non-Greek background who are in separate Greek classes. The Coptic and Maronite schools teach Arabic as a second language but do not employ it as a language of instruction, a situation similar to that in the Islamic schools, which, however, are multi-ethnic (e.g. children of Turkish, Arabic, Somali, Malay and Urdu background). In the Islamic schools, Arabic has a significance as a sacred rather than a spoken language. Only about 1% of students from Muslim communities attend Muslim schools in Australia (Irene Donohoue Clyne, pers. comm.).

The significance of the language programs at school is that the community context in which the speaking of the relevant community language is valued encourages the children to view language maintenance and community language use positively. The fact that a school is an ethnic school does not make its programs better or more successful than those of other schools. In fact, the best language outcomes at matriculation examinations in Arabic in Victoria are at state schools.

Stage 4b. Xish programs in Yish schools.

The acquisition of languages other than English is compulsory in the State of Victoria throughout primary school and in the first four years of secondary school. The types and quality of program vary greatly. Some of the major community languages, such as Italian, Greek and Vietnamese, are taught in mainstream Victorian schools, in addition to Mandarin and German, which are widely used community languages as well as international ones. In a worldwide survey, Vignuzzi (1986: 185) found that 15.1% of students of Italian in Australia were learning the language for 'affective reasons', as compared to 8.6% over the rest of the world. At times of economic austerity or when, as at the present time, economic matters take precedence over social and cultural ones, there is a danger that programs with sociocultural objectives will be threatened. For instance, programs in less 'important' community languages have been reduced in recent years and, in 1999, the Aboriginal bilingual education programs in Northern Territory state schools were under threat from the Northern Territory because they allegedly did not lead to sufficiently impressive results in English.

Most of the forty-three languages assessed at the Matriculation level are community languages. Usually students are taught in programs of the Education Department's Victorian School of Languages conducted in twenty state schools on Saturdays. There are equivalents in New South Wales and South Australia. A number of languages are taught at each centre.

Stage 3. Xish work spheres.

Most workplaces are multilingual with English as a lingua franca and a range of other languages employed. This, however, does not contribute in any substantial way to arresting or reversing LS between generations, as Fishman (1991: 269) has indicated. Temporary exceptions are family businesses and retail shops, run by recently arrived families. Such businesses are usually intended to provide the economic means to enable the younger generation to study and enter the professions with the result that Fishman's conditions for intergenerational language continuity are not achieved. A more indirect incentive for multilingualism in the workplace is government policy (sometimes termed 'productive diversity', see section 1.6) promoting multilingual skills at work.

Stage 2. Mass media and government spheres.

Fishman's (1991) distinction between local and national media does not apply well to Australia. Ethnic newspapers tend to circulate nationally irrespective of where they are published, and it is not always clear to the listener whether a broadcast is local or national. There is a government-financed television network transmitting films in community languages with English subtitles and satellite news broadcasts in a range of languages, and a government-financed radio network broadcasting in sixty-eight languages. There are also public multilingual radio and television stations in various parts of Australia in which the programs are made by the communities themselves. While this provides some people with output opportunities, it detracts from the programs as input – there is frequent criticism of regional varieties, non-standard forms and mixed code. The more 'professional' radio programs as well as the newspapers have a norm-setting function for some members of some communities. There are now seventy-five radio stations, transmitting in a total of ninety-seven community languages for nearly 1,400 hours weekly, and 117 newspapers in community languages published in Australia, mainly weekly and bi-weekly but including five dailies in Chinese and one in Italian. However, younger people – and especially the second generation – generally find radio programs and community language newspapers unappealing, rendering them ineffective as a resource for reversing LS. Television is somewhat more generally popular, but some of the films are regarded by many as outdated or too avant-garde and there is an absence of children's films in community languages. Young people tend to prefer cable television and videos to satisfy their 'community language diet' (on the media, see, for example, Fishman 1991; Clyne and Kipp 1999[13]).

The allocation of radio time corresponds to a large extent to the number of language users and could therefore both reflect and perpetuate language maintenance/shift rates.[14]

Stage 1. Higher education, regional/central government activities

Most government business is carried out in English though government departments employ bilinguals to deliver services in community languages; such employees receive a special loading which provides an incentive to maintain and develop bilingual skills. Public notices in community languages are issued on elections and voting procedures, health, safety and social security, legal questions and rights, traffic codes, the education system and library facilities. The languages are chosen according to perceived needs so that notices on child care and care of the aged may be in different languages for demographic reasons.

In response to the experience of various scholars working with his RLS model in various parts of the world, Fishman (2001c) has emphasized a number of points, especially the intention that his model should be an instrument for diagnostic and programmatic location of a particular language and that it should provide the basis for the development of linkages between higher- and lower-order stages of RLS. The scales should enable people to identify where their language stands and what needs to be done to improve the situation. A number of colleagues throughout the world working with Fishman's model have found the categories and sequencing less clearcut than they might appear. Fishman has clarified (2001c: 476) that some languages 'function across several stages simultaneously. Some even stage-jump . . .' He also addresses a number of topical points, declaring that, 'without an *actual* ethnolinguistic community home', virtual interactive community use on the internet 'will not augur nearly as well for the future of Xish . . .' (2001c: 466). Fishman's model is useful and appropriate for the description, explanation and prediction of RLS, especially with the refinements presented in Fishman (2001d). It is important to emphasize that the 'power-sharing' stages 1 to 4, especially the non-educational ones, may not have an implicational relationship with the 'diglossic' stages 5 to 8, thereby removing the implicational relationship between these two groups of stages.

There are two underlying problems in relating the RLS model to community languages in Australia. Most immigrants have come to the country in order to improve the life chances of their children. The experience of immigrants (including refugees) in postwar Australia has been one of socioeconomic mobility – starting at the bottom of the escalator and moving up while being replaced at the bottom by more recently arrived groups; starting in depressed inner-city areas and dispersing (cf. section 1.5.8). Many of the measures suggested by Fishman would tend to detract from this socioeconomic mobility and would therefore not appeal to most, even in the interests of longterm language maintenance. It is perhaps significant that the groups (Amish, Old Order Mennonite, Hasidim in the US, see Fishman et al. 1985, Fishman 2001b) who provide the best conditions for language maintenance owe their very existence there to their desire to remain aloof from mainstream society. Moreover, the multiculturalism concept, which promotes and encourages the maintenance of community languages, rests on multiple interaction rather than the ethnic separatism required to overcome Stage 6 (though the latter is not outlawed!). The tolerant attitude towards the use of community languages in Australia in recent years, the availability of language programs, and the input opportunities in various domains, particularly the media, can aid language maintenance and RLS as long as they are taken up and utilized by the younger generation. The political context and standing of the language in Australia and beyond, discussed in relation to some of the other models, could provide incentives (or obstacles) for the various stages in RLS.

2.5.7   Smolicz: cultural core values

The crux of this model (Smolicz, e.g. 1981) is that each group has particular cultural values fundamental to its continued existence as a group and members rejecting these values run the risk of exclusion from the group. Language is such a value for some groups (e.g. Greeks, Poles and Chinese according to Smolicz) and not for others (e.g. Italian, Irish, who have family cohesion and Roman Catholicism respectively as their core values). Smolicz, Secombe and Hunter (2001), taking into account distinctions between individualist and collectivist cultures, show that dialect is integral to the southern Italian family rather than the family being the 'supporting agency' for the transmission of the dialect. For Poles, collectivist family patterns and language go hand in hand, while family, language and religion are mutually supportive core values in Greek culture, and Mandarin has become the symbol of Chinese identity.

The core value theory has the potential of explaining the LS differential. However, it has to be stressed that attitudes do not necessarily correspond to actual LS. Smolicz and Secombe (1989) differentiate between:
(i) general positive evaluation – regarding the language as a core value but not being prepared to learn it;
(ii) personal positive evaluation – putting the commitment into practice.

However, this distinction may detract from the original usefulness of the theory.

One point to be made is that language is usually most effective as a core value where it is linked with other core values such as religion and/or historical consciousness and where such intertwined core values necessitate the use of the language for particular purposes. For instance, Arabic, Greek and Macedonian all (at least in older varieties of the language) have respective claims to authenticity as the language of the Qu'ran, of the New Testament and European Antiquity, and the Slavonic Liturgy. The revival of Hebrew as the official language of Israel was undoubtedly greatly helped by such a claim to authenticity as a 'religious classic' (Fishman 1991: 360). Religious ideology or commitment leading to bilingual schools in nineteenth-century Victoria (Kipp 1980) and to the exclusion of Hebrew from the secular curriculum (Klarberg 1976) has been more successful than stronger language ideology of other groups in maintaining German and Yiddish respectively. It is the authenticity of Greek as a medium of religion that makes third-generation Greek-Australians feel that it is inappropriate to pray in a language other than Greek (Katsikis 1997: 52–3).

Guus Extra (pers. comm.) has observed that Dutch culture in Australia is seen but not heard, for many Dutch-Australian families display their ethnicity through Delft shoes on the mantle-piece and a birthday calendar in the toilet, but do not maintain their language. In the case of young Spanish–English bilinguals in Australia, Spanish music, especially songs, has sometimes rekindled an interest in Spanish language and culture among young people, notably those in their late teens (Clyne and Kipp 1999: 73).

There are a number of other issues requiring attention:

(i) Some groups are defined *around* language, in many others language is a possible carrier of the culture. The former applies particularly to the speakers of pluricentric languages which are national languages with different norms in different countries, e.g. French, German, Arabic, Spanish, who meet in a third country (see, for example, Clyne and Kipp 1999). A commonality of interests creates and/or supports language programs in schools, electronic media, ethnolinguistically specific social welfare programs. However, individual groups will have differing attitudinal relationships to the language. For example, the German-speaking community in Melbourne encompasses:

(a) Templars, with longstanding core values of pietist, non-dogmatic religion and Swabian dialect, supported by dense networks (including in-marriage until about twenty years ago), their own infrastructure for religion, social and cultural activities. High language maintenance rates have only yielded in an effort to keep up the religion and community in exogamous contexts.

(b) Postwar German and Austrian immigrants with exogamy, geographical mobility and low concentration, compounded by initial anti-German attitudes in the wider community.

(c) Prewar refugees with problems of multiple identity and multiple exclusion (see section 1.3).

(d) Swiss-Germans, who identify with a dialect and do not regard Standard German as their language (Clyne 1995: 42–3).

Religious, class, national or regional identity within a 'language group' may determine a variation in attitudes to the language, e.g. Lebanese Maronites or Muslims see Arabic as a liturgical language or as God's language respectively, urban or rural dwellers and people of different levels of education identify with different varieties.[15] One level of identification within an existing multiple identity is often abandoned to make room for 'Australian'. According to McNamara (1987), Israelis find themselves in a new 'minority' situation in Australia (having not been primarily identified as 'Jews' in Israel, where this is an unmarked category). They also bear the brunt of a stigma for leaving Israel. All this leads to their negative attitudes to the Hebrew language and a high LS in a context where the language is highly regarded by the Jewish community.

(ii) Language contact context. The comparative study by Boyd et al. (1994; see above, section 2.2.8) which shows the same immigrant language maintained far better in one country than in another suggests that the core value may need to be explored differentially in relation to sociodemographic factors. (See also above, section 2.5.3 on language status.)

(iii) Intergenerational variation. Katsikis (1997) found that, of her fifteen third-generation Greek-Australian case studies, nine believed that ethnic identity could survive without the Greek language, four were not sure and only two disagreed. This contrasts with Katsikis's earlier study of the second generation (1993). Katsikis (1997: 184) relates the high status of the Greek language as a core value in the second generation to family cohesion. For the second generation, Greek is the language in which to honour the parents; this is usually not the case in the third generation.

Across the three pluricentric language communities, Arabic, Chinese and Spanish, it emerged (Clyne and Kipp 1999) that those under the age of thirty-five (and especially the second generation) were far less committed to the position that language was central to their culture than were the older first generation, even though the main function of the community language among the second generation was symbolic rather than communicative. Intergenerational variation in core values is acknowledged by Smolicz et al. (2001).

(iv) Ethnic revivals. We have referred (section 2.1) to Fishman's notion of the 'ethnic revival' in relation to mother-tongue claiming in US censuses, reflecting general change in societal attitudes to languages other than English. The major changes mentioned under section 1.4 and specific efforts among Macedonian speakers to propagate their language is an Australian parallel. Many Greek migrants of the 1930s changed their surnames, married Anglo-Australians and/or did not pass on the Greek language to their children. Re-ethnization accompanied more recent Greek 'ethnolinguistic vitality'. An example where an ethnic revival came too late to save a community language is the Sorbian[16] Heritage Movement. Descendants of German-Sorbian (Wendish) bilingual settlers who had co-settled with Germans in rural areas found that they had been misidentified as Germans by both the in- and out-group. They conduct visits to the homeland and learn together about Sorbian culture (including cuisine) but there are few opportunities to acquire the language, which is under threat in the core area.

(v) 'Ownership'. This is another way of viewing the 'core value' issue.

It needs to be investigated to what extent ethnic groups which recognize language as a cultural core value also claim exclusive propriety over their language. This is the case for Australian Aboriginal languages where there is a very close link between language, land, identity and culture (Dixon 1980). The degree of propriety differentiates the attitudes of Greek and Italian communities in Australia. Until recently, there were more Greek ethnic schools (almost exclusively attended by children of Greek descent) than those of other ethnolinguistic groups combined. Some Italian communities, on the other hand, decided in the 1970s to abandon part-time ethnic schools and put their resources (provided principally by the Australian and also by the Italian government) into Italian programs for all students in state and Catholic primary schools. Such sharing of languages with those from outside the ethnic group is fundamental in the case of German and French, and the German- and French-speaking communities expect their languages to be available to all students. It may be that speakers of less-used languages see the 'ownership' of their languages in a different way to those of languages of wider communication. Some ethnolinguistic groups, such as Czechs, Norwegians and Hungarians, tend to believe that no one outside their communities would want to acquire their language. There is probably no automatic connection between language maintenance/shift and the propriety issue.

With an increasing number and diversity of groups and subgroups under investigation, this model can complement Fishman's and others' in the explanation of LS differential.

2.5.8   Cost benefits

(Perceived cost benefits are both an individual and a group factor.)

The following remarks are intended to complement the above consideration of factors and models. At the beginning of section 1.1 we referred to four major functions of language. It could be argued that language shift constitutes an often subconscious decision that, all in all, the disadvantages of language maintenance to the individual at the time outweigh the advantages. Among the disadvantages are the negative baggage or burden on one's self-identity and imposed identification from outside, and the perceived burden of time and money involved in maintaining or using it. The advantages include the value of effective communication and solidarity in family and community, the self-fulfilment of speaking the language, the opportunity for expressing multiple identity verbally, and the market value of the language for one's self and the wider community. The idea of market value of a language is developed by various scholars, including Haugen et al. (1980: 114), Coulmas (1992), Jaspaert and Kroon (1988) and van Avermaet and Klatter-Folmer (1998), the latter two following Bourdieu's (1982) notion of the linguistic marketplace. They postulate two linguistic markets, one for interethnic communication (in the majority language), the other for intraethnic communication (with a choice of languages). Individuals have to weigh out the continuing benefits of LM as they become incorporated into the interethnic marketplace. De Vries (1999) shows the importance of a knowledge of English and French as linguistic capital in Canada. The commodification of languages is becoming increasingly significant with the domination of market forces in all domains of society serving as a modern myth to complement the myth of God's language (see above, sections 2.5.1, 2.5.7). Grin (1996) rightly argues that language cannot be projected in purely economic terms (given its symbolic value) and is critical of economic terminology as an extended metaphor only. Nevertheless, the market value of languages other than English (including their use on the internet) should not be underestimated despite the dominance of English as an international lingua franca. Many young Australians from bilingual backgrounds have seized job and business opportunities in their family's former homelands in Asia and eastern Europe, and new technologies have put immigrants and their descendants in touch with the original homeland and emigrant communities in other countries. McClure (2001: 185) shows how language maintenance in the scattered Assyrian community all over the world has benefited from the use of the internet. Several contributions to Fishman (2001a) indicate that the internet is enhancing the position of minority languages such as Ainu, Frisian and Yiddish. However, Fishman (2001c: 458) argues for a need to differentiate between real and virtual community.

Many of the issues discussed in this chapter relate to the interaction between two democratic rights – the right to maintain and the right to shift. In the long run, it would appear that perceived cost-benefits will tip the balance in favour of the latter. But how and when this occurs is subject to a great deal of variation.

2.6   Concluding remarks

In this chapter, we have seen the effects of *individual factors*, such as generation, age, exogamy, gender, socioeconomic mobility and English proficiency, *group factors*, such as community size, cultural distance, religion, premigration experience and situation in the homeland, and *general factors*, such as time and place, on language shift and language shift differential. LS has emerged as a product of premigration and postmigration experiences mediated through culture. We have also considered the applicability of a number of models to the study of LS dynamics, using Australia an example – Kloss's, Conklin and Lourie's, and Edwards's taxonomic-typological ones; Giles et al.'s ethnolinguistic vitality model; Fishman's predictive and reversing language shift models; and Smolicz's one on core values. Each of them – whether taxonomic, quantificational or quasi-implicational – is able to depict part of the language shift process in a very significant way: Kloss in its open-ended approach demonstrating that the same factors may work in different directions; Conklin and Lourie's more extensive enumeration of factors; Edwards in setting up the basis for a relationship between factors and settings;[17] Giles in introducing the highly relevant notion of perceived ethnolinguistic vitality; Smolicz in initiating the core values issue; Fishman et al. (1985) in the provision of a more exact and predictive model; and Fishman (1991) in its focus on the disruptive factors giving rise to LS and in enabling the programmatic discussion of reversing LS. These models also have their shortcomings – Kloss and Conklin and Lourie in their limited possibilities of combining factors, Edwards in its vagueness, Giles in its selection of components of ethnolinguistic vitality and in its reliance on binary relations between the minority and the majority, Smolicz in its rather monolithic view of communities, Fishman et al. (1985) in its emphasis on numbers of institutions, and Fishman (1991) in its quasi-implicational assumptions, including a somewhat linear relationship between the 'diglossia' and 'power-sharing' factors. The way in which language use is conditioned by the culture and history of the group and its members, their present-day needs and their current environment will be subject to considerable variation and change especially over time and generation. This means that taxonomies and components of models need to be kept open-ended as combinations of factors can change the influence of any individual factor. Moreover, language use reflects people's multiple identities, different constituent parts of which may be emphasized at various times and in different places.

3   On models and terms

3.1   Introduction

In this chapter, I will attempt to provide a context for the corpus-based discussion of some of the dynamics of convergence. Models, terminology and the preoccupations of recent research literature will be explored and a rationale proposed for my own treatment of language contact phenomena.[1]

3.2   The troublesome terminology around 'code-switching'

Before we discuss various theoretical frameworks, let us consider what 'code-switching' has come to mean. There are three main ways of conceptualizing code-switching:

i. in contrast to 'borrowing';
ii. subsuming 'borrowing';
iii. with indexical (or other discourse) function only, for instance indicating group membership or 'otherness' (in conversational analysis, in contrast to language switching).

Ever since Haugen (1953) gave prominence to 'switching', it has been customary to differentiate between 'borrowing' (also called 'importation') and 'switching' (Haugen 1956: 50 actually worked with a trichotomy 'importation'/'integration'/'switching'). Gumperz (1964) introduced the term 'code-switching' for switching with a discourse function (see below, section 5.2). However, over time it was employed increasingly for any kind of switching, irrespective of its functions. 'Code' there simply means 'language' or 'variety'. However, some conversation analysts (e.g. Alvarez-Caccámo 1998; Meeuwis and Blommaert 1998) have recently reclaimed the term and advocate making explicit the distinction between *code-switching*, where the code and the switch have emblematic meaning and discourse functions, and *language* or *variety switching* or *alternation* where the 'codes' and the 'switch' may not necessarily be communicatively meaningful. Meeuwis and Blommaert suggest that the 'codes' may not be two distinct languages but may be, for instance, two lects, one of which is mixed and one of which is not.

Some scholars, such as McClure (1977), Kachru (1978), Sridhar (1978), Pfaff (1979) and Bokamba (1988) differentiate between 'code-mixing' and 'code-switching' – some on the basis of whether it is intersentential [code-switching] or intrasentential [code-mixing] (e.g. Kachru), some on contextual criteria (i.e. 'code-switching' marks a change in the social situation, e.g. Kachru, Sridhar). Auer (1990, 1998) distinguishes between 'code-switching', where there is an alternation between languages or a preference for one language or another with a meaning discernable through sequencing, and code-mixing (the community's code), where there is no such alternation or preference in the community. Boeschoten (1998) expresses misgivings about the isolation of some 'code-switching' research from language change and other language contact phenomena.

Some (e.g. McClure) have 'code-switching' as the umbrella term, while Muysken (2000), for instance, employs 'code-mixing' as the generic term, being more neutral, and 'code-switching' for 'rapid succession of several languages in a single speech event' (Muysken 2000: 1). His 'code-mixing' includes what many others term 'code-switching' and Muysken often employs 'switch' as the verb corresponding to 'code-mixing'. Many scholars have decided on one or the other term. Mufwene (1994) argues that, as an umbrella term, 'mixing' is more appropriate than 'code-switching' because some phenomena currently included under the latter are ones contributing to mixed languages. However, the general tendency is to regard 'code-switching' as the generic category of language contact. This has been accompanied by a marginalization of phonetic/phonological and prosodic transference (Cruz-Ferreira 1999).

There is a great deal of disagreement in recent literature as to what determines clearcut instances of both 'borrowing' and 'code-switching'. In recent years also, there has developed a consensus among some linguists (e.g. Myers-Scotton 1992; Treffers-Daller 1994; Backus 1996; Mahootian 1996; Boyd 1997) that there is no clear dividing line between 'code-switching' and 'borrowing', that they form a continuum. Schatz (1989) provided a list of shared and discrete features of 'borrowing' and 'code-switching' based on the state of the field at the time. While the term 'code-switching' is employed for both single-word and multi-word elements, 'borrowing' is limited to the former. Phonological or morphological integration is likely in borrowing but not in 'code-switching'. Myers-Scotton (1993a: 180) has argued that borrowing as well as 'code-switching' shows both complete and incomplete grammatical integration but that there may be a quantitative difference. Schatz's summary of the literature shows that monolinguals or bilinguals can 'borrow' but only bilinguals 'code-switch'. Myers-Scotton (1993a), for instance, argues that other language contact phenomena operate on similar principles as 'code-switching' in the way in which forms or constituents from one language are embedded in another. But borrowings are part of the lexicon of the matrix language and code-switches belong to the embedded-language lexicon. A distinction is often made (e.g. Myers-Scotton 1993a; Muysken 2000: 69) between 'code-switching/mixing' – embedding other-language words or constituents into a clause – and 'borrowing' – entering (them) into the lexicon. I would contend that a rigid 'borrowing'/'code-switching' distinction would tend to accentuate the discreteness of the systems when we are dealing with a dynamic relationship between languages that are interconnected and constantly changing (see chapters 4 and 5).

The most prominent protagonist of the 'borrowing'/'switching' distinction is Poplack. The important question of how central the 'transferred' item has become in the recipient language (or any idiolect of it) is addressed in the terminological framework of Poplack and her associates (e.g. Poplack 1980; Poplack, Sankoff and Miller 1988; Poplack, Wheeler and Westwood 1989; Poplack and Meechan 1995, 1998) who introduce 'nonce borrowings' (single-item switches used in individual cases) as a third category beside 'borrowing' and 'code-switching' (see below, section 3.4.2). This category, while sharing features with code-switching, does not conform to the proposed constraint. Myers-Scotton (1993a) and others reject the category as superfluous: 'a resting-place out of harm's way for single lexemes which are not clearly established as borrowings' (Myers-Scotton 1993a: 23). Muysken (2000: 79) deals with Poplack's 'nonce borrowings' rather as a category smaller than a full determiner phrase, such as a NP. There is a long-standing differentiation between intersentential and intrasentential code-switching. Myers-Scotton (1993a) has introduced for her analysis the notion of intra-CP^2 switching, i.e. within the complementizer of projection, often corresponding to the clause.

If the terms are on a continuum and the main reason for the distinction is the need for a term other than 'code-switching' denoting a high degree of acceptance into the recipient language, then it might be better to start from a term that can include this. The term 'code-switching' has now become so polysemous and unclear that it is necessary to find more precise terms to map out the boundaries and interfaces. This would free 'code-switch(ing)' to be used for emblematic functions between symbolically significant codes – or more loosely, as it sometimes is today, without affecting debates where preciseness is required (see also Boeschoten 1998). In section 3.3, I will try to build a framework based on the umbrella term 'transference', which I have been employing (in slightly varying forms) since the 1960s (e.g. Clyne 1967). It will cover *some* aspects of 'code-switching' as employed in a general sense today, and diachronic as well as synchronic dimensions. (An instance of 'transference' is termed a 'transfer'.) However, it may be desirable to preserve a term such as 'borrowing' in historical linguistics, lexicography and language planning in the discussion of stability and codification of the items. If 'borrowing' does not require the speaker to be bilingual, it is perhaps not an appropriate term for issues concerning specifically plurilinguals.

It could perhaps be argued that 'borrowing' may also be more useful in stable bilingual situations such as Brussels and Strasbourg (cf. Treffers-Daller 1994; Gardner-Chloros 1991) than in the description of highly variable corpora such as the ones dealt with in this monograph. Backus (1996) observes more lexical transference among the intermediate generation (generation 1b) than other generations of Turkish–Dutch bilinguals. (Dutch does not play an important role for the first, Haugen's generation 1a, and there is more switching in the second.[3])

The degree of integration, i.e. the position of transfers between the centre and the periphery of the receiving language system, must remain part of the agenda, but since this is a complex issue involving typological differences and further continua, it should be addressed through subcategorization (see section 4.5.1). Also, the 'centrality' of the item should perhaps be determined at the individual level – is it a central part of the individual's system in that particular language? With 'code-switching' now sometimes being regarded as the generic language contact phenomenon, research runs the risk of being distracted from semantic and phonological language contact phenomena which coexist and interact with lexical and syntactic ones. A coherent terminology could contribute to a recognition of this.[4]

3.2.1 Different types of 'code-switching'

Let us consider where the differentiation between 'borrowing' and 'code-switching' has been sought and how 'code-switching' has been subcategorized. 'Integration' and 'frequency' are the main criteria employed to establish 'borrowing' (I shall return to this point under section 4.5.1). In addition to the dilemmas and problems in differentiating between 'code-switching' and 'borrowing', 'code-switching' is not a uniform category, and different scholars have emphasized different aspects of the phenomenon. The subcategorization into three types of 'code-switching/ mixing' has been the achievement of Muysken (1997, 2000). The first type is *insertion*, involving the embedding of a constituent, either a single-word or a multiple-word item, usually in a nested ABA structure (A and B designating the two languages). For instance:

(1)   Yo anduve IN A STATE OF SHOCK por dos dias
        'I walked in a state of shock for two days'
        (Spanish–English, Pfaff 1979, cited for categorization by Muysken
        1997)

In relation to nominal constructions, examples of such switching, are, according to Muysken (2000: 60): Noun, NP (ADJ + N, N + CONJ), DGNP (NPs marked for number, gender and definiteness), and DP (full DET phrase).

The second type is *alternation*. This is where two languages remain relatively separate (Muysken 2000: 96), for example:

(2)   Andale pues AND DO COME AGAIN
       'That's alright then, and do come again'
       (Spanish–English, Peñalosa 1980, cited for categorization by Muysken 1997)

A variant of alternation is where the switched string is preceded and followed by elements not structurally related from the other language (Muysken 2000: 97), for example:

(3)   Bij mijn broer Y A UN ASCENSEUR en alles
       'At my brother's place there is a lift and everything'
       (Dutch–French, Treffers-Daller 1994: 204, cited for categorization in Muysken 2000: 97)

Muysken's third category, *congruent lexicalization*, is where the two languages share a grammatical structure which can be filled lexically with elements from each language and there is planning in both languages simultaneously, for example:

(4)   't geet *vaak* AUTOMATISCH BIJ JOU
       'It often goes automatically with you'
       (Switching between Ottersum dialect and Standard Dutch)
       (Giesbers 1989: 149, cited for categorization by Muysken 2000: 131)

We will return to Muysken's classification and reconceptualization of 'code-mixing' in section 3.4.4 and section 5.3.

3.2.2   Multiple transference

My earlier terminology employed 'lexical transference' for the transference of individual lexical items (Clyne 1975) and 'multiple transference' for the transference of whole stretches of speech, beyond the single lexeme from one language to the other (Clyne 1967). The latter includes combinations of adjective and noun that could be regarded as a compound noun, for example:

(5)   Wir machen hier MIXED FARMING
       We do   here mixed   farming
       'We do mixed farming here' (MGP 8m)[5]

two or three consecutive words, which could in some cases, constitute a phrase, e.g.

(6)   Hier sind einige CLUMPS OF TREES
        'Here are several clumps of trees' (MGP 103m)

and a complete change to the other language in the form of what is often designated as 'intrasentential code-switching', for example:

(7)   Der *Farmer'* S GOT[6] Schafe
        'The farmer's got sheep' (MGP 123m, generation 1b)

Although there is not complete sharing of syntax, the German equivalent being 'Der Farmer hat Schafe', this can be regarded as an instance of Muysken's congruent lexicalization. (5) and (6) would be instances of insertion.

(8)   Am Montag seh' ich am liebsten *'The Nelsons'* AND THEN 'Doctor
        Kildare' AND THEN WE TURN IT OFF
        'On Monday I like to see "The Nelsons" most and then "Dr Kildare"
        and then we turn it off'
        (MGP 26f, talking about the television programs she watched)

In considering such examples, (5) and (6) are utterances in which a single lexical item is transferred and should be regarded as a subset of lexical transference. However, in (7), the lexeme *Farmer* seems to have triggered *'s got*. The phenomenon of triggering is discussed in section 5.3. Similarly, in (8), *and then* and *and then we turn it off* appear to be triggered by the names of English-language television programs, which are used in German discourse too. *Farmer* in (7), like the names of the television films in (8), are not part of the 'switch' but items of the overlapping area between the two languages. Example (8) would be a candidate for alternation in Muysken's framework.

It will be clear that, in (8), in contrast to the other examples, we have an entire clause (corresponding to a large degree to CP – Complementizer of Projection – in Myers-Scotton's terms based on Government and Binding Theory) in the other language, but the first transfer was before this. In (7) and (8), the speaker is crossing over into the other language rather than transferring *something*, a lexical item or unit, from one language to another. We may be dealing here with a process that is psychologically different to other kinds of lexical transference. This needs to be specially labelled in a way that distinguishes it from the lexical transference commonly referred to as 'code-switching'. Moreover, as we will be arguing that lexical transference may facilitate transversion (section 5.3), it would be confusing to refer to both as 'code-switching'. In section 5.3 below where I will discuss this, I will refer to it as 'transversion'. In the terminological dilemma in which I find myself, two possibilities present themselves – the use of 'code-switching' in a more restricted way than that used by many colleagues, which can be confusing, or the coinage of a new term, which denotes what I wish to express. The coinage of any new term is sometimes considered superfluous and distracting, so I invite readers to substitute 'code-switching' if they prefer this but to take into account that 'transversion' only covers some of the meanings of the now polysemous term. It differs from fixed expressions such as *up and away* or compound nouns such as *mixed farming*, which are multiple transfers. Transversion includes both intra- and interclausal (CP or sentential) switching. It enables us to express 'crossing over' *to* the other language rather than alternating *between* the languages. Moreover, 'alternation' is employed by conversation analysts in a more general sense as they restrict 'code-switching' to the indexical function (Auer 1998). Also, 'alternation' is one of the two categories described by Muysken (1997, 2000) which cover our 'transversion', the other being 'congruent lexicalization'. Muysken (e.g. 2000: 274) shows a strong differentiation between insertion on the one hand and alternation and congruent lexicalization on the other in relation to types of contact phenomena and to language change.

3.3   A terminological framework – transference at different levels of language

The first part of my model builds on a terminological framework based on 'transference'. A 'transfer' is an instance of transference, where the form, feature or construction has been taken over by the speaker from another language, whatever the motives or explanation for this. 'Transference' is thus the process and a 'transfer' the product. The terms have the advantage of covering lexical, semantic, phonetic/phonological, prosodic, tonemic, graphemic, morphological and syntactic transference, and any combinations of any of these (e.g. lexicosyntactic; see also section 5.2, section 5.3.3, below). They enable us to label which aspects of language have been affected by transference. This kind of terminological framework has served me well for my purposes. I respect and appreciate the terms used by colleagues because they consider them appropriate for their data and the objectives of their studies. I am grateful to readers for their continuing acceptance of terminological flexibility.

Lexical transference – the transference of lexemes (i.e. words in form and content), for example:

(9)   German:
         Die *Apricots* in unserem *Backyard* sind so *beautiful* (MGPR 43f)

This includes instances of varying degrees and types of integration, e.g. *Gumtrees* and *Gum*bäume [gumbɔymə]. These are subcategorized in section 4.5.1.

Multiple transference – the transference of a number of collocated lexical items, whether in fixed expressions or not, for example:

(10)   German:
         Hier sind einige CLUMPS OF TREES
         'Here are several clumps of trees' (MGP 103m; see section 3.2.2)
(11)   Croatian
         tako da to sve.. bi bilo FOR FREE
         'so all that would be for free' (MCr 26f, from Hlavac 2000)

Morphemic transference – the transference of bound morphemes, for example:

(12)   English:
         Düsseldorf*er* boat
         (*-er* transforms German proper nouns into adjectives)
         (English speaker living in Germany, Clyne 1969)

Morphological transference – the transference of a morphological pattern, e.g. the generalization of the *-s* plural in Dutch: klant*s* for klant*en* 'clients' (MD 66m), stam*s* for stammen 'stems' (MD 202m), hoofleiding*s* for hoofleiding*en* 'mains' (MD 62m). (As we will discuss in section 4.4.3, this can be seen as morphological change in which transference plays a part.)

Semantic transference – the transference of meanings from words in one language to words in another with some morphemic or semantic correspondence,[7] for example:

Greek *depozito* (tank) used in the sense of Eng. *deposit* (Greek *katatheto*) (Tamis 1986).

Italian *fattoria* (small farm) used in the sense of Eng. *factory* (It. *fabbrica*).

Dutch *speciaal* (special) used in the sense of Eng. *specially* (Du. *vooral*), for example:

(13)   speciaal toen we in de *hills* kwamen
         'especially when we came in the hills'
         Homeland Dutch:[8] vooral toen we naar de heuvelen kwamen

Spanish *oficio* (office – task, job) used in the sense of Eng. *office* (workplace – Sp. *oficina*) (Kaminskas 1972).

German *sehen* used in the sense of Eng. *see* (visit), for example:

(14)   *sehe* CLIENTS WHICH, mit denen ich in Verbindung bin
         'see clients which . . . with whom I am in contact'
         Homeland German: treffe ich mich mit Kollegen, mit denen ich im
         Kontakt stehe (*treff mich* – meet) (MGP 193m)

Syntactic transference – the transference of syntactic rules, for example:
Spanish ADJ + N used instead of N + ADJ: *la mas vieja casa* (Homeland Spanish: la casa mas vieja) (Kaminskas 1972).

Dutch V2 in statement sentences and SOV in subordinate clauses replaced by English SVO construction:

(15)   Dutch:
Maar als wij *praten* in het Hollands, ze *verstaan* drommels goed
'But if we speak in Dutch, they understand damned well'
Homeland Dutch: maar als wij in het Hollands *praten, verstaan* ze drommels goed (MD 199m)

Lexicosyntactic transference – the transference of one or more lexemes and the syntactic constructions:

Transference of English conjunction and the SVO word order to replace SOV in subordinate clause:

(16)   Dutch:
BECAUSE die Grieksen *hebben* een hele typische inslag
'because those Greeks have a very typical streak'
Homeland Dutch: omdat de Grieksen een heel typische inslag *hebben* (MD 48f)

Morpheme-for-morpheme transference of an idiom and of one of the lexical items:

(17)   German:
einen   kühlen   DRINK   *haben*
a   cool   drink   have+INF
'have a cold drink'
Homeland German: Etwas kühles trinken
(MGP 69m) (German uses a verbal construction and English a nominal one)

Semanticosyntactic transference – the transference of meanings and the syntactic construction of the whole syntagmatic unit (idiomatic expression):

(18)   Dutch:
Ik ga uit voor een drive
'I go out for a drive'
Homeland Dutch:
Ik   ga   een   auto   tochtje   maken
I   go   a   car   excursion+DIMIN   make+INF (second generation)

Phonological transference – the addition or deletion of phonemes because of the phonemic structure of the other language, e.g. /ts/ replaced by /s/ in third-generation German-English bilinguals.

Phonic transference – the transference of phones from language to language, e.g. /r/ in final position not realized in second-generation Italian speakers in

North Queensland (Bettoni 1981a) or second-generation Polish speakers not voicing final stops, centralizing all unstressed vowels and diphthongizing and/or lengthening stressed vowels (Sussex 1982a).

Graphemic transference – the transference of English phoneme–grapheme relations, e.g. <ie> for <ei> as in z*ie*chnen (for z*ei*chnen); the dropping of distinctive graphemes, e.g. <u> for <ü> as in St*u*hle (for St*ü*hle); the dropping of distinctive sequences, e.g. <sch> as in *Sh*atten (Schatten) (second generation).

Prosodic transference – the transference of Australian English rising intonation for statements in German, Greek, Italian and Polish.

Tonemic transference – the transference of tones or the absence of tones from another language, e.g the dropping of highest and lowest tones in Vietnamese by young bilinguals in Melbourne (Tuc Ho-Dac, pers. comm.).

Pragmatic transference – the transference of pragmatic patterns, e.g. informal forms of address in situations where the formal form would normally be required; discourse markers, such as *well*; or more 'indirect' Australian English request patterns, as in:

(19)   Polish:
        Mamo czy mozèsz mi prosze dác soku?
        'Mummy, can you please give me a drink of juice?'
        Homeland Polish: Mamo daj mi prosze soku?
        'Mummy, give me please a drink of juice?'
        (Wierzbicka 1985: 202; see also Wierzbicka 1991; Kasper and Blum-Kulka 1994)

3.3.1   Convergence and its relation to transference

Convergence means different things to different researchers. I am employing it as a general term to denote making languages more similar to each other (including through transference). However, when preceded by an adjective, e.g. syntactic, phonological, it will be used in Weinreich's (1953: 41–2) sense of partial similarity increasing at the expense of differences. This does not necessarily mean *both* languages converging (cf. Silva-Corvalán 1994). Myers-Scotton's and Jake's (2000) sense of 'convergence' – morphemes from one language and 'lexical structures' from another – overlaps with my semantico-syntactic transference. In order to distinguish between transference and convergence, let us consider a pair of syntactic examples. Two ways of expressing 'we went to school in Tarrington':

(20)   Standard German:
        Wir *sind*   in Tarrington zur   Schule *gegangen*
        we   AUX+be in Tarrington to.the school go+PAST.PT

indicate the difference between syntactic convergence and syntactic transference.

(21)   a. Wir *haben*   zu Schule *gegangen*   in Tarrington
           we AUX+have to school go+PAST.PT in Tarrington
           (MGWD 2m)

        b. Wir *haben gegangen* zu Schule in Tarrington
           we have   gone   to school in Tarrington

While (21b) shows a morpheme-for-morpheme correspondence with the English, and thus constitutes syntactic transference, there is no morpheme-for-morpheme correspondence in (21a), which converges towards the English.

Convergence includes phonological and prosodic compromise forms, such as [ɔf] < German auf/English of; [hai'drant] < German [hy'drant]/English [haɪdrənt].

3.3.2   Transversion

Transversion was mentioned under section 3.2.2 as referring to a crossing over from one language to another rather than a transference of an item, feature or construction. This is crucial in the discussion of facilitation processes such as triggering:

Triggering – transversion as the result of trigger-words, words at the intersection of two language systems.

A detailed discussion of this may be found in section 5.3.

3.4   Some language contact frameworks

A recent preoccupation in language contact research has been with the development of constraints on 'code-switching'. The precursor of this direction was Hasselmo (1974: 48–9), who found that his Swedish–English bilinguals in the US observed regularities in the ways in which they employed items in their Swedish, e.g. for 'foxyness' they used *foxyness* or *foxighet* not *foxigness* or *foxyhet*; and for 'tough guys', *tougha guyer* and *tougha gubbar* but not *tough guyar* and *tough gubbar*. However, he did not make claims that extended beyond contact between Swedish and English in a particular setting. In the late 1970s and 1980s, there were attempts to postulate constraints that were valid universally, across contact language pairs and groups. This was followed by a quest for constraints 'resulting from the interaction of universal principles and aspects particular to each code mixing situation' (Appel and Muysken 1987: 126). The most recent stage has been the development of overall theories embracing constraints, notably Myers-Scotton's Matrix Language Frame Model.

In order to understand the similarities and differences between my emphases and those of others working in the field, I will briefly summarize the frameworks of a number of colleagues.

3.4.1   Myers-Scotton and Jake: Matrix Language Frame model (MLF)

This model, developed by Myers-Scotton (1993a) and elaborated by her and Jake, is the most comprehensive and influential current framework in this field. It has constantly undergone modifications to account for new data and in response to criticisms (e.g. Jake and Myers-Scotton 1997; Myers-Scotton and Jake 1995, 2000; Jake et al. fc, see section 3.4.7). It is designed to explain grammatical and lexical choices and 'constraints' in a universal framework. More recently, Myers-Scotton has restricted the model to what she terms 'classic code-switching', where the speaker can produce well-formed utterances in both (all of) the languages. The MLF model does not address intersentential code-switching, for example, because the construct of a ML is not relevant there. The most important principles of the MLF model are:

i. One of the languages in contact is the matrix language (ML) which sets the morphosyntactic frame for constituents within a CP (complementizer of projection) involving both the matrix language and one or more embedded languages (ELs). Each CP has one matrix language.

ii. Morpheme order principle – in mixed constituents, the morpheme order principle requires a morpheme order which is that of the matrix language.

iii. System morpheme principle – in mixed constituents, those system morphemes external to their head constituent come from the matrix language (see below).

Myers-Scotton and Jake work with three types of 'code-switching' constituents:

i. mixed ML + EL constituents, with morphemes from two or more languages;

ii. ML islands, constituents from the ML only and in accordance with its grammar;

iii. EL islands, constituents from the EL only and in accordance with its grammar.

Code-switching will occur, among other things, where there is a lack of congruence due to differences in the syntax of the two languages. As single-word switches and multiple-word switches both constitute embedding onto an ML, they are treated together as 'code-switching'. Other forms of language contact phenomena can also be treated in much the same way. The ML and EL can change roles over time. This is termed a 'turnover' (see section 4.6).

Myers-Scotton and Jake postulate a blocking hypothesis whereby EL content morphemes are blocked if they do not meet the conditions of ML lemmas.[9] Subsequently, Myers-Scotton and Jake (2000) have developed an Abstract Level providing a framework for linking the (modular) production of surface lexemes to abstract information in lexical entries at three levels of complex lexical structure – conceptual, functional, positional (see chapter 6).

Myers-Scotton and Jake (2000) also postulate four types of morphemes – *content morphemes*, directly elected and activated at the lemma level, and three types of system morphemes differentiated according to how they are elected, thereby proposing a link between the surface structures and their relative accessibility in production. *Early system morphemes*, like content morphemes, are activated conceptually. They are realized without going outside the maximal projections, e.g. a definite article is within the NP maximal projection, and its form depends only on the content morpheme with which it is used (like -*s* in *apricots*). Early system morphemes are activated at the lemma level but do not assign (like most verbs, some prepositions) or receive thematic roles (most nouns and adjectives). They are elected by content morphemes. *Late system morphemes* are not activated at the lemma level. There are two types – those which depend on information other than the head within the maximal projection (*bridge morphemes*, e.g. Ger. genitive -*s* in *Bruders*) and those which depend on information outside their own maximal projection (*outsider system morphemes*, e.g. the -*t* in Dut. hij spreek*t* 'he is speaking' or the *niente* in It. non so niente 'I don't know anything', dependent on *hij* and *non* respectively). In addition, the revised model attempts to explain how intentions are related to surface forms. This is done by demonstrating asymmetries in code-switching, such as plural marking in both matrix and embedded languages, difficulty in inserting verbs from English into an Arabic grammatical frame, the preference for Swiss German nouns with Italian determiners in Italian–Swiss German switching, and the tendency for full English NPs not to occur in a Spanish morphosyntactic frame. All these can be attributed to the languages in contact having equivalent morphemes processed at different stages. Double marking, not just with plurals but also inflections on both auxiliary and participle, for instance, occurs frequently in Dutch–Turkish bilingualism (Backus 1996: 353–5). Hlavac (2000: 127–8) has instances in his corpus from second-generation Croatian–English bilinguals in Australia, for example:

(22)   imam moja Mam*in's* sestra je tu
         I have my   mum's   sister be here
         'I have my Mum's sister here'

where the possessive marker from both Croatian (*in*) and English (*s*) are added. There are also examples of only the English possessive being added to a Croatian kinship term, for example:

(23)   moj tata*'s* family je sve u Zagreb
         'my father's family is all in Zagreb' (same speaker)

Two other instances of double marking cited by Hlavac (2000) from second-generation Croatian–English bilinguals are:

(24)   Azija*n*sku hranu
         'Asian food'

where both an English (*n*) and a Croatian adjectival marker (*sku*) are applied, and

(25)   skrim*dijo*
         scream+PAST+3sg
         'she screamed'

where both English (*d*) and Croatian past-participle inflections (*ijo*) are added to the verb. Hlavac offers three possible explanations of the last example:

a. feature checking for tense and election of morphemes of English-origin Croatian verbs;
b. *skrimd* is unanalysed;
c. *skrimd* is the 'desired' form which is being repaired.

Bare (uninflected) forms, one of the consequences of interlingual asymmetry, will be discussed in section 4.4.

The four morphemes (4M) model has illuminated the effectiveness of the System Morpheme Principle. In studies of Hungarian–English child bilingualism, Bolonyai (2000) has demonstrated the usefulness of the early–late system morpheme distinction to explain why nominative and accusative morphemes (late SMs) are produced less accurately than oblique or lexical case morphemes. It also facilitates an understanding of Hungarian preverbs which are at the same time early and late SMs and are produced accurately more in the latter function. On the other hand, Schmitt (2000) notes the absence of late SMs in her Russian–English child bilinguals except for English EL islands. The late SMs are from the ML, even if some part of the abstract-level structure is mapped from the EL (i.e. there is semantic and/or syntactic transference). This she explains by the lack of a necessary Russian slot in a frame as opposed to the use of the English system of case marking in a Russian grammatical frame. On the basis of her data from Pennsylvania German, which shows hardly any late SMs from English, Fuller (2000) argues that the early–late SM distinction makes it possible to predict the route of structural convergence in language shift.

Myers-Scotton (1993a: 17, 25–6) indicates that there are two issues which the MLF does not deal with – convergence and triggering. The former, however, had to be tackled in time because it was sometimes difficult to designate the embedded and matrix languages due to what I term 'syntactic convergence' and 'syntactic transference'. Jake and Myers-Scotton (1997, Myers-Scotton 1997a) have revised their model to accommodate bilingual speech in which the morphosyntactic frame derives from more than one source language,[10] i.e. the matrix language is not any *specific* language but a composite matrix language and the speakers are not 'classic code-switchers'. Syntactic convergence is discussed under section 4.4, section 4.4.8.

Jake (1994) has used the 4M model to demonstrate why pronouns rarely participate in code-switching. Among other things, it can be attributed to pronouns having different status in the 4M model in different languages in contact.

3.4.2   Poplack

In her quest for a formula for how languages in contact 'fit together in code-switching', Poplack was one of the pioneers of the study of universal constraints on code-switching. It has thus been very important for her to clarify any ambiguities between 'code-switching' and 'borrowing' in relation to 'lone items', as 'borrowing' is constrained differently from 'code-switching'. This remains one of the ongoing tasks facing her and her colleagues (e.g. Poplack and Meechan 1998). The category of 'nonce borrowings' (used only once) enables them to deal with incidental items in such a way that they do not need to abide by the constraints. 'Code-switching', according to Poplack, operates on the grammatical constraints of both languages while 'borrowing' is constrained grammatically by the recipient language. That is an important distinction from the MLF Model, which has the matrix language providing the morphosyntactic frame of mixed constituent code-switching.

Poplack (1980) postulates two constraints:

1. Equivalence – the syntax on either side of code-switching must be grammatical for the language concerned, for example:

(26)   El MAN que CAME ayer   WANTS JOHN comprar A CAR nuevo
        the man who came yesterday wants John to.buy a car new
        'The man who came yesterday wants John to buy a new car'
(27)   Tell Larry QUE SE   CALLE   LA BOCA
        tell Larry that he+REFL shut + SUBJ+3sg the mouth
        'Tell Larry to shut his mouth' (Examples from Poplack 1980: 587)

2. Free morpheme – there is no switch between the bound morpheme and the lexical form unless the latter is phonologically integrated into the language of the bound morpheme, e.g. * EAT-iendo (Poplack 1980: 586; see also section 4.5.1).

The prevalence of counterevidence from a range of language contact dyads and situations (see, for example, the references in Clyne 1987) demonstrates that, expressed more cautiously, these are not universal constraints but strong tendencies. In other words, the Equivalence Constraint really indicates that syntactic overlap facilitates 'switching', not that lack of structural overlap prevents such switching. Evidence in favour of this will be presented below, in section 5.3.3. There is by now a strong general preference for 'tendencies' rather than 'constraints' in various branches of linguistics (e.g. Harris and Campbell 1995; Muysken 1995; to some extent Halmari 1997; see below).

The papers in Poplack and Meechan (1998), by scholars working within a variationist framework (with careful quantification) on a range of languages in contact with English (Turkish – Adalar and Tagliamonte, Ukrainian – Budzhak-Jones, Igbo – Eze, Iranian – Ghafar Samar and Meechan, and Acadian French – Turpin, all in Poplack and Meechan 1998), generally support the code-switching/borrowing dichotomy on the basis of the language imposing constraints – the recipient language in borrowing, the source languages in code-switching. Another significant finding (Ghafar Samar and Meechan, Eze) is that, in their corpus, bare forms that are borrowings do not occur proportionately more than bare forms do in monolingual speech (but see sections 4.4.6, 4.5.1.3). Most lone-word items, including 'nonce borrowings', turn out to be 'borrowings' according to Poplack et al.'s criteria (see, for example, Ghafar Samar and Meechan 1998).

3.4.3 Other models and constraints proposed

3.4.3.1 Government
In the 1980s, a number of other constraints were proposed, by other colleagues (see Clyne 1987). The most important of these was the *Government Constraint*, hereafter GC (Di Sciullo, Muysken and Singh 1986), which runs according to more abstract hierarchical relations than the surface and linear constraints proposed by Poplack and Sankoff. The GC holds that switching is possible only between elements not related by government (for example, V governs O and P governs the NP in a PP). This constraint proved to be too powerful and eliminated large numbers of examples (Bentahila and Davies 1983, Arabic–French; Clyne 1987, German/Dutch–English; Nortier 1990, Arabic–Dutch). Muysken (1995) discarded this constraint in favour of pluralistic explanations and (Muysken 2000: 25) admitted that it was too powerful. However, it is reinstated in a revised form by Halmari (1997). She downplays the universal validity of the constraint by describing it as a 'probabalistic tendency' (p. 191) based on the properties of the particular languages in contact, especially their government relations. She argues that it may find different manifestations in different contact languages and needs to be supplemented by sociolinguistic, discourse and pragmatic factors as explanations. The governed element has to be tied to its governor by a language carrier (e.g. Finnish inflection) that matches the language of the governor. A reformulation is also proposed by Muysken (2000: 25) involving the incorporation of functional elements as governors.

Halmari uses American Finnish data to argue that switches between NPs and VPs (previously disallowed by the GC) can be explained by government together with the language carrier. For instance, a normally unacceptable switch between a case-assigning verb and an object-determiner phrase becomes acceptable when a Finnish case morpheme is added to an English noun. Thus the degree of morphological integration paradoxically becomes a criterion of 'code-switching', which was traditionally contrasted with borrowing on the basis of integration. Among arguments for the GC is backtracking, where speakers are correcting violations of the constraint. Examples are:

(28)   Mir nehmen[11] unse Bücher für FOR FOUR *periods*
         'we take our books for (Ger)/ for four (Eng) periods' (MGP 92f –
         generation 1b)

where a young German–English bilingual backtracks to the beginning of the PP where she realizes that the head word was going to be a lexical transfer from English; and

(29)   Wir lernen Englisch (A) / und WELL, WE LEARN ENGLISH,
         GEOGRAPHY, HISTORY, SCIENCE (MGP 123m, generation 1b)

where another young bilingual, enumerating her school subjects, realizes that she lacks some German vocabulary and returns to the beginning of the sentence.
    Perseveration is used to *break* the GC in:

(30)   IT SHOWS es IT SHOWS den großen Unterschied zwischen
         einer richtigen Großstadt und einer REAL typischen australischen
         CONSERVATIVE CITY
         'It shows it it shows the big difference between a real metropolis and
         a real typical Australian conservative city'
         (MGP 192m, talking in German about a picture of an Australian city
         street)

where a switch back occurs between V and NP.
    Halmari argues that languages with rich inflections (e.g. Finnish and Turkish) do not discard them in code-switching. (Her criterion for 'code-switching' is phonological.) This is supported by Boyd's (1997) comparison of Swedish–English and Swedish–Finnish bilingualism in Sweden. However, this could also be seen in terms of the integration conventions of the more richly inflected language and the range of integration options (see below, section 4.5.1).

3.4.3.2   Belazi/Pandit

Belazi et al. (1994) propose a constraint on switching between functional heads and constituents in the maximal projection, viz. COMP and IP, INFL and VP, NEG and VP, DET and NP, quantifier/number and NP. Belazi et al.'s constraint permits switching between ADJ and N, PREP and complements of PREP, their relationship not being one of functional head and complements. Where

ADJ + N order clashes between the languages, the word obeys the order of the language from which it is derived. Pandit (1990), also working within a Universal Grammar framework, postulates that code-switching must not violate the grammar of the head of the maximal projection within which it takes place.

3.4.3.3 Mahootian

Mahootian (1996) has built her competence model on Pandit's (1990) postulation that a model does not require any special treatment for bilingual speech. Mahootian does not differentiate between 'borrowing' and 'code-switching' as she claims that the latter can be dealt with by assigning it to one or the other languages. For instance, in the sequence ADJ + N, the language of the adjective determines its position, and in a VP, the word order is guided by the language of the verb. This is certainly not the case with participles transferred and integrated into German (or Dutch), for example:

(31)   Wir haben inzwischen   schon   ein Haus gerentet.
         we   have   in the meantime   already   a   house   rent+PAST.PT
         'Meanwhile we have rented a house' (MGP 97f)

Presumably Mahootian would regard the participles as German. But in an example from Hlavac (2000: 353), the Croatian sentence does not take its word order from the verb *supervise* transferred from English:

(32)   Ne, on radi taj   posao I   ja njega SUPERVISE
         no, he does that job   and I him   supervise
         'No, he does the job and I supervise him'

The language of the adjective does not always appear to provide the word order either, as will be evident from the following sentence from our Italian–Spanish–English trilingual corpus:

(33)   No porque quiero   disprezzare a   mi LANGUAGE ITALIAN
         not because seek+1sg undervalue+INF my language   Italian
         'not that I want to undervalue my Italian language' (ISE 16f)

as opposed to:

(34)   Maria allora tiene una TEACHER italiana en la   scuola.
         Maria now   has   a   teacher   Italian   in the school.
         'Maria now has an Italian teacher at school' (same informant)

However, in (33), where the adjective, *Italian*, does not provide the word order, that word could be construed as a noun in apposition to *language (my language, Italian)*, which facilitates switching. The word order of (34) does agree with that of the adjective.

Thus, like other constraints, Mahootian's may be general tendencies.

3.4.4   Muysken: three types of 'bilingual speech'

Muysken (2000) draws not only on his own work on Quechua–Spanish and Papiamentu–Dutch switching but also on a range of corpora from other scholars, including French–Dutch, Dutch–Arabic, Dutch–English, dialect–standard Dutch, Swahili–English, Finnish–English and Frisian–Dutch. As has been mentioned in section 3.2.1, Muysken differentiates between three types of bilingual speech, which require different solutions:

Insertion – including most of Myers-Scotton's embeddings (constituent insertions), Poplack's 'borrowings' and 'nonce borrowings', and our lexical transfers – is characterized by constituent structures, the adjacency principle (based on Annamalai 1989) whereby switched elements would preferably be analyzed as one unit, and nested ABA structures.

Alternation may be found quite frequently where there is shared word order between the languages, but here the two languages remain relatively separate in an ABA sequence. It occurs, for instance, in Treffers-Daller's French–Dutch data from stable bilinguals in Brussels. Among the characteristics of alternation are: adverb modification, switching at the clause periphery, flagging, tag switching, (sometimes) long constituents, self-repair, doubling (of morphology) and the use of syntactically unintegrated discourse markers.

Congruent lexicalization is characterized by an abundance of bilingual homophones acting as trigger-words and general structural equivalence, making 'code-mixing' possible without necessary lexical correspondence. Convergence and code-mixing of this type have a mutual influence on one another. Muysken also categorizes mixed collocation with this pattern of 'code-mixing' (cf. section 5.4). Neutralization occurs so that code-mixing can occur. This is the type of 'code-mixing' where there tends not to be a clear-cut matrix language, there appear to be no constraints and switching is bi-directional. In fact, this switching pattern may convey the impression that no constraints hold. Muysken's is the only overall model which takes triggering into account. He locates the switching patterns I discuss in previous publications within his congruent lexicalization type (cf. below, section 5.3).

One of the ways in which Muysken differentiates between the categories is that, if a switched fragment forms a constituent selected by an element in the fragment in the other language, it is likely to be an insertion or congruent lexicalization; if no selection takes place, alternation is more probable.

Muysken attributes the patterns to typological differences between the languages in contact and differences in the bilingual and sociolinguistic contexts (including attitudes) and interactional settings. In particular, Muysken attributes the distinctive types of 'code-mixing' to:

Structure – very closely related languages promote congruent lexicalization; but it is also prevalent in the speech of Arabic–Dutch and Malay–Dutch

bilinguals, while the speech of Turkish–Dutch bilinguals contains more alternation and that of more recent groups in the Netherlands more insertion.
Dominance in use – increased period of residence promotes a continuum from insertion via alternation to congruent lexicalization.
Attitudes – according to Muysken, congruent lexicalization is indicative of a non-purist attitude.

Muysken resolves the controversy on whether 'code-mixing' is an indicator of a high or a low level of bilingualism (according to Poplack 1980 and Nortier 1990, high; cf. Bentahila and Davies 1983, Backus 1996, low) by alluding to the different code-mixing patterns. Bentahila and Davies study insertions and Poplack and Nortier alternations.

Muysken provides a basis for understanding some of the contradictions in the findings and interpretations in language contact studies, particularly at a time when there is an interest in establishing universals.

3.4.5 Conjunction and PP constraints

As there are two diametrically opposed versions of the conjunction constraint – that the conjoined clause conjunction must be in the language of the second clause (Gumperz 1976) or that it must be from the language from which the conjoined sentence is introduced (Kachru 1978) – its validity must be questioned. Pfaff (1979) and Bentahila and Davies (1983) find that both are possible. Pfaff's (1979) semantic constraint which allows for PPs which are temporal or figurative but not locative to be switched is not borne out by our Dutch and German anticipationally facilitated transversions where locative switches predominate (see section 5.3.1.2 and Clyne 1991: 201).

3.4.6 Johanson: code-copying

Johanson's code-copying model (1999) is less well known than the models described above. Like Myers-Scotton, he demonstrates the role of each of the languages in contact, a basic code (Myers-Scotton's matrix language) and a model code (embedded language). He projects them as a 'weak code' A and a 'strong code' B. The three procedures which Johanson categorizes are:

  i. B moves (i.e. changes, influences) A; language A is influenced but maintained: adoption of copies ('borrowing/calquing', my semantic transference), i.e. my lexical or semantic transference.

  ii. A moves (i.e. changes, influences) B; imposition of copies – expressions and syntactic structures, i.e. my syntactic, semanticosyntactic transference.

  iii. B removes A: code-shift, but language B is influenced by A substratum.

Language change and language shift are thus included in the same process. Johanson also differentiates between *global copies* (affecting combinational properties), e.g. *alles klar* 'OK'; and *selective copies* (single properties of material, 'of a combinatorial, semantic or frequential nature', producing phonological, syntactic and semantic transference, are copied). There are also mixed copies (such as 'loan blends', e.g. from our corpus: Ger. *Beach*landschaft 'beach landscape', *Ledger*buch 'ledger-book', Dut. *different*heid 'different-ness'. He postulates a rank ordering of adopting copies:

a. global copying, where the copied elements are (phonological/ morphological/ phraseological) segmental units, e.g. *alles klar* (based on 'all clear'), Norwegian Turkish *klatre-yap* 'climb-do', cf. below, section 4.5.1.3.

b. copying as isolates, where copies are used productively along with native elements, e.g. *per dag* (Lat. per + Eng. day).

c. selective copying, when it only involves single properties, e.g. *rt* realized with retroflex in Norwegian Turkish.

The most salient are copied most. These bear on both the language of the contact group and the ethnolect of the new language following code shift. This model is a little broader than the others, more useful as a diachronic theory, but less so for a syntactic theory.

3.4.7   MacSwan

On the basis of studies of data on Nahuatl–Spanish bilingualism, MacSwan (1999) contends that there are no special constraints on 'code-switching' other than the requirements of the mixed grammars and that the bilingual speaker's competence does not differ from that of monolinguals. Working within a minimalist framework, MacSwan argues against all the constraints discussed in the previous sections. Constraints to him are basically a conflict of lexical features. MacSwan concludes from his analysis of code-switching data based on minimalist principles that bilinguals have discrete lexicons, phonological systems and internal word-formation principles (e.g. for past tense) for each language. The syntactic operations, however, are shared by the languages. Code-switching theories are code-switching-specific constraints and problematic because syntactic operations should, according to MacSwan's position, be sensitive to lexically encoded language-particular parameter settings and not to identities of particular languages (p. 230). Convergence and code-switching occur where there is a mismatch, e.g. between phi (gender, case, number) relations. 'Checking' of this takes place as in monolingual speech. MacSwan does determine, on the strength of his data, what is 'allowed' (e.g. switch between Spanish pronoun and Nahuatl verb in third person) and what is 'not allowed' (e.g. switch between Spanish pronoun and Nahuatl verb in the first and second persons). This is dealt with through the PF (Phonetic Form) Disjunction Theorem which ranks constraints or orders rules. 'Borrowed' forms are those subject to rules of word formation internal to the lexicon of the recipient language – with phonological rules sensitive to affixal material. MacSwan attaches importance to determining 'code-switching' grammaticality on the basis of speakers' judgments. As chapter 5 will show, our data defies grammaticality criteria. Meechan (2001) rightly casts doubt on the reliance on speakers' judgments on 'code-switching'. As will be clear from chapter 6, the kinds of issues we are dealing with do not enable us to work with common models for monolinguals and plurilinguals.

Jake, Myers-Scotton and Gross (2002) argue that the role of the Matrix Language, which has universal status, can best explain what occurs in bilingual speech, especially linguistic mismatch in phi features, and can do so without consigning most bilingual data to 'borrowing'. They recast the MLF model in terms of minimalist grammar, introducing as a universal construct their Uniform Structure Principle, which gives any language a uniform abstract structure for constituents and a requirement of well-formedness for this constituent type. This is fulfilled by there being a matrix language. Jake et al. (fc) claim that their model is particularly suited to accommodate phi features. On the basis of degrees of integration varying, they reject MacSwan's claim that phonological systems cannot be mixed in 'code-switching'.

3.4.8 Grosjean: modes

Grosjean (e.g. 1997, 1998, 2001) has drawn attention to the multiple modes of the plurilingual speaker, representing the level of activation of each language at the time, determined by such factors as the language proficiency, attitudes, usual mode of interaction, kinship relations and socioeconomic status of the interlocutor; the setting (location, presence of monolinguals, degree of formality); form and content of message; function of the linguistic act; type and organization of the stimuli (e.g. book read, TV program watched). So a bilingual may fluctuate between two monolingual modes (one for each language), a bilingual mode and intermediate modes between the bilingual and monolingual modes on each side. A trilingual may have several bi-, monolingual and intermediate modes and sometimes also a trilingual one. In the bilingual mode, both languages are activated but the base (comparable to Myers-Scotton's matrix) language is activated more. As the mode is determined by the language, a certain degree of circularity is introduced.

Grosjean's modes are supported by an experiment he conducted (Grosjean 1995) and a study by Treffers-Daller (1998) in which different switching practices are adopted by Turkish–German bilinguals for the same content with different interlocutors. The concept of mode presents a challenge to much data collection in this field, e.g. telling people to speak a particular language with a bilingual interlocutor or hiding the interviewer's bilingualism. Grosjean also argues that, when speakers are in the monolingual mode, switches are unintentional, while they are conscious and deliberate in other modes. According to Grosjean, no claims can thus be made about the independence or interdependence of the user's linguistic systems in the bilingual mode. (As language is the determinant of the language mode, some circularity is introduced.) This is supported by the tendency for immigrant bilinguals to switch in the direction of another language understood by the interlocutor. Grosjean acknowledges that a speaker's attitude to 'code-switching' will influence the mode.

I would argue that attitudes to convergence and divergence of languages promote different modes, involving 'separation' of the systems (including inter-CP transversion), 'mixing' (unintegrated lexical transference) and 'adaptation' (integrated lexical transference, semantic and syntactic transference); and that type and degree of integration and non-lexical (e.g. syntactic, pragmatic, even phonological) forms of transference are also established as part of the mode.[12] As I will show in chapter 5, the default mode is determined at the beginning of an interaction but there may be considerable changes in the course of the interaction. The way in which mode is adjusted from 'separation' to 'mixing' is seen by a comparison between two sections from an interview with MGP31m. There is not a single lexical or semantic transfer when he talks about a city scene in Melbourne, but in an account of a day's activities, his trip to Phillip Island, near Melbourne, evokes an Australian context for which he requires the bilingual 'mixing' mode, for example:

(35)   Aber nachher, als wir auf der ISLAND gewesen sind, hat's uns gut gefallen. Es war so *gut*, daß wir uns für unsere HOLIDAY einschrieben 'But afterwards, when we were on the island, we liked it. It was so good that we booked for our holidays'

3.5   The treatment of morphological and syntactic transference and convergence

Few grammarians today would doubt, like Max Müller (1862: 74) did, that grammatical transference occurs ('*Es gibt keine Mischsprache*', 'there is no such thing as a mixed language'). There are so many known examples ranging from the transference of even system morphemes such as the personal pronouns *their* and *them* into English to the many syntactic transfers across unrelated as well as related languages in the Balkans (e.g. Birnbaum 1965, 1966, 1999) and on the Indian subcontinent (e.g. Gumperz and Wilson 1971; Emeneau 1965/1980), which function as *Sprachbünde*. The opposite view to Müller's ('*Es gibt keine völlig ungemischte Sprache*', 'There is no such thing as a completely unmixed language') was taken by Hugo Schuchardt (1884). His examples of Slavic–German, Slavic–Italian and Balkanese contact constitute what is termed 'substratum', where a language continues to show features resulting from earlier, pre-shift language contact. Mühlhäusler (1985, 1997: 142ff) goes as far as to suggest that morphology may be the first 'victim' of language contact. Louden (1994) argues that phonology and lexicon are more resistant to change because of their communicative salience. Greater consciousness of these than of syntax is due to their function in marking social identities. Nevertheless, J. Milroy (1998) comments on the concentration of historical linguistics on *internal* change, emphasizing the monolingual norm, parallelling the stress on *standard* varieties and on sudden, *spontaneous* change. Milroy proposes a more speaker-centred approach, with 'change only becoming change when it spreads to other speakers' (J. Milroy 1998: 315). In our data, it is difficult to prove such spread. Harris and Campbell (1995) have expressed objections to extreme positions, such as the total rejection of syntactic transference and the 'fanciful explanations that all otherwise unexplained syntactic eccentricities' (p. 120) can be attributed to it.

3.5.1 Internal and external change

The old problem of differentiating between external (contact-induced) and internal (natural) change, which was addressed in the section on phonological transference (section 4.3.2, below), is very relevant to morphology and syntax. Sometimes external change may reinforce and accelerate an internal one already in progress, as Silva-Corvalán (1994) has demonstrated, especially with auxiliary use, in Los Angeles Spanish. The acceleration of change in contact situations is also discussed by Schmidt (1985) for the Queensland Aboriginal language, Dyirbal, and by Maandi (1989) for Estonian in Sweden, to name just two further examples. As Aikhenvald (2001) has aptly put it, contrasting 'healthy' and endangered or obsolescent languages, the difference in their language change 'lies not in the *sorts* of change . . . (but) in the *quantity* of change and in the *speed* (of change)'.

Mufwene and Gilman (1987) have shown how universals, African language substrata, the influence of southern states English and internal developments, have all contributed to the structure of Gullah. Internal changes already in progress in the heartland of the language may be accelerated by external (contact) factors. There is also evidence, for instance, in Dal Nagro's (n.d.) work on a (Walser) German dialect in northern Italy, that some features of the system live on and new creative aspects come to the fore.

It is hoped that, here too, by comparing the impact of English alone, or together with another language, on languages of various typologies, we can learn more about both language change and typology.

3.5.2   Thomason and Kaufman and others

Thomason and Kaufman (1988) also wish to redress the emphasis on internal
linguistic change in a model that is informed by and addresses whole communities or polities rather than individuals and families in language contact
situations. Those discussed include ones resulting from conquest or mass immigration. However, some of their model can be very usefully applied in the
immigrant situations which provide the context for most of the data discussed in
this book. The model proposed by Thomason and Kaufman is intended to predict what types of contact-induced changes would occur when (1988: 13). They
maintain that change is gradual and affects all levels of language, something that
is confirmed by Harris and Campbell (1995: 149) who assert that, given time,
any transference can occur. The data discussed in the next chapter will show
how quickly this can happen. Thomason and Kaufman differentiate between
shift and maintenance situations and postulate a borrowing scale, encompass-
ing the effects of different types and degrees of socially conditioned contact
with the dominant group on language change, covering lexicon, morphosyntax
and phonology. 'Shift-induced change' is related to imperfect learning of the
target language after a shift has occurred from the original language. This is
the basis of the ethnolects which are discussed in section 4.6. Thomason (fc)
argues that syntactic and phonological changes rather than 'code-switching' are
responsible for this.

   Largescale structural change will occur with asymmetrical dominance relations and large discrepancies in population sizes, as we have in Australia
(cf. section 2.2). As may be seen in chapter 2, all the community languages in
Australia are subject to language shift over a short period, but there is a varying
degree of maintenance along the way. Thus, the distinction between 'maintenance' and 'shift' is not relevant to our urban 'immigrant' data. It would appear
that the Australian data characterize, mainly, two of the stages on Thomason
and Kaufman's Language Maintenance scale:

Intensive contact, including much bilingualism among borrowing-language speakers:
MUCH LEXICAL BORROWING; MODERATE TO HEAVY STRUCTURAL BORROW-
ING, especially phonology and syntax.

   The change tends to be moderate and not heavy, as will be evident from
chapter 4, and is not related to intense contact 'over a long period of time' as
suggested by Thomason and Kaufman.

   Thomason and Kaufman list the borrowing of non-basic vocabulary as an
early stage of change stimulated by casual contact and little bilingualism on the
part of the borrowers. On their borrowing scale (pp. 74–6), the four points on
the continuum which most adequately describe the transferences of the bi- and
trilinguals we are referring to are:

1. Casual contact: lexical borrowing only.
2. Slightly more intense contact: slight structural borrowing.
3. More intense contact: slightly more structural borrowing. The Thomason and Kaufman description includes some transference of derivational morphemes and of personal and demonstrative pronouns and low numerals. This point on the continuum includes such structural features as syllable-structure features and transference of prepositions into a postpositional language such as Hungarian (Endrody 1971), but not a complete change from SOV to SVO.
4. Strong cultural pressure: moderate structural borrowing. The changes are described as ones that are major but 'cause little typological change' (Thomason and Kaufman 1988: 75). New morphological categories will be added to L1 words especially if there is structural overlap between the languages.
5. Very strong cultural borrowing: heavy structural borrowing. This includes 'major structural features that cause significant typological disruption' (1988: 75) such as the adoption of ergative morphosyntax or a change from flexional toward agglutinative morphology.

It would seem that immigrant languages in Australia do not survive for long enough for massive structural change to take place and that, in the former enclaves, where longterm maintenance of German did occur, the infrastructure of the settlement was sufficiently strong and well developed for a very heavy restructuring to be prevented. However, with the typological variation of the languages and varying distance from English on the one hand and the differential in community language use patterns discussed in chapter 2, conditions for change are not constant, something that will be taken up in chapter 4.

Queen's (2001) study of the intonation patterns of Turkish–German bilinguals in Germany would call for some extension of the Thomason and Kaufman framework as she identifies three patterns:

i. German and Turkish intonation in the respective language;
ii. 'interference' patterns;
iii. 'fusion', where patterns are employed which are not possible in either system but resulting from both without any convergence taking place.

The issue of internally motivated vs. contact-induced change is reintroduced in a recent paper by Thomason (fc). She points to similarities in their consequences – feature loss, feature addition, feature replacement. She differentiates between four causes of change:

i. ordinary internally motivated change (no simplification or convergence);
ii. 'borrowing' alone;
iii. 'attrition' only (simplification but no convergence);
iv. 'borrowing' and 'attrition' (simplification and convergence).

However, Thomason contends that the internal change/contact-induced change dichotomy is a false one, arguing that there is frequently multiple causation. (There is no shortage of studies that confirm the reinforcement of one factor by another, e.g. Mufwene and Gilman 1987; Clyne 1991: 187; Salmons 1994). According to Thomason (fc), change is best accounted for by either 'borrowing' or (markedness-governed) simplification or both. In the latter case, attrition or non-acquisition plays an important role.

Andersen (1982) and Campbell and Muntzel (1989) differ on what changes are predictable. Andersen classifies the following as predictable – fewer distinctions, the preservation of distinctions common to the languages in contact and the longer survival of distinctions with high functional load. These are considered by Campbell and Muntzel to be of uncertain predictability. According to them, the certain categories are paradoxically: overgeneralization of unmarked or marked features; the development of variability; the development of regularity by extremes of regularization; and morphosyntactic reduction.

In using the term 'change' in relation to the contact situations discussed in this volume, I will be considering it for individuals rather than for an entire speech community. A 'diachronic' approach is therefore not appropriate; it would be preferable to conceptualize the issue of change as 'dynamicized' (Aristar 1999), i.e. it is based on synchronic data, explanations and theoretical generalizations.

3.5.3   Language death

Much progress on language contact and change has taken place within the paradigm of 'language death' (Dorian 1977, 1981 and subsequent publications), an advanced stage of language shift, inferred from the presence of 'non-fluent semi-speakers'. I do not, however, intend to differentiate between 'semi-speakers' and 'fluent speakers' as Dorian does. The term 'semi-speaker', which gives the impression of precision, actually represents one end of a continuum (Dorian 1981: 114–21), and membership of the categories is determined by testing (Dorian 1981: 109) and the intuitions of older 'fluent speakers'. While the distinction between 'fluent' and 'semi-speakers' may be crucially important in the study of some communities, the speakers in our community-based corpora are rather fluent and generally now not available for testing.

3.5.4   Drift and typology

A theory of language which many linguists continue to draw on is that of Sapir: 'Language moves down time in a current of its own making. It has a drift' (1921: 150). The continuing trend to develop in the same direction (e.g. loss of morphological endings) is attributed, by Thomason and Kaufman (1988: 9), to 'structural imbalances' in the system. Hawkins (1986: 4) demonstrates that English and German, for instance, are differentiated due to 'major readjustments' in all the major areas of grammar and that there is a set of generalizable typological principles which unites these contrasts. This can be related to work on universals and typology initiated by Greenberg (1963). He constructs typologies based on the position of Subject, Verb and Object relative to one another, of adjective and noun, of dependent genitive and noun, and of adverbs and adjectives that they modify, and the existence of prepositions and postpositions. He develops a set of forty-five universals, including the likelihood that SOV languages are postpositional, languages in which genitive follows governing noun also have the order N + adjective, and languages do not have more gender categories in the non-singular numbers than in the singular. Lehmann (1974), who applies this model to historical linguistics, shows that it is rare to find a highly consistent language in typological terms. He demonstrates that the history of Indo-European typologies is neither static nor unidirectional. The overall pattern of change from Proto Indo-European to its descendants is overwhelmingly from SOV to SVO.

The linkage between features of linguistic subsystems (e.g. morphology, syntax) involving change has been commented on by Sapir (1921), Keenan (1978), Hawkins (1986: 40–51), Thomason and Kaufman (1988: 55), and others, and this is consistent with the interrelations on which we will be focusing in chapter 4. Keenan (1978: 120–1) uses the term 'covary' to express the notion that the more a language has of one process (e.g. case morphology), the less it has of another (e.g. fixed word order). A change to a more fixed order is usually associated with a typological change to SVO order. This is why language contact between languages of different typologies has so often resulted in SVO (Whitney 1981; Hyman 1975 on Niger Congo; Lalor and Blanc 1988 on Adyge–Russian contact). Incidentally, this also applies to most Pidgins, although Romaine (1989: 377) gives Hiri Motu (OSV), Trader Navajo (VSO) and Eskimo Trade Jargon (SOV) as exceptions.

Perhaps the best-known case of change from SOV to SVO alongside loss of case markings and an increasingly fixed order is that of English. Hawkins refers to an analysis by Saitz (1955, cited in Hawkins 1986: 50–1) of English word order in the ninth and twelfth centuries, showing that a far higher case syncretism went hand in hand with a much more fixed SVO order, and studies by Bean (1963) indicating that early examples of SVO occur where Subject and Object are morphologically ambiguous. Thomason and Kaufman (1988: 55) assert that SOV, SVO, etc. are susceptible to change because they all perform the same basic syntactic function – 'identification of subject and object by their position relative to each other and to the verb'. Hawkins (1986: 125) argues that all languages are both grammatical and pragmatic, but that English has become increasingly grammatical and less pragmatic in its word order, 'drifting uniformly towards a more fixed word order and towards the more extensive use of more limited formal means' (Hawkins 1986: 127). This drift is not occurring in German and marks one of the contrasts between the languages. It will be argued (section 4.4.7) that, in this respect, the drift of Dutch is in the same direction as that of English but not to the same extent. Vennemann (1974, 1975) regards V2 as an intermediate stage between SOV and SVO. However, it should be stated too that it constitutes a continuation of at least some aspects of pragmatic word order.

According to Givón (1971: 413), 'today's morphology is yesterday's syntax'. But it seems that yesterday's and today's morphology can also have a substantial effect on syntactic change and so can alternative means of emphasizing pragmatic functions, such as the time, location or sufferer of the action.

3.5.5   Levelling and markedness

Thomason and Kaufman (1988: 51) point out, 'in general, universally marked features . . . are less likely than unmarked ones to be transferred in language contact'. Among other things, they are less easy to acquire. Andersen (1977) claims that markedness relations can be observed in every type and stage of language change. However, the ill-defined term 'markedness' is open to many interpretations (Mufwene 1991; Smith 1999), such as optimality, less elaborate form, less salient, more general meaning, more salient and occurrence in absolute neutralization. Some of the definitions are arbitrary or circular (Smith 1999). 'Markedness' does, however, make it possible to contrast the more basic, natural and/or frequent forms of constructions in a language. For instance, in English *sheep* is more basic and therefore unmarked and *ewe* marked as it refers to the female sheep only. Similarly, OSV order in English (e.g. *This I cannot accept*) is marked, in contrast with the more general SVO. Smith offers a more specific explanation in relation to the loss of agreement between the past participle and the direct object in compound past tenses with 'have' auxiliary in the Romance languages, e.g. French *J'ai écrit les lettres* < Latin *habeo scriptas epistulas*.

Smith considers the agreement in a number of implicational hierarchies (e.g. position of direct object, identity of preceding direct object, person of clitic pronoun) as well as the loss of agreement. The preferred explanation is the actualization (mapping out of consequences of reanalysis) of a change in the underlying structure of the syntactic pattern. I would see the advantage of this way of conceptualizing the issue in two ways: (1) it is in harmony with the notion of drift; (2) it is consistent with processing implications.

Smith (1998) draws on Durie (1995):

When a potentially discriminative linguistic structure is only an option in particular contexts, yet compulsory in others, the contexts where there is greater flexibility could be characterized by less functional pressure on this particular coding device for discrimination. (Durie 1995: 284)

The levelling that ensues from this kind of process does not necessarily result in a return to a kind of core grammar, Universal Grammar or biogrammatical features, as has been suggested by Mühlhäusler (1980: 328), Bickerton (1981: 293) and Givón (1979: 26–7) respectively. In relation to pidgins and creoles, Mufwene (1991) argues that unmarked strategies may be those shared by most of the languages in context or ones to be particularly salient in only some of them, especially where there may have been a conflict in markedness values.

3.6   Some notes on the languages in our corpus

The languages in our corpus are characterized by typological or genetic differences as well as demonstrating variation in language shift in the Australian context. They therefore represent opportunities for a comparative analysis of the structural effects on transversion among bilinguals and trilinguals as well as the types and pace of morphosyntactic change, in terms of transference, convergence or simplification.

German and Dutch, as West Germanic languages, are closely related to English. Although they both share a considerable amount of lexicon with English, the overlap between Dutch and English is greater than between German and English, due partly to the consonantal shift known as the High German Sound Shift. Also, unlike Dutch and English, German has an elaborate system of case- and gender-marked articles/adjectives (for the accusative, dative and genitive, though the latter is not so prevalent in the spoken language; and some dialects do not differentiate between dative and accusative). German has three grammatical genders (masculine, feminine, neuter) while Dutch has retained only two (neuter, non-neuter).

German and Dutch are best described as V2 languages (Mallinson and Blake 1981) as they require the verb to be in second position, regardless of whether the subject, object, indirect object or adverb/adverbial phrase are in initial position. There is an older German tradition of describing German as a language with the verb in the 'centre', e.g. Drach (1937 (1963)), Boost (1964). The word order in German (and Dutch) is more pragmatically determined than in English (Thompson 1978; Givón 1979). In each of the following sentences, a different phrase is in first position but the verb is always in second position:

(36)   a. Ich habe gestern   morgen meinen Freund vom   Bahnhof abgeholt.
        I   AUX yesterday morning my   friend from.the station   fetch+PAST.PT
        'I picked up my friend from the station yesterday morning' (unmarked)

b. Gestern   morgen   habe ich meinen Freund vom   Bahnhof abgeholt.
yesterday morning AUX I   my   friend from.the station   fetch+PAST.PT
(Emphasis on time)

c. Vom   Bahnhof habe ich meinen Freund gestern   morgen   abgeholt.
from.the station   AUX I   my   friend yesterday morning fetch+PAST.PT
(Emphasis on place)

In the main clause, the constituents, AUX and participle are discontinuous. In embedded clauses, the main verb is at the end.

d. Ich sagte ihr,   daß ich gestern   morgen
I   told   her+INDIR that I   yesterday morning
meinen Freund vom   Bahnhof abholte
my   friend from.the station   fetch+PAST.PT

However, there have been descriptions of German and Dutch which have assigned them the word order SVO on the basis of the unmarked main clause word order (Hartung 1964; Isačenko 1965), or SOV on the basis of embedded clause word order and deep structure postulations (e.g. Bach 1962; Bierwisch 1963; Heidolph 1964). The main difference in word order between them is in the unmarked order of AUX and PARTICIPLE in embedded clauses. The AUX precedes the infinitive in sentence-final position in Dutch but follows it in German, for example:

(37)   German:
Ich weiss nicht, ob sie *kommen kann*
I   know not   if she *come   can*
(38)   Dutch:
ik weet niet, of ze *kan komen*
I   know not   if she can come

Both languages have an adjective + noun order (German *der runde Tisch*; Dutch *de ronde tafel* 'the round table').

While German offers a diverse system of plural allomorphs (e.g. *e, er, en*, (¨)*e*, (¨)*er*, (¨)*φ, s*), Dutch uses two main plural allomorphs (*en, s*). Dutch shows less variety in verbal endings (three allomorphs) than German (four) but far more than English (one). As was shown in chapter 2, language shift is very high among Dutch speakers and substantial but not quite so high among German speakers.

The Romance languages, Italian and Spanish, share much of their lexicon with each other and a considerable amount with English. They, like English, are SVO languages, but unlike English, they show the order N + ADJ (e.g. Italian *la casa bianca* / Spanish *la casa blanca* 'the white house'). Both tend towards pro-drop (e.g. Italian *tornano alla campagna*/ Spanish *tornan al campo* 'they (DELETED) return to the country'. Both languages have two genders (masculine and feminine) but no case markings. Chilean speakers of Spanish show a relatively low shift. The shift from Italian is medium, moving to fairly high in the second generation.

Croatian, a South Slavic language, is more distantly related to English. The inflectional system is rich, with three grammatical genders (masculine, feminine, neuter), seven cases (nominative, accusative, dative and locative – between which syncretism of nominal and pronominal forms has occurred – genitive, vocative, instrumental). For example, (for masculine stem) singular:

zákon	nominative
zákone	vocative
zákon	accusative
zákona	genitive
zákonu	dative
zákonom	instrumental
zákonu	locative

The basic typology is SVO, with pro-drop and A DJ + N order. Croatian is a well-maintained language (Clyne 1991: 67).[13]

As a Mon-Khmer language, Vietnamese is completely unrelated to any of the other languages on which we are drawing. It is a tonal language; it is also an isolating language, i.e. it has no inflections (although there are various clitics). Typologically it is SVO, including mainly N+A DJ, for example:

(39)   dau thân thê
         pain physical
         'physical pain'
(40)   lãnh chính tri
         leader potential
         'potential leader'

Although we do not have precise statistics on this (see sections 2.2.1, 2.2.2), Vietnamese is one of the best maintained of the community languages (Clyne 1991: 67–8; Ho-Dac 1996).

Hungarian is a Finno-Ugrian language and therefore not related to English and the other Indo-European languages. While typologically SOV, it is highly pragmatic in its word order. It has a rich morphology and elaborate case markings, based largely on postpositions, which express local and other relations. Descriptions of Hungarian disagree on the number of cases – they range from seventeen to twenty-one (Loránd and Samu 1972) to twenty-seven (Tompa 1968). Abandolo (1988) concurs with Loránd and Samu's lower estimate, while Fenyvesi (1994), in her work on Hungarian in America, works with twenty-four cases. Some examples of the case system:

ház	'the house'	nominative
házat	'the house'	accusative
háznak	'of the house'	genitive
(The dative 'to the house' has an identical case marking)		
házban	'in the house'	inessive
házból	'from the house'	elative
házba	'into the house'	illative
házon	'on the house'	superessive
házról	'from the top of the house'	delative
háznál	'near the house'	adessive
házig	'up to the house'	terminative

There are no gender distinctions.

Hungarian has vowel harmony, 'agreement among vowels in successive syllables in respect of one or more features' (Matthews 1997: 400). All the vowels within a word are either front or back. For instance, the accusative of *ház* 'house' is *házat* but that of *nyelv* 'language' is *nyelvet*.

3.7   Concluding remarks

These characteristics will, it is hoped, enable us to consider some of the issues discussed under section 3.4. They will make it possible to study the impact of typological variation on contact-induced language change and on bilingual and trilingual speech production. Otherwise, this chapter was intended to provide a context based on the research literature for the study of language contact and change in chapters 4 and 5.

4 Dynamics of convergence and transference

4.1 Introduction

This chapter is about how bilinguals and trilinguals make their languages more similar (convergence) – and how some of them, having done this, try to differentiate them in particular ways (divergence). The chapter utilizes Australian data from bi- and trilinguals as an example to focus on the following issues:

1. The ways in which the resources of two or more languages are employed and how these ways might be connected.
2. How the language systems converge and how such convergence is resisted by some speakers.
3. How languages change differentially in the context of, and under the influence of the same language in contact.
4. How and to what degree material from one language is integrated into another.
5. What facilitates transference from one language to another and how this varies between languages in contact.
6. The applicability of current models to the above issues.

Clearly there are many other issues that can be dealt with using a comparative corpus, but time and space require a selection.

Issue 1 above is the main concern of virtually all linguistic studies of language contact. Issue 4 is of paramount importance in some publications because it is a special issue in contact between certain pairs of languages (e.g. Backus 1996; Boeschoten 1998; Halmari 1997) and because traditionally it underlies the distinction between 'code-switching' and 'borrowing'. Some discussion on current models and their applicability may be found in chapter 3. It is hoped that a contribution of the present monograph will be to establish the relationship between issues 2, 3 and 4 and their contribution to 1.

We will attempt to move away from the common hidden assumption that bilinguals are 'double monolinguals' and stress the *variable* nature of languages in contact. I concur with Mühlhäusler (1985) that dynamic models are needed to deal with languages in contact. Some of the issues enumerated above have been present in the discussion since the 1950s and 1960s, but with more corpora from a bigger range of languages, new dimensions have emerged, with some other issues moving into the background. This will have become obvious with the debate on terminological and theoretical frameworks (see chapter 3).

As Dixon (1997) puts it, migration is a situation that 'punctuates the equilibrium' of a language. As we have seen in chapter 2, among the dynamics bringing about a continuum of LS from very low to very high are the complementarity of communicative need and the will to maintain a language or to shift from it. Need and will are also both complementary and conflicting forces when it comes to actual language contact phenomena. The need to communicate with 'monolinguals', limitations of one's own language proficiency, and the perceived exigencies of the setting play a role as does the determination to 'keep the languages apart'. We have already intimated that there is, in language contact research, an interaction between language systems, social and communicative factors, and psycholinguistic processing. The focus in this chapter on the dynamics of the language *systems* in contact is to clarify some of the categories. This should, however, not be interpreted as an indication that I consider the social and/or communicative functions of language contact phenomena to be less important. They have been given much consideration in other works and are summarized in section 4.3.

4.2   Convergence[1]

Convergence occurs at the phonetic, morphophonemic, and prosodic as well as the syntactic levels.

4.2.1   *Phonetic/morphophonemic/prosodic bilingual convergence*

Among the occurrences in the data are:

Ger. [haɪˈdrant] < Ger. [hʏˈdrant] + Eng. [ˈhaɪdrənt]

Ger. [gɛnɛˈratsioun] < East Central Ger. [gɛnɛraˈtsioun] + Eng. [ˈdʒɛnɛreiʃn]

Ger. [ˈpʀoblem] < Ger. [pʀoˈble:m] + Ger. [ˈpɹɔˈbləm]

Ger. [ˈkɔntinɛnt] < Ger. [kɔntiˈnɛnt] + < Eng. [ˈkɔntinənt]

Dut. [ˈsɪste:m] < Dut. [sɪste:m] + Eng. [ˈsɪstəm]

Ger. [ɔf] < Ger. [aʊf] + Eng. [ɔv]

Ger. [ʃɪːf] < Ger. [ʃaːf] + Eng. [ʃiːp]

Dut. *hijs* or *hijn* < Dut. *zijn* + Eng. *his*

(e.g. *in hijn boek*, MGD 102f, second generation)

Cr. [taːt] < Cr. [tata] <tata> + Eng. [dæd] <dad>

Cr. [ʃkots] < Cr. [ʃkoti] <skoti> + Eng. [skots] <Scots>

(Croatian examples from Hlavac 2000)

Either stress comes from one language and vowels and/or consonants from the other, or vowels and consonants are derived from different languages. Such compromise forms add to the number of bilingual homophones, which may facilitate transversion (see below, section 5.3.1).

4.2.2 Trilingual convergence

In our trilingual corpus derived from conversations with Dutch–German–English, Hungarian–German–English, and Italian–Spanish–English trilinguals (and some informal self-taped conversations with their family or friends), two forms of main convergence are evident:
– adoption in the third language of pattern shared by two languages (section 4.2.2.1);
– conversion formulae (section 4.2.2.2).

4.2.2.1 Interlingual identification based on bilingual commonalities
The tendency for trilinguals to extend to the third language a feature shared by two of their languages is found at the lexical, semantic, syntactic, morphemic, phonological/prosodic levels.[2] For instance, in (1), *pronunciazone* is used rather than *pronuncia* in Italian, making it closer to English *pronunciation* and Spanish *pronunciación*. The tendency is regardless of the acquisition order of the languages.
Lexical –

(1)   It. pronunciazone
        Models: Eng. pronunciation; Sp. pronunciación
        Homeland Italian: pronuncia (MTISE 4f)
(2)   Hung. perfektul ['pɛrfɛktul] (inflected)
        Compromise between Eng. ['pœfɛkt] and Ger. [pɛr'fɛkt]
        Homeland Hungarian: tökéletes (MTGHE(P) 9f)

Here the Hungarian compromise takes over the vowel from German, and from English the lexical stress corresponding to the Hungarian norm. The English and German models are cognates.

(3)   Ger. Das ist nicht so provinzial
        Models: Eng. That isn't so provincial; Dut. Dat is niet zo provinciaal
        Homeland German: Das ist nicht so provinziell (MTGED 1f)

The German lexical item is formed by analogy with that in the other two languages.

Semantic –

(4)   Eng. Without paying a cent and without making notice of it
       Models:
       Sp. sin   pagar   un centésimo y   sin
           without pay+INF a   cent+DIM and without

           haciendo   caso de esto
           make+PRES.PT notice of this

       It. senza   pagare   un centessimo e   senza   fare
           without pay+INF a   cent+DIM   and without make+INF

           caso   a questo
           notice at this

       Native English: 'without paying a cent and without taking notice
       of it' (MTS-I-E13f)

The meaning of 'make' is based on that in the Spanish and Italian idioms.

(5)   It. affetava (in the meaning 'affected')
       Models: Eng. affected; Sp. afectaba
       Homeland Italian: meaning 'cut off' (MTISE 04f)

(6)   Hung. Szép napos nap van
             nice sunny day is
       Models:
       German
       Es ist ein schöner sonniger Tag
       it is a   nice   sunny   day
       'It's a nice sunny day'
       Homeland Hungarian
       Szép napos idő   van
       nice sunny weather is
       (Hung. nap = sun, day) (MTGHE(P)9f)

German and English provide the model for 'day' being used for 'weather'.
Syntax –

(7)   Eng. The garden like it my wife
       Models:
       Italian
       Il   giardino piace   a mia moglie
       the garden   please+3sg   to my wife

Spanish
El jardin le gusta a mi mujer
the garden it taste+3sg to my wife
Native English: 'My wife likes the garden' (MTISE 23M)

In both Spanish and Italian, verbs of liking require what is liked to be in the subject position while the experiencer is marked as a recipient.

(8)   Hungarian
        Sok emberek napoznak   meg mennek a   vizbe   úzni
        many man+pl sunbake+3pl and go+3pl the water.into swim+INF
        Models:
        German
        Viele Menschen sonnen sich   und gehen ins   Wasser schwimmen
        many people   sun   themselves and go   in.the water swim+INF
        Eng. Many people are sunbaking and go and swim in the water
        Standard Hungarian
        Sok ember   napozik   meg megy vizbe   úzni
        many man+sg sunbake+3sg and go+sg water.in.the swim+INF
        (MTSwissG/HE16m)

The addition of the plural morpheme -ek, as in emberek here, is ungrammatical after an adverb of number in Hungarian. The plural forms of the verbs follow the ungrammatical plural. In our data, there are numerous examples of this phenomenon with numerals. Csernicskó and Fenyvési (2000) report the same phenomena from Hungarian in Sub-Carpathia. Istvan Lántsyák (pers. comm.) has pointed out that sentences with numerals plus plural nouns may be heard in Hungary but are considered marginal (though they may be on the increase). The incidence of this among trilinguals may therefore be attributed to multiple causation.

Morphological –

(9)   Ger. meist normale
        Models: Dut. meest normale; Eng. most normal
        Homeland German: normalste (MTDGE 2f)

Dutch and English both have analytic comparatives for most adjectives and this pattern is transferred to German.

(10)   Hungarian
        Mikor én tizennyolc éves voltam,   én egy francia
        When I eighteen   years was+1sg I a   French

családnál   laktam
family+ADESSIVE lived+1sg
Models:
Ger. Als *ich* achtzehn Jahre alt war, wohnte *ich* bei einer
französischen Familie
Eng. When *I* was eighteen, *I* stayed with a French family
(MTH/GE(PR)1f)

The use of the first-person-singular pronoun in the above example would be considered unnecessary, unusual and stylistically inferior but not ungrammatical and could be promoted by its use in both English and German (pers. comm. Tibor Endrody).

Phonology/prosody –

(11)   German
        alle drei Kinder mit einem ['ɛksɛnt] aber ungarisch
        all   three children with an   accent   but   Hungarian
        'but all three children speak Hungarian with an accent'
        Hung. initial stress, Eng. initial stress, Ger. stress on second syllable
        in this case
        Homeland Ger.: Akzent ['aktsɛnt]; Eng.: accent ['aeksent]; Hung.:
        ékezet ['e:kɛzɛt] (MTH/GE(PR) 5f)

In studies of second- and third-language acquisition, Dewaele (1998) found that third-language learners of French were influenced less by their L1, Dutch, than second-language learners. The former were influenced by their L2, English. (For psycholinguistic implications, see chapter 6.)

A feature limited to one language is sometimes the cause of confusion. An example is the *er* construction in Dutch, which combines with a preposition to form a complement but can be split into discontinuous constituents (e.g. *for it, about it*), (Donaldson 1981: 237–8), for example:

(12)   Dutch
        In principe ben ik wel   voor
        in principle am I indeed for
        Models:
        Eng. In principle I am in favour of it
        Ger. Im Prinzip bin ich dafür
        Homeland Dutch:
        In principe ben ik *er* wel   voor
        In principle am I there MOD.PRT for (MTEGD 2m)

Er 'there' is combined with a preposition such as *over* to make a pronominal adverb the pronoun.

(13)   Ik ben tweezijdig over
        I   am   twosided   over (it)
        Models:
        Eng. I am two minds about it
        Ger. Ich bin darüber unschlüssig
        Homeland Dutch: ik ben *er* tweezijdig over (MTGED 3f)

These phenomena could have occurred under the influence of one of the languages but the coincidence of the features (or their absence) in two of the
languages is likely to reinforce the influence.

4.2.2.2 *Conversion formulae*

The other main convergence phenomenon among our trilinguals is the operation of conversion rules to transform an item from one language to one in
another language. These occur among many of the Dutch–German–English
and Italian–Spanish–English trilinguals who have developed their competence
in a subordinate language through a closely related one (Weinreich 1953: 10),
i.e. these occur among Dutch–German–English and Italian–Spanish–English
trilinguals where signs in L2 are linked with signs in a closely related language rather than directly with meanings. This occurs also in bilinguals – as is
shown in Schmid's (1994) study among Italian–Spanish bilinguals and Häcki-
Buhofer and Burger's (1998) on Swiss-German children acquiring Standard
German. Nordenstam (1979) describes conversion rules among Norwegian-
Swedish bilinguals, based on markedness principles. They involve past tenses
of verbs, articles and plural allomorphs. Recent studies such as Cenoz et al.
(2001), Hammarberg (2001) and De Angelis and Selinker (2001) demonstrate
how a related language is used as a base for the acquisition of another language. Herwig (2001) shows how a number of related languages are multifar-
iously linked through associative chains but, to some extent, can be independently accessed. In our Dutch–German–English and Italian–Spanish–English
trilinguals, there is contact between closely related languages in which a subordinate relationship is more likely than between the somewhat less closely
related languages.

However, the fact that many trilinguals no longer feel the need for one language to support another suggests the automaticization of a direct relationship
between signs and meanings in the later acquired language with time and practice. However, in a small number of cases, repairs and hesitations indicate the
points at which monitoring still leads to the application of conversion formulae,
for example:

(14)   Zehn Jahren wenigstens (A) fifz   fünf fünfzehn
        ten   years   at least   (A) fift   five fifteen (MTDE/G 22m)

where the informant is evidently converting English *fifteen* and Dutch *vijftien* according to sound changes (ij -> i, t -> ts).

(15)   No, für die beide la [læ]   (A)   Zahl   (A)
         no   for the two   la..(Eng.) (A) (Ger.) number (A) (Ger.)

         Sprache   macht   kein   Unterschied
         language makes   no   difference

         'No, which of those two languages I speak doesn't matter to me'
         (MTDE/G 11f)

The English lexical transfer *language* is articulated incompletely, monitored but replaced, after hesitation, by German *Zahl* 'number', a conversion from Dutch *taal* 'language' in accordance with the sound change. After further monitoring, manifested in a filled pause, it is corrected to *Sprache*, German for 'language', and *taal*.

There are some instances where the repair is to replace an item or construction common to two or three languages by one that is specific to the 'matrix language', for example:

(16)   Voordat ik studeerde..   ben   gaan   studeren
         before I study+PAST+1sg AUX go+INF study+INF
         'before I studied . . .'(MTGDE 15m)

Here a uniquely Dutch construction *ben gaan studeren* expresses the inchoative – aspectually marked as the beginning of an action – to diverge from *studeerde*, which corresponds to German *studierte*. This trilingual marks his multiple identity by his determination to employ the specific resources of each language. A similar explanation can be attributed to the replacement of *matematica* (cognate with German *Mathematik* and English *mathematics*) with the more common Dutch lexical item *wiskunde*, usually employed for the school subject:

(17)   Ondanks dat ik op de school matem..(A) wiskunde
         despite that I at the school math..   mathematics

         gedaan   heb
         do+PAST.PT have+AUX+1sg

         'In spite of doing mathematics at school' (MTGDE 9m)

It should be noted that the trilingual speakers of both sentences had German as L1 and Dutch as L2. It is therefore not surprising that they would want to differentiate Dutch from German and thereby identify with the Dutch language, the language of their new country and the L1 of their spouse.

Among trilinguals, the language providing the basis for the conversion rules may change as Dutch and German or Italian and Spanish reverse roles as the more frequently used language.

Some other examples:[3]

(18)   Dut. Grondlage [x]; Ger. Grundlage; Std Dut. Grondslag (MTDEG 17f)
(19)   Ger. Programma [g]; Ger. Programm; Std Dut. programma [x] (MTGDE 15m)
(20)   Ger. Bauerei; Dut. boerderij; Ger. Bauernhof (MTDE/G 5m)

4.3   Facilitation of different types of transference

In this section, we will discuss lexical, semantic, multiple, phonological, graphemic and (inasfar as it is feasible) prosodic transference – but not morphosyntactic transference as it is bound up with the more general issue of structural change to be discussed in section 4.4, or pragmatic and discursive ones which are the focus of chapter 7. Transference phenomena at different levels of language may coincide and affect each other, or they may occur in variation.

4.3.1   Lexical transference

The motives for lexical transference are many and varied and have been discussed in the literature progressively over a long period (e.g. Haugen 1953, 1956, Weinreich 1953). An obvious one is lexical renewal in order to be able to express the realities of living in a new environment. Lexical transference may compete with *semantic expansion*, e.g. *Eisschrank/Eiskasten* 'ice-chest' for *Kühlschrank* 'refrigerator' (prewar refugees) and *Luftschiff* 'airship' for *Flugzeug* 'aeroplane' (descendants of settlers in former German enclaves), and *neologisms* drawing on the morphological devices of the language, e.g. *farmerieren* 'to farm' (literally 'to farmer' Ger. *Landwirt sein*), *gärtnerieren* 'to garden' (*den Garten machen*) in place of German nominal constructions in former enclaves, or *vaftis* 'painter' based on *vafo* 'I paint (walls)' and *-is* (masculine professional term), cf. Homeland Greek *boghjakis* (Tsokalidou 1994: 138).

Archaisms are perpetuated either because the contemporary lexical item in the country of origin is not known or because it is unacceptable due to its political connotations. This applied to Hungarian, Croatian, Polish, Latvian and other refugees of the late 1940s and early 1950s. In our corpora, lexical transfers are employed:

1. To express items that do not have real equivalents in the other language, concepts or objects that did not exist at the time of immigration and changes in lifestyle and outlook. The following are lexical transfers found in the German of pre- and postwar immigrants and the Dutch of postwar immigrants listed according to domain:

Landscape: beach, gum-tree, creek.
Australian Housing: double-fronted, brick veneer.
Food: vegemite, meat pie.
Leisure: farm, fence, paddock, enjoy, relax, sun-bake, TV/ television, jog, fielding and bowling.
Work: accountant, overlocker, equipment, overtime, shift, check, examine, deliver, relieve, vacuum, busy, desperate.
Shopping: chemist, milkbar, newsagent.
School: spelling, PE (physical education), SOSE (study of society and the environment), assembly, roll, mark.
Cars: gear shift, oil change.
Administration: rates, council.

(21)   Well, um neun Uhr   haben wir meistens *Form Assembly* . . .
         well, at   nine o'clock have   we usually   form assembly

         da   ist die ganze *Sixth Form* zusammen
         there is the whole sixth form   together

         . . .da   wird   die *Roll gemarkt*
         . . . .there AUX+PASS+3sg the roll   mark+PAST.PT

         'Well, at nine o'clock we usually have Form Assembly. Then all of
         the Sixth Form is together, then the roll is marked'
         (MGP 46m, generation 1b, relating school procedures)

Most of these items support Backus's (2001) finding for Turkish–Dutch bilinguals in the Netherlands that the first generation will most frequently transfer lexical items with a high degree of semantic specificity. Bilinguals in former rural German enclaves employ in their German *car, railway, electricity*, and other lexical transfers denoting aspects of modern living, for example:

(22)   Das war eine..war bloß eine kleine *car*[4]
         'That was a ..was only a little car'
         (MGWD 6m, talking about his first car)

2. In view of the above, to cope with the interpenetration of domains where, say, the home domain is predominantly L1 and the work domain English, for example:

(23)   Diese Arbeit besteht in (A) . . . ich kann es Ihnen nicht auf deutsch
         sagen, was ich . . . CHECKING OF CATALOGUING . . . und (A) die
         Times . . . London Times durchsehen und anstreichen und GENER-
         ALLY . . . RUN THE LIBRARY . . . und (A).
         'This work consists of (A) . . . I can't say it in German, what
         I . . . checking of cataloguing . . . and look through and mark (A)

The Times . . . London Times and generally . . . run the library . . . and (A).'
(MGPR 34f, a librarian talking about her work in her home language)

3. To express concepts the equivalent lexical items for which may have become unavailable in the community language in the process of language attrition, e.g. Hungarian:

(24) Ez egy modern ház egy . . . again . . . swimming pool (H) and . . . egy
      egymeletes ház valószimüleg a . . . egy *bedroom* az első emeleten[5] van
      I don't know bedroom anymore.
      'This is a modern house a . . . again . . . swimming pool (H) and . . . a
      single-storey house a really . . . one bedroom on the top floor I don't
      know bedroom anymore.'
      (MT HG/E (PR)5f)[6]

4. To express in one word something that has two or more equivalents in the community language, e.g. in the German of some postwar immigrants:
      put(ten) (+causation) (+direction) (+position), used in preference to
      the equivalents –
      setzen (+causation) (+direction) (+horizontal) (−upright)
      legen (+causation) (+direction) (+position) (+capable of sitting)
      stellen (+causation) (+direction) (+position) (+upright)
      hängen (+causation) (+direction) (+position) (+suspended)
– providing that the position of the 'putting' is not significant in the communication.

Plumber for *Spengler* 'tin smith' or *Installateur* 'person who installs and repairs water systems' or *Monteur* 'person who fits systems' (different functions); *happy* for *froh* 'actual, state', *fröhlich* 'potential, quality'; *change(n)* for *sich umziehen* 'change clothes'; *ändern* 'change condition or state of someone or something'; *tauschen* 'swap'; *wechseln* 'change money'.

A variant of this category is where there is no supraregional item but several alternative regional items in the language, with the English lexical transfer preferred in interregional communication in Australia, e.g. *butcher* for *Metzger* (West German), *Fleischer* (East German), *Fleischhauer* (South German, Austrian); *rubbish-tin* for *Mülleimer* (North German), *Mistkübel* (Austrian), *Misteimer, Abfalleimer* (Central German).

Hawkins (1986: 29–31) demonstrates that German generally has more items than English in a lexical field, but with more restrictive meanings. The drift of English has been towards the 'more extensive use of more limited formal means' (Hawkins 1986: 127). The resulting complexity is not an issue in our bilinguals because of the economies in lexical fields.

5. To express something verbally with less complex valency relations, e.g. *remember(n)* – in preference to German *sich erinnern* requiring the reflexive pronoun, following preposition *an* and accusative. A parallel case is the use of Croatian *sjeam* (remember) + ACC in Hlavac's corpus of second-generation Croatian–English bilinguals, instead of with a reflexive clitic *se*, the agent in the nominative, and the patient/recipient in the genitive as in 'Homeland Croatian', for example:

(25)   ..to   je   možda   najbolje   što   sam
         that is   perhaps best+NEUT+NOM.sg   that+NOM   be+AUX+1sg

         ja, što   ja rememba   yeah [jeə]
         I   that+NOM I   remember   yeah

         Homeland Croatian:
         ..to   je   možda   najbolje   što   sam
         that is   perhaps best+NEUT+NOM.sg   that+NOM   be+AUX+1sg

         (ja), doživio čega   se
         I   experience+MASC.3sg+PAST.PT   that+REL.P+GEN

         sjećam
         REFL+ACC remember+1sg+PRES (Hlavac 2000: 398–9)

6. Quotation words, e.g. in bilingual family communication (parents speak German, children respond in English), the German keyword characterized prosodically and through discourse prominence is picked up by the child in the English response, for example:

(26)   Parent: Wenn du *allein* gehst.
         Child: But I'm not going *allein* (twelve-year old)

4.3.1.1 Multiple transference
Multiple transference (or Myers-Scotton's Embedded Language Islands) may be the result of the process of transversion (see section 5.2, section 5.3) or it may be simply phrases or idioms transferred interlingually, for example:

(27)   Ich bin Bankangestellter. Zur Zeit   arbeite   ich am
         I   am   a bank employee   at the moment   am working   I   at

         Schalter   ON THE RELIEVING STAFF
         the counter on the relieving staff

         'I am a bank employee. At the moment I am working at the counter on the relieving staff' (MGP 45m)

Because of production in chunks (Levelt 1983; Clyne 1967; Azuma and Bales 1998; see also section 6.3.1.1), phrases are prevalent in multiple transference. This is most conspicuous in Ho-Dac's Vietnamese corpus, for example:

(28) Mình vẫn có thee̋ A LOT OF FRIENDS AROUND hông
      I   still can   a lot of friends around   question+PRT
      'I still have a lot of friends, haven't I?' (MV2f, 1b, Ho-Dac)
(29) Ong là salesman ông đi DOOR TO DOOR bán
      He is salesman he go door to door   sale
      'He is a salesman selling from door-to-door' (MV4m, Ho-Dac)
(30) Cái PROBLEM của ổng tức cái
      CLA problem of him mean CLA

      PERSONAL HAPPINESS ông không có
      personal happiness he no   have

      'His problem is that he does not have personal happiness' (MV4m,
      Ho-Dac)

However, multiple transference of a phrase is often, across all languages
under consideration, the result of anticipational triggering (see section 5.3.1).
It can also be considered support for Azuma and Bales's (1998) Stand-alone
Principle whereby any chunk – anything that can stand alone – can be 'code-
switched'. Closed-class items cannot stand alone and therefore are not usually
'code-switched' but may be a structural cue. Nevertheless there are many instances of system morphemes that are switched from Dutch into English, e.g.
al 'all', *dat* 'that', *de* 'the', *en* 'and', *een* 'a, an', *je* 'you', *wat* 'what' and, to a
lesser extent, *dit* 'this', *met* 'with', *uit* 'out', *van* 'of', *hoe* 'how' and *want* 'for,
because'. In German–English bilinguals who migrated as mature adults, *mit* is
the preposition most frequently transferred into English.

4.3.2 Phonetic/phonological/prosodic aspects of transference

As Rayfield (1970) points out, the phonological level of the L1 is usually the last
to be affected by contact with an L2. Where such phonological transference occurs, this is usually an identity marker of second- and especially third-generation
bilinguals. Then salient features of Australian English replace the community
language equivalents. Among the distinctive features are the alveolar [ɹ], the
velar [ɫ] and, to a lesser extent, the diphthongization of monophthongs such
as /o/, /e/ and /u/ *in most community languages*, the substitution of /ts/ and
/ç/ by [s] and [k] in German, the omission of /r/ in postvocalic position (e.g.
parla, prima) and substitution of unstressed [ə] for [o] as in *ancora* (Bettoni
1981a) in Italian, centralization of unstressed vowels to [ə], devoicing of final
stops and underdifferentiation of *ss, cc, dz*, in Polish. (This already affects the
first generation – Sussex 1982a.) The potentially most feasible study of phonological transference would be that of data from the former German enclaves
as they constituted the longest-standing immigrant language contact situation
in Australia. The problem is that most of the deviations from the 'standard'

German norm are shared with the East Central German base dialects of most of the original settlers:

Unrounded vowels [e:] [i:] for [ø][y], e.g. [le:zən] *lösen*, [fy:lən]*fühlen*
Diphthongs [ɛi] [əu][ʉ]for [e] [o] [u], e.g. [lɛɪzən] *lesen*, [gɹəus] *groß*, [məʉt] *Mut*
Fricatives for affricates [f] for [pf], [s] for [ts], e.g. [fɛ:ət] *Pferd*, [sa:n] *Zahn*
Alveolar [ɹ] (alongside [r]), e.g. [ɹɛɪgən] *Regen*

These features should therefore not *necessarily* be attributed to Australian English influence. Where the realization does not correspond to East Central German (broader diphthongs such as [au], [ai]; triphthong [æu]), Australian English influence can be surmized. This demonstrates that, even where there is overlap between features attributable to contact-induced and internal change, the contact situation promotes a greater convergence between the languages.

4.3.2.1 Prosodic transference
Various scholars (e.g. Bettoni 1981a: 80–2 for Italian; Tamis; 1986: 197 for Greek; and Waas 1996: 160 for German) have observed anecdotally the use of the characteristic Australian English high-rise terminal in community languages. I am not aware of any study of the effects of the majority language on the prosody of an immigrant language.

4.3.3   Graphemic transference

The types of graphemic transfers are similar to those of phonological transference but the former is far more prevalent and there are far more examples of it. This may be attributed to the 'academic' nature of orthography, the time lag between many bilingual children's acquisition of the spoken and written forms of the community language, the far more restricted corrective influence of the school, and the limited exposure to it through the media, public use and so on. (The examples are based on Clyne 1972a: 41–7, German; Kaminskas 1972: 206–9, Spanish; Clyne, Fernandez, Chen and Summo-O'Connell 1997, German, Italian and Chinese):[7]

  i. the transference of English phoneme–grapheme relations, <oo> for Sp. <u>, as in: *toocha* for *ducha*; <ei> for Ger. <ie> as in: *seiben* for *sieben, speilen* for *spielen, veilen* for *vielen,* <ɪ> for It. <e> as in: *amici* for *amiche* (masc. for fem.);

 ii. the dropping of distinctive graphemes or grapheme sequences in the community language, e.g. Sp. <cqu>, Ger. <ä>, <ö>, <ü>, <sch>, as in *querdo (acquerdo), lachelnd (lächelnd), Sohne (Söhne), Stuhle (Stühle), Shatten (Schatten), swimmen (schwimmen)*;

iii. extension of phoneme–grapheme rules from variable (contextual) to general rules, e.g. It. *li* for *gli*, Ger. *fon* for *von*. Similarly, in Chinese, words are replaced by their homophones (according to research by Chen in Clyne et al. 1997: 98, 101, 115). Thus, the parallels between phonological and graphemic transference are the tendency to eliminate the distinctive units, realizations and sequences characteristic of the community language, and the extension from the specifically variable or contextual to the general.

4.4   Grammatical convergence, transference and other changes

In this section, we will take up some of the issues raised in section 3.4. In particular, the role of convergence and transference and of drift and the evidence for multiple causation will be considered in relation to aspects of morphosyntax for which our data lends itself to some interlingual comparison.

There are a number of examples of levelling based on 'markedness' – gender markings on the adjective, demonstrative pronoun and participle in Italian, and the 'have' auxiliary in a number of Germanic and Romance languages are some examples. Also related to markedness is the greater tendency for SVO generalization to take place in main clauses than in subordinate ones in Dutch and German. A change that does not affect the basic typology is that of adverbial word order from time–manner–place in German and Dutch to place–manner–place based on English, for example:

(31)   Ich hab   (A) zu meiner Mutter gesprochen   gestern   morgen
        I   have+AUX   to my   mother speak+PAST.PT yesterday morning
        'I spoke to my mother yesterday morning'
        Homeland German: Ich habe gestern morgen zu meiner Mutter gesprochen (MGW 17f)

In data from the twelve informants from a former German enclave in the Wimmera whose recordings included several different multi-adverbial utterances, fifteen of twenty-four instances of such utterances had them in an English word order.

Among prewar refugees, only four out of eighty-one multi-adverbial utterances transferred the English order of adverbials. In one case the particular is placed before the general instead of the reverse as in Standard German:

(32)   Mein Mann   fängt   um drei Uhr   an zum
        my   husband start+3sg at three o'clock   to

        Arbeiten   *jeden Tag*
        work-VERBAL NOUN every day

        'My husband starts work at three o'clock every day'
        Homeland German: Mein Mann fängt *jeden Tag* um drei Uhr an zu arbeiten (MGPR 15f)

Two instances have the direct object preceding instead of following the time adverbial:

(33)   Habe   Frühstück um sieben Uhr
        have+1sg breakfast   at   seven o'clock
        'I have breakfast at seven o'clock'
        Homeland German: Esse um sieben Uhr das Frühstück (MGPR 33f)
(34)   Verlassen wir das Haus gegen neun
        leave+1pl we the house about nine
        'We leave the house about nine'
        Homeland German: Wir verlassen gegen neun das Haus
        (MGPR 32m)

In colloquial homeland German, the word order in examples (32) to (34) would not be impossible.

In the speech of postwar Dutch immigrants, in contrast, there are twelve converged adverbial orders out of twenty-one multi-adverb utterances, for example:

(35)   Ik ben   in Parijs zelf   nooit geweest
        I   am+AUX in Paris myself never be+PAST.PT
        'I have never been in Paris myself'
        Homeland Dutch: Ik ben nooit zelf in Parijs geweest (MD 193m)
(36)   Ik zou   niet weten, waar   er   water moet hier zijn.
        I   would not know   where DUMMY water must here be+INF
        'I wouldn't know where there was water here'
        Homeland Dutch: Ik zou niet weten, waar er hier water moet zijn
        (MD 45m)

4.4.1   Auxiliary

One of the common features of a number of languages in contact with English in Australia is the competition between 'have' as the unmarked auxiliary for the perfect and pluperfect (coinciding with English) and 'be' as the marked auxiliary (for verbs denoting either movement or change of place or state). The former occurs in some speakers of German and Dutch (Clyne 1967, 1977a), French (Ludwig-Wyder 1982) and Italian (Bettoni 1981a). Thomason and Kaufman (1988: 128) point out that historically the French 'marked' auxiliary was due to the German substratum, and the Italian to French influence. In the Italian of our Italian–Spanish–English trilinguals, there are numerous instances of *andare* 'go' (from three speakers), *arrivare* 'arrive' (from two), *emigrare* 'emigrate', *nascere* 'be born', *sembrare* 'seem' and *venire* 'come' (from one informant each) employing *avere* instead of *essere* as an auxiliary. Of the eight of the third-generation urban German–English bilinguals who used the perfect, three used *haben* as an auxiliary throughout, for example:

(37)   Die Mutter *hat*   eingeschlafen
        the mother have+AUX+3sg   fall.asleep+PAST.PT
        'The mother has fallen asleep'
        (MGG3–19f; thirteen-year-old who speaks German to all four grandparents but not to her parents, describing a picture sequence. However, an eight-year-old who speaks German to the mother, and whose father does not speak German, uses *sein* as the aux with *einschlafen* twice in similar sentences.)

(38)   Ich habe   nach Stawell in der
        I   have+AUX+1sg to   Stawell in the+DAT+FEM.sg[8]
        Grampians gegangen
        Grampians go+PAST.PT
        'I went to Stawell in the Grampians'
        (MGG3–18f, describing a holiday; she speaks German to the grandparents)

Three of these speakers employed *sein* in all the relevant cases, one employed *haben* in three out of four relevant instances, and one in one out of three. All of the examples were from the verb *gehen* 'go' (or its compounds) except for two single instances of *bleiben* 'remain' and *einschlafen* 'to fall asleep'. In our postwar corpus, only one second-generation and two generation 1b children generalized *haben* consistently. The overgeneralization of *hebben* (i.e. used instead of *zijn*) may be found in sixteen Dutch–English bilingual informants (thirteen first generation and three second), seven of whom used it consistently. It is also reported in Dutch in Brazil (Schoenmakers-Klein Gunnewiek 1998) and in Afrikaans, the 'have' auxiliary displaced 'be'. The latter is attributed by Valkhoff (1972: 173) to 'confusion' in seventeenth-century Dutch.

Thomason and Kaufman (1988: 58–9) are right in questioning the position that rejects external change as an explanation simply because the same phenomenon can be attributed to internal change in another language or variety. In the case of Dutch, there are dialects where *hebben* is the sole auxiliary but they are not spoken in the northwestern, northeastern and southeastern areas which provided Australia with its Dutch-speaking immigrants. Moreover, the merger is not part of a historical development, as there has been a recent increase in the use of *zijn* as an auxiliary (De Rooij 1988). Bettoni (1981a: 72) suggests the influence of regional and popular varieties in the parallel development in Italian in Australia, but it is likely that the two influences – dialect and English – reinforce each other. Spanish has two auxiliaries corresponding to 'be', *ser* and *estar*, which Kaminskas (1972: 109–11) found to be merging in some speakers in Melbourne, something that was also reported by Silva-Corvalán (1994) in Los Angeles. While the levelling is not extremely widespread, it is part of a general tendency towards the abandonment of the marked feature or construction.

As was mentioned in section 3.5.5, Smith (1998) has proposed actualization and reanalysis as an explanation of the agreement loss in Romance language compound tenses with a 'have' auxiliary. The extended loss of agreement with 'be' could be regarded as part of a drift that is accelerated in the contact situation with English. (This line of argument will be developed for word-order typology under section 4.4.7.) Smith considers agreement between direct object and past participle in a number of implicational hierarchies (e.g. position of direct object, identity of preceding direct object, person of clitic pronoun) as well as the loss of agreement. He prefers sentence-processing strategies and the notion of recoverability to markedness as an explanation.

4.4.2   Gender agreement on Italian modifiers and verbs

Bettoni (1985, 1991), in her studies of second-generation (Venetian) Italian speech in Sydney compared to that of their parents, found that masculine suffixes on articles, adjectives, pronouns and past participles of verbs taking *essere* were sometimes used invariably to cover the feminine, even in natural gender, e.g. *che belo che era l'Australia* (Homeland It. *che bella che era l'Australia* 'how beautiful Australia was'), *questi macchine elettronichi* (Homeland It. *queste macchine elettroniche* 'these electronic machines'), *sia andato* (Homeland It. *sia andata*), even *el capitale* (*la capitale* 'the capital'), *i sorelle* (*le sorelle* 'the sisters'), *coi droghe* (*colle droghe* 'with drugs'). This may be an extension of the functionally unmarked masculine gender, i.e. it is used where the natural gender is unknown or both genders are represented (Aikhenvald 2000: 50–1). This does not occur much in our Italian–Spanish–English trilinguals as they are first-generation speakers of at least one of the Romance languages and due to the protection that the overlap between Italian and Spanish offers against changes promoted by English (cf. section 4.2.2.1 above). Nevertheless there are a few Italian instances, for example:

(39)   Siamo   stato   un   mese
         be+AUX+1pl go+MASC.sg+PAST.PT one   month

         il   primo anno
         the first   year

         'We went for one month the first year'
         Homeland Italian: stati (plural marking) (MTSIE 13f, relating a trip
         to Italy)

(40)   Si   quando   siamo   arrivato   a   Australia
        Yes   when   AUX+1pl   arrive+MASC.sg+PAST.PT   in   Australia
        siamo   andato   a   Northcote
        AUX+1pl   go+MASC.sg+PAST.PT   in   Northcote
        'Yes, when we arrived in Australia, we went to Northcote'
        Homeland Italian: arrivati (plural marking) (MTS/IE 2m)

4.4.3   Plural affixes in German and Dutch

A clearcut case of Category 3 in Thomason and Kaufman's schema would be the overgeneralization of -s as a plural allomorph. As we saw in section 3.6, Dutch has two main plural suffixes, -en and -s, while German has five. In our bilingual Dutch corpus, twelve of the informants (including ten generation 1a), employed -s instead of -en in a total of fifteen nouns of indigenous origin, but there were only two examples of -en for -s substitution. Moreover, four of the nouns given an -s plural instead of -en were not homophones of English equivalents: koei 'cow', zondag 'Sunday', hoofdleiding 'main', lantaarnpaal 'lamp post' (unlike kamps 'camps' or mijls 'miles' for instance). Almost all English lexical transfer plural nouns retained the -s allomorph. Thus, implicationally, this is the hierarchy:

a. -s for English lexical transfers;
b. -s for native Dutch nouns that have English homophones; and
c. -s for other native Dutch words.

There is only a single instance in our comparable German corpus of -s being affixed to a German noun (almost in category (b) due to the similarity of hundert and hundred):

(41)   hunderts und hunderts OF Leute
        'hundreds and hundreds of people'
        (spoken by a generation 1b informant, MGP 169f)

Of seventy-four second-generation German–English Saturday school bilingual children whose German morphosyntax was studied specifically (Clyne 1970c), four generalized the -en plural and one the -(¨)e plural (e.g. Bäumen, Leuten, Männe), but none the -s allomorph. Twenty-five of the children were tested on plurals and used -e inappropriately thirty-seven times, -(e)n thirty-three times, -er six times and -s only four times, of which two instances were a cognate of English boot. Monheit (1975), in similar elicitation, found twenty-three inappropriate uses of -s, alongside eighty-five of -er and sixty-eight of -(e)n, among sixty-eight second-generation children. Although -s was assigned far more than in the 1970 study, -s generalization still only represented 13% of the total instances. In the third generation, there is a remarkable tendency towards a zero plural, recorded by nine out of twenty informants for *Auto*, along with six instances of plural *Hund* and five each of *Haus* and *Stuhl* as plurals. In each instance, the noun was preceded by a numeral. Four of the informants, all of whom were under the age of ten, speak German habitually at home and three are in a content-based primary school German program. The *-s* overgeneralization occurs in *Hockers, Tiers* and *Hunds* in one informant and in *Türs* in another. Schmid (fc) found a tendency towards zero plural in German-born refugees in the UK and US who were not actively using much German.

Among Dutch–German–English trilinguals, the common non-standard forms are *-en* to replace *-e* as in *Freunden* (for *Freunde*), *Jahren* (for *Jahre*) and *Leuten* (for *Leute*), on the assumption that German *-en* corresponds to Dutch [ə]. But other informants transfer Dutch *-e* [ə] to replace German *-en* (e.g. *Straßenbahne, Zeitunge*). What there is no sign of in the Dutch and German of the trilinguals is the overgeneralized *-s* plural so common among the bilinguals.

4.4.4   Gender marking on German and Dutch articles

Another less drastic change is the tendency to overgeneralize one article. Thomason and Kaufman (1988: 82) refer under Category 3 to the trend to assign English lexical transfers to the feminine in some German enclaves in Australia. And, as we will see under section 4.5, the integration of English transfers in Dutch into the common gender (definite article – *de*) rather than the neuter (definite article – *het*) is well attested.

As far as native German words are concerned, there were only ten gender re-allocations in our postwar corpus – three to each of the genders and one variably to the masculine and the neuter. Only one of our (second-generation) informants had developed a generalized pattern; she used *de* (cf. *the*) for all nouns. This has been reported elsewhere only in research on the Apostolic German settlement in Hatton Vale, Queensland, whose original settlers came from Braunschweig, Westphalia, and Berlin (Bleakley 1966). In the Victorian and South Australian German settlements, the feminine was the preferred gender of a few widely adopted lexical transfers from English but this did not affect German-origin words. The fluid situation among German–English bilinguals was confirmed in direct testing of definite articles of nouns among generation 1b and second-generation children attending German Saturday schools. In one study (Clyne 1970c), native nouns were inappropriately allocated to the masculine twenty-one times, to the neuter twenty-two times and to the feminine sixteen times. In the other study (Monheit 1975), there were 103 inappropriate assignments to the masculine, sixty-seven to the neuter, and sixty-three to the feminine. In the two studies, out of the misallocations, this represented 42.25% to the masculine, 30.4% to the neuter and 27% to the feminine. Almost all the nouns were inanimate and many of the children had no clear conception of gender allocation. In the feminine nouns, the dative-gender article *der* (identical to masculine nominative article) may have confused some children. A more distinct gender tendency was not found until a study of the German speech of twenty third-generation urban German–English bilinguals (Clyne 1997a), fourteen of whom were under the age of twelve. Most of the informants generalized *das* as the definite article of *inanimate* objects whose gender they were uncertain of. Of thirty-eight inappropriate gender assignments, twenty were neuter, ten (including three from one informant) were feminine and only eight masculine. Nine out of ten of the informants who employed a pronoun referring to particular nouns used *es* instead of another pronoun at least once, six informants four times and two three times. This included some of the most fluent German speakers. This tendency, which may be a stage in the development of a *das* generalization in the third generation, is already strong in the second generation as is evident from informal conversations between the bilingual parent and the third-generation speaker. The use of *es* in this way is also recorded in data from former German enclaves, for example:

(42)   Interviewer: Sie haben einen schönen Garten
        Informant: Ich weiss nicht, ob *es* so schön ist, aber es ist ein großer
                    Garten (MGWD 28f)

Here, in response to the interviewer's comment 'You have a nice garden', the elderly (third-generation) informant replies 'I don't know if it is so nice but it's a big garden.' *Garten* is masculine but she refers to it by the neuter pronoun *es*. In our third-generation urban data, there were indeed eighteen misappropriations to *das*, eleven to *die* (four of them from one informant) and eight to *der*. (There were only twenty informants and the amount of data was less than for the second generation above.)[9]

The tendency to overgeneralize *de* for native Dutch nouns even to the point of reduction of grammatical genders to one occurs in some speakers. Fifty-two different *het* nouns were assigned to the non-neuter gender (*de*) in the speech of thirteen generation 1a and thirty second-generation and generation 1b of our 200 Dutch speakers, while only nine *de* words were assigned to the neuter. Thirty-four of the fifty-two nouns whose gender had been changed bear phonetic similarity to the English equivalents, e.g. *bed, café, land, soort, werk*, but eighteen do not, including *gebouw* 'building', *gedeelte* 'part', *gezin* 'family', *paard* 'horse', *verhaal* 'story'. Two explanations need to be considered, an internal and an external one. *De* is already by far the most frequently used definite article (van Berckel 1962), as most Dutch nouns are non-neuter and *de* is also the plural article. In fact, the overgeneralization of *de* as an article also occurs in early first- as well as in second-language acquisition (Extra 1978). Moreover, the similarity between *de* and *the*, particularly in the realizations of some first-generation bilinguals, increased the likelihood of a lexical transfer being assigned a non-neuter article, either by themselves or by members of their family or community. Of 174 transferred nouns with a clearcut article assignment, 150 were used with *de* and twenty-four with *het* (cf. below, section 4.5.1.1). Both of the explanations are valid contributing factors. The implicational scales proposed for plural allomorphs thus appear to hold even more for gender allocation:

a. for lexical transfers from English;
b. for bilingual homophones;
c. for other Dutch nouns.

Bilinguals in areas of Dutch concentration in the rural and semi-rural areas of Victoria, where networks spread innovation, assign two-thirds of their lexical transfers to the non-neuter. Convergence between Dutch and English is promoted by the morphemic correspondence and the phonetic similarity between /də/ and the Dutch non-neuter /ðə/ as realized by first-generation Dutch–English bilinguals. Also, the fact that the historic masculine-feminine differentiation no longer occurs in Dutch (except in pronoun reference for the animate, and for the inanimate in some southern dialects) means that the Dutch gender system and its markings may not be perceived as sufficiently salient to preserve. The unified typology of German contrasts (cf. Hawkins 1986) with that of English too much for the same convergence to take place as between Dutch and English. The crystallization of this development cannot be assessed because of the rapidity of language shift among Dutch-Australians, but the increasing tendency toward single gender *de* may be seen as part of the drift of Dutch.

4.4.5   Case loss and restructuring

Case reduction has been attested in a number of immigrant contact situations, e.g. the loss of the dative for nouns and of the dative, instrumental and locative for adjectives in Polish in New York (Preston 1986: 1020–1), and a reduction to a three-case paradigm in the case marking of prepositional phrases in Slovenian in the US (Meyerstein 1969: 64–6). Durović (1983) developed a retention continuum for Serbo-Croatian in Sweden:

Nominative, Accusative, Genitive, Instrumental, Dative, Locative

with the last lost first. This is confirmed by Hlavac (2000: 463), who found 21% ungrammatical dative nominal case marking, mainly changing to nominative, and 26% ungrammatical locative nominal case marking, mainly changing to accusative, in his second-generation Croatian-Australian sample.

Typically, the changes were in the masculine plural (dative) and feminine plural (locative).

In Finnish in the US, Larmouth (1974) found that case reduction is environmentally sensitive but the most vulnerable nominal cases are the accusative, allative and partitive. In Fenyvési's (1994) study of Hungarian in Pittsburgh, accusative endings are by far the most likely to be omitted, followed by inessive and superessive.

In our data from Hungarian–German–English trilinguals, there are seventy-five instances of the nominative – the unmarked, suffix-less case – being substituted for another case (e.g. twenty-three instances of accusative suffix deletion, especially in describing photographs; twelve of the inessive, twelve of the possessive, four of the superessive, and one to three instances of delative, essive, illative and other suffixes being deleted). There is therefore a limited tendency towards a uniform nominative–accusative with an analytic form, for example:

(43)   Á német,   azt úgy   tanultam,   mint második
        the German+NOM that really learn+PAST+1sg as   second

        anyanyelvem
        mother-tongue

        'I really learned German like a second mother tongue'
        Homeland Hungarian: A németet . . . (accusative) (HTH/GE (r)11m)

(44)   Minden   mi csinálunk
        everything+NOM we do+1pl
        'We do everything'
        Homeland Hungarian: Mindent . . . (acc.) (MTHSwGE13m)

This corresponds to the findings of Fenyvési (1994) among first- and second-generation Hungarian Americans in McKeesport, Pennsylvania. The Hungarian–English and Finnish–English bilinguals Kovács (2001) has studied in Australia also show a tendency to substitute the unmarked (nominative) case for the Hungarian accusative and the Finnish accusative and partitive respectively.

The other case that is overgeneralized considerably in our corpus is the accusative, which replaces the nominative, perhaps hypercorrectly, four times, and other cases (delative, essive, illative) replace the nominative a total of four times in the trilingual data. This reflects the uncertainty of many trilinguals in the expression of logical and spatial relations. One suffix not affected by this is the instrumental. We have not included many instances of the illative replacing the inessive as this also occurs in monolinguals (cf. Fenyvési 1994), probably attributable to nasalized vowels and the dropping of the final -n, as in *városba(n)* 'in the town'/*városba* 'into the town'.[10] Thus, there appears to be some restructuring rather than case loss due to attrition. It should be noted that our informants are almost entirely first-generation, linguistically aware trilinguals. It would be interesting to follow this issue up with a sizeable group of second- and third-generation Hungarian–English bilinguals. In a study of postpositions among first- and second-generation Hungarian–English bilinguals in Australia, Endrody (1971) found frequent deviation, especially in the expression of spatial relations, such as Melbourne-*en* 'on Melbourne' for Melbourne-*ben* 'in Melbourne', rather than transference. This phenomenon was attested frequently by Fenyvési (1994) and in the second-generation informants in Kontra's (1990) research on Hungarian speakers in South Bend, Indiana. The 'on' forms are not usually employed for non-Hungarian place names, but, as Fenyvési (1994: 93–4) explains, the usage in the contact situations could be due to the change in the sense of homeland. However, the most frequent change in the case system in our corpus, and also in Kontra's, is the deletion of the suffix making accusatives and sublatives, for instance, effectively into nominatives.

Studies of the German of bilingual enclaves in Pennsylvania, the American Mid West and Texas (Gilbert 1965; Salmons 1994; Huffines 1989; Louden 1994; Keel 1994) report syncretism of cases. Generally there is a reduction to a common case, in Plain Pennsylvania German, or to two cases, nominative and oblique, largely by the generalization of accusative forms in the dative in the other groups and areas, with marked case forms for both. The masculine oblique case form *den* is also employed for the neuter singular (*das*). Salmons (1994) points out that this is in line with the cross-linguistically most common distinction and concurs with a basic principle of the theory of Natural Morphology (Wurzel 1989), that the usual direction of change is towards system congruity with less markedness and more 'naturalness' in nominal case morphology.

In a sample of Settlement German from ten informants from the Western District of Victoria (third generation or half second and half third generation) who were selected because their recorded data contained many opportunities to use the dative or the accusative, the dative plural was the form which was most 'non-standard'. By dative plural -*n* suffix deletion, acusative and dative plural nouns are syncretized, for example:

(45)   Leute   saßen   überall   im   Park auf..auf Bänke
        people   sat around   all over   in the   park   on   seats
        'People sat around on seats all over the park'
        Standard German: auf Bänke*n* (MGWD 42f)

(46)   Mit   meine   Kinder
        with   my+ACC.pl   children+ACC.pl
        Standard German: mit mein*en* Kinder*n* (MGWD 35m)

Table 4.1 *Use of dative in a subsample from the Western District*

	Dative singular	Dative plural	Dative forms after prepositions taking accusative or dative
Standard	64 (56.14%)	17 (30.91%)	51 (53.13%)
Non-standard	50 (43.86%)	38 (69.09%)	45 (46.88%)

Mit takes the dative in Standard German. The addition of the *-n* to nouns is unique to the dative plural. But there are also instances of accusative substitution involving articles only, for example:

(47)   Aber welche von *die* Jungen, die   wollen wieder Deutsch lernen
        but   some of   the boys, they want   again German learn
        'But some of the boys, they want to start learning German again'
        Standard German: von *den* Jungen (MGWD 14f)

About half the 'non-standard' forms used are dative singular forms and nominal case endings after prepositions taking the dative or the accusative, depending on whether the object is stative or active (see table 4.1).

Of the ten informants, only four had a majority of standard forms for the dative singular and six for the instances where there was a choice between accusative and dative after prepositions. Standard forms occurred most frequently in idiomatic expressions, such as *am Leben* 'alive', *zum zweiten Mal* 'for the second time', or verbs taking the dative, notably the frequent verb *geben* 'give', *einem gefallen* 'to like' and *einem leid tun* 'to feel sorry for someone', often used in polite everyday conversations and probably acquired as formulaic routines. Among standard forms are also contracted dative forms such as *zum* and *zur* (< *zu dem, zu der*), *am* and *im* (< *an dem, in dem*). There is considerable variation in the same story told by the same informant, for example:

(48)   Mit *dem* Wagen
        'In the wagon'
        (Standard German) (MGWD 1)
(49)   Da   kommt der Vater gefahren   mit *'nen*   großen Wagen
        there comes the father travel+PAST.PT with a+ACC big   cart
        'Then the father comes along in his big cart'
        Standard German: mit einem (MGWD 1)

Otherwise there was a high incidence of accusative or uninflected forms for the dative, for example:

(50)   Wir haben alles   müssen   mit *die*   Hand drehen
         we   have   everything must+INF with the+ACC hand turn+INF
         'We had to turn everything by hand'
         (Eng. by hand, Std Ger. mit *der* Hand; *die* is accusative)
         (MGWD 4f, describing conditions on the farm in the old days)

(51)   Sie wohnten mit *mein*   Vater auf *denselben*   Farm
         they lived   with my+ACC father on   the-same+ACC farm
         'They lived with my father on the same farm'
         Standard German: mit mein*em* Vater auf *der*selben Farm (This can
         be construed as either also non-standard gender allocation for *Farm*
         or *den* as oblique feminine (the only instance of this in the small
         sample); *mein* could be *mein'n*, accusative; or *mein*, uninflected,
         therefore nominative.) (MGWD 34f)

(52)   Das kommt aus *das* Laub
         'That comes from the foliage'
         Standard German: aus *dem* Laub; *das* is nominative/accusative
         (MGWD 41m)

(53)   Ich denke, der hat sechs Kinder in *die* Familie
         'I think he has six children in the family'
         Standard German: in *der* Familie; *die* is nominative/accusative (MGD
         41m)

Mit and *aus* always take the dative in Standard German, while *auf* and *in*
take the accusative in active objects and the dative in stative ones. There was
only one instance of a move to an analytic system:

(54)   Ich geb's *zu die* Katze
         'I give it to the cat'
         Standard German: Ich geb's *der* Katze (MGWD 33f)
         Zu takes the accusative; *die* is nominative/accusative

The former enclaves were largely settled from East Central German areas
in which the generalized accusative (though not the syncretism of neuter and
masculine ACC/DAT.sg) were normal. School and church provided a corrective
influence in the direction of Standard German in the settlements, resulting in a
'mixed' outcome.

In our urban data, the case system is still intact in the first generation. As in
the colloquial German in the countries of origin, the genitive is not employed
much, possession being usually expressed by *von* 'of'. In the second generation,
there is an occasional transference of the *-s* possessive from English, e.g. *zu
ihre Mutters Grab* (from a fourteen-year-old girl, talking about a book she had
read in English).[11] This is far more common in former German settlements,
especially when speaking about family relationships, for example:

(55)   Das war meine Großeltern, mein Mutters Eltern und mein Vaters Eltern
        'That was my grandparents, my mother's parents and my father's
        parents'
        Standard German: Das waren meine Großeltern, die Eltern meiner
        Mutter und die Eltern meines Vaters (MGWD 29f, referring to a picture
        on the wall)

Other instances include: *meine Fraus Schwester* (Std. Ger. *die Schwester
meiner Frau*). (MGW 2m); *meine Mutters Vater* (MGW 107m); *meine Mutters
Seite* (MGWD 35m). There are some examples which may have been inspired by
a convergence between English and archaic (e.g. biblical) German, e.g. *in mein
Großvaters Haus* (archaic German: *in meines Großvaters Haus*) (MGW 49f).
    The two syncretism tendencies (accusative for accusative and dative, and
masculine accusative as generalized accusative) reported in the US are also to
be found in the third-generation urban data, for example:

(56)   Wir müssen bis   halb vier in *die*   Schule sein
        we   have   until half four in the+ACC school be+INF
        'We have to be at school until half past three.' (Std. Ger. in *der*)
        (MGG3–17f)
(57)   Wir haben ein Klavier in *den*   Wohnzimmer
        we   have   a   piano   in the+ACC living-room
        (*den*, MASC.ACC.sg; but *Zimmer* is NEUTER; Std Ger. NEUT.DAT.
        sg *dem*) (MGG3–7m)
(58)   Sie liest   noch einmal *den* Buch
        she is reading again once   the book
        'She is reading the book again.'
        (*den*, MASC.ACC.sg; but *Buch* is NEUTER; Std Ger. NEUT.ACC.
        sg *das*) (MGG3–8f)

This is not attested in German dialects, and there are no family regional background factors correlating with this tendency. Nine of the seventeen informants
who could have used datives, substituted accusatives for most of them, and
one employed only accusatives in such instances. *Den* was generalized for the
neuter as well as masculine accusative and dative by three of the informants.
    There are regional varieties with an oblique case based on forms that are ac-
cusative in Standard German, but none of the families of these third-generation
bilinguals speak such a dialect. The accusative tendency in our informants
is strongest with prepositions such as *in* and *auf* that take the accusative
or the dative according to whether they denote direction or position. For
example:

(59)   weil   wir in *die*   zwölfte   Klasse sein
        because we in the+ACC twelfth+ACC grade be+INF
        'Because we are in the twelfth grade'
        Standard German (stative): weil wir in *der* zwölf*ten* Klasse *sind*;
        die is accusative (MGG3–3f)

A few informants who generalize the accusative in this way also tend to use transitive verbs (e.g. *fragen, wecken*) with the dative, for example:

(60)   Kannst   du   mir   morgen   früh   wecken?
        can+2sg you   me+DAT tomorrow early wake+INF
        'Can you wake me up early tomorrow?' (MGGG3–17f, aged 14)
(61)   Mummy   hat   mir   gerade   gefragt.
        mummy   AUX me+DAT just   ask+PAST.PT
        'Mummy just asked me' (Same informant)

It is possible that some of the syncretism in the German of the Western District may have already occurred prior to their family's immigration to Australia. But this does not apply to the urban families' third generation. Aikhenvald (2000: 415) notes that children have more difficulties with three-gender systems where gender markers interact with numbers and case. Myers-Scotton's and Jake's 4M model (Myers-Scotton and Jake 2000, see above, section 3.4.1) makes it possible to explain both the accusative–dative syncretism and the masculine–neuter accusative syncretism. The fact that, according to the 4M theory, gender system morphemes are processed early and case system morphemes late, makes German nominal morphology very difficult to process. German has much overlap in the marking of features (case, gender, number). Particularly plurilinguals who are accustomed to more economic processing from their other language simplify the system by making a form unique to either gender or case marking. This is part of the change that typically takes place in the third generation, which Gonzo and Saltarelli (1983) describe in terms of simplification, restructuring and replacement based on a second-generation system which is already based on simplification, restructuring and replacement. The masculine–neuter accusative syncretism also adds support to natural morphology (Salmons 1994).

The above developments are in contrast with the generalization of *de* in Dutch, a language where articles are processed early and there is no overlap between gender and case features as in German.

4.4.6   Uninflected forms of Dutch verbs

Dutch still has two personal endings other than zero for verbs in the present tense: *-t* for second- and third-person singular and *-en* (usually realized as shwa) for the plural (as opposed to four endings in German and one in English). The drift in Dutch towards uninflected forms of verbs is therefore a more gradual one than in English. As the pronoun is not dropped, the endings are generally redundant from a communicative point of view. There is a small amount of evidence of the development of zero-form conjugations by some second-generation Dutch–English bilinguals, who employ forms such as *eet* 'eat', *kan* 'can', *houd* 'hold, keep', *kijk* 'look' and *moest* 'had to' for the first- and third-person plural, which would take *-en* in Homeland Dutch (*eten, kunnen, houden, kijken*), and forms such as *heb* 'have', *ga* 'go', *lijk* 'seem' and *raak* 'become' in the third-person singular (Standard *-t, heeft, gaat, lijkt, raakt*), for example:

(62)   Al de mensen *zit* op straat.
       'All the people sit on the beach'
       Homeland Dutch: zitten (MD 175m)

(63)   En dan *heb*   hij geen geld   in zijn bank.
       and then have+ZERO he no   money in his bank
       'And then he hasn't any money left in the bank'
       Homeland Dutch: heeft (MD 1m)

This seems to indicate an avoidance of the personal endings altogether. The zero form in Homeland Dutch is actually used for the first-person singular. Reduction in verbal inflections is also reported in Dutch in the US (van Marle and Smits 1997: 181). The most consistent development is in Afrikaans, which has only invariant analytic forms of the verb. This is the only example of a Thomason and Kaufman Category 5 change in our corpus. However, even here there are parallels in early first-language acquisition (Extra 1978).

Such instances of a general change from second-generation bilinguals must be distinguished from 'bare forms' where a stem form instead of an inflected one is employed in a situation of incongruence between structures in the two languages (Myers-Scotton 1993a: 125–6; Jake and Myers-Scotton 1997: 33–5). One example from our corpus is:

(64)   dat ze, zeg maar,   niet (A) *you know*, dat die niet
       that they say MOD.PRT not (A) you know that they not
       PISS OFF BY THEMSELVES
       piss off by themselves
       'So that they don't piss off on their own'
       Dutch: (zo) dat ze niet alleen opdonderen. (MGD 197m)

The speaker in (64), a first-generation bilingual in his fifties, is talking about a photograph of a drover driving sheep. He has chosen the multiple transference of an English taboo expression, the Dutch equivalent of which is not taboo. Another reason for the transversion is that Dutch requires a verb-final construction with the separable prefix and the infinitive merging (e.g. *offpissen*). The second-generation bilinguals who employ uninflected forms of the verb do so under circumstances not involving non-congruence, such as simple statement sentences.

A slight tendency towards a one-article system, a generalized *-s* plural and analytical verb forms has been noted (Stolz 1987) in other contact situations: New Jersey Dutch and, to some extent, in Mohawk River Dutch, and these are features of Afrikaans. As Dutch is hardly ever maintained into the third generation in Australia (cf. chapter 2), we cannot assess if, in time, the Australian contact situation would lead to a Dutch similar to Afrikaans.

4.4.7   Emerging typological change to SVO and fixed word order

Thomason and Kaufman (1988: 55) assert that SOV, SVO, etc. are susceptible to change because they all perform the same basic syntactic function: 'identification of subject and object by their position relative to each other and to the verb'. Actually in Dutch and German, SOV expresses dependence/subordination, adverb-VSO emphasis on time, manner or place, and OVS emphasis on the sufferer of the action rather than the actor.

Though only an emerging tendency, SVO generalization is a second- and later-generation phenomenon in German (if it occurs at all), but occurs quite frequently in the first-generation in Dutch–English bilinguals. In our postwar German–English bilingual corpus, the 193 first-generation (including generation 1b) and seven second-generation informants between them, overgeneralized SVO eight times. In the comparable Dutch–English bilingual corpus, first-generation informants produced ninety-three instances of SVO generalizations (seventy-six generation 1a, eighteen generation 1b) and the second-generation bilinguals seventeen instances. The lower incidence of SVO in the second generation can be attributed to the small numbers of fronting and subordinate clauses in their Dutch. Of the 110 SVO generalizations in Dutch that could be classified in a single category, sixty-eight (61.81%) were after fronting in the main clause and forty-two (38.18%) in subordinate clauses. SVO after fronting in the main clause was, relatively speaking, even more common in generations 1b (72.22%) and 2 (88.29% of SVO generalization) than in 1a (53.23%). It should be noted that seventeen of our thirty-nine second-generation bilinguals produced only simple sentences with no adverb to the left of the subject. Thus, in the second generation, there is very little pragmatic focus expressed by word order where SVO is generalized. The contrast between German and Dutch means that the typological change to SVO is more advanced in the Dutch bilinguals than in the German ones (see table 4.2).

Table 4.2 *SVO overgeneralization in German and Dutch postwar corpus*

German			Dutch		
Gen 1a	Gen 1b	Gen 2	Gen 1a	Gen 1b	Gen 2
–	5	3	76	18	17

Table 4.3 *Types of SVO overgeneralization in German and Dutch postwar corpus*

	German	Dutch
Fronting	6	68
Subordinate clause	1	42
Both	1	1
Total	8	111

Two possible explanations present themselves for the difference between the German and the Dutch data. One is that Dutch is used less than German, and the English pattern becomes much better established among Dutch speakers (section 2.2.1, section 2.2.2). There is, however, also a typological argument. While Dutch is traditionally described as being morphologically between English and German, and syntactically closer to German (Van Haeringen n.d.), it would be more appropriate to see morphology and syntax as working hand in hand and the Dutch changes as part of a 'package'. Because Dutch, like English, has lost its case markings, it too potentially has to rely on word order to express syntactic relations. Thus, it needs to ultimately adopt a grammatical word order rather than a more pragmatic one as it currently has, similar to that of German. This distinction also constitutes one of the differences between 'syntactic' and 'pragmatic' mode in Givón (1979). In her study of syntactic change in Middle Dutch, Burridge (1993) shows the change to more grammatical word order developing since the Middle Ages. She records two 'different but intrinsically connected typological drifts' (Burridge 1993: 238) – one towards subject (rather than topic) prominence, the other towards a more uniform SVO-type syntax.

Thus the tendencies in our data could be part of the 'unified contrast' (Hawkins 1986) between German and Dutch, with the former maintaining its use of morphology for marking case and of syntax to express focus, and the latter being a sort of latent SVO language. However, this has only started to affect European Dutch. In ongoing research on the syntax of contemporary

Table 4.4 *SVO generalization in Dutch–German–English trilinguals*

	Dutch		German	
After fronting	32/1565	(2.0%)	41/1023	(4.0%)
In subordinate clauses	41/1080	(3.8%)	56/857	(6.53%)

Table 4.4a *SVO generalization in Dutch–German–English trilinguals (35 informants)*

	Dutch		German	
After fronting	32/1565	(2.0%)	38/1020	(3.72%)
In subordinate clauses	41/1080	(3.8%)	45/846	(5.32%)

colloquial Dutch by the Meertens Institute, SVO constructions have surfaced in subordinate clauses in West Flanders, e.g. *dat ik heb de auto gewassen* 'that I (have) washed the car', and throughout the Netherlands with adverbs of time and also with *waarschijnlijk* 'probably' and *helaas* 'unfortunately', *dat ik heb de auto gewassen gisteren* 'that I washed the car yesterday' and before PP complements, *ik denk, dat Jan wacht op de brief* 'I think (that) Joan is waiting for the letter' (Sjef Barbiers, pers. comm.). Thus, contact with English in Australia seems to stimulate the continuing drift of Dutch.

Let us then see what effects English and German have on Dutch among trilinguals. Here the change is stronger than in German–English bilinguals but not as strong as in Dutch–English bilinguals. The SVO overgeneralization occurs more in German than in Dutch, in both main clauses and subordinate clauses, suggesting that the two languages are being treated the same (see table 4.4).

This is the case far more for Dutch L1 speakers than for German L1 speakers (Clyne and Cain 2000). Moreover, the results are skewed by one Dutch L1 trilingual, who employs about a fifth of the examples of the Dutch L1 subgroup in German subordinate clauses. Without this informant, the figures would be as in table 4.4a.

But, in general terms, the data from the trilinguals does suggest that German has a conservative influence on the typological drift in Dutch in what becomes a tug-of-war between the shared conservatism of German and Dutch syntax and the shared progressiveness of English and Dutch morphosyntax. For fronting this applies especially not only to those with Dutch as L1 (German SVO overgeneralization 5.12%, Dutch SVO 2.71%) but also, though to a lesser extent, to those with German as L1 (German SVO overgeneralization 2.94%, Dutch

1.75%). For German subordinate clauses, the overgeneralization occurs mainly in those with Dutch L1 (whose Dutch may still be the basis of their German competence) (German SVO overgeneralization 9.1%, Dutch 2.95%) as opposed to German L1 speakers (German SVO overgeneralization 2.8%, Dutch 3.8%).

One can only speculate whether the strong presence of German speakers in the Dutch/Afrikaans-speaking community in South Africa was in any way responsible for V2 order alongside the radical morphological developments mentioned (section 4.4.1).

The development towards a fixed SVO order in the Hungarian–German–English trilinguals is not as strong but there are signs of such a tendency. Because SVO is sometimes grammatical in both Hungarian and German, some of our informants, regardless of their acquisition order, overgeneralize this word order in both their other languages. In Hungarian this will lead to a word order which in the given pragmatic context is unusual because the item focused should come immediately before the finite verb, for example:

(65)   Vagy szeretek írni   leveleket
        or   like+1sg write+INF letter+pl+ACC
        'or I like to write letters'
        Homeland Hungarian: Vagy szeretek leveleket írni (MTH/G/E 2f, second generation)

(66)   később csináltam *a tanárképző* kurzust
        later   made+1sg   the teacher   course+ACC
        'Later I took part in a teachers' course'
        Homeland Hungarian: később a tanárképzőtanfoyamot csináltam (MTH/GE(PR) 5f)

4.4.7.1 Adjective–noun order
One of the features of an SVO language is Noun + Adjective order. This is not characteristic of languages such as English which were originally not SVO. Some movement towards ADJ + N is reported in Spanish (Kaminskas 1972), for example:

(67)   la mas vieja casa
        'the oldest house'
        Homeland Spanish: la casa mas vieja

Among trilinguals, there are a small number of instances in Italian and Spanish, for example:

(68)   Bosniaca nazione
        'Bosnian nation'
        Homeland Italian: nazione bosniaca (MTISE 27m)

(69)   simpatico uomo
'likeable man'
Homeland Italian: uomo simpatico (MTSIE 02f)

The slight tendency can be explained by the existence of that construction in both Italian and Spanish for pragmatic reasons, e.g. *la dishonesta campagna* is marked and therefore stronger than *la campagna dishonesta* 'the dishonest campaign'. The resistance to a substantial change towards A DJ + N in the trilinguals can perhaps be attributed to the sharing of what is an essential feature of SVO languages by two of the languages in accordance with the principle described in section 4.2.2.1.

4.4.8   'Composite Matrix Language' and syntactic convergence

One of the changes to the Matrix Language Frame Model (section 3.4.1) has been the recognition of a Composite Matrix Language (CML) – 'bilingual speech disguised as monolingual speech' (Bolonyai 1998: 23). Jake and Myers-Scotton (1997) analyse convergence in terms of compromise strategies, and subsequently adopt the term employed by Bolonyai. This enables much of our data to be accommodated within the MLF model even when it does not have a clear matrix language according to the 1993 model of the MLF (Myers-Scotton 1993a; see below).

The following example is from a second-generation Dutch–English bilingual:

(70)   En dan ga ze *questions asken   about it*
and then go she questions ask+IN F about it
'And then she goes and asks questions about it'
Homeland Dutch: En dan *gaan* ze er vragen over stellen
(MGD 101f, describing a classroom situation)

Features of the Dutch morphosyntactic frame *gaan* + IN F 'to go and ask', position (V2) of main verb (*ga*), are combined with ones of the English frame: uninflected verb (cf. bare forms, see section 3.4.1), extraposition of 'about it' after the infinitive, avoiding the discontinuous *er – over*. Thus there is morphological, syntactic and lexical transference as well as a transversion.

The notion of a CML is a broad one, characterized mainly by 'long embedded island switches', and what we term semantic, syntactic and morphological transference, which are disparate phenomena and may or may not be interrelated in particular instances.

An example of what I call 'syntactic convergence' is:

(71)   Das kann fotografiert   sein   im   Norden *of* Victoria
        this can photograph+PAST.PT be+INF in.the north of Victoria
        Homeland German: Das kann im Norden von Victoria fotografiert sein
        (MGP 192m)

This sentence constitutes convergence towards 'This could be photographed in the north of Victoria', but not transference because of the position of auxiliary and infinitive.

A similar instance in Dutch:

(72)   Ook hebben *we* haar geleerd Nederlandse versjes
        also have   we her taught Dutch   little verses
        'And we taught her Dutch rhymes too'
        (MD 105m, talking about his daughter's language development)

which converges towards 'We taught her Dutch rhymes'. The word order in Homeland Dutch would be: *We hebben haar Nederlandse versjes geleerd.*

Both of these examples involve proximity-promoting strategies, i.e. ones to bring discontinuous constituents closer together. As was mentioned above, such strategies are employed by both first- and second-generation German and Dutch speakers. While there is a tendency, in colloquial speech in both languages, to relax the participle-final constructions in the interests of ease of processing (Lockwood 1968: 264; Bierwisch 1963: 57), this does not lead to changes of the magnitude of those in our data. In the following example from a generation 1b speaker, there is an almost morpheme-for-morpheme translation from English:

(73)   Mummy hat gesagt die Wörter für mich
        mummy has said   the words for me
        'Mummy (has) said the words for me'
        Homeland German: (Die) Mami hat mir die Wörter vorgesagt (MGP
        188m, Gen.1b)

(74)   Währenddem sie hat ihr *lesson*, hab' ich gemacht
        while   she has her lesson have I   made

        einen Schaukasten im   foyer vom   Chevron Hotel
        a   showcase   in.the foyer of.the Chevron Hotel

        'While she had her lesson, I made a showcase in the foyer of the
        Chevron Hotel' (MGPR 36m)

Example (74) constitutes syntactic convergence insofar as the first clause has English word order, and the second a compromise between Standard German *hab' ich im Foyer vom Chevron Hotel einen Schaukasten gemacht* and English 'I (have) made a showcase in the foyer of the Chevron Hotel'. Syntactic convergence and transference in the interests of proximity (i.e. the bringing closer together of discontinuous constituents) occurred twenty-two times in first-generation German–English bilinguals and twenty in the second generation. In the Dutch bilingual corpus, there were twenty examples in the first generation (fourteen from generation 1a and six from generation 1b) and seven in the second. The difference may be due to the fact that some relaxation of the sentence bracket is grammatical in spoken Standard Dutch but not in its German equivalent.

4.4.8.1 *Variation between syntactic convergence, syntactic transference and lexicosyntactic transference*

In our corpora, instances of syntactic convergence, syntactic transference and lexicosyntactic transference, and Standard German syntax occur side by side (cf. Clyne 1987: 750–3). Some examples from talk about the old days in the settlements:

(75)   Ja   sie   hatten keine Maschine so daß sie   *konnten*
        yes they had   no   machine   so that they could+3pl+PAST

        den Weizen ausdröschen
        the wheat   thresh+INF

        'They had no machine to thresh the wheat'
        Standard German: Ja sie hatten keine Maschine, womit sie den
        Weizen ausdröschen konnten
        (Syntactic convergence) (MGWD 41m)

(76)   Ja   es war so dick *that* du *konn'ste*   nicht
        yes it was so thick that you could+PAST not

        mit ein Wagen durchfahren
        with a   cart   travel.through+INF

        'Yes, it was so thick that you couldn't go through it with a cart'
        Standard German: Ja es war so dick, daß du es nicht mit einem
        Wagen durchfahren konntest (Lexicosyntactic transfer, SVO)
        (same informant)

(77)   und denn wurden   sie in (A) ... in ein Gebäude
        and then AUX+PAST+PASSIVE they in (A) ... in a   building

        gsch.. (A)   ge..fahren.. so *daß* es sie   es trocken
        FALSE START driven   so that it that they it dry

        halten   konnten (standard word order)
        keep+INF could

        'and then they were driven into a building so that they could keep it dry' (Same informant, MGWD 41m)

Thus, this speaker employs both SOV and SVO in a subordinate clause, SVO occurring after a German or transferred conjunction.

(78)   und sagte.. daß wir das nun nicht mehr *tun*   *könn'*..
        and said   that we it   now not   more do+INF can

        daß meine Schwester *sollte* 'n Operation *haben*
        that my   sister   should an operation have

        und daß es *wird* nicht mehr *geben*
        and that it will no   more happen+INF

        'and said that we couldn't do it any more..that my sister was to have
        an operation and it won't happen any more'
        (First sentence Standard German word order, second SVO in
        subordinate clause) (MGWD 5f)
(79)   weil wir *haben* dieselbe Lieder in Englisch
        'because we have the same songs in English'
        (Syntactic transfer, SVO) (MGW 98f)
(80)   weil   wir letzte   Jahre *sind*
        because we (the) last years are
        'because we are the last years'
        (weil + SOV, Standard German word order) (Same speaker)

The speaker employs SVO (79) and SOV (80) after *weil* which traditionally
requires a verb-final construction.[12]

(81)   Wir haben in Berlin eine Straße, welche *is'* Unter den Linden
        we   have in Berlin a   street   which is Unter den Linden
        Homeland German: Wir haben in Berlin eine Straße, die Unter den
        Linden heißt (SVO) (MGP 192m)
(82)   Typisch australische Bäume, welche wir im   Continent nich' *haben*
        typical Australian trees   which we in.the continent not   have
        'Typical Australian trees which we don't have on the Continent'
        (SOV order as in Standard German) (Same speaker)

This appears to show a syntactic change in progress in the informants with
variation between the German and the contact-induced form, and that this is not
necessarily due to 'code-switching'. In fact, as we will argue in section 5.3.3, it
is more likely transversion is promoted by syntactic transference, which is more
common. Syntactic transference probably also facilitates lexical transference,
as the transferred lexeme in lexicosyntactic transference makes the subordinate
clause in German or Dutch grammatical,[13] for example:

(83)   BECAUSE die wisten niks   meer van papa af,   hé?
        BECAUSE they knew   nothing more about papa AFFIX, you see
        Homeland Dutch: omdat die niets meer van Papa afwisten, hé? (MD 38f)

The lexicosyntactic transference entails SVO instead of SOV in a subordinate
clause, as in the German example (83) above.

In (84) on the other hand, the lexical transfer introduces further lexicosyntactic transference:

(84)   ik was achtenzestig jaar B E F O R E ik *kon* G E T mijn PENSION
         'I was sixty-eight years (old) before I could get my pension'
         (MD 28m) (Homeland Dutch would require the auxiliary and PAST.PT
         to go to the end: Ik was achtenzestig jaar, voordat ik mijn pensioen
         kon krijgen)

4.4.9   Implicational scales?

For the second-generation Dutch–English bilinguals, a search was undertaken
to ascertain if the informants who used uninflected forms of one or more verbs
were also those who overgeneralized SVO and those who used *de* as a definite
article for *het* nouns and, if so, which of these features was the more basic. As
it was, there was no clear implicational relation between the three phenomena,
twenty-five using analytic forms of the verb, including eleven of the fifty-eight
informants who overgeneralized SVO. Of the twenty-five, fifteen overgeneralized *de*, and only seven showed examples of all three features.

4.4.10   Transference at several levels of language

In section 3.2, we introduced a number of types of transference involving different levels of language. They too are facilitated for particular reasons. The
lexicosyntactic transference in (83) above is an example of this. Such instances
may be found in all the groups of plurilinguals. In the following examples
from Hungarian–German–English trilinguals, the lexical items transferred are
subject to extraposition:

(85)   Ezen   a képen   látom   a *beachet*
         this+LINKER+LOC the picture+LINKER+LOC see+1sg the beach+ACC
         'On this picture I see the beach'
         Homeland Hungarian: Ezen a képen egy tenderpartet látok (MTH/GE(PR) 1f)

The sentence would ordinarily require SOV. The lexicosyntactic transference
comprises SVO and the transference of *beach*.

(86)   aber ich will nicht hören   die *tape*
         but I   want not   hear+INF the tape
         'but I don't want to hear the tape'
         Standard German: Aber ich will das Tonband nicht hören
         (MTH/GE 1m)

This type of transference is motivated by an avoidance of an ungrammatical construction if purely syntactic transference were to occur. It is typical of situations in which the languages are converging and/or the languages in contact show what Myers-Scotton (1993a) terms 'lack of congruence'. Semantic–syntactic transference, on the other hand, takes place in order to retain the unique way that one language expresses something in the other, i.e. not just the semantic transference of idioms but the entire construction as well. Convergence can also cut across levels of language, for instance phonoprosodic convergence (section 4.2.1) resulting in compromise forms is the product of psycholinguistic stress between the phonic and prosodic aspects of the two languages.

4.4.11   A note on theoretical implications

In the above sections, we showed that convergence can occur between two or more languages in bi- and trilinguals. It can take place at any level of language. From the above, it will be evident that languages with certain common structural features, and especially those whose drift in Hawkins's (1986; section 3.5.4) sense lends itself to certain changes (e.g. SVO word order, gender system, synthetic vs. analytic structures, adjective agreement), will converge in a contact situation and/or will do so faster than those where this is not the case. Whether this is described as 'levelling', 'preference for the unmarked variant' or 'actualization of reanalysis', language contact facilitates the overgeneralization of the more basic or usual variant in one language which is the only alternative in the other language (and especially two of the other languages). Evidence for this has been found in verb endings (Dutch), object-verb order (German, Hungarian), ADJ-N order (Italian, Spanish), gender (Dutch), case (German, Hungarian, Croatian), plural allomorphs (Dutch), auxiliaries (German, Dutch, Italian, French) and adjective, demonstrative and particle marking (Italian), as well as convergences across many areas of the languages of trilinguals. It will be evident from the above that convergences affect only some language pairs/groups. The more overlap or potential overlap there is across linguistic levels, the more likely it is that convergence will occur and increase the overlap. This supports the notions of drift and unified contrasts as well as the interaction of internal and external factors and of different levels in language change. Most of the changes constitute a continuation of a drift especially if the language in contact has already moved faster in the same direction. Drift may prevent contact-induced change if it is in conflict with another simultaneous language contact in trilinguals. The tendencies generally represent points 1 to 4 on Thomason and Kaufman's 'borrowing scale', but the SVO generalization in Dutch and the analytic verb forms could be perceived as 5. However, here it is in harmony with the general drift and in accordance with very high LS.

Maher (1991) enumerates as features of 'attrition':

a. a reduction in the number of allomorphs and an increase in paradigm regularity;

b. the replacement of synthetic structures by analytic ones; and

c. progressive reduction in inflectional morphology.

As we see from the above, these features are the product of the typologies of the languages in contact. Our data has shown a progressive reduction of categories but also the variation mentioned by Campbell and Muntzel (1989, see section 3.5.2). Some other contact situations are characterized by gains as well as losses, as Aikhenvald (2002), dal Negro (n.d.) and Dorian (1999) have indicated.

The role of convergence in transversion will be considered in section 5.5.

4.5   Divergence

So far in this chapter, we have discussed numerous phenomena involving convergence of forms in the community language towards English. However, in section 4.2.2, when we considered evidence for conversion formulae employed by some of our trilingual informants to develop multilateral competence, we found it in repairs aimed at divergence. In language contact situations such as the ones where our corpora were collected, some bilinguals and trilinguals will take great care to avoid convergence.[14]

The most important type of divergence is integration at various levels of language. It is on the conceptualization of 'integration' that a crucial aspect of the discussion on the distinction between 'borrowing' and 'code-switching' (section 3.1) hinges.[15]

4.5.1   Integration[16]

Integration is important in the discussion of transference insofar as it makes possible a centre–periphery continuum – of how much the word is treated as part of the recipient language – and of how stable or variable is its use of an item. In broad terms, it is a classic aspect of embedding into an ML or of Muysken's 'insertion', except that in the case of dummy verbs (section 4.5.1.3 below), Muysken (2000: 184–220) argues for a bilingual grammar for Indian languages.

There are three aspects of variation in integration – type, degree and stability.

(a) *Type of integration*, e.g. semantic, phonological, morphological, prosodic (in terms of stress), tonemic, graphemic. The Matrix Language Frame Model and Poplack's research focus on grammatical integration into the matrix or recipient language. Halmari (1997), on the other hand, views prosody and phonology as indicators of integration.

The type of integration possible or necessary is determined partly by the structures of the languages in contact. For instance, English transfers will usually be integrated morphologically in Hungarian and Turkish (agglutinative structure) but not in Mandarin and Vietnamese (isolating). Nouns may and verbs usually will be integrated in German, French, Italian and many other languages, but adverbs and conjunctions will not. Transferred adjectives are inflected in Croatian, usually in German, and in Dutch except in the neuter after an indefinite article or possessive pronoun. There is a tendency, even in Standard (homeland) Italian, to employ unintegrated transferred adjectives, for example:

(87)   Omicidio *gay* sul video *hard*
        'Gay homocide on hard video'
        (Headline in *La Repubblica*, 6 April 2000, p. 19)

Transfers from English in languages with gender marking assign gender most frequently according to perceived synonymity but also according to perceived homophony and other phonologically related factors (Clyne 1991: 170–2). English transfers may be integrated phonologically and/or tonemically in Vietnamese by the loss of final *-t* and/or the use of a particular mid or high tone, but they do not require any grammatical integration as it is an isolating language. Almost all our Hungarian–German–English trilinguals mark English lexical transfers and even proper nouns morphologically in Hungarian but they do not integrate them into German because this is not required, for example:

(88)   szép swimmingpool*al*
        'a nice swimming pool' (MTH/GE 8f)
(89)   egy opshop*ba*
        'into an op-shop' (MTH/GE 8f)
(90)   Acland Street*re*
        'to Acland Street'
        (Sublative – looking to) (MTH/GE 3m)
(91)   Prahran*ben*
        'in Prahran' (MTH/GE 3m)
(92)   voltam oversea*n*
        'I was overseas'
        (locative marking added to adverb treated here as a noun)
        (MTH/GE 9f)

as opposed to the uninflected: *shop, swimming pool, Flinders Street Station, overseas, aeroplane, computer* in German.

Only five of our thirty-six informants, one of whom was born in Australia, regularly use unintegrated lexical transfers in their Hungarian. Examples of unintegrated transfers in Hungarian are: *brick veneer, courtyard, deputy principal, holiday, shop, social work, swimming pool(s)*, as well as some place names and personal names. Many of these items are preceded by a filled or unfilled pause.

Unintegrated nouns and adjectives are found in mixed collocations (see section 5.4), for example:

(93)   és   később csináltam a   Melbourne   egyetemen –
        and   later   did+I   the Melbourne+NOM university+LOC
        The appropriate affix on Melbourne would be -*ei*. (MT HE(PR) 5f)
(94)   szép suburban ház
        nice suburban house
        Homeland Hungarian: szép külváros*i* ház, with -*i* as the appropriate
        adjectival affix (MT HG/E(P) 6f, in a description of a picture)

Non-integration at the phonological level is generally a marker of belonging to the second generation among Croatian–English bilinguals in Australia (Hlavac 2000). Stoffel (1981, 1994) found that lexical transfers are generally morphologically integrated in first-generation Croatian–English bilinguals in New Zealand but less so in the second generation. One problem in assessing the integration of first-generation bilinguals' transfers is that it may simply reflect the L1-influenced phonology of their English, so in phonology, integration is dependent not only on structural differences between the languages but also on the level of acquisition of the phonology of the source language. Here the regional variety also needs to be considered; this may determine whether an English item with an original /s/ is integrated into German.

Integration may be necessitated by a different script and may then reflect phonological integration (e.g. Greek ΜπΑΔΖΕΤ < budget).

(b) *Degree of integration*, e.g. *mixed up* (no grammatical integration), *abgemixt* (high degree of grammatical integration), Ger. [tʃatʃ] 'judge' (high phonological integration), [dʒadʒ] (no phonological integration). This varies according to integration type, for instance, an item may show high phonological and no morphosyntactic integration, e.g. Ger. *Swimming pools* [ʃwimiŋkpu:ls], Dut. *fridge* [frɪts]; or low phonological integration and high morphosyntactic integration, e.g. Hung. *komputerfirmnál* [kɔmpju:tafirmnal] 'at the computer firm'. A factor in the degree of phonological integration among generation 1a bilinguals may be the speaker's level of competence in the phonetic aspects of L2. Apart from different *types* of integration, there may be differences of *degree*. English *control* (verb) transferred into German may simply be given an -*n* suffix but this will indicate a low level of grammatical integration whereas the -*ieren* suffix as with borrowed verbs from Romance languages will reflect a higher degree of grammatical integration as such verbs are now regarded as an integral part of German vocabulary (*realisieren/realizen*).

While *Carpenter* or *Plumber* will be integrated by receiving the masculine gender marking on the article in the singular, its plural may be unintegrated (-*s*) or integrated (zero), and in *shrinken*, the weak participle (*geshrinkt* < *shrink*) is less highly integrated than the strong one (*geschrunken*) which indicates an original indigenous item. Combinability with a morpheme in the recipient language which has a morphological function is an indicator of a high degree of integration, e.g. *flokje* (Eng. *flock* + Dut. diminutive *je*), *milkbaraki* (Eng. *milkbar* + Greek diminutive *aki*), *bus- ista* (Eng. *bus* + It. *ista* to denote an occupational term, all used in Australia) (Greek and Italian in Australia, from Tamis 1986, Bettoni 1981a respectively).

Realisieren in the sense of 'apprehend as real' extends the meaning of an established transfer in German. This example shows that semantic transference can be regarded as phonologically and grammatically highly integrated lexical transference. The term *Semantic transference* covers the transference of a meaning from a homophone or synonym in the other language, e.g. *smal* (in the meaning of 'small', Dut. *narrow*); *Likör* (in the meaning of 'liquor', Ger. *Alkohol*), *libreria* (in the meaning of 'library', Sp. *bookshop*); *bosco* (to mean 'bush, forest', It. *bush, shrub*); *weten* (to mean 'know a person', Dut. *know a fact*), *gehen* (to mean 'travel by plane, car, tram or train or on foot', Ger. *go on foot*), for example:

(95)   Wir sind mit dem Auto nach Bright *gegangen*.
         'We went (lit. 'walked') to Bright by car' (MGP 158f, generation 1b).

It contributes to *morphosemantic transference* – morpheme-for-morpheme translation of compound nouns and idioms, e.g. *oppikken* (to mean 'pick up a language', Dut. *natuurlijk verwerven*); *Textbuch* (to mean 'text book', Ger. *Lehrbuch*); *kijken achter* (to mean 'look after', Dut. *oppassen*), *für Examen sitzen* (to mean 'sit for exams', Ger. *Examen machen, schreiben*).

(c) *Centrality and stability in the system of the recipient language.* In models requiring differentiation between 'borrowing' and 'code-switching', to indicate that 'code-switching' has not taken place, it needs to be shown that the item is regarded as part of the recipient language. That can be determined by its stability within the system, for instance, its semantic integration in terms of having a discrete place in the semantic field, used consistently in a particular meaning, and not in variation with the item from the other language. The embedded language items may serve as hyponyms or co-hyponyms of the matrix language item, e.g. *Footy* for Australian Rules football and German *Fußball* for soccer, *farma* for an Australian farm and *campagna* for an Italian one – cultivated land owned by others. In Italian speech in Australia, *fattoria* (Standard Italian meaning: small farm) has generally taken on the meaning of *fabbrica* (factory) while *farma* has filled the gap vacated by this semantic shift.

The degree and stability of integration are partly conditioned by social networks. Oksaar (1972) rightly argues that people are more likely to employ highly integrated transfers, including semantic transfers, when speaking to members of their social networks than when speaking to others. They will often be avoided outside these networks because such items are not always readily identifiable (without warning). A recent immigrant to Australia may not comprehend *Hetmeister* for 'headmaster' (Ger. *Rektor*), used by a second-generation bilingual, and the phonologically highly integrated *Brücken* (for 'bricks', Ger. *Ziegel*) and *probäblich* (for 'probably', Ger. *wahrscheinlich*), employed by individual first-generation bilinguals.

In the data from former German enclaves, reflecting relatively stable bilingualism before largescale LS, some lexical transfers were used and integrated in the same way by the same community. As in American-German settlements (Aron 1930), frequently transferred nouns were generally assigned the feminine article *die*, e.g. *die Fence, die Car, die Road, die Railway line, die Yard, die Post office*, probably under the influence of the accented form of the definite article [ði:] (Clyne 1981: 17–18). All of these items except *Road* were assigned another gender by more recent immigrants on the principles outlined below. In the former enclaves, the integration was sometimes completed by the addition of an *-e*, which complied with the feminine gender, e.g. *Bande* ('band'; Ger. *Blaskapelle*), *Kappe* ('cup', Ger. *Tasse*). Different German-Australian settlements integrated the same word in different ways, e.g. gum tree became *Gumbaum* [gumbaum] in Western Victoria, *Gummibaum* (literally 'rubber tree') in the Barossa Valley, an area of early German settlement in South Australia, and *gum (tree)* [gam] in the Wimmera (Northwestern Victoria), *die Car treiben* (*treiben* normally used for driving livestock) in Tarrington and *die Car fahren* in the Barossa Valley. There was individual variation in the use of (phonologically unintegrated) lexical transfers representing the era after German had been regularly spoken in the district, e.g. *electricity, television, motor-bike*. The more a transfer is associated with a close network, the more likely it is to be highly integrated, e.g. *Swamp* becomes *Schwamm* [ʃwam] around Buckley's Swamp and *swamp* [swɔmp] in the less immediate vicinity. There was a much greater incidence of morphologically and phonologically integrated nouns in the Western District (around Tarrington and Tabor) than in the Wimmera, which was a less closely settled, more heterogeneous and more recent enclave area (settled about twenty years after Tarrington and Tabor). All former German enclaves which had very dense networks with strong ties are characterized by less variability in gender assignment of lexical transfers than other German-speaking groups (e.g. *die* instead of *der/das Paddock, der/das Car*).

Tamis (1988: 89) shows that Greek tends more towards integration of transfers in Sydney (*zipa* 'zip', *masinja* 'machines') than in Melbourne (*zip, masines*) and that the degree of integration of English transfers in the US is sufficiently high to cause communication breakdown with Australian speakers of Greek (American *biti* vs. Australian *bit*; *klopi* vs. *club, kredito* vs. *credit*). The Sydney–Melbourne variation may be related to the denser concentration of Greek within Sydney than within Melbourne.

4.5.1.1 Principles of gender assignment[17]

Nouns tend to receive their genders according to the following criteria which concur with the literature, from Aron (1930) to Zubin and Köpcke (1986), examples from Bettoni (1981a), Kaminskas (1972), Ludwig-Wyder (1982), Tamis (1986) as well as from our own studies of German and Dutch in Australia:

i. Natural gender, e.g. Italian *il boss*, Greek *o bosis*, German *der/das teacher*, Spanish *la nursa*, French *une chamber-maid*, Italian *una secretary*.

ii. The gender of a synonymous noun in the recipient language, e.g. Spanish *el ocean* (*el océano*), Dutch *de shop* (*de winkel*), Fr. *un job* (*un travail*), Ger. *der* or *das shop* (*<der Laden, das Geschäft*), *der fridge* (*der Kühlschrank*), Greek *to milkbar* (*to bakaliko, to magazi*). It is possible that a competence for integration is developed in a community. This might explain why people who do not know or cannot recall the target language equivalent assign its gender to the transfer (cf. Bettoni 1981a: 66). However, 84% of the nouns in Bettoni's corpus of North Queensland Italian are assigned to the masculine (see (vi) below).

iii. The gender of a homophonous noun with a different meaning in the recipient language, e.g. *der Schauer* (Ger. *die Douche, der Schauer* < rain shower, shudder), *to karo* (Gk. *to aftokinito, to karo* cart) *il carro* (It. *la macchina; il carro* cart).

iv. A choice between (ii) and (iii), e.g. *roof* integrated as either *das* (< *Dach* 'roof') or, more commonly, *der* (*<Ruf* 'reputation').

v. A suffix, e.g. French words ending in *-ie* are feminine, hence la bakery (ie); similarly Ger. das Depart*ment*, Gk. oi roula (ruler), It. *il* tichet*to, la* marchet*ta*, Sp. la dictat*ión*, el record*or*, Croatian joiner*y* (masculine).

vi. A general tendency, where no clear motivation exists or predominates. This will vary according to the most common article in the language or the gender to which borrowings are traditionally assigned: masculine in French, Italian, Spanish, Russian and Croatian, feminine in the German of former enclaves (see above), neuter in Greek and Romanian, non-neuter in Dutch (albeit attracted by the homophony of the non-neuter article *de* and the pronunciation of the English definite article by most first-generation Dutch-English bilinguals). Monosyllabic transferred nouns that resemble a verb stem sometimes take the masculine, e.g. *der Bell* (despite *die* Glocke; *die Bell* is actually more frequent).

Sixty-four of our Dutch–English bilinguals used *de fence* and sixteen *het fence* (probably by analogy with the neuter *het hek*, Dutch for 'fence'). Thirty-three employed *de beach* and only three *het beach* (probably by analogy with the Dutch equivalent, *het strand*). All in all, thirty words were assigned to the non-neuter when their equivalent is neuter, and ninety-four of the two hundred subjects assigned all transferred nouns to the non-neuter (Clyne 1977a). In the corresponding corpus from postwar German-speaking immigrants and their children, there was much variation in keeping with the ternary choice in German with the variation explicable by alternative equivalents (e.g. *der Shop < Laden, das Shop < Geschäft*) or alternative explanations (e.g. *die Building < ung,* cf. *das Gebäude*). The main exception is the widespread use of *die Beach* despite *der Strand.* (Three postwar German-speaking informants out of two hundred used *der Beach.* All came from North Germany.) The beach scene, in a picture employed for stimulus, would perhaps be expressed by *das Meer* by people from beyond the coastal strip of Germany. *Die Beach* is perhaps the only example in the postwar corpus of a feminine gender assignment not motivated by the above-mentioned factors. Gender also affects the marking of the oblique cases. e.g. German:

(96)   Das ist in Frankston an *der* Beach (feminine dative)
        'That is in Frankston on the beach' (MGP 81m)
(97)   bei ein*em* klein*en* River (masculine dative)
        'on a little river' (MGP 158f, generation 1b)

In Hungarian, where there is no gender marking on article, the marking of oblique cases is one form of morphological integration, for example:

(98)   Akik   armchair*ben*   ülnek (inessive)
        those.who armchair.on.the (INESSIVE) sit+3pl
        'Those who are sitting in armchairs' (MTHGE 9m)

Phonetic shape determines the pluralization rule as part of the integration process. There is some variation between *-s* plural (unintegrated) and zero in Italian (e.g. *film/films, tram/trams*), and in German for nouns ending in *er* or *or* [ə] (e.g. die *Plumbers/Plumber, Tractors/Tractor* (despite *Traktoren* in 'homeland German'). Generally German and Dutch speakers in Australia employ the *-s* affix to form plurals of nouns transferred from English (cf. section 4.4.3 above). This plural ending is one of the options in both languages though in German it does indicate original borrowing from another language. There are exceptions in both bilingual corpora, e.g. Beach*en*, Umbrell*en* (Ger.), beach*en*, fens*en*, tree-*en* (Dut.) indicating a higher level of morphological integration. Greek and Italian nouns are allocated plurals in accordance with gender assignment as with indigenous nouns, e.g. Italian farm*e* (farms), tichett*i* (tickets), Greek oi machinist*es* (machinists), to boks*ia* boxes) (Tamis 1986). In Russian, transferred nouns are assigned to the first masculine or second feminine declension, thereby determining their pluralization (Kouzmin 1973). Nouns ending in a consonant or a final *-i* or *-u* are assigned to the masculine, those ending in *-a* to the feminine and those ending in *-o* and *–e* to the neuter in Croatian (Hlavac 2000: 122).

Transferred verbs are generally allocated to a particular conjugation, *-er* in French (Ludvig-Wyder 1982), *-are* in Italian and *-ar* in Spanish. Muysken (2000: 54) makes the point that *eatiendo*, cited as a violation of the Free Morpheme Constraint, was actually assigned to an inappropriate conjugation type and might rather appear as *eateando*. English verbs are usually integrated also in Croatian, using one of the infinitive suffixes *-irati*, *-ati* or *-ovati* (Hlavac 2000: 124, 163). In German and Dutch, transferred verbs are usually assigned to the weak conjugation (e.g. German past participle *gejoint, upgeroundet*; Dutch *getind, opgemixt*), with strong conjugation (e.g. *geschrunken* rather than *geshrinkt*) constituting a higher level of integration and the absence of the *ge-* prefix morphological non-integration (e.g. *parked* rather than *geparkt*),[18] for example:

(99)   Autos sind *parked*   an der   Straße
         cars   are   park+PAST.PT on the+DAT street
         'Cars are parked on the street' (MGP 90m)

(100)   Autos an der   linken Seite *geparkt*
         cars   on the+DAT left   side park+PAST.PT
         'Cars parked on the left-hand side' (MGP 186f)

This all demonstrates the complexity of the integration issue and the need for detailed description of integration type and degree. Simple answers as to whether an item is or is not 'integrated' do not, in my opinion, provide a dividing line between, or evidence of, two profoundly different language contact phenomena ('borrowing' and 'code-switching').

Grosjean (1995) has shown the importance of integration and frequency of use in the recognition of 'guest words' in 'mixed speech'. Boyd (1997) demonstrates a complementary role of social networks and typology in integration in Scandinavian and African contact studies. This issue could benefit from comparative study across language dyads/triads and sociolinguistic contexts (as is recommended in Muysken 1997).

4.5.1.2   Some markers of non-integration

The other forms of integration also entail consistent use and not free variation with the 'native' item or variation in the type of level of integration (unless it is then regarded as a separate item). On the other hand, as Haugen (1953), Poplack (1985) and Kinder (1986) have demonstrated, unintegrated transfers are sometimes flagged as such by metalinguistic comments such as 'as they say in English' or 'I don't know the word in X'. Gafaranga (2000) differentiates between 'medium-repair' (i.e. repair in the base or matrix language) and 'other language repair'. The former explicitly states that a transversion will take place, the latter simply 'repairs' in the 'other language'. In our data, explicit metalinguistic comments can be in either language, e.g. (101) and (102) below.

(101)   Ich weiss nicht, wie man das nennt.
          'I don't know what you call it'
          (MGP 115f)

Hlavac (2000) did find, among his second-generation Croatian–English bilinguals, some flagging (such as filled and unfilled pauses, laughter, discourse markers), coinciding with integration at the phonological and/or morphological levels (30% incidence of the flags compared to 61% for unintegrated items). Unintegrated lexical transfers are also sometimes identifiable as such by the change in prosody. An example is (41) in section 5.3.1.8, where the speaker's intonation rises on *secondhand-dealer* which she uses, having unsuccessfully searched for a German equivalent. There is a drop in pitch in the transversion after the lexical transfer. In (102) below, there is a rise at the lexical transfer *really* but the higher tone is continued in the subsequent transversion:

(102)   Ich habe (A) nicht sehr viele deutsche Freunde *really* AND I DON'T
          KNOW IT'S A (A)
          'I have (A) not very many German friends really and I don't know it's
          a (A)'
          (MGP 43m)

It should be stated, however, that a high-rise terminal is characteristic of Australian English and is often indicative of chunking (Guy and Vonwiller 1989; Allan 1984) and, in any case, there is no general tendency in the prosody of lexical transfers.[19]

4.5.1.3 Dummy verbs

Although dummy verbs, which do not have a meaning of their own, do not occur as integration devices in the main languages of our corpus, they are a good example of an integration device which saves a lexical transfer from being morphologically integrated, i.e. inflected.

One of the compromise strategies discussed by Jake and Myers-Scotton (1997) is *bare forms*. Some instances can be attributed to lack of congruence between the grammars of the two languages, as discussed by Myers-Scotton (1993a). Others, however, can be regarded as morphological transference from the uninflected or less inflected language or perhaps an acceleration of a slow development of the language towards uninflected verbs as in the case of Dutch–English bilinguals (section 4.4.6). This does not apply to the bare form of a verb transferred from another language used together with a dummy verb based on the equivalents of 'do' in Turkish, *yap-, et-,* and *olm-* in Turkish, 'do' or 'become' in Greek, *kano* and *yino* respectively, or 'make' in the Indian languages, e.g. *kərnaɛ* or *kərdadɛ* used together with a bare form of the verb transferred from another language (see section 4.5.1, above). Examples of this phenomenon may be found in Turkish–Dutch, Turkish–English, Turkish–German, Turkish–Norwegian, Punjabi–English and Greek–English bilinguals (see Kurtböke 1998a: 255–63, 1998b; Pfaff 1991; Türker 1998; Romaine 1995: 137; Tamis 1986: 169–70; also Haig 2001).

(103)   Turkish:
         delivery yapilir
         delivery do+PASSIVE
         'delivery can be arranged' (Kurtböke 1998a: 256)

Kurtböke argues that *delivery* and *yapilir* co-select. Kurtböke (1998a: 20) gives *yap* as meaning 'do, make, create, give rise to, build, constitute, repair, apply, set to rights, and make ready' – depending on the collocation. Backus (1996: 264ff) views *yap* as either an affix or a stem.

Australian-Greek examples of delexicalized verbs:

(104)   Greek:
         kano   *enjoy*   ti   douleia   mou
         do+1sg   enjoy   the   work   mine
         'I enjoy my work'
(105)   Greek:
         γinoume   *retire*
         become+1pl   retire
         'we will retire'
         (Tamis 1986: 169) (first generation, Greek–English bilinguals)

According to some unpublished data on Sinhala in Australia collected by Dipemala de Silva, *kərən wa* 'make' has a similar function:

(106)   *drive/fix/start/drive* (etc.) kərən wa
         make+1,2,3sg/pl[20]

In Korean in Australia, *ha* is used to form similar constructions, for example:

(107)   ma   neun   *drive* – jal-ha-eyo
         I   well   drive (Choong-Woon 1990)

Ha, used in Korean to transform nouns into verbs (Young-a-Cho, pers. comm.) is employed here to integrate English items into the Korean grammatical system.

    While I would consider such strategies as the above part of the integration process, Nortier (1990), in her Arabic–Dutch study, sees bare forms as an intermediate stage between code-switching (with Dutch morphological characteristics) and 'lexical borrowing' (with Moroccan Arabic characteristics).

Muysken (2000: 197–211) draws on several corpora for Indic languages in contact with English or Dutch to dispute that this construction is based on one in the recipient language as the leftmost item would not be a verb there. He argues that this requires a bilingual grammar to construct.

4.6   Ethnolects

Myers-Scotton (1993a) has drawn attention to what she calls 'turnover', where the matrix and embedded languages change roles. In Australia, this is often associated with a shift (in progress or completed) from a community language and the transfer of the function of a symbolic identity marker to an ethnolect of Australian English. Historical linguists have long been studying the phenomenon of substratum where a language used by particular communities contains features of a language previously spoken by the group. (See Oksaar 1984 and Schuchardt 1884, the latter of which, however, was sceptical of the term and a blanket explanation.) Irish English, Indian English and Singapore English are well-known examples of this phenomenon. Ethnolects may be characterized by lexical, syntactic, phonetic and/or prosodic features.

4.6.1   The case of a disappearing ethnolect

The English ethnolects of former German enclaves such as Tarrington (Hochkirch) and Tabor in Western Victoria were marked phonetically, lexicosemantically and syntactically. Among the *phonetic features* were (Clyne 1994a; Clyne, Eisikovits and Tollfree 2001):

- Final devoicing of /d/, /z/, /b/, /g/, /ŋg/, /ʒ/, as in: brothers [bɹaθas], *is* [ɪs], *guild* [gɪlt], *bag* [bæk], *everything* [ɛvɹɪθɪŋk], *change* [tʃɛ:ntʃ].
- /e/ realized as [ɛ] (lower than in the Australian English of the time), e.g. *breakfast*.
- Use of [ø] for /ɜ/ e.g. *girls* and [ɛ] for /æ/, e.g. *granted, answer*.
- A tendency towards monophthongs [e], [i] and [o], e.g. in *lady, seem, so* (even though the German of the area generally had diphthongs).
- Use of close [ɔ] e.g. *all*; but use of [o:a], e.g. *course*.
- Use of velar [ɰ] for /r/, sometimes in variation with alveolar [ɹ].
- In particular environments: *pasta* for *pastor*; short [U] in *Lutheran*, overgeneralization of the accented form of the definite article [ði] in unaccented positions:

(108)   Open *the* door. You ask me *the* questions.

Semantic differences also distinguished the ethnolect from mainstream Australian English, e.g. *yet* for *still* (Ger. *noch*):

(109)   I'll show you something else too *yet* (MGWD 1m)

• Overuse of 'already' (Ger. *schon*), for example:

(110)   My wife is dead forty years *already* (MGWD 40m)

• Different for 'several' (Ger. *verschieden* has both meanings)

(111)   This has happened *different* times (MGWD 29m)

• *Bring (come, take) with* (Ger. *mitbringen, -kommen, nehmen*) in the sense of 'bring, come, take along'.
• Prepositions semantically transferred, for example:

(112)   Warrayure was a congregation *from* the Tarrington parish
         (Ger. *von* corresponding to both 'of', 'from') (T40m1)
(113)   What's meant *with* times where we've gone away
         (Ger. *mit*, Eng. *by*) (T30m1)

Syntactic features of the ethnolect included:
• The deletion of the indefinite article before an occupational designation, for example:

(114)   She was teacher (Ger. *sie war Lehrerin*) (MGWD 28f)

• The construction (relative) TO X as in:

(115)   He's an uncle to David Schulz.
         (Mainstream Aust. Eng.: He's an uncle of David Schulz's; colloquial
         Ger.: Er ist dem DS sein Onkel)[21] (MGWD 29m)

• The addition of the definite article with the names of languages (*the German, the English* [optional in German]), for example:

(116)   I'm bad enough in *the* English to make sentences, let alone *the* German
         (MGWD 2m)

This ethnolect was typical of a generation that was born before 1904, raised and schooled bilingually and that has, for the most part, now died out. However, the study of the English of three generations of four families in the Tarrington–Tabor districts as part of a project on rural Australian English (Clyne et al. 2001) showed that the most salient features continued into the present grandparent generation (late seventies and eighties) who still spoke some German at home. These included the final devoicing of /z/ only, the use of [e] for /æ/, and [ø] for /ɜ/, the distinctive use of *yet, already* and *different*, and the verbs with *with*, as well as some nonce occurrences, such as *relationship* for *Verwandtschaft*, *borrow* for *lend* (Ger. *leihen* can mean both) and *oftener* as a synthetic comparative of *often*. These can be identified as ethnolectal (Australians of German descent), dialectal (part of Victorian Western District) and sociolectal (Lutheran), reflecting multiple identity. By the present middle generation, only *yet, already*, relative T O X, the pronunciations of *Pastor* and *Lutheran* and sometimes the *with* verbs have survived, and these are not to be found in the younger generation (present children and adolescents). It should be noted that these are in the domain of religion or family and that the features are semantic, syntactic and especially phonetic. There is little evidence of lexical transference from German. The incidence of syntactic and semantic transference support Myers-Scotton's argument of turnover in 'code-switching'. But syntactic and semantic transference also confirm a continuing multiple identity and a long-standing position favouring integrated rather than unintegrated (conspicuous) transference ('adaptation' rather than 'mixing', section 5.8) among speakers in German-Australian enclaves. This early predetermining development of a position on language concurs with Mufwene's (2001) founder principle in pidgins and creoles.

4.6.2   More recent and emerging ethnolects

Ethnolects are becoming common in more recently migrated families of non-English-speaking background. Sometimes they are used by the younger generation to the older generation to express solidarity, instead of or alongside the community language. I have previously (Clyne 1981) presented data from Australians from four families, of German, Greek and Hungarian descent. The ethnolects in all families are phonetically marked. In three families there is also syntactic marking, and in one of them also semantic transference. Speakers of the ethnolect will speak it only to older members of their own ethnic group, sometimes also to members of other non-English-speaking groups but not usually to their own age peer group. The syntactic marking may include simplification, such as auxiliary or pronoun deletion, for example:

(117)   No love, 'I don't like it'
(118)   You makin' pita? 'Have you been making pita?'

or syntactic transfers, for example:

(119)   I speak faster English 'I speak English faster'
           based on: Ich spreche schneller Englisch

All the speakers believe that they use the ethnolect to ease communication with their parents or grandparents. Their Australian English is generally indistinguishable from that of the mainstream. The ethnolect in three of the families may derive from the original English acquired within home and ethnic community, before 'mainstream English' was acquired, which may be retained as the home and ethnic community 'we-code' (cf. Mufwene's 2001 founder principle).

This contrasts with the 'we-code' developed through linguistic divergence from the home-based variety and social integration, which the younger generation shares with the wider community. The ethnolect may also be a way of addressing bilingual communication in the home, where children responding in English take up key words from their parents' community language discourse (item 6 under section 4.3.1 above). In this way, the ethnolectal and mainstream varieties of Australian English symbolize the person's multiple identity.

In the minority of families where the ethnolect is used alongside the community language (Clyne 1981), the ethnolect eases the communication of experiences and information from the work, school and institutional domains in the home.

The ethnolect may be identified by the younger family members, typically third-generation, as the community language. Many third-generation Italian–Australians regard the ethnolect as their Italian though it may only embed a small number of items of food and family relationship, e.g. *zia, nonna, marinara*, into English, confirming turnover, sometimes with the speech marked with Italian phonology and prosody. Cavallaro (1997: 279–80) gives examples of second-generation input to the third generation in 'bilingual' families, for example:

(120)   You've gotta go and do SONNINO
         'You've got to go and take a nap'
(121)   Take it off the paper Dora, Jenny, PIANO hey Jenny
         'Take off the paper . . .quietly . . .'
(122)   Not going to tell you

    This reflects Italian pro-drop structure:

(123)   non vado   dirti
         not go+PRES+1sg tell+INF+you
         'I'm not going to tell you'

These were probably influenced by bilingual communication in their own parental homes and some turnover within the second generation.

Jewish ethnolects have been reported for a range of languages, e.g. Fishman (1987) in general; Gold (1981) for American English; Jacobs (1996) for Viennese German of the 1920s. Benor (2000) has shown how religiosity and Zionism have been sources of Hebrew and Yiddish influence in an American-Jewish ethnolect. Data collected by Eisikovits within an Ultra-Orthodox Jewish community where the community language had been Yiddish suggests that Yiddish has left a phonological, lexical and grammatical impact on their Australian-English ethnolect (Clyne et al. 2001). The main phonological features are the tendency to add a voiced stop and [ə] to a velar nasal at the end of a word and a uvular [ʀ]. Yiddish lexical items are integrated into English sentences according to the principles of the Matrix Language Frame Model, for example:

(124)   I don't like the SHLEPPING but what can I do?
        (<Yiddish *shleppen* 'to drag around')
(125)   SHMECKEN the LUFT!
        'Smell the air' (<Yiddish *shmecken* 'to smell')

The lexical transfers tend to be in the domains of religion, family life and food, for example:

(126)   I had no more tomatoes or onions in the house so Harry had to get from Rose on the way home from SHUL (*shul* 'synagogue')
(127)   We had KNEIDLAKH tonight (*kneidlakh* 'dumplings')

The most salient syntactic feature is the absence of the direct-object pronoun, as in:

(128)   Question: Do you want some fruit?
        Response: I've got.
        Mainstream Aust. Eng.: I've got some.

Expressions such as *Zey gesunt!* 'Be well' occur in the English of descendants of Yiddish speakers, regardless of whether they themselves speak it or not.

Data collection for the Greek ethnolect suggests that it is used widely among students at a Greek Orthodox community secondary school but among students from other schools only in ethnic in-group communication, especially in the family (see also below).

The main distinctive phonetic features of the Greek ethnolect (based on Tollfree's analysis in Clyne et al. 2001) are:

* [ɯ] in GOOSE.
* /ə/ advanced to [ɛ] in closed syllables, e.g. *houses*.
* The diphthong in FACE has an open starting point, [eːɪ] e.g. *day*.
* KIT is close, which contradicts the current development in Melbourne English among comparable young people. NEAR has an open finish [ia] or with glide insertion, [ija], e.g. *here*.
* The final nucleus in COMMA is consistently open [back a], e.g. *soccer, longer*.
* Heavy aspiration of /k/, e.g. *cold, soccer*.
* Perceptual voicing of voiceless stops and fricatives, e.g. /t/ in *together*, /t/ in *Tuesday*, intervocalic /p/ in *properly* and /s/ in *baseball*.
* The frequency of /t/ tapping is higher than in comparable speakers from other backgrounds.

Syntactic marking is limited to in-group communication, especially with parents.

• Ellipsis reminiscent of pidginization and foreigner talk.
• Auxiliary deletion, for example:

(129)   How you know?

• Preposition deletion, for example:

(130)   We'll go movies.

• Quantifier deletion (some), for example:

(131)   Can I have money?

Ongoing data collection involving separate conversations within the extended family and with out-group members confirms the ethnic in-group nature of lexical marking in ethnolects (corresponding to bidirectional switching) and the identity function of phonetic marking (Clyne et al. 2001). Myers-Scotton (1998a: 300) emphasizes turnover as an explanation of 'syntactic borrowing'.

Warren (1999) has studied a stylized variety developed for dramatic purposes by some young second-generation Australians of Greek, Italian, Turkish and 'Yugoslav' background acting in ethnic Australian theatre known as 'wogshows'. She identifies phonetic features such as [a] in final syllables of words such as 'pleasure', the replacement of 'th' by [d], and the avoidance of reduced vowels, as well as some grammatical features such as double negatives. This 'pan-southern European-ethnic Australian' variety is one with which Australians of similar backgrounds will identify.

As we have seen, turnover, as discussed by Myers-Scotton (1998a), is one of the possible components of the ethnolects, but there are others too – pidginization, semantic transference, phonetic features (cf. Thomason fc). It is most likely that there are prosodic features of the ethnolects which would warrant investigation.

4.7   Concluding remarks

In this chapter we have shown how the drift of a language is utilized and extended through language contact, and how the various levels of language work together in the convergence of the systems. Lexical and syntactic transference co-operate to facilitate grammatical word order in the community language and/or to achieve interlingual convergence. Semantic and syntactic transference work together to enable speakers to express themselves in an idiomatic way particularly appropriate to their multiple identity. Compromise forms arise from the combined effects of phonic and prosodic transference.

A high degree of integration is a type of divergence, which counteracts the convergence and transference. As Thomason and Kaufman (1988) indicate, degree and period of contact, together with typology, are key factors in contact-induced changes. Existing typological proximity to English and a drift in a similar direction promote convergence in our data. 'Markedness' (or actualization of reanalysis: Smith 1998, section 3.5.5) plays a role in the decrease in distinctions evidenced in semantic transference, syntactic convergence and transference. The extension of SVO, the preservation of distinctions shared by two of the trilinguals' languages, the levelling of adjectival endings in Romance languages and the overgeneralization of 'have' auxiliaries are instances of this as are the incidence of 'bare verbs' in Dutch and of 'bare accusatives' in Hungarian. However, the increasing variability (e.g. SVO/ accusative–dative) is a product of the same change. Most of our data indicates a position between Levels 1 (casual contact but only 'lexical borrowing'); 2 (slightly more intense contact/some structural borrowing); and 3 (more intense contact/slight structural borrowing, including derivational morphemes) on Thomason and Kaufman's scale. However, some (particularly second-generation Dutch) shows indications of Categories 4 and 5 (especially SVO, bare verbal forms). The contact has been overwhelmingly more than 'casual' and there is more than 'little bilingualism'. The restriction of the impact of L2 to the lexicon, however, does apply to many of the informants.

5   Dynamics of transversion

5.1   Introduction

In chapter 4, we focused on mechanisms of transference, convergence and integration in contact-induced change. Data was drawn from languages with different typological features, in contact with English. Chapter 5 complements this. It will develop and illustrate across languages some principles for the structural facilitation of transversion, including the role of convergence. The discussion will focus on facilitators rather than constraints. The chapter utilizes Australian data from bi- and trilinguals as an example to focus on transversion between languages and how this varies between languages in contact and the applicability of current models to this.

In this chapter, it will not be possible to separate the linguistic and psycholinguistic dimensions completely as the latter helps elucidate the former. However, the psycholinguistic implications will be drawn in chapter 6.

This chapter develops from earlier studies (e.g. Clyne 1967, 1972a, 1977a, 1980b) where the facilitation of switching was considered mainly a lexical issue. In this chapter, the role of facilitation at the prosodic and syntactic levels will also be explored. Also, it will be argued that what had previously been described in terms of grammatical constraints could realistically be conceptualized in terms of facilitation. It is hoped that this chapter might stimulate more discussion of typological variation in switching phenomena.

5.2   Sociolinguistic and discourse motivation for transversion

In this section, we will discuss the way intraclausal transversion may be facilitated by lexical and structural overlap and convergence. The explanation for interclausal transversion, on the other hand, lies largely in the discourse, in the sociolinguistic setting (interlocutor, domain, topic, role-relationship, venue, channel of communication, interaction type), or in the speaker's preference for separating languages (Clyne 1972a: 99–101). As the emphasis in this chapter is on structural facilitation of transversion, we will not discuss sociolinguistic and discourse motivation in detail, there being many excellent treatments of this issue (see, for example, Auer 1998). Moreover, there are grounds for Gardner-Chloros's (1995: 68) fear of a new orthodoxy by differentiating skilled code-switching from 'the aberrant manifestations of bilingualism', namely interlingual influence. However, below are some examples of various categories of discourse-motivated transversion in our data:

    i. *Quotation*, for example:

(1)   Dann später kriegte ich ein Brief von England.. von Mrs Borgers..und die schrieb zu mir: 'DO YOU REMEMBER? YOU'RE COMING TO VISIT ME'
    'Then later I got a letter from England.. from Mrs Borgers and she wrote to me . . .' (MGWD 44f)

The speaker is quoting from an English letter and, recognizing the interlocutors' bilingualism, does not see a need to translate the citation.

    ii. *Change in constellation of participants*, for example:

(2)   'Checkerboard' habe ich gestern gelesen. *Can you follow*?
    'I read "Checkerboard" yesterday. Can you follow?' (MGP 187f)

The switch was to address an Indian friend who had just walked in.

    iii. *Topic/comment*, for example:

(3)   *Topic*: Ich kann nicht kegeln oder Squash spielen.
    'I can't play badminton or squash'
    Comment: Only fifth and sixth formers can do that.
    (Templar, second generation)

Here the comment is in the 'other' language.

    iv. In terms of Gumperz's (1982) notion of metaphorical switching, a switch from one language to another or from one language to a mixed (bi/trilingual) code may constitute a switch from the they-code to the we-code, for example:

(4)   Manchmal wenn ich deutschsprachige Bekannte treffe, spreche ich deutsch, OTHERWISE I SPEAK ONLY ENGLISH
    'Sometimes when I meet German-speaking friends, I speak German, otherwise I speak only English' (MGP 61m)

This is code-switching in the true sense of the term, as indexical functions are expressed, with each language expressing a different identity. There is a juxtaposition of the old and the new we-identity.

(5)   Ich wollte anfangs bloß zwei Jahre bleiben. Jetzt bin ich schon acht Jahre hier. I THINK THAT SPEAKS FOR ITSELF

'I originally only wanted to stay for two years. Now I have been here for eight years . . . I think that speaks for itself' (MGP 107f)

The transversion indicates a positive attitude to Australia, the break with the German past. In most immigrant families, the we-code of the first generation generally became the they-code of the second. The we-code of the younger generation is the one to which they transverse when they merge the domains, i.e. when they discuss something from the school domain or the institutional domain in the context of the home domain, for example:

(6)   Wenn mir in die Schule kommen, tu mer unse Bücher weg (A) . . . da
        geh mer zu dem . . . Locker . . und mir nehmen unse Bücher für
        vier . . . FOR FOUR *periods* . . .[1] und . . . denn gehen mer zu unsen
        Raum und warten, bis der Lehrer 'reinkommt und fangen an. Mir lernen
        Englisch (A) und . . . .*Well* WE LEARN ENGLISH, GEOGRAPHY,
        HISTORY, SCIENCE[2]
        'When we come to school, we put our books away (A) . . . then we go to
        the . . . locker . . and take our books for four . . . for four periods . . . and
        then we go to our room and wait for the teacher to come in and start. We
        learn English (A) and . . . Well we learn English, geography, history,
        science (A) and . . .' (MGP 92f)

All this contributes to giving expression to the speaker's identities. Conversation analysis focusing on relevance and procedural consequentiality of code-switching has advanced the understanding of this. (See, for example, Auer 1998, especially Sebba and Wootton 1998, Li Wei 1998b, Alfonzetti 1998.) Both Li Wei (1998a, b) in his work on two Chinese communities on Tyneside (England) and Rindler-Schjerve (1998), in her research on Sardinian–Italian bilingualism, demonstrate that speakers in the more open networks transverse more than members of more closed networks. Space does not permit me to give more emphasis to this approach here.

In her study of second-generation Greek–English code-switching in Melbourne, Tsokalidou (1994) finds a much greater incidence of code-switching in young women than in young men in single-sex participant observations (there females produced 61.69% of 'code-switches', cf. males 38.21%), but about the same amount in mixed groups (females produced 49.33% of the 'code-switches', males 50.67%). Moreover, the motives for code-switching vary, with the females accommodating to interlocutors and males asserting their language choice. Males tended to switch to use slang and swearwords and make comments, and females to quote or imitate. There was more 'code-switching' in the speech of those with closer friends in the Greek community than among the others.

Gumperz (1982) differentiates between the following functions of code-switching in conversations:

Referential (lack of facility with language)
Directive (involving the hearer directly)
Expressive (expressing mixed identity)
Phatic ('metacomment')
Poetic (puns, jokes)

5.3   Facilitation as a concept

In earlier publications (e.g. Clyne 1967, 1972a, 1980b), I drew attention to the way certain lexical items triggered a switch (transversion) from one language to another. It would be appropriate to say that they *facilitated* transversion as the lexical items may not be solely responsible. In this section, I will attempt to develop facilitation within the lexical level using trilingual as well as bilingual data and extend it to the prosodic and syntactic levels. I will present some principles of facilitation. The notion of facilitation may be seen as a more appropriate alternative to constraints.

Muysken (2000: 16) rightly comments that my data on Dutch and German in Australia will have given rise to different experiences from those of the language pairs that Myers-Scotton and Poplack worked on originally. Through cross-linguistic and cross-corpus comparisons it will be possible to show how typological and sociolinguistic factors impact on the facilitation process.

5.3.1   Lexical facilitation

According to Facilitation Principle 1, lexical items that can be identified as being part of more than one language for the speaker or for some section of, or the entire speech community, may facilitate a transversion from one language to another. Such words are phonologically unintegrated lexical transfers (or ones with a low level of integration), proper nouns, bilingual homophones (words that sound the same or nearly the same in the two or more languages or in the speaker's idiolects in the two or more languages). Broersma (2000: 18–20) is correct in imputing that many colleagues have misinterpreted the trigger-word to be the result rather than the cause of 'code-switching'. (The need to differentiate the trigger-word from its consequences is a reason for not employing the latter ambiguous term in the present discussion.)

5.3.1.1   Trigger-words
Lexical transfers In (7) below, an example from a conversation on values, *human being*, while a transfer from English, has become part of the informant's

Dutch, and brings the speaker to a point where he can continue in either language:

(7)   Wat er gebeurt met de gewone werkers, die er eigenlijk uitgeschopt worden, die niet meer nodig zijn. ALSO WHAT *wat* wij er aan kunnen doen als *human being* OR IN MY CASE AS CHRISTIAN 'What is happening to ordinary workers who are actually kicked out, who are not needed any more. Also what what we can do about it as human being or in my case as Christian' (MD172m, talking about social problems in the modern world)[3]

The same applies to the following Croatian example:

(8)   ima ovaj, razne te, kao ovu *colleges* AROUND, THERE ARE A COUPLE OF CAMPUSES
        'there is this these various like these colleges around, there are a couple of campuses' (MCr 65f, from Hlavac 2000)

(9)   Ik ga, ik moet   (A).. dingen van de   *shops*   EINKAUFEN
        I   go, I   have to (A).. things from the (Dut.) shops (Eng.) buy+INF (Ger.)
        'I go, I have to buy things from the shops' (MTDEG 17f)

Here *shops* is a lexical transfer from English in both the German and Dutch of the informant, with the equivalents *winkel* and *Laden/Geschäft* not employed in the recording. *Shops* facilitates a transversion from Dutch to German. It is further facilitated by syntactic overlap between German and Dutch. (Cf. section 5.3.3, below.)

(10)   Ich muss   ab und zu   in einem   *Dictionary*   KIJKEN
        I   have to every now and then in the (Ger.) dictionary (Eng.) look+INF (Dut.)
        'I have to look in the dictionary every now and then' (MTGED 25f)

In this example, *dictionary* is apparently a lexical transfer in both the speaker's German and Dutch and facilitates a transversion, this time from German to Dutch. It is interesting that, in both examples (9) and (10), facilitation of transversion occurs from their chronological L1 to their L3. Again there is secondary facilitation due to syntactic overlap between German and Dutch.

(11)   Nhủng mà *based* ON REAL CHARACTERS ồngoài ông *based*
        but   based on real   characters   outside he   based
        ON LIFE EXPERIENCE ông viêt
        on life   experience   he   write
        'He based his writing on real characters and life experience' (MV 3f, generation 1b, from Ho-Dac 1996)

This informant transverses three times after *based* in the one interview. The obligatory *on* acts as a link with the subsequent complement.

Bilingual homophones Like lexical transfers, bilingual homophones are part of the speaker's two or more languages:

(12)   Imam puno zadaca I sutra mi igramo *tennis*..THAT'S ABOUT ALL
        'I have a lot of assignments and tomorrow we are playing *tennis*..that's about all' (MCr 38m from Hlavac 2000)

This second-generation Croatian–English bilingual from Hlavac's corpus is using *tennis*, a well-established part of homeland Croatian vocabulary, making it part of both languages, and it facilitates the transversion. As *tennis* is the normal and only word for the sport in Croatian, this is not a lexical transfer of the speaker.

In previous treatments of triggering, I distinguished between the more unusual category 'compromise forms' such as [ɔf] (between German [auf] and English [ɔv], and bilingual homophones (homophonous diamorphs). As the compromise forms are, in fact, bilingual homophones to the speakers, I stress by using the term 'bilingual homophones' that they may be items that are common to the two systems of all bilinguals using the respective languages or ones that in the idiolect of some speakers have become common due to convergence. An example of the latter is (13):

(13)   Keine Apfelsinen. Wir haben se gehabt BUT oh großes Feuer *come*
        THROUGH AND KILLED ALL THE TREES
        'No oranges, we had them but oh big fire come through and killed all the trees' (MGWD 40m, talking about his garden)

This third-generation bilingual from a former German enclave, talking about his garden, uses *come* [kam] for both Ger. [ka:m], past tense, and Eng. [kam] present and (non-standard) past tense. (In earlier publications I described such a phenomenon as a 'compromise form', but for this speaker it is a bilingual homophone.)

(14)   En we reckoned Holland was too *smal* VOOR ONS. Het was te benauwd allemaal
        'and we reckoned Holland was too narrow/small for us. It was all too oppressive everything' (MD 198f)
        Smal (Dutch 'narrow') and English *small* are both pronounced [smɑl] by the speaker.

Thus phonetic convergence contributes to the category of bilingual homophones and therefore to the facilitation of transversion, in this case from English back into Dutch. It should be noted, however, that the informant pronounces *Holland* and *was* in much the same way in the two languages, contributing further to the facilitation of transversion.

The close similarity between German, Dutch and English means that there are trilingual homophones that can have facilitative effect, for example:

(15)   Denke ich   *in* DUITS   *en..*   *and so on*
        think   I (Ger.) in German and (Dut.).. and so on (Eng.)
        'I think in German and so on' (MTGED 25f)

where the informant is reflecting on the languages in which she thinks. *In* is common to the three languages, German *denke* and Dutch *denk* are very similar, and *en* is both Dutch and an unaccented variant of English *and*.

Proper nouns Most proper nouns are used in both (all) the speaker's languages and therefore contribute to the facilitative potential:

(16)   Die die jüngste ist in *Portland* THAT'S RUBY, GLADYS IN
        NEW ZEALAND, STELLA HERE IN WARRAYURE, VIDA IN
        BENDIGO AND EL AND und Sylvie in Hawkesdale und Elsie in
        Südaustralien.
        'The youngest is in Portland that's Ruby, Gladys in New Zealand,
        Stella here in Warrayure, Vida in Bendigo and El and and Sylvie in
        Hawkesdale and Elsie in South Australia' (MGWD 34f)

The place name *Portland*, supported by the preceding *in*, facilitates the transversion in this enumeration of the speaker's children, which constitutes a comment on the discourse topic in the previous clause. Further personal and place names and bilingual homophones (*in, here*) maintain the transversion.

(17)   Ik heb gelezen '*Snow White come home*' IT'S ABOUT A WINTER
        PET
        'I have read: "Snow White come home" it's about a winter pet'
        (MD 101f, second generation)

The title of an English book read by the informant and talked about in Dutch facilitates transversion – between topic and comment.

(18)   Flinders Street đây OPPOSITE STATION a
        Flinders Street there opposite   station   PRT
        'The place is in Flinders Street opposite the station' (MV 13f, from
        Ho-Dac 1996)

In (18), the name of the station facilitates the transversion.
    There is a tendency for conjunctions to be in the same language as the proper nouns that they conjoin in a multiple transfer, for example:

(19)   Die Housing Commission in Werribee, Broadmeadows AND Laverton
        (MGP 97f)

The words facilitating a transversion, which I have termed trigger-words (e.g. Clyne 1967), introduce the transversion but are not part of it, just as the proper nouns in (17)–(19) are not part of the transversion themselves.

5.3.1.2   Anticipational transversion

Generally transversion follows the trigger-word but in many instances it precedes and anticipates it at the start of a unit of speech planning, as in this instance involving Italian, Spanish and English:

(20)   io ho abitata   EN   *Sydney* (Interviewer: Che bello! Quando?)
        I   have live+PAST.PT (It.) in (Sp.) Sydney (How nice! When?)

        FROM *Argentina hemos*   ido   tutti a in Sydney dieci.. no
        from   Argentina have+1pl go+PAST.PT (Sp.) all to in Sydney ten.. no

        otto   anni.
        eight years (It.).

        'I have lived in Sydney since we all came to Sydney from Argentina ten no eight years ago' (MTSI/E3f)

(The inflection of *abitata* is non-standard.) *From* is more likely to be triggered by *Sydney* (consequential) than by *Argentina* (anticipational) because it is pronounced [arɣ ɛnti:na] in Spanish. *Sydney* also probably facilitates anticipational transversion (*en*).

(21)   htila bi malo vidit od ALL THE *states*
        'I would like to see all the states' (MCr 22f, from Hlavac 2000)

Another speaker in Hlavac's study transverses in anticipation of the use of the same lexical transfer *states*, producing the same phrase, *all the states.*[4]

The following trilingual example is characterized by both consequential and anticipational facilitation:

(22)   Drie, *nou*, IT'S *Three Double Y R* NENNEN SIE DAS
        three now it's three double y r call   they that
        'three now, it's Three Double YR they call it' (DE/G 22m)

The informant had been speaking Dutch. *Nou* [nɑʊ] is a bilingual homophone (Dutch–English), *Three Double YR* an English proper noun, *IT'S* is facilitated by both *nou* (consequentially) and the proper noun (anticipationally). As this proper noun is common to all the three languages, it in turn triggers a transversion to German.

Another instance is example (6) above, where the anticipation of *periods* facilitates transversion.

Table 5.1 compares the relative incidence of consequential and anticipational switching.

Table 5.1 *Type of facilitation*

Group	Consequential		Anticipational		Both	
German – postwar	68.37%	(67)	27.55%	(27)	4.1%	(4)
German – prewar	60%	(24)	35%	(14)	5%	(2)
German – settlements (sample)	41.52%	(71)	49.12%	(84)	9.36%	(16)
Croatian	76.19%	(32)	23.8%	(10)		
Dutch	86.3%	(88)	13.7%	(14)		
Vietnamese (sample)	81.3%	(13)	18.7%	(3)		
Italian	92.3%	(12)	7.69%	(1)		
Spanish	66.66%	(4)			33.33%	(2)
German (HGE trilinguals)	63.04%	(29)	32.61%	(15)	4.5%	(2)
Hungarian (HEG trilinguals)	66.67%	(4)	16.67%	(1)	16.67%	(1)
German (DGE trilinguals)	90%	(18)	10%	(2)		
Dutch (DGE trilinguals)	93.75%	(15)	6.25%	(1)		

Both anticipational and consequential facilitation of transversion occur in all language dyads/ triads. Irrespective of typology, consequential facilitation predominates in all groups of bilinguals and trilinguals except those in the former enclaves. To a lesser extent, prewar refugees also show a considerable amount of anticipational facilitation. This is due to either locative prepositional phrases anticipating a proper noun,[5] or the English indefinite article anticipating the trigger-word, for example:

(23)   Der war zwei..zwei Tage FROM *Tarrington* kam   er   TO   *Warrayure*
        He   was two..two   days from   Tarrington came he to   Warrayure
        'He was two days he came from Tarrington to Warrayure' (MGWD 29m,
        talking about his schoolteacher)

(24)   Das ist *a* STOCKMAN
        'This is a stockman' (MGPR 10, talking about a picture of an Australian
        scene)

In German–English bilinguals from the Wimmera, 44.2% of anticipational facilitation occurred before a proper noun (including some instances of facilitation by both a proper noun and a bilingual homophone) but only 25.7% of consequential facilitation occurred after a proper noun (or a proper noun and a bilingual homophone). The high incidence of bilingual homophones and of phonological convergence between Dutch and English coincides with both anticipational and consequential facilitation. It should be remembered that the Croatian speakers and the settlement German speakers are later-generation bilinguals, while the other groups are predominantly first generation. Some of these (e.g. prewar German speakers and, to a lesser extent, Dutch postwar migrants), having been in Australia for longer at the time of data collection than others (e.g. postwar German speakers) (for details, see section 1.4), had had longer to automatize collocations. Anticipational and consequential facilitation occur together in a small number of instances (such as (22)) where a word sandwiched between two trigger-words is in English.

The slightly greater incidence of facilitation of transversion from Italian than from Spanish in the trilinguals may be attributed to the slightly larger potential of bilingual homophones in Italian and English and the greater public use of the language in Australia than in Latin America, many of the informants claiming that their Italian has been revived in Australia.

5.3.1.3   Lexical facilitation and Muysken's 'congruent lexicalization'

Muysken (2000) views our facilitation of transference as consistent with his category of 'congruent lexicalization' and the interlingual sharing of structures within the utterance in which 'code-mixing' occurs. On the whole, this is so. However, there are also facilitated instances of his category 'alternation' – examples include (16) above, (17), the first part of (22) and to some extent (15), as well as example (5) in chapter 7, and the Vietnamese examples to be discussed under section 5.3.2. Of the 103 instances of triggering in the data from our Dutch–English bilinguals, seventy-one fit into Muysken's category of congruent lexicalization and thirty-two are alternations.

But there are also instances where a repair takes place or (in very dense transversion, section 5.6) when the structure is not shared and no repair occurs, for example:

(25)   Dan *soms*   TIMES GO FOR 'N *(voor'n)* HOUR nog in bed
        then sometimes (Dut.) times   go   for'n   hour   still in bed
        'Then sometimes go back to bed for an hour' (MD 17f)

A compromise form comprising Dutch *soms*, already meaning 'sometimes', and English *times* (from *sometimes*) facilitates a transversion. Though Dutch is not a pro-drop language, the subject pronoun is lost through the non-congruence between Dutch and English word order. The tonal facilitation of Muysken's 'alternation' will be discussed under section 5.3.2 in relation to Vietnamese–English.

I would reword Muysken's argument that there are no constraints in congruent lexicalization as follows: the facilitation process, notably triggering, invalidates constraints. Congruent lexicalization makes it very difficult to discern a specific matrix language.

5.3.1.4   The switch back

Like Rindler-Schjerve's (1998) Sardinian–Italian bilinguals, our informants rarely remain in the language of the switch for long. Sometimes the same or a similar trigger-word will facilitate reversion to the original language. This is commented on by Muysken (2000: 132), who attributes it to the absence of a dominant matrix language in what he terms 'frequent back-and-forth switches'.

(26)   'ne Strandszene in *Droman..*I THINK NO*..Dromana/* mit ein paar Häusern.
        'A beach scene in Droman..I think no..Dromana..with a few houses'
        (MGP 135m, talking about a picture of a beach scene)
(27)   Alle die Umgegend hier..nicht..bloß hier..nicht for Meilen und Meilen
        'all the area here..not only here..not for miles and miles' (MGWD 42m)

where the bilingual homophones *hier/here* and *Meile/mile* mark the limits of the transversion. That *Meile* and *mile* are perceived by the speaker as bilingual homophones is clear from another example of transversion facilitation from the same speaker, again speaking about his district:

(28)   Das war ungefähr eine Meile oder *Meil* 'ND A HALF nach Norden
        'That was about a mile or mile 'nd a half to (the) north'

In the trilingual example (20) above, *Argentina* is likely to have facilitated both anticipational transversion of *from* in English and consequential transversion of *hemos ido* in Spanish.

5.3.1.5 Comparative analysis
Though lexical facilitation of transversion is not very widespread in most bilinguals, it is of considerable significance in the way it counteracts the effects of other phenomena (see below, section 5.3.1.7). It might be assumed that because all dyads/triads of languages have proper nouns, especially in the Australian context, and lexical transfers from English, facilitation would occur between all languages. But this is not necessarily so. Relatedness and structural correspondence contribute as they increase the potential for overlap. Bilingual homophones have a facilitative effect because of phonetic correspondence and lexical overlap.

The examples above are representative of the speech of bilinguals and trilinguals, several generations of people from former enclaves as well as different immigrant vintages and a range of language contact dyads/triads. The breakdown of trigger-words facilitating transversion does vary according to languages, vintage and plurilingual situation, as may be seen from table 5.2.

Table 5.2 confirms that lexical transfers function as trigger-words across all language dyads and triads. It also shows that bilingual homophones facilitate transversion, particularly between closely related languages. Dutch, in particular, offers much overlap with English, especially because the realization of English phonemes by adult Dutch immigrants (*That's* becoming a homophone

Table 5.2 Types of trigger-words in a number of plurilingual groups[a]

Groups	Lexical transfer		Proper noun		Bilingual homophone		Bilingual homophone with PN		Bilingual homophone with LT	
German: postwar	62.24%	(61)	14.28%	(14)	23.47%	(23)				
German: prewar	70%	(28)	27.5%	(11)			2.5%	(1)		
German: settlements (sample)	47.34%	(81)	31.54%	(54)	7.6%	(13)	8.77%	(15)	4.09%	(7)
Croatian	76.19%	(32)	21.43%	(9)	2.81%	(1)				
Dutch	36.89%	(38)	10.68%	(11)	44.66%	(46)	1.94%	(2)	5.83%	(6)
Vietnamese (sample)	50%	(8)	50%	(8)						
Italian (trilinguals)	76.92%	(10)	7.69%	(1)	15.38%	(2)				
Spanish (trilinguals)	66.66%	(4)	33.33%	(2)						
German (HE trilinguals)	67.39%	(31)	19.57%	(9)	13.04%	(6)				
Hungarian (trilinguals)	66.67%	(4)	33.33%	(2)	–	–				
German (DGE trilinguals)	66.67%	(8)	0	(0)	33.3%	(4)				
Dutch (trilinguals)	50%	(8)	25%	(4)	25%	(4)				

[a] As has been mentioned for example (15), a bilingual homophone can have a facilitative effect together with other categories of trigger-words.

of *dat's*; *the* of *de*; *new* of *nieuw*) provides opportunities for convergence between the Dutch and English items. In the sentence

(29)   *Dat's* ONE OF *de nieuwer* plaatsen *in Holland*
        'That's one of the newer places in Holland' (MD 197m)

only *one of* and *plaatsen* are clearly in one language or the other.[6] (Even *of* is also a Dutch word, meaning 'or'. English *of* is often transferred into Dutch, with or without transversion.) Thus, each of the bilingual homophones increases the potential of transversion.

(30)   Ik hebt   een kop of tea OR SOMETHING
        I   have+3sg a   cup of tea or something
        'I have a cup of tea or something' (MD 109m, second generation)

Again there are multiple potential transversion facilitators, the bilingual homophones *kop of* (cup of), homophones not in the speaker's Dutch but in his parents' Dutch and English which provided his model and the lexical transfer *tea*. As will be seen from table 5.2, there are a number of instances in the speech of Dutch–English bilinguals where several bilingual homophones or one homophone and a lexical transfer or proper noun can facilitate transversion.

The relatively high incidence of bilingual homophones in postwar German-speaking immigrants, whose English is characterized by phonological transference, giving rise to more bilingual homophones, such as *café* [kafe:] or *taxi* [teksi] and compromise forms such as *of* < German [auf] / English [ɔv], may have a facilitative effect. But this occurs far more in first-generation Dutch–English bilinguals. The trigger-word facilitating more than one transversion from Italian to English is *in*. Perhaps the absence of transversion facilitated by bilingual homophones from Spanish to English in the same informants is due to the Spanish equivalent being *en*.[7]

Proper nouns will facilitate transversion across languages, but less so in Croatian which often requires more morphological integration of such items than does German, Dutch or Vietnamese. The greater incidence of proper nouns as trigger-words in the former enclaves than among postwar German speaking immigrants and their descendants can be attributed to the earlier use of both languages in the local situation where people and places were the topic of conversation, as was the case in the recording sessions. In the case of Vietnamese, it may be attributed to the proper nouns being in the 'tonal range' corresponding to English (see section 5.3.2).

Well triggered transversion to English 14% of the times it was used by postwar German-speaking immigrants and *anyway* did after 11% of its occurrences in the same group. But one of the informants transversed every time *well* was collocated with *then*.

An important variable is whether there are conventions in the language community requiring integration. For instance, in Hungarian (as also in Turkish and Finnish, for example; cf. section 3.5), the degree of morphological integration is so high that lexical transfers (and even proper nouns) are less likely than they are in German to facilitate transversion. Table 5.2 indicates the low facilitation potential of Hungarian (six instances) as compared to German (forty-six) in the same trilingual informants. Hungarian and English do not have bilingual homophones. The same types of items that facilitate transversion from German to English, including the names of streets, suburbs, and people, for example:

(31)   Was wir heute wissen, *alongside* FLINDERS STREET STATION und bis zu Jolimont
        'What we today know alongside Flinders Street Station and up to Jolimont' (MTH/GE 10m)

(32)   Es ist *by* ERICA YOUNG
        'It is by Erica Young' (MTH/GE 4f, referring to a book)

do not have the same effect on the Hungarian speech of the same informants. Also, Hungarian has postpositions, not prepositions.

The differential facilitation potential is due to the actual or perceived similarity of items in the community language with the English items. Even communities with particular conventions of integration, such as former stable bilingual enclaves (see above, section 4.5.1, on integration patterns) may thereby reduce the likelihood of facilitation.[8] The facilitation of transversion by what I have termed 'trigger-words' has been reported in studies of different language contact dyads from all over the world, both related and unrelated (Norwegian–English in the US, Haugen 1953; Swedish–English in the US, Hasselmo 1961, 1974; Dutch–English in the US, Schatz 1989; Serbian–English in the US, Savić 1995; dialect and standard in the Netherlands, Giesbers 1989; Sardinian–Italian in Sardinia, Rindler-Schjerve 1998; Latin–sixteenth-century German, Stolt 1964; Latin–Ancient Greek, Wenskus 1998; Latvian–Swedish in Sweden, Rūke-Dravina 1967; Turkish–Dutch in the Netherlands, Backus 1996; Finnish–English in the US, Halmari 1997) as well as in Australia (German–English, Clyne 1967; Spanish–English, Kaminskas 1972; Russian–English, Kouzmin 1973; Dutch–English, Clyne 1977a; Italian–English, Bettoni 1981a; Russian–Yiddish–English and Slovak–Hungarian–German, Rót 1985: 203; Greek–English, Tamis 1986; Croatian–English, Hlavac 1999, 2000; Romanian–English, Beligan 1999; Finnish–English, Kovács 2001). Gardner-Chloros, Moyer, Sebba and van Hout (1999) found that (Cypriot) Greek–English data contained significantly more 'triggered switches' than did comparable Punjabi–English data. They suggest that Punjabi–English transversions are less influenced by the lexis and more intrinsic to the speech mode of the group. A question perhaps worth asking is whether typological contrasts might also play a role in the differences in transversion patterns which they discuss. A small amount of data collected recently by Meredith Bartlett and Sandra Leane among bilinguals using Auslan (Australian Sign Language) and English suggest that finger spellings, comparable to lexical transfers (see Battison 1978; Lucas and Valli 1989), can trigger transversion between these languages, as can a vocalized quotation. This is a promising area for further research, especially where informants both sign and vocalize since the two languages are then employed simultaneously.

From the above discussion, it will be evident that facilitation reflects the unified typology of the languages (see section 4.4, above) and the use made of the resources of the two languages.

5.3.1.6   Bi- and trilinguals
From examples (9), (10), (15), (20) and (22) above, it will be evident that facilitation of transversion between three languages operates on similar principles as that between two languages, except that for the former, the cross-linkages are more complex. Also, because each pair of languages offers a different degree of potential for transversion through the extent of overlap and cross-linkage, some trilinguals function as double bilinguals for this purpose. In a very similar corpus, lexical facilitation of transversion occurred forty-six times from German into English but only six times from Hungarian into English in the same Hungarian–German–English trilinguals.

5.3.1.7   Lexical facilitation and the contravention of grammatical constraints
Lexical facilitation constitutes one of the reasons why grammatical constraints are contravened.[9] For instance, the Free Morpheme Constraint is 'violated' after a trigger-word, for example, in:

(33)   That's what *Papschi* MEIN's to say
        'That's what Papschi means to say'
        (Trigger-word – kinship name used to address the person in both languages) (MGPR 18f on her father's opinions)
(34)   Moj *tata*'s FAMILY
        'my father's family' (MCr 27f from Hlavac 2000)

Hlavac (2000) argues that *tata* is the normal designation of the father in the Australian ethnolect of the informant, is therefore common to the two systems, and likely to trigger a switch.

There are also instances where transversion occurs between the two morphemes of a compound noun, one of the morphemes being a lexical transfer:

(35)   dat de arbeids*space* WAS VERY MUCH SLOWER THAN IT IS IN HOLLAND
        'That the work pace was very much slower than it is in Holland'
        (Note that *was* can be regarded as a bilingual homophone) (MD 5m)

Anticipational facilitation is one of the reasons why the Government Constraint (section 3.3.3.1) is 'violated', for example:

(36)   Wir packen alle die alte Kleider, das für THE *missions*
        we   pack all   the old   clothes that for THE MISSIONS
        (Switch between prep and NP) (MGW98 talking about charitable work)
(37)   D'r ben'   NO, daar ben'   lampen ON *de bridge*
        there be+1sg/3pl no   there are/am lamps on de bridge
        'There are, no, there are lamps on the bridge'
        (MD 181f, second generation,[10] talking about a picture) (Transversion at
        the start of PP)

Here the similarity between *on* and *op* and between *the* and *de* may further facilitate the transversion.

As consequential facilitation can occur anywhere, it is responsible for the contravention of the Government Constraint, for example:

(38)   You don't see dat in Australië
        'You don't see that in Australia' (MD 17f)

where *dat* and *in* are bilingual homophones as well as cognates in the idiolects of this informant and trigger *Australië*.

Exceptions to the Conjunction Constraint demonstrate the uncertainty as to where a 'switch' begins. Example (38) would usually be construed as supporting Gumperz's Conjunction Constraint (see section 3.4.5).

(39)   I don't know wat [vɑt] het exactly is
        I don't know what   it   exactly is
        'I don't know what exactly it is' (MD 61f)

However, the facilitation model would suggest that *wat*, which is common to the speaker's two languages, facilitates transversion.

The Matrix Language Frame Model explicitly accounts for embedded language (EL) islands through violations of its own morpheme order principle. It does not, however, enable 'code-switching' to be explained by facilitation as it does not consider overlaps between languages. In examples such as (38) and (39), the products of closely related and converging languages in contact, a differentiation between matrix and embedded language is not feasible.

5.3.1.8 Hesitation and transversion

It had been observed (Clyne 1987: 744) that, when 'switching' occurred, trigger-words were frequently preceded by unfilled or filled pauses. In real time, a pause increases the time since the last item that was unambiguously from one language or the other. This enables the speaker to move into the other language. When this was tested against our data, it was found that pauses before or after a trigger-word could have this effect. This is in spite of the expectation that the hesitation pauses might constitute the monitoring that would enable speakers to find the appropriate word in the desired language (or mode).

(40)   Wir gehen . . . oh . . . BY *car*
         'We went[11] by car'
         (*Car*, which was an established lexical transfer in the settlements, facilitated *by*)
         (MGW 25f)

(41)   Ich les   grad eins.. das handelt von   einem alten . . . *secondhand dealer*
         I   read just one.. it   is   about an   old . . . secondhand dealer
         AND HIS SON
         and his son

         'I am just reading one, it's about an old secondhand dealer and his son' (MGP 136f)

In both these examples, the pause gives the speaker time after the item of ambiguous affiliation to forget which language they are in.

5.3.2   Tonal facilitation

According to Facilitation Principle 2, lexical items in a tonal language whose tone is identified with the pitch and stress of the non-tonal language in contact are liable to facilitate (though not necessarily cause) transversion, i.e. the fact that the item(s) is/are in the same tonal range increases substantially the likelihood of transversion.

On the basis of perception tests, Vũ Thanh Phượng (1986) is able to demonstrate that pitch height and movement play the most important role in the identification of Vietnamese tones. This corresponds to pitch and stress in English.

In his study of the speech of fifty first-generation (including generation 1b) Vietnamese–English bilinguals, Ho-Dac (1996, 2002) found that 85.46% of switches occurred where the Vietnamese item immediately before the switch was in a mid to high pitch tone (32 to 35)[12] – 33.41% in Tone 1 (high pitch) and 51.95% in Tone 2 or 3 (mid pitch). These are the tones which Vietnamese speakers are likely to equate with English pitch and stress – unstressed syllables with mid tones and stressed syllables with high tones. Words with these tones bring speakers into the tonal range which is also possible in English, i.e. which overlaps in the two languages.

(42)   Nhùng mà nếu IT'S VERY EXCITED MAYBE I JUST SO (A) CAUSE I
         but   if   it's very excited maybe I just so (a) cause I
         GOT NOTHING ELSE TO DO
         got nothing else to do

         'But if it's very exciting maybe I just like it because I haven't got anything else to do'
         (MV 2f, generation 1b woman, talking to much older man, from Ho-Dac)
         (Transversion immediately preceded by Vietnamese word with high tone)

(43)   Rồ'i   xong cái   (A) THAT'S THE END OF THE STORY
         already over CLA (A) that's the end of the story
         (MV 7f, generation 1b woman in interview)
         (Transversion immediately preceded by Vietnamese classifier with high tone)

(44)   Không có về đây   thì   bây giờ   I'M TAKING OFF A COUPLE OF YEARS
         I   won't come back here now I'm taking off a couple of years

         ..EXPLORE MY FUTURE
         ..explore my future

         'I won't come back here now. I'm taking off a couple of years to explore my future'
         (MV 2f, from Ho-Dac)
         (Transversion immediately preceded by Vietnamese word with mid tone)

The transversion appears to be eased by a syntactic rearrangement – the addition of (optional) emphatic particles of a high tone (such as *cái*, a classifier, *nếu* 'if' and *đó* 'that') where the lexical item before the particle has a low tone and would ordinarily not be followed by a transversion, for example:

(45)   Mây biêt   cái   THE THE WORK WE INVOLVE.. a hông
         you   know CLA the the work we involve   PRT
         (MV12m, generation 1b, from Ho-Dac 2002)

Each of the above examples would fit into Muysken's category 'alternation' rather than 'congruent lexicalization'.[13]

In Mandarin–English language contact, it is falling tones, fourth (53), half-third (35) and neutral that facilitate transversion (and transference). Among second- and young first-generation Mandarin–English bilinguals in Melbourne, Zheng (1997) found that 96.49% of switches came after such a tone, corresponding to English pitch and stress, for example:

(46)   tā xiǎng yào   GET A STICK
         It think want get a stick
         'It (the panda) wants to get a stick'
         (MM4–2, SC2 from Zheng 2000, based on pictures) (Tone 4)

(47)   yǒushí   lǎoshī   ràng nǐ   RESEARCH SOMETHING
         Sometimes teachers let   you research something
         'Sometimes the teacher lets you research something'
         (MM2–5, SD3, on school activities, from Zheng 1997) (Tone 3)

(48)   xǐhuan kěyǐ   FIND SOMETHING
         like   can find something
         'Yes, I like it because I can find something'
         (MM3–2, SD4, from Zheng 1997) (Neutral falling tone)

35% of switches from Mandarin to English occur at Tone 4, 16.35% at Tone 3, and 45.14% at the neutral falling tone. But many of Zheng's examples are of 'single word switches', lexical transfers in our terms, 'insertion' in Muysken's. Thus, tonal facilitation operates on similar principles to lexical facilitation. By using any tonal language items that are in the same tonal range as the non-tonal language, the speaker activates that whole language which is in this tonal range. This increases opportunities for transversion. The Mandarin–English examples are predominantly insertion or congruent lexicalization, with (46) to (48) belonging to the latter category, in contrast to the Vietnamese–English ones which tend to fit into Muysken's category of alternation, with some congruent lexicalization, for example:[14]

(49)   Nó BOTHER em A LOT lắm a
        it   bothers me a lot   very PART
        'It bothers me very much' (MV 2f)

It is possible that, in the type of transversion prevalent in Ho-Dac's corpus, it is conversational rather than structural issues that are responsible for alternation. Both Mandarin and Vietnamese, while recent immigrant languages, share word order with English. According to Muysken (2000; see section 3.4.4), shared word order is a factor facilitating congruent lexicalization and recency of migration a factor working against it.

5.3.3   Syntactic overlap/transference/convergence (secondary facilitation)

The third type of facilitation is syntactic overlap, often due to syntactic transference. It will be recalled that Sankoff and Poplack (1979) and others postulated, and still adhere to a constraint requiring that the syntax on either side of a 'switch' be 'grammatical' in the language concerned. In section 5.3.1.3, it was shown that lexical facilitation sometimes caused violations of grammatical constraints (further discussion, Clyne 1987). Thus it is not that *no* transversion occurs if there is not syntactic equivalence. It is rather that transversion is *facilitated* by such equivalence there. I have previously (Clyne 1987, 1991: 200) argued that it is mainly syntactic convergence that makes for the success of the constraint in relation to our German and Dutch corpora in Australia, i.e. it makes for very similar syntactic structures which enable bi- and trilinguals to transverse in and out of their languages. This is what Muysken (1997, 2000) terms 'congruent lexicalization'.

That is, according to Facilitation Principle 3, if syntactic rules overlap between the languages or previously divergent syntactic rules converge in the individual grammars of the speakers, switching is facilitated.

The idea of 'code-switching' being the basis for understanding other language contact phenomena (Myers-Scotton 1993a and subsequent publications) is appealing, especially as syntactic, semantic, semanticosyntactic and lexicosyntactic transference can sometimes be the result of relexification as in pidgins, that is, substituting lexical items from another language in the same syntactic frame, for example:

(50)   Je (A) je heb te look voor een ander job
         Homeland Dut. je moet een andere baan gaan zoeken
         'you have to look for another job' (MGD 197m)

or a partial relexification, for example:

(51)   Ich mag gerne BIT WIDE offene Flächen zu haben
         I   like   bit wide open spaces to have+INF
         'I like to have a bit of wide open space' (MGP 36f)
         ('Zu haben' is redundant.)

However, it is just as likely that syntactic convergence will provide enough syntactic overlap to facilitate multiple transference for the phrase *for lunch* or anticipational facilitation of transversion:

(52)   Wir haben   aus *FOR LUNCH* gegangen
         we   have+1PL out for lunch go+PAST.PT
         Ger. Wir sind zum Mittag ausgegangen
         'we went out for lunch' (MGP 161f; second generation)

but not complete overlap, which would have entailed moving the past participle ahead of the adverbial phrase.

Syntactic convergence and transference then function like other forms of convergence and overlap due to perceptual identification between items in the two languages as a potential *facilitator* of switching.

In her Serbian–English data from the United States, Savić (1995) also observes the cooccurrence of code-switching with syntactic convergence (e.g. the perfect as the 'default' past tense, *be* deletion, subject pronoun in positions where it is usually deleted). Treffers-Daller (1994) does not find evidence of code-switching accompanied by syntactic convergence in her Brussels French–Dutch data. That may be due to the stable and longstanding nature of the contact.

(53)   Das ist ein Foto gemacht an der *beach* (A) COULD BE kann
         this is a   photo made   on the beach (A) could be   can
         BE kann sein in Mount Martha
         be can be   in Mount Martha
         (MPG 135m, describing a picture)

In (53) the lexical transfer *beach* facilitates transversion but it is co-facilitated by the syntactic transfer *gemacht an der beach* (Std Ger. *das an der Beach gemacht ist*). It takes two attempts to relexify the transversion but the syntactic transference is kept.

5.3.4   Closing remarks on facilitation

In this section, we have illustrated three facilitative principles in switching – two of primary facilitation:
  I. Lexical
  II. Prosodic
and one of secondary facilitation:
  III. Syntactic

Thus, not only do typological factors further convergence as we have seen in earlier sections of this chapter, they also play a key role in facilitating transversion. Sociolinguistic factors (such as settlement pattern) influencing phonological transference in either direction and choice of lexical item can be responsible for variation in the facilitation of switching. Multiple transference of ADJ/N and V/N collocations constitute an emerging type of transversion and can also be attributed to structural factors (e.g. absence of inflections in matrix and embedded language) as well as sociolinguistic ones.

5.4   Collocations

The repeated use of one item in collocation with another increases the availability of the collocation. This is so not only in the facilitation of transversion by trigger-words, as we have shown above. Often constituents such as V + N, ADJ + N are switched in chunks (Annamalai 1989; Nattinger and De Carrico 1992) or prefabricated patterns (Pawley and Syder 1983) without one of them acting as a trigger-word, giving rise to what Myers-Scotton (1993a and subsequent works) terms 'embedded language islands'.

Adjective– Noun collocations:

(54)   Cây này nó là TYPICAL AUSTRALIA nè
        this tree is   typical Australia   PRT
        (MV2f, talking about a picture, Ho-Dac 1996)

(55)   Das ist ein Problem in Amerika mit den COLOURED PEOPLE
        'That is a problem in America with the coloured people'
        (MGP 107f, discussion of a book she had read)

(56)   Io parlo WOG LANGUAGE
        'I speak wog language'[15] (MTI/SE 5f)

Table 5.3 *Adjective + noun (or noun + adjective) collocations*

Group	English EL islands (multiple transf.)		Mixed constituents (Eng. and other language/s) (lexical transf.)		Ambiguous or both	
German: postwar	18.75%	(6)	78.13%	(25)	3.13%	(1)
German: prewar	32.6%	(31)	67.4%	(15)		
German: settlements	34.83%	(31)	65.16%	(58)		
Croatian	30%	(117)	70%	(268)		
Dutch	41%	(146)	59%	(210)		
Vietnamese (sample)	77.8%	(7)	22.2%	(2)		
Italian (trilinguals)	–		100%	(4)		
Spanish (trilinguals)	50%	(3)	50%	(3)		
German (HGE trilinguals)	20.93%	(9)	79.07%	(34)		
Hungarian (HGE trilinguals)	28.57%	(11)	71.43%	(35)		
German (DGE trilinguals)	25%	(24)	75%	(24)		
Dutch (DGE trilinguals)	56.1%	(46)	43.9%	(36)		

Verb–Noun (Phrase) collocations:

(57)   Samo, ah plešu   kolo, u hrvatskiom selu,
        Only, ah dance+3pl+PRES kolo in (a) Croatian village,
        nešto..   ah.. CELEBRATE SOMETHING
        something.. ah.. celebrate something
        'They're only dancing kolo [ring dance] in a Croatian village, some-
        thing.. ah.. celebrate something'

(58)   tiānqì   hen rè,   hěnduō rén   dōu WEAR SHORTS
        weather very hot, many   people all   wear shorts
        'The weather is very hot and many people are wearing shorts'
        (MM3–5, SA3, Generation 1b, from Zheng 2000)

It would appear that such multiple transference of collocations is activated together (see chapter 4) and is thus a phenomenon akin to transversion facilitation. Tables 5.3 and 5.4 indicate cross-linguistic variation in the English EL islands and mixed constituents (i.e. multiple vs. lexical transference) of ADJ + N/ N + ADJ and V + N(P) collocations.

These comparisons enable us to study the impact of three factors on the relative incidence of multiple and lexical transference of ADJ /N, V/N constituents (EL islands and Mixed constituents) – the structure of the language(s) in contact with English (see section 3.5), a tendency towards anticipational facilitation, and immigration vintage/generation of plurilinguals. A possible explanation would be Myers-Scotton's (1993a) attribution of EL islands to lack of congruence between the languages in contact. From that I would predict that:

Table 5.4 *Verb and noun collocations in VP*

Group	English EL islands		Mixed constituents		Ambiguous or both	
German: postwar	23.91%	(11)	73.91%	(34)	2.17%	(1)
German: prewar	10.3%	(4)	84.6%	(33)	5.1%	(2)
German: settlements	4.44%	(6)	95.56%	(129)		
Croatian	1.56%	(2)	98.44%	(126)		
Dutch	21%	(9)	79%	(30)		
Vietnamese (sample)	75.6%	(31)	24.4%	(10)		
Italian (trilinguals)	2.57%	(1)	97.43%	(38)		
Spanish (trilinguals)	25%	(1)	75%	(3)		
German (HGE trilinguals)	22.22%	(2)	77.78%	(7)		
Hungarian (HGE trilinguals)	0%		100%	(4)		
German (DGE trilinguals)	0%		100%	(25)		
Dutch (DGE trilinguals)	3.22%	(1)	96.78%	(30)		

(a) ADJ – N EL islands would occur relatively more than mixed constituents in Italian–Spanish–English trilinguals because Italian and Spanish have N+ADJ sequences, and the same would apply to a lesser extent to Vietnamese–English bilinguals;

(b) bi- and trilinguals with Hungarian, Croatian, German, Italian, Spanish and, to a lesser extent, Dutch, as one of their languages would prefer V + N EL islands because the verb is inflected, but Vietnamese–English bilinguals would tend towards mixed constituents because Vietnamese is an isolating language and English only inflects third-person singulars.

However, an alternative prediction in keeping with the findings on the impact of typology on our data (see above, section 4.4, especially section 4.4.7) would be that:

(a) where the other language is more isolating than English, i.e. no inflections are required, EL islands occur in both ADJ /N and V/N collocations;

(b) where the other language(s) in contact with English requires more inflection than English, mixed constituents are preferred.

In addition, on the basis of language use, we could predict that:

(c) those who use English most at the time of recording (second- and later-generation plurilinguals, those in former German enclaves, and speakers of Dutch) are the ones most likely to employ EL islands, because they would employ the collocations habitually; and

(d) a relatively large number of EL islands would coincide with a high incidence of anticipational facilitation because this type of transversion is largely bound to collocations.

The high incidence of multiple transference of EL islands in the isolating language Vietnamese could be evidence in favour of the lack of congruence argument (Myers-Scotton 1993a) when it comes to ADJ/N collocations. This is not supported by the data from Italian–Spanish–English trilinguals. However, there are not sufficient examples of either EL islands or mixed constituent collocations in this data to argue a case.

What is more important is the incidence of V/N collocation EL islands in Vietnamese bilingual speech, which is much higher than that of the ADJ/N collocations. In V/N collocations, Vietnamese and English share the same word order. Also, Vietnamese is more isolating in structure than English. There are no third-person-singular -s forms in the V/N collocations in the Vietnamese data. In the case of V + N(P), the explanation of the mixed constituents in the Croatian, Hungarian and the discourse of the most of the German-speaking vintages may be the relative absence of morphologically unintegrated verbs, except in the first-person singular in German (e.g. *Dann start ich das Abendbrot* 'Then I start dinner', *ich watch TV*). Even in such instances, the constituents are usually mixed. This points to typology (isolating vs. inflected language, see (a), (b) above) as a predominant factor. However, the sociolinguistic factor (c) also needs to be considered. The high incidence of multiple transference in V + N collocations among the postwar German speakers relates to new habitual activities related to job (*Ich change mein Dustcoat*) or leisure (*ich watch TV*). As was shown in chapter 2, Dutch is used less in Australia than German. This could be a reason why Dutch has a relatively high incidence of multiple transference, especially in ADJ + N collocations, among bilinguals. It should also be noted that, in Dutch but not in German, adjectives qualifying neuter nouns after indefinite articles and personal pronouns are uninflected (e.g. *een goed boek* 'a good book'; *mijn klein dochtertje* 'my little daughter', cf. German *ein gutes Buch, mein kleines Töchterchen*). The much higher incidence of ADJ/N EL islands in the Dutch than in the German of Dutch–German–English trilinguals would suggest that the structural factor may be the more salient one. The varying results between vintages for German ADJ + N could be related to the amount of use of English, with the settlement bilinguals, who by the time of the interview spoke English virtually all the time, and earlier-vintage bilinguals producing a larger proportion of EL islands than more recent arrivals. The Croatian speakers are all second generation, with English as their dominant language. This may influence the comparatively high rate of multiple transference for ADJ + N despite the inflected structure of Croatian.

The Italian–Spanish–English trilinguals are all first generation. In the case of Italian and Spanish, as the unmarked order is noun + adjective, it is not surprising that most of the examples are English noun and Italian adjective or involving an adjective such as *piccolo* which usually precedes the adjective. The 50–50 divide between English and mixed constituents in Spanish may be related to the lower incidence of solely consequential facilitation.

The strong tendency towards multiple transference among German-speaking prewar refugees and the settlement bilinguals could also be at least partly attributed to their tendency towards anticipational facilitation of transversion, factor (d). For the rest, typological factors and the amount of use appear to be the main explanations for collocation behaviour.

It is interesting that Muysken (2000: 134) regards mixed constituent insertions, based as they are on shared structures, as congruent lexicalizations, which he also associates with triggering, especially ragged switching. However, it is EL islands that are frequently part of the process of anticipational facilitation (triggering). In her study of the Turkish of the Turkish press in Australia, Kurtböke (1998a) discovers that lexical transfers from English may collocate with different items from their originals in the source language or their equivalents in the recipient language. One of the prominent examples she gives is *delivery*, which is frequently collocated in Australia with *yapilir* 'is made, is done', to express the meaning of 'delivery can be arranged'. This, she argues, means that lexical transfers have to be considered in their collocative environment.

Backus's (1996: 118ff) analysis of Turkish–Dutch 'code-switching' leads him to postulate a specificity continuum with proper nouns and, to a lesser extent, cultural borrowings (specific objects identified with a particular place or culture) leading to the greatest collocational entrenchment. The specificity continuum is the opposite to the awareness continuum, where some of his informants – especially the original Turkish immigrants and the second generation – consciously keep the two systems apart where there is little triggering potential. Triggering is seen by Backus (1996) as a non-conscious type of switching. We have already suggested that the collocations discussed above may be examples of a phenomenon close to triggering (lexical facilitation of transversion).

5.5 Directionality of lexical transference and transversion, especially in elderly bilinguals

The Matrix Language Frame Model (Myers-Scotton 1993a and subsequent publications) assumes unidirectionality of 'code-switching' with the possibility of a turnover of matrix and embedded languages. In this respect it concurs with the large amount of data gathered in situations where speakers are consciously avoiding switches to the minority language or transference from the minority language because the minority is bilingual and the majority is monolingual and unable to comprehend material from the other language. There is no need to invoke typological factors, as Halmari (1997: 201) does, alongside what she calls 'status' factors to explain unidirectional switching. Bidirectionality of transference and transversion do occur, however; for instance, where a speaker is constantly within a bilingual setting. This is the case with some elderly Dutch–English bilinguals in Australia, for example, who move in a circle of bilinguals after retirement and after their children have left home. There is transference of L1 (in this case) Dutch words into English discourse (see section 4.3.1), including words expressing concepts reminiscent of the Netherlands, e.g. *gracht* (canal in Dutch town), *gevel* (gables on Dutch houses), *bromfiets* (moped), *lantaarn* (old-style lamp), and transversion from English into L1 Dutch in English discourse or in interaction with monolingual English speakers, for example:

(59)   Because de KIPPENMEST is very very (A) BELANGRIJK VOOR
        MEST EN HET GRAS
        'because the chicken manure is very very important for manure and
        the grass'
        (MD 28m, a farmer talking about his activities)

Such phenomena are often popularly identified as L2 attrition inherent in elderly bilinguals (see also the Dutch–English text under section 5.6). A longitudinal study of Dutch–English bilinguals (De Bot and Clyne 1989, 1994) does not confirm the hypothesis of such a general tendency. A sample of our Dutch–English bilinguals, recorded in the early 1970s, was recorded a second time, most of them in 1987. The group who were recorded in 1987 were selected because they were considered to have a strong competence in both languages in the first data collection. However, subsequently some others from the 1970s were also interviewed again, in the early 1990s. The study underlines the importance of social factors, such as involvement in the ethnic or wider community, absence from children, and church now attended (whether there is an ethnic concentration in it), motivating language-use patterns – and suggests a strong relation between attrition and the earlier level of L2 proficiency. It appears that there is a threshold of competence in both languages in middle age that at least partly determines if attrition will occur with the ageing process. This is confirmed also in the analysis of a German–English bilingual who was taped thirty, thirty-four and thirty-eight years after arriving in Australia between the ages of fifty-six and sixty-four. The use of present for past tense of English verbs increased over this time and she employed no third-person-singular -*s* allomorphs in the third interview. Her English grammar, not well developed, appears to have reverted to an earlier pidginized stage (Clyne 1977b).

An analysis of lexical richness in the Dutch–English bilinguals (De Bot and Clyne 1994) showed that, in the use of lexical items, these had not really changed between the 1971 and 1987 data collection. English adverb order (Place–Manner–Time) has increasingly influenced significantly Dutch order (traditionally Time–Manner–Place) (cf. section 4.4). SVO generalization had increased but not significantly, while lexical transference and the overgeneralization of *de* had actually decreased. The informants had moved more in the direction of Dutch frequency distribution of words rather than away from it. It was suggested that ethnic radio and multicultural TV may have played a part. In cross-sectional studies (e.g. Clyne 1977b), childhood bilinguals do not experience attrition. This leaves features of elderly bilinguals' speech in cross-sectional comparisons – especially the bidirectionality mentioned above – best explained as less disciplined deactivation of the language not required at the time or the unmarked choice of a bilingual mode (Myers-Scotton 1993b; Grosjean 1998, 2001; see below, section 5.7).

5.6   Very dense transversion and convergence

On the whole, the Australian corpora affirm the notion of a single matrix language (Myers-Scotton 1993a) of any CP, seeing that this allows for a Composite Matrix Language (Jake and Myers-Scotton 1997). In the case of closely related languages, two of the languages of trilinguals may have converged so much that the boundaries of the languages are difficult to ascertain. This applies to many of our Italian–Spanish–English trilinguals who migrated from Italy to Latin America as children (section 1.3.3). For instance, twelve of the thirty-six employ forms with [i] from Italian:

il, 'the' (masc. sing.)
mi 'me' (object)
di 'of'
in 'in'

and *si* 'if' from Spanish consistently in stressed positions and, in a few cases, forms with *e* (*el*, *me*, *de*, *en* from Spanish and *se* 'if' from Italian) as unstressed. On the other hand, it should be pointed out that a local or regional variety (dialect) may be so distant from the standard or near-standard variety that the two are always regarded as autonomous systems. Very dense transversion between Italian and Spanish occurs especially in those with the acquisition order, ISE. This is comparable to the variety known as Cocoliche in Argentina (e.g. Whinnom 1971). A characteristic of the speech of our group of trilinguals is the transference of verbs from Spanish into Italian, for example:

(60) **No ve'no**   c'era   nessuno   **nadie   entonces** che **la**
      not see+PRES+3sg.not there.was nobody (It) nobody so (Sp) that it

      vi'mal   la **que quiere   decirle**   troppo male **no sabìa**
      see+PAST.bad what   want+3sg tell+INF.it too   bad   not know+PAST+1sg

      parlare   solo parlavano   espáñolo italiano **no** capivo
      speak+INF only speak+PAST+3pl Spanish Italian not understand+PAST

      niente perchè   m'avevo   dimenticato   tutto   no no
      nothing because me.have+AUX+ISG forget+PAST.PT everything no no

      c'era   qualche italiano y   no me **capìa**   **porquè**
      there.was some   Italian and not me understand+PAST+3sg because

no sabìa   **como no . . . no no   podìa**   **hablar**
not know+PAST+1sg how   not . . . not not could+PAST+3sg speak+INF

màs en italiano perchè m'ero   dimenticato
more in Italian because me.be+PAST+1sg forget+PAST.PT

tutto   no? **entonces tuve   que** las memoria
everything no so   I.(had).to that the memories

'I didn't see there wasn't anybody so I didn't like it you know didn't like it at all I
didn't know how to speak because they only spoke in Italian Spanish, I didn't
understand anything because I had forgotten all my Italian. There were some Italian
and could not understand me because I didn't know how I couldn't speak Italian any
more because I had forgotten everything, right? so I had to (remember)' (MTISE 17f)

Here, even in the first CP, *Ne ve'no . . .*, there is a return to Spanish *nadie*, which
preserved the ML.

(61)   se   sente   male allora se te   stanno sette otto dieci quindici
        (one) feel+3sg bad   so   if you be+3pl seven eight ten   fifteen

        te   più   allegra più   come s/ più con un'altra**manera**
        you more happy more like   s/ more with another.way

        di **vivir**   **no es** una come **no es** una persona sola **es**
        of live+INF no is one like not is one person only is

        la unione   per esempio de Europa per me **està** bene sta
        the unification for example of Europe for me is   good is

        bene per tutto   **no** per una cosa sola
        good for everything not for one thing only

        porquè dice   hay   molti
        because (it) say+PRES+3sg there.are many

        '(if you are alone) you feel bad so if there are seven, eight, ten, fifteen you feel
        happier more how do you (say) more with another way of living. It is not like only
        one person, it is the unification of Europe for example, for me it is alright for
        everything not only for one thing because there are said to be many people'
        (MTISE 19m)

(62)   **no** uno sì un'altra guardi   e'spiaggia **no puedo**   dire
        not one yes another look+sg+IMPER it.is.beach not can+1sg say+INF

        come **distinguir**   de   una parte all'altra   gente che è
        how distinguish+INF from one side to.another people who is

        nuda   gente vestita   tutto   quello e' sabbia e   mare è
        naked people dress+PAST.PT everything that   is sand   and sea is

        'No one, yes someone else listen! It is a beach. I cannot distinguish between one
        place and another. People who are naked and some who are dressed – sand and
        sea are all that there is' (MTISE 19m)

(63)   Io l'italiano l'ho   continuato sempre a parlare pure en Argentina
        I the Italian it have+1sg kept   always to speak even in Argentina

        lo   parlavamo   fra   di noi quindi ci trovavamo   fra
        it+OBJ speak+1sg+PAST among of us so   we find+1pl+PAST among

italiano **si**   **tocaba**   il   piano si   parlava   in italiano
Italian REFL play+3sg+PAST the piano REFL speak+3sg+PAST in Italian

si estaba   qualche argentino o **de habla**   **hispana**
if there.be+3sg+PAST any   Argentinian or of language Spanish

si   parlava   espagnolo
REFL speak+3sg+PAST Spanish

'I kept talking Italian always, even in Argentina as well. We spoke it among ourselves, so we found among ourselves we played the piano, we spoke Italian. If there were any Argentinians present, we would speak Spanish' (MTISE 13m)

This frequent phenomenon in the trilinguals contrasts with earlier frameworks (e.g. Klavans 1983) which have the verb determining the matrix language.

Hasselmo (1961) refers to Swedish–English bilinguals in the US whose speech is characterized by dense transversion (in both directions) at the grammatical and lexical levels, facilitated by a large number of lexical transfers and compromise forms, syntactic convergence in one or both directions, and a phonic pattern based on L1. This phenomenon, which he later termed 'marginal passages', can be found in some of our elderly Dutch–English bilinguals. For instance, in the following passage from an 83-year-old first-generation bilingual (MD 17f), a woman from a small country town with a large settlement of Dutch Calvinists, English items for numbers (especially with years) and occupations, and English kinship terms are usually employed in both languages, and *de*, *en* (and *'n*), *is* and *nou* are perceived to be the same in the two languages because of the informant's phonic pattern being Dutch, while the word order of English quotes tends to be Dutch converging towards English. Compromise words and quotes as well as the transfers common to both subsystems of the individual facilitate the transversion that is characteristic of this mode. The language of the conversation was Dutch:

(64)   MY SON *was* daar, hij *was* FIRST *here* op de ANZ Bank en hij STUDYde nog bij voor 't *bookkeeping* AND AFTER THAT HE GO TO *de ANZ Bank* . . . FOUR AND A HALF YEARS toen had ie een overplaatsing naar Geelong en toen was die in Geelong en toen was hij (eh) op *de* DAY was ie op *de ANZ Bank*, maar 's avonds deed hij study in de college van de Reformed Church en zo heeft ie dat zo FOUR YEARS gedaan en toen is die (eh) nou verder heeft ie nog TWO YEARS hebben wij voor hem te PAY dat wij eh dat hij wou minister worden. En hij is minister geworden en heeft gestaan in Ulverstone en Toowoomba en nou is die nu, hij was in Nieuw Zeeland, in Auckland, in Hamilton *en* ALSO in nog *een* OTHER PLACE. En nou zit ie ook in de andere eiland, eerst was 'ie Nelson en nou zit 'ie Richmond Nelson dat is 't andere. Hij was vierentwintig september was die vijfentwintig YEAR minister. Dus heel. . . .[16]

[Dat is een lange tijd, he?] I HAVE SEVEN CHILDREN *en* MY OTHER SON *was* eerst een electrisch man, maar hij zegt 'MUM, I DON'T LIKE IT MORE TO DO'. Hij had SEVENTEEN YEARS DONE, hij zegt, hij zegt 'I ZAL study something else'. Nou, toen ging die voor (eh) . . . .voor HOUSE(n) TO SELL [estate] ESTATES AGENT agent heeft 'ie ESTATES AGENT geworden. Nou is die ESTATES AGENT [en vindt 'ie dat beter?] Ja . . . . . je hebt hier *een* LOT OF . . . allemaal BUY THEM *en* dan CLEAN *'t* op en hij is en dan RENT'T OUT.

The discourse of this speaker may be seen as an example of Jake's and Myers-Scotton's notion of the Composite Matrix Language. While there are some clear instances of Dutch syntax employed in sentences with mixed constituents, for example:

(65)   Nog TWO YEARS hebben wij voor hem *te* PAY
         Still two years   have   we for him to pay
         'We had to pay for him for another two years'

many instances of converged Dutch and English compromise word order are to be found, for example:

(66)   dat hij wou   minister worden
         that he wanted minister be
         'that he wanted to be a minister'[17]
         Standard Dutch: dat hij dominée zou worden
(67)   I don't like it more to do
         'I don't like doing it any more'
         Standard Dutch: ik wou het niet meer doen
(68)   Toen ging hij voor house to sell
         'Then he started selling houses'
         Standard Dutch: Toen ging hij huizen verkopen.
(69)   een shop van zich zelf
         'a shop of his own'
         Standard Dutch: een eigen winkel
(70)   I zal study something else
         (English word order)
         Standard Dutch: Ik zal iets anders (gaan) studeren

There are also instances of bare forms in English (*go, live*), perhaps reflecting earlier stages of second-language acquisition.

Data described among Danish–English bilinguals aged over eighty in the US (Kjær and Bauman-Larsen 1974) as lacking any structural patterns or constraints appears to constitute similar 'marginal passages'. Such convergence and transference facilitating transversion in this 'unmarked code' (Myers-Scotton 1993b) – or default mode (see sections 3.4.8, 5.7) – may be limited to plurilingualism in related languages and speakers who are constantly in plurilingual situations.

Ho-Dac's (1996) data from first-generation Vietnamese–English bilinguals in Melbourne contains fairly dense transversion (often facilitated by Facilitation Principle 2, section 5.3.2) and demonstrates that the English component of such a code can be based on rather ungrammatical English, for example: (42) under section 5.3.2 and:

(71)   Thây khoảng năm sáu tháng nữa mới TOTALLY RECOVERY .. SO I
         THINK THAT'S WHY EVERYBODY'S SO SCARY
         'You need about five or six months to totally recover. That's why
         everybody's so scared' (MV 2f, generation 1b, from Ho-Dac)

The speakers we have referred to do not contrast this 'mixed code (or bilingual mode)' with a 'monolingual' one, the situation which we will discuss in the next section.

5.7   Modes

Our data was collected in interview-type conversations.[18] How informants view the mode which they intend to be in is identifiable through repair, filled and unfilled hesitation pauses, and flagging, e.g. 'I can't think of the Italian' or 'How do you say that in Dutch?' or 'I am talking English again' (cf. section 4.5.1). It is also confirmed in follow-up conversations with some of the informants after the interview in which the tape is played back to the speaker who then commented on the interview.

For the first generation this is generally an intended monolingual mode in which the other language is not completely deactivated, particularly since a completely monolingual mode is not feasible in talk about the Australian situation. Many of the informants switch mode during the interview. Many choose to 'adapt', i.e. integrate lexical transfers or use semantic transfers for at least part of the time. They speak what they consider to be language X as they use it in Australia. The recordings in former German enclaves are a special case – here most informants have not spoken German regularly for many years. They are using the variety of German that they recall speaking (including some stabilized transfers), but they do change the 'matrix language', in Myers-Scotton's terms, for asides because they are aware of the interlocutors' bilingualism (section 4.2) and need to adopt a bilingual mode to talk about modern concepts (e.g. new types of communication or transport) which appeared on the scene after the community's shift to English. A monolingual English mode is also used to address someone in the room who does not understand German. Most of the generation 1b and second-generation informants have only a bilingual mode available and select 'mixing', or 'adaptation', or use interclausal switching for 'separation'. About 60% of our postwar German–English bilingual sample are in a monolingual mode for most of the time. The other 40% include almost all the second and 1b generation but also some generation 1a. The bilingual mode is very prevalent among second-generation Croatian and generation 1b Vietnamese speakers. But where the first generation engages in a bilingual mode, as in the Dutch community,[19] the second generation may tend more than the parents to exercise the option of separating the modes insofar as their linguistic resources permit. While Waas's (1996, see section 1.3.2) findings indicating L2 transference in the German of German immigrants in Sydney are clearly influenced by use and availability, 'mode' probably plays a role in the variation patterns. Those who have retained German citizenship and are 'ethnically affiliated' may be choosing a more monolingual mode.

Hlavac (2000) is, to my knowledge, the only study which explicitly considers the effects of the relationship between the researcher-interviewer and participant on the speech. He found that the average number of switches per turn was least where the informant was known to the interviewer and highest if they had been referred through an ethnic organization or school. However, the latter category had the lowest number of words per turn. Those known or referred through a friend or relative tended to accommodate to the interviewer while those referred by an ethnic organization or school tended to diverge more. All this is likely to vary according to community, interviewer, informant and situation, but it demonstrates the importance of taking factors such as the above into account.

5.8   'Code-switching', turnover and language shift

There is sometimes an assumption (Thomason and Kaufman 1988; Johanson 1999) that 'code-switching' is part of the process of language shift or even promotes it. On the other hand, Rindler-Schjerve (1998) even argues that switching protects a language with minority status from shift as it continues to be used. Similarly, McConvell (1991), writing on endangered indigenous languages in Australia, describes three functions of 'code-switching':
(a) to mark relations between bilingual insiders and monolingual outsiders;
(b) to identify speakers, listeners or both within a social group; and
(c) to contrast world-views.

The retention of these functions helps preserve the threatened language. Myers-Scotton (1993a) also maintains that switching is not necessarily a precondition for LS, i.e. that LS does not necessarily constitute a turnover.

Backus (1996) considers scenarios where:
(a) turnover is a step towards LS; or
(b) where the shift is arrested, the old embedded language becoming the new dominant language, the outcome being a fossilized bilingual vernacular (e.g. Mous (1994) and Gurindji Children's Language and Tiwi (Dalton et al. 1995)).

The above discussion (section 4.6) would suggest that Backus's (1986: 398) doubts whether insertional switching is necessarily present after the 'alleged turnover' in LS are well-founded.

5.9 Concluding remarks and reassessment of models

In this chapter we have shown how the various levels of language, working together in the convergence of the systems, provide structural facilitators of transversion. The convergence will sometimes blur the boundaries of the 'Matrix' and 'Embedded' languages. Compromise forms arise from the combined effects of phonological and prosodic transference. Phonetic convergence increases the already existing potential for bilingual homophones which, in turn, facilitate transversion. The perception of correspondence between particular tones in one language and pitch-stress patterns in another further facilitates transversion. Morphological correspondences can lead to syntactic convergence which is a secondary facilitator of switching. Multiple transference (ADJ + N in NP and V + N in VP) is based on habitual-use patterns and as such provides parallels to the lexical facilitation of transversion (triggering). Certain commonalities in syntactic typology will also have a facilitative effect on collocations. More isolating languages lend themselves more to the formation of English EL islands than more inflected languages. Similarly, a recipient language requiring a high degree of morphological integration of lexical transfers and proper nouns does not lend itself to English EL islands and as much transversion facilitation as ones not requiring morphological integration.

The field of language contact studies is fortunate in having available to it versatile models which can be employed to test the specificity and universality of a range of phenomena.

The Matrix Language Frame Model is a very comprehensive framework which enables us to explain the contribution of the languages in contact to mixed constituents. However, it does not offer the possibility of explaining exactly what in one language is affecting what in the other language, something that is not within the intention of the model. Sometimes there are also some difficulties in differentiating between related and/or converging matrix and embedded languages (as in what Muysken terms 'congruent lexicalization').

Poplack's framework aims to show how languages in contact 'fit together'. In accordance with Poplack's position, our data requires a distinction between single-word transfers (or compound nouns) and larger unit transfers because of the possibility of grammatical integration of the former and particularly because such a distinction is essential to an understanding of the lexical facilitation of transversion. Our data also demonstrates the overall validity of the equivalence constraint providing that the syntactic acceptability allows for syntactic convergence. In the Australian corpora to which we are referring, the counterevidence against all constraints is stimulated by the transversion facilitation phenomena discussed in this chapter. The role of syntactic equivalence (including that arising from convergence) makes for a more positive interpretation of the equivalence constraint as facilitation. Neither the MLF nor Poplack's model nor any of the others mentioned in this chapter describe facilitation and indicate which was the facilitator and which was facilitated.

Muysken's trichotomy of 'insertion', 'alternation' and 'congruent lexicalization' goes a long way to account for longstanding contradictions and discrepancies in the literature, especially in relation to constraints. He relates the three categories to the entire body of research on language contact. In particular, the category of 'congruent lexicalization' enables Muysken to discuss issues of this chapter, convergence and transversion facilitation. Our data confirms Muysken's (2000: 231) own understanding of the categories not being completely watertight. The Australian data, especially Dutch–English, suggests that 'alternation' as well as 'congruent lexicalization' may be facilitated by the same processes. I would see 'insertion' as both facilitator and individual transfer.

None of these frameworks accommodates language contact phenomena under a single umbrella with subcategorizations for the aspects of language affected and affecting one another. The continuum of degrees and types of integration is also not inherent in any of the models, all of which tend to give a rather peripheral place to phonetic and prosodic aspects. Some of those issues discussed in this chapter and to be treated in the following ones are not dealt with through the above models because any model addresses issues of special importance to those devising it. It is hoped that the above analysis of convergence, transference and facilitation of transversion will contribute in some way to an understanding of the influence of typological variation on switching. In chapter 6, an attempt will be made to relate the questions discussed in this chapter to processing.

6 Dynamics of plurilingual processing

6.1 Introduction

Chapters 4 and 5 discussed how the resources of two or more languages are employed by plurilinguals and how these convergence, transference, integration (divergence) and transversion phenomena are facilitated by typological/ structural factors. This chapter considers what questions these findings pose for psycholinguistic processing models. As the present research is not informed by its own experimental studies, we will examine some existing models and studies for answers. An attempt is then made to develop an integrated model.

The issues need to be considered from two points of view – how can psycholinguistic models help us understand what is going on in plurilingual language processing, and what does language contact contribute to an understanding of speech processing? Psycholinguistic studies of language contact are concerned largely with access to and storage of the languages in contact as well as with the development of the two or more languages in contact. The key issues are:
1. What goes on in the mind when people use language?
2. How is thought turned into language?

Some speech processes can be observed more clearly in plurilinguals than in monolinguals because the former have more than one set of representational symbols. Model building in speech processing has taken much of its impetus from studies of errors. There are some correspondences between errors and the facilitation of transversion insofar as speakers are sometimes forced into saying something that they had not originally planned. However, there are also phenomena of choice and change to consider.

6.2 Demands on processing models

The following issues arise from the previous chapters and require consideration in the choice of an appropriate model for plurilingual speech:
1. How are the two or more languages of a plurilingual stored – together or separately? Or are different aspects (e.g. sounds, lexicon) of the languages stored together and others separately? Does this vary between two and more than two languages?

2. How are the two or more languages accessed? Does that change during 'attrition'?

3. Are the items belonging to each network tagged in some way so that they can be identified with the 'right' language? How then are the items that facilitate transversion tagged? If items are tagged according to language, how is the language changed midstream in the processing?

4. At what point does the speaker decide which way to juxtapose the languages? Does the way of juxtaposing change within a stretch of discourse? How does this relate to Grosjean's notion of 'modes' (see above section 3.4.8, section 5.7)?

5. At what stage do lexemes have to be processed for transversion to be facilitated?

6. How does syntactic convergence occur?

7. How does the right lexicon go with the right syntax? How does this relate to the facilitation of lexicosyntactic transference?

8. How does subordinate bilingualism work?

9. How do speakers process divergence to avoid transfers?

10. How does tonal facilitation work in terms of processing? How does this relate to syllables? How are tones stored and accessed, in particular in plurilinguals?

11. How do limitations on mental load affect some of the above issues?

6.3   Models and what they can tell us

There are currently two overall processing models available, Levelt's modular computational model and Dell's parallel distributed processes, or activation spread model. Neither model was devised with plurilinguals in mind but both of them have been adapted for this purpose. However, Levelt's has been utilized far more for plurilingual speech.

Several of the available processing models, including the two overall processing models, help us resolve some of the issues enumerated above. No one model contributes all the answers and there are a number of key phenomena described in this monograph which do not fit with current processing models.

6.3.1   Levelt

Levelt (1989) represents the culmination of much speech processing research since the 1960s and, seeing the speaker as a 'highly complex information processor' (1989:1), postulates three functions:

1. Conceptualizer – which generates messages, selecting information (macroplanning) and deciding on speech acts, on the marking of given and new information, and assigning topic and focus (microplanning);

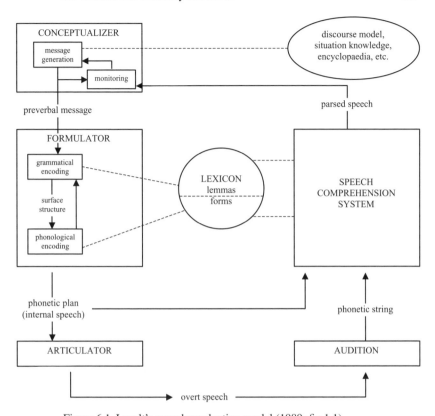

Figure 6.1 Levelt's speech production model (1989: fig 1.1)

2. Formulator – which encodes; and
3. Articulator – which executes phonetic planning through neuromuscular instruments.

   Each of the three components operates independently (although some feedback is possible in Levelt et al. 1999 – see below). Lemmas, which are stored in the mental lexicon and are processed at the formulation stage, contain the syntactic relations (and, in the 1989 version of the model, semantic information) of the lexical concept, while the lexeme comprises morphological and phonological information.

6.3.1.1 Adaptations and applications
De Bot (1992) adapts Levelt's model for bilingual language processing. The three functions are performed thus:
1. The complementizer performs universal macroplanning and language-specific microplanning (see above).

2. The formulator is language-specific, i.e. different procedures are applied to the grammatical and phonological encoding of each of the languages. It works with a single lexicon, with the languages stored together, and lemmas tagged according to language.[1] Lemmas carry syntactic information and gender information in the case of nouns, for instance, and separate lemmas are necessitated for a concept common to two or more languages since different information has to be accessed.

3. The articulator stores the possible sounds and prosodic patterns of all the languages of the speakers.

This processing model satisfies many of the needs which we have considered under section 6.2. In De Bot's adaptation:

i. The lexicon is stored together.

ii. Sounds and prosodic patterns of all languages are also stored together.

iii. Lemmas are selected neutrally on the basis of meaning but with some specifications for the terms of special reference. Syntactic information is contained in the lemmas while morphological and phonological information is retrieved during the formation of the surface structure.

Lemma selection and joint storage of sounds and prosodic patterns provide a means of explaining lexical transference, lexical and prosodic facilitation of transversion on the basis of common sounds and tones, phonological transference, phonological integration of lexical transference, and also phonetic/prosodic compromise forms. They do not provide us with answers concerning grammatical convergence and the relation between lexicon and syntax and between grammatical convergence and other language contact phenomena. In a paper subsequent to De Bot's adaptation of Levelt's model to bilingualism, De Bot and Schreuder (1993) propose that information on language choice is contained in the preverbal message as a language cue, raising activation levels of that language, though not enough to avoid transference. Also, De Bot and Schreuder (following Bierwisch and Schreuder 1992) add a verbalizer between conceptualizer and formulator to divide the message into lexicalizable chunks for lexical access. This chunking will vary according to language. Anticipational facilitation of transversion and English embedded islands comprising A D J + N or V + N offer evidence in favour of chunking.

Also in the spirit of the Levelt model is Myers-Scotton and Jake's (2000) abstract (sub-)model to explain 'how two languages come together in code-switching' (2001: 86). The processing model comprises:

a. Lexical-conceptual structure, the semantic and pragmatic mappings of intentions and choice of language provided by the conceptualizer.

b. Predicate-argument-structure, the formulator-driven mapping of thematic structure onto grammatical relations.

There is a progression from lexical selection via morphosyntactic procedures to morphosyntactic frames.

c. Morpheme realization patterns with the realization of lexemes called by lemmas; assignment of phonological structures and surface-positional information (e.g. word order, agreement) enabling content to be translated into a matrix language, perhaps with items embedded from another language. Myers-Scotton and Jake's (2001) 4M (sub-)model is discussed under section 3.4.1.

6.3.1.2   Challenges and revisions
There is potentially a problem linking facilitation of transversion to a model based as Levelt's (1989) was on three independent processing components, i.e. with no feedback between them. That is the question – how can transversion be facilitated by trigger-words if information about lexical items then needs to be available at the lemma, i.e. pre-phonological stage?

The facilitative effect of bilingual homophones (section 5.3.1.1) and perception of tonal overlap (section 5.3.2) on transversion, and the role of phonetics/phonology in convergence (section 5.3.1.1) would suggest some simultaneity between the phonetic plan and the conceptualization (including language choice) and formulation, requiring feedback from the 'later' to the 'earlier' stages of processing. Wheeldon and Levelt (1985), in their studies of internal speech monitoring, demonstrate that the representation underlying the monitoring response is phonological and syllabified. This would entail a considerable amount of bottom-up as well as top-down interaction even though this does not agree with the Levelt model in its original form. However, in the revised model (Levelt et al. 1999), there is provision for some two-way activation spread between the levels, in particular between lemmas and lexical concepts, but only within a specific language. This provision makes it possible for a lemma in language A selected through meaning to spread activation to a lemma in language B, or for a lemma in language A to spread activation to the concept in that language and from that to the concept in language B and finally to the lemma in language B. Thus there could be activation from the concept 'smallness' to English *small* to Dutch *smal* 'narrow'. However, there is no similar provision for feedback from a phonological code to a lemma to allow for the speaker to identify Dutch *smal* and English *small* and for the former to facilitate a transversion to English (example (14), section 5.3.1.1). But there may be perceptual feedback from one language to the other. Levelt et al. (1999) state the assumption that active phonological segments in the perceptual network affect the state of activation of the corresponding nodes in the production network. They also make the second assumption that a spoken distractor can affect corresponding nodes at the lemma level. The perceptual and productive systems are shared from the lemma level upwards. The way of dealing with 'triggering' according to the Levelt et al. model (pers. comm., W. J. M. Levelt, 8 January 2001) would be for phonological production in one language to act through an

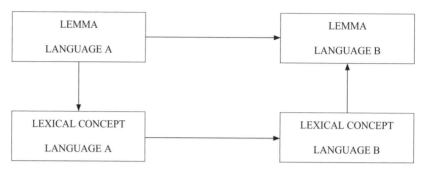

Figure 6.2 Adaptation of Levelt's model to feedback from one language to another

'internal loop' as perceptual stimulus for the production system of the other language. The internally perceived phonological word *tennis* in Croatian in example (12), in section 5.3.1, is self-perceived internally, and activates the English item *tennis*, and the whole system of which it is part. With only a slight modification of the second assumption, a self-perceived (pre-articulated) item can also activate the lemma in another language, with all its syntax, and from there, activation can spread to the level of lexical concepts in that language. The same applies to all the facilitation of transversion by lexical transfers, proper nouns and bilingual homophones, which are part of the speaker's two or more languages (networks).[2]

Tonal facilitation, however, challenges the Levelt model and De Bot's adaptation, in which lexeme forms are activated only as linguistically unique forms or bilingual ones tagged per language.

The Wheeldon and Levelt (1985) experiments also explain the phonological–prosodic compromise forms among the examples in section 4.2 which are compromise forms, composites between English and other-language syllables (where both languages are activated).

6.3.2   Dell et al. – parallel distributed processes

In Dell's (1986, 1995; Dell and Reich 1980) activation spread model, each level of encoding (syntactic, morphological, phonological) has a set of rules defining the possible combinations of units at that level. The rules generate frames with categorized slots (in a sentence such as *Die Studenten spielten* 'The students played': DET, N, V PAST; stem, affix; vowels, consonants). Retrieval begins with the node with the highest activation level; this decreases after selection (to prevent its being selected again) and spreads to the next node down. The advantages of interactive spreading activation models over modular ones for transversion facilitation and other language contact phenomena are that:

a. they allow for feedback between the levels, especially phonological feedback to lexical selection; and

b. they provide a basis for representing feedback from neighbouring items (target competitors) in the other language (cf. Martin et al. 1996 in their study of aphasic and normal monolinguals).

However, as has already been mentioned, Dell's model has been applied less to plurilinguals, while Levelt's models are used quite widely and offer a more comprehensive approach from concept to articulation. It may be possible to combine models since Dell's is intended as a computational representation of language processing.

Let us consider some adaptations and potential applications of Dell's model to bilingualism.

6.3.2.1 Adaptations and applications

Grosjean's (1988, 1995) Bilingual Model of Lexical Access based on McClelland and Elman's (1986) parallel distributed process (spread activation) TRACE model provides an alternative starting point to De Bot's (based on Levelt) for an understanding of switching. Grosjean (1995: 291) postulates two language networks, one for each language. In this model:

i. both languages are activated but one (the base language, comparable in many ways to Myers-Scotton's matrix language) more strongly than the other;

ii. two corresponding items (phonetic units or words) in the two languages may be activated because of their similarity;

iii. activation of the items increases the overall activation of that language network, and activation of words similar in the two languages will normally slow down the recognition of 'guest words' (phonologically unintegrated lexical transfers). But:

iv. the activation of words specific to one language increases the overall activation of a network, as occurs in 'triggering' (Grosjean 1988).

This model offers the opportunity to extend (ii) and (iii) above to accommodate facilitation through bilingual homophones, lexical transfers and perceived tonemic overlap to bring about overall activation of the 'other' language. The model has the potential for extension to cover more than two languages.

One linguist considering the application of the activation spread model to language contact is Riehl (1998, 1999, 2001: 278–80). She postulates how activation is spread from an item in one language to its neighbouring item from the other language in a network of semantic equivalents, and how in turn that can activate the entire system of which this item is part. The semantic component of a word activates the phonetic code, thereby activating more items from the 'other' language. However, it does not enable the phonetic item itself to be the trigger. This Riehl (1999) explains through monitoring. She refers to the internal monitor (pre-articulatory editing) where the speaker listens to their 'inner voice' (internally perceived phonological code) and the external monitor, where they listen to their output. Not only repair but also anticipational facilitation of transversion could then be regarded as the result of pre-articulatory editing, and consequential facilitation can follow a kind of post-articulatory editing. This has not been tested experimentally. Riehl cautiously comments that the framework is not yet able to deal with syntax. Our data (section 4.4.8.1, section 4.4.10) would suggest that the syntactic and lexical units are connected in their processing, and this could potentially be interpreted to confirm activation spread.

6.3.3   Paradis – storage hypotheses

The neurolinguist Paradis (1981) considers four alternative hypotheses concerning storage:

1. An extended system hypothesis, where phonemes and syntactic systems from L2 are incorporated into the L1 system. (This does not cover people with more than one L1.)
2. A dual system hypothesis.
3. A tripartite system hypothesis, where identical items in the language are represented by a single neural substrate and the others separately, each with their own neural representation.
4. The subset hypothesis, which assumes the use of a single storage system where the same-language elements are linked. The links are strengthened through habitual use. According to this model, speakers have one set of neural connections for each language and, in addition, one larger set from which elements from each language are available. This is a combination of hypotheses 1 and 2 and follows the approach of activation spreading models (see below, section 6.3.2).

The subset hypothesis has special appeal for the interpretation of our data from bi- and trilinguals. It is useful to address anticipational facilitation and EL collocations which are similar in that they promote syntagmatic unity after a transversion facilitation. The tripartite hypothesis would represent the facilitation of transversion in which some elements of the two or more languages will be more closely linked than others because of their similarity. It could also explain how some speakers repair to divergent forms to avoid risking 'unwanted transfer' (cf. section 4.2.2.2). Subsequently, Paradis (1987) formulated a storage hypothesis relating language distance to the question of joint or separate storage. This makes possible the use of the same procedural or lexical knowledge when speaking either (or any) of the languages, and also provides a basis for considering the conversion rules addressed in section 4.2.2.2.

The subset hypothesis is not incompatible with the tripartite system hypothesis and the combination would be the most useful neurolinguistic model to represent the phenomena on which I have been focusing.

6.3.4   Green – inhibition/mental load

Green (1986) postulates not only the languages as separate subsystems of a language system but also three activation levels of languages – selected (actually used at the point of time), active (but not selected) and dormant. In attrition, the dormant language cannot be activated sufficiently. A bilingual needs to ensure that the language chosen is activated more than competing languages. The other language(s) should be inhibited. Inhibition of items from the other active language(s) increases mental load. Items are tagged according to language. This model is developed further in Green (1998). The model, derived from a language task schema, inhibits potential competitors for production at the lemma level and selects according to language tags. Green postulates Supervisory Attentional Systems which help mediate conceptualization of messages. A binding-by-checking method to keep the right lexeme for the right concept is taken over from Levelt's model. However, Green suggests that items with the same meaning across languages may be activated as the lemmas are linked, but that this is sorted out through checking before articulation. Green's inhibition model thus informs divergence to avoid transfers and also conversion formulae (chapter 4).

Green (1986) also suggests that bilinguals produce two plans simultaneously, one for the selected language and the other for the (other) active one. This idea is taken over by De Bot (1992) but considered with some scepticism by Poulisse (1999) who raises the questions: how can two plans be produced simultaneously if one language is activated especially in the preverbal stage? If this is because the other language is activated from before, how can the languages be kept apart? Poulisse and Bongaerts (1994) object that simultaneous speech plans are not needed as it is individual items and not the subset that activates code-switching. Broersma (2000) considers the simultaneous speech plans unlikely as it is wasteful of energy. On the other hand, our data – such as that on convergence, transference and transversion discussed in chapters 4 and 5 – makes simultaneous speech plans very plausible. In this way, speakers can make use of both syntactic patterns simultaneously and easily transverse. Even multiple plans on the part of tri- and multilinguals are likely, considering the examples of trilingual convergence (section 4.2) and trilingual transversion (section 5.3.1, section 5.3.1.6). One of the plans may be based on a conversion process from the other.

Green (1998) argues that language contact phenomena in general can be attributed to inhibition caused by the mental load of competition between two languages with items tagged for language. This is crucial to facilitation of transversion as well as all types of convergence and transference.

Green has pointed out to me (pers. comm. 12 June 1998) that, from his model's point of view, mental load (i.e. other concurrent demands) and the relative availability of an item in another language as compared to the one currently used are decisive in the facilitative effects of trigger-words in transversion. Mental load limits the possibility of monitoring and inhibiting competing alternatives while relative availability affects the nature of the competition. Green's (1998) contention that relative availability affects the nature of the competition would also explain lexical transference.

6.4   Detailed plurilingual issues

The above discussion has shown that many of the issues raised in section 6.2 can be dealt with through the above models. There are, however, some matters arising from our data for which we need to go beyond the models and experimental evidence for further ideas.

6.4.1   Syntactic convergence

So far, we have no means of including syntactic convergence in a processing model. On the basis of data collected by Bach, Brown and Marslen-Wilson (1986), Vosse and Kempen (1989) discuss the cognitive architecture for syntactic aspects of sentence processing. They find that centre-embedded structure (as in German subordinate clauses with auxiliaries) is harder to process than centre-serial structure (Dutch equivalent, see section 3.6) and right-branching (English) is easiest. This confirms earlier studies and the recognition model proposed by Fodor, Garrett and Bever (1968: 453–4), where it is implied that SVO aids comprehension. This is the construction that both Dutch and German speakers converge to, and it is further aided and accelerated by the drift of Dutch and slowed down by two left-branching languages used by trilinguals (section 4.4.7). Håkansson (2001) and Naumann (1997) present evidence of processing difficulties in verb–subject languages. Thus, we are back in the arena of reducing mental load. This issue will be taken up again under section 6.4.3.

6.4.2   Tonal transversion facilitation

Chen, Chen and Dell (2002) have conducted experiments on word-form encoding of disyllabic words in Mandarin Chinese, using implicit priming on the first syllable, examining syllable and tone as hypothesized units. On the basis of their experiments, they were able to sketch a model of word-form encoding with the activation of a lexical unit or lemma. The results show that syllable-only produced priming whereas tone-only and syllable-onset do not. As each character/morpheme unit is activated, it receives a syllable and a tone. Syllables are stored units associated with lexical items but the syllable representation lacks tone. Chen and Dell conclude that:

a. syllable plus tone is a unit in word production;
b. syllable without tone can act as a separate planning unit at the phonological level but the encoding requires the tone to be completed;
c. tone probably functions like stress as constituting part of the Mandarin metrical frame.

This would suggest that:

a. tone is like lexically stored stress;
b. the syllable is likely to be a lexically stored unit in Mandarin, which here could act as a test case for tonal languages.

But the fact remains that Chinese and Vietnamese speakers go from the syllable to the stress and then decide that this is a point where they could be in either language. This applies especially to the Vietnamese–English data where there is so much transversion.

6.4.3   Mental load, selection and facilitation

We have already referred to Green's work on mental load (section 6.2.5). There is also the issue of chain effects. Embarrassment and stress surrounding transference causes perseveration. This is due to the high mental load imposed by the combination of monitoring stress, the competition between the languages, and the planning and articulation of the next stretch of speech (cf. Zipf 1948; Goldman-Eisler 1968). The outcome can be a chain of interlingual and intralingual speech errors surrounding transversion, for example:

(1)   Hier sehe ich ein'n großen   Baum . . . (Was für einen Baum?)
       Here see   I   a   big+ACC   tree   (What kind of a tree?)
       gum [gam] Euc [juːk] Eukalyþtus*tree* [ɔikalyptustɹiː]..AND IN THE
       BACKTREE I SEE SOME SIMILAR BUT MOSTLYS EVERGREENS
       (MGP 99m, generation 1b)

The psychological stress and embarrassment generated by the uncertainty of lexical choice seems to trigger not only transversion but also backtracking to the word *tree*, the 'source of the error'. It reappears in place of *ground* in *background*. All this increases mental load and detracts from the monitoring of performance errors, such as the allomorph *s* of *evergreens* anticipated in *mostlys*.

The next example shares some characteristics with this:

(2)   Das ist ungefähr   die RIGHT   rechte   Proposition [prɔpɔzi'tsioːn],
       that is approximately the right (Eng) right (Ger) proposition

       die   man hier hat   bevölkerungsmäßig zu den SHEEPS
       which one here has   population-wise   to the sheeps

       'That is the right proportion here of sheep to people that they have here' (MGP 188m)

In this example, there is no indication of stress or embarrassment. Here *right* (which is phonemically possible in both languages) and its inappropriate repair *recht* (semantic equivalent: *richtige*) leads to confusion resulting in a performance error *(Proposition* for *Proportion)*. This chain reaction may influence a morphological error *(sheeps)* due to increased mental load. The informant had used *Schafe* in the previous sentence.

Example (3) comes from a Dutch–German–English trilingual:

(3)   wie man sagt, MORE PAUSISCH   dan(n) de   Paus
       as one says more   popish   than the pope

       der   de   der   *Paus*
       the (Ger.) the (Dut.) the (Ger.) pope

       German: wie man sagt, päpstlicher als der Papst

The informant MTDE/G 2m, who is talking about linguistic purism, is trying to find the German equivalent of *roomser dan de Paus* 'more Roman than the Pope', finds an appropriate morphological equivalent rule (add [iʃ]) but adds it to Dutch *paus* 'pope' instead of German *Papst*, which actually forms an adjective with *lich*. However, he forms the comparative analytically with English *more* instead of synthetically (with the addition of *er)* as in Dutch and German, and there is fluctuation between the Dutch and German definite articles. Apparently he cannot decide if he has transversed or is still converting Dutch into German. Finally, *Paus* receives the German definite article *der*.

Goffman, in his paper, *Radio Talk* (1981: 204), drawing on the work of Simonini (1956), also contends that 'the production of faults can be progressive. The occurrence of one imperfection increases the chance of another, and that in turn increases the chance of consequent ones.' He also observes that, as errors can be traced both forward and backward, speakers premonitor what they formulate.

6.4.4   Access – conceptual and phonological

Under section 6.3.1.2, we considered the possible activation spread between the conceptual and the phonological through perceptual feedback for production. In her study of slips of the tongue in the L2 speech of Dutch second-language learners – which has far reaching implications for bilinguals – Poulisse (1999) argues that both L1 and L2 lemmas and L1 and L2 lexemes may be activated simultaneously and that phonologically related lexemes from different languages may spread activation to each other. This concurs with lexical facilitation of transversion as well as semantic transference. However, in Poulisse's study, L2 morphemes were used invariably when L1 lemmas were unintentionally activated.

Experiments conducted by Jescheniak and Schriefers (1997) and Peterson and Savoy (1998) confirm that near synonyms are phonologically encoded in a language, something that is challenged, however, by an experiment by Hermans, Bongaerts, De Bot and Schreuder (1998). Our data, suggesting feedback through self-perceived phonological representation, would support the notion of phonological encoding.

In Green's (1998) model, activation of a Language A lemma and its lexical concept activates a language-neutral representation which can in turn activate a lemma in Language B via its lexical concept. In the facilitation of transversion, many decisions are taken through direct connections within a lexical network.

The 'concept' has received a considerable airing from Pavlenko (1999/2000) and her respondents in *Bilingualism* 3 (1), 2000.

6.4.5   Broersma's critique

In a comprehensive critique of the triggering model (Facilitation Principle 1 under section 5.3.1), Broersma (2000) notes that the model does not fit into any contemporary processing model as the surface structure would have to be processed before the language choice. In the Levelt framework, the conceptualizer would have to know what was to be articulated at the conceptual stage. The lexemes would have to be known before the planning of lemma. These issues have been discussed above (see above, section 6.3.1 and also section 6.4.1 to section 6.4.4) and will be addressed in the model proposed below.

Broersma revises the triggering model so that it is the *conceptual* overlap that determines choice of language. This assumes that the degree of conceptual overlap between what she calls 'cognates' (bilingual homophones and proper nouns) is greater than between items of conceptual overlap in general. However, it is not necessarily the case. It is unlikely that *window* and its Dutch counterpart *raam*, for instance, have less conceptual overlap than, say, *huis* and *house*. She includes 'loanwords' in one of two analyses. The emphasis on conceptual overlap is problematic because it would give 'trigger-word' status to pairs/groups of items without phonetic correspondence. It would also render tonal facilitation impossible.

Broersma tests the original triggering model and her revision of it – based on Levelt's idea (section 6.3.1) that it is the basic clause that is the unit of processing. She wants to establish if (potential) trigger-words do facilitate code-switching by checking the incidence of (potential) trigger-words with and without code-switching and code-switching with and without (potential) trigger-words. While any lexical transfer could be regarded as a potential trigger-word the way it has been conceptualized in earlier publications and in section 5.3.1.1 (but see below, section 6.4.5.1), Broersma considers any 'cognate' (bilingual homophone) a potential trigger-word (pers. comm., 6 July 2001). The decision on cognates was made on the basis of standard pronunciation. She uses code-switching to include our lexical transference and Muysken's insertion (pers. comm., 6 July 2001). I would contend that no assumption can be made about bilingual homophones since this is dependent on the speaker's identification of their own realization of the Dutch and English items. Broersma (2000) found that consequential but not anticipational triggering occurs significantly in a small random sample from Boumans's (2000) Arabic–Dutch corpus and a sample of speakers from Hulsen's (2000) New Zealand Dutch–English data who 'code-switch'. However, Broersma (2000) found sufficient evidence of a flow-on effect of trigger-words beyond the basic clause in Dutch–English but not in Dutch–Arabic, probably due to the greater number of additional trigger-words between Dutch and English. In our data, it is not at all unusual for the trigger-word to be at the end of a basic clause and for it to facilitate transversion in the following basic clause and even the next sentence, for example:

(4)   Steh morgens um sechs Uhr auf, habe einen Kaffee mit Brot. . . nimm
         mein Brot . . Butter . . *put* es in die Tasche . . AND OFF I GO. I GET
         A TRAIN, SOMETIMES I RUN FOR TOO, IF I'M LATE.
         'Get up at six o'clock in the morning, have a coffee with bread . . . take
         my sandwiches . . butter . . put it in my bag. . .'
         (MGP 90m, describing his day's activities; see also example (1) above.)

Broersma's suggestion that there might be yet unknown processes involved, perhaps feedback between the 'speech plan' and the grammatical encoding level (i.e. presumably from the articulator to the formulator), is consistent with our position. The revision of the model has actually reinforced the need or the conditions for such a new model.

6.4.5.1   On the impossibility of generalizing specific potential trigger-words
It is probable that individuals have their own trigger-words and that not all potential trigger-words have facilitative effect. This is a plausible interpretation of the individuals' bilingual homophones and the probable explanation, in an experiment on the perception of transversion, of the presence or absence of trigger-words not being a significant factor in successful perception (Clyne 1972c). Fifty German–English balanced bilinguals were played thirty-two ten-word sentences with a transversion in the middle, presented in random order, read on tape by a bilingual. They were asked to repeat what they had heard. They were distracted by 25% compression (increasing the rate of production) and some music before their response. Correct recall correlated highly significantly with transversion at the clause boundary (irrespective of the presence of a trigger-word). As the informants had the meaning right but many could not

recall where the transversion came, there appears to have been language-neutral conceptual de- and recoding.

6.4.6   Grosjean – modes

In section 5.7, we discussed Grosjean's notion of monolingual, bilingual, etc. modes largely from a methodological and sociolinguistic point of view. Grosjean, however, is a psycholinguist and his model has important processing implications.

One of the problems with the 'monolingual' mode is the likelihood that the other language(s) will not be totally deactivated when one is activated, as Green (1998) shows and Grosjean (see also 2001: 1) himself points out. Input and output mechanisms and language knowledge and language processing may not be in the same mode. I would suggest that some speakers would be in the bi/trilingual or a monolingual mode in spontaneous speech regardless of the setting because of their personal disposition. The intermediate modes between the bilingual and either monolingual mode are probably the ones where facilitation is most likely to take place since this is where lexical transfers and potential trigger-words occur and cluster. Grosjean (1995) suggests that the same surface phenomena might have different explanations in the monolingual and bilingual modes and (Grosjean 2001) that the continuum of modes might make it possible to differentiate between intentional and unintentional transference. Dewaele (2001) shows that, among Dutch–French–English trilinguals, the degree of formality of the situation is an important factor in promoting the multilingual mode though there is substantial individual variation. The dichotomy could offer a link between sociolinguistic motivations of language contact phenomena, processing models and actual linguistic phenomena. It might help explain the unidirectionality of transference phenomena (cf. Myers-Scotton 1993b and subsequent publications) in some bilingual and multilingual situations and the bi- or tridirectionality in others. Hoffmann (2001: 12) draws our attention to the likelihood that trilinguals will rarely use all seven of the modes available to them.

Grosjean (1997) contends that, in the bilingual mode, involving in our corpus elderly bilinguals such as the speaker of text (64) in section 5.6, no claims can be made about language independence or interdependence or 'automatic interlingual influence'. I sense a difficulty in the perception perhaps arising from the dichotomy that the modes at the extreme are monolithic when they are variable and thus in pinning down the various modes as much as will be necessary for experimental purposes.

6.4.7   Use and attrition

This monograph has been a little cautious about the notion of language attrition. Our data (De Bot and Clyne 1989, 1994; see above, section 5.5) suggests that there is no *inevitable* attrition in normal (non-clinical) speakers. However, as has been shown in numerous examples in chapter 4, many of our bi- and trilinguals do grope for a word or expression, and attrition is one of the causes of lexical transference. This is confirmed by flagging of transfers. Long unfilled as well as filled pauses are a clear indication of uncertainty.

Contact phenomena in Dutch in Australia are attributed by Ammerlaan (1996) to changes in access to knowledge of Dutch and tip-of-the-tongue type errors on the one hand and changes in stored information due to practice involving different information (i.e. English), on the other hand. Ammerlaan argues that certain Dutch structures and words are probably not acquired and practised sufficiently before disuse to escape the influence of the predominant use of English on lexical processing. Ammerlaan makes the important point that it is not so much period of residence in Australia but rather the limited period of residence in the country of origin that correlates with attrition. This explains the incidence of lexical and syntactic phenomena in generation 1b and of course second- and third-generation bilinguals.

As De Bot (1998) expresses it, actual attrition (which he defines as 'language knowledge loss over time in individuals') is unusual. 'Attrition' in the literature is the result of inavailability, i.e. a weakening of links in the memory, and is mainly a question of recall speed and a decline in the effectiveness of access mechanisms, a deactivation of knowledge, not an inhibition or erasure of it (De Bot 2001). Decline in use also causes a deterioration of internal monitoring (De Bot 2001).

Among the bilinguals from former German enclaves in Australia, long periods of non-use of German might be expected to have caused attrition, and it is remarkable that most of the informants still speak German very fluently. However, particularly in such settlements, lexical transfers should not be identified with attrition. Certain transfers are likely to have been stabilized (e.g. *car, post-office, fence, paddock, railway-line*), having been part of the community's shared experience in Australia. Transfers employed by only some individuals also largely denote concepts that were not part of the community's experience through German (e.g. *bus, trams, caravan, diploma, sprinklers*).

I would like to complement our findings with those of two other studies – one in the US and one in Australia, both of which provide evidence for attrition related to reduced use over time. Kenny (1996) found that, for his Palestinian-Americans, unfilled pauses functioned as a direct result and filled pauses[3] as an indirect result of a 'malfunction' of the Ll speech mechanism, where resulting gaps were filled to keep the channel open. The informants increased the use of both unfilled and filled pauses in their Arabic speech after twenty-one years in the US. The less educated used fewer pauses after fourteen years in the US but the more educated (and presumably more language aware) increased the use of filled pauses after fourteen years.

Ammerlaan (1996) has studied the reactivation of skills in Dutch among those for whom it has become a 'dormant' language in Australia. He administered a battery of tests, including Cloze procedure, word naming, text editing and phonological and semantic cues. Summarizing the literature he concludes that the following variables affect encoding (Ammerlaan 1996: 11):
- The subject's motivation to remember the information.
- The time available for analysing the information.
- The interval between encoding and recovery.
- Subject's knowledge and analytic skills.
- The nature of the information and previous experience.
- Cross-linguistic similarity.

Phonological and morphological similarity proved a very important factor in Ammerlaan's dormant bilinguals who were trying to retrieve an item. On the other hand, words 'too similar' to English were sometimes rejected. This strategy is at the crux of divergence (section 4.2.2, section 4.5). In the phonologically similar items, the probability of a facilitatory effect was enhanced by the number of syllables being equal across the languages. However, items in the same lexical field were also frequently used as an aid. Morphological dissimilarity inhibited access and retrieval processes in Dutch, but phonological and morphological partial similarity proved more of a disruption than dissimilarity, especially in the single-stem items. Using data from second-language acquisition, De Bot and Stoessel (2000) confirm Ebbinghaus's (1885) assumption that words once learned are never really lost. They can be relearned much faster than newly learned. This applies to items learned either long ago or more recently. It has far-reaching implications such as the challenge of finding short-cuts for those reacquiring a language. There are different levels of activation, e.g. for active and passive knowledge. Ammerlaan, like Waas (1996), in her study of German–English bilinguals in Australia, recorded metalinguistic comments expressing hesitation and lack of confidence in grammatical and lexical choices.

In general, lexical and tonal facilitation would serve as evidence in favour of Green's model of simultaneous plans and Grosjean's notion of 'mode', determined at the start of the interaction but with the possibility of change.

6.4.8 Progress summary

Which issues then are resolved? Which are still waiting for answers? Our brief journey through current models complemented by experimental results shows that there is the basis of a framework of a processing model to address the facilitation, convergence and transference phonomena we have been discussing – covering storage, access, tagging, modes of combining or not combining the resources of several languages, syntactic convergence, divergence, mental load and tonal as well as lexical transversion. We shall return to this in section 6.6.

Those matters that require further consideration are feedback between the formulator and the articulator, the relation between lexicon and syntax, tones, and the differences between bi- and trilingual processing (cf. Hoffmann 2001).

6.5   Integrating the sociolinguistic into a processing model

Before proposing a processing model consistent with the findings of the previous chapters I would like to discuss the integration of socio- and psycholinguistic aspects into a single framework. This has been done by De Bot (2001; see section 6.4.7) when he shows the relation between use and attrition. A processing model which embraces a number of key sociolinguistic and social psychological dimensions is that of Walters (2001). His model includes two components which can be utilized at any point of the processing. They are *language choice*, arising from social and motivational factors, and *affective information* – motivation, wants and needs – linked to the speaker's multiple identity. These are to enable a bilingual model to deal with the changes that lead to language attrition. Linguistic phenomena can often be explained by societal patterns of language use and by identity changes. His proposal weights differentially the sources 'setting', 'interlocutors' and 'genre'. Walters also adds an *intentional/contextual* component at the beginning of the processing model which specifies the sociopragmatic information and illocutionary forces governing message selection. The lexicopragmatic concepts, modified by language contact, and its underlying factors, motivation, needs and social networks, rather than lemmas and lexical contexts, are what, according to Walters, underlie language attrition. Among the other features of Walters's model is an emphasis on the broad concepts of invitation, based on recognition and recall, and variation, derived from discrimination and classification. This model provides in embryonic form some further input for both the sociolinguistic and psycholinguistic aspects of the facilitation process (cf. figure 6.3).

6.6   Towards a model of plurilingual processing

In the following proposals, my indebtedness to such scholars as Levelt and his associates, Green, Myers-Scotton and Jake, Poulisse, De Bot, and Walters will be evident (see above). I take over from Levelt the three stages, of conceptualization, formulation and articulation. At the conceptualization stage comes the intention to express particular content and illocutionary force, including scripts and speech act fields. A language, usually in the form of a mode in Grosjean's sense, is chosen for the purpose. In practice the mode is based on a recognized language or variety or some not precisely defined combination of two or more languages or varieties. The choice is taken on the basis of context (e.g. setting, participants and genre), identity and other attitudinal issues. What is established at the start of the interaction is the default or unmarked mode for the interaction. Once a speaker has decided to speak in the ('monolingual mode' of a) particular language, this raises the activation threshold of one system, but does not totally inhibit the other(s) (see section 6.3.4).

Plurilinguals activate and deactivate their languages to varying degrees so that their position on the mode continuum may change during the interaction. So, within the discourse, due to group dynamics or the exigencies of the topic or some other reason, more divergent or convergent strategies may be implemented (see sections 4.2, 4.4, 4.5), the former through inhibition. Thus the mode used may include fewer lexical transfers or more, and/or the syntax may converge more or less towards that of another language (or other languages), or there may be separation of codes through transversion or adaptation of transferred items through integration strategies. This is done through self-monitoring, which, among other things, can also increase the potential for facilitation. Lexical transfers are the result of multiple or perhaps non-language tagging of lemmas. Not only does mental load limit the possibility of monitoring and inhibit competing alternatives (as Green has convincingly argued). Self-monitoring itself increases the mental load, as is illustrated in section 6.4.3.

The grammatical encoder (Levelt 1989; Levelt et al. 1999) contains procedures for accessing lemmas and constructing syntax. Lemmas, which are stored in the mental lexicon, contain syntactic information, and lemmas sharing such information may be related to each other. The lemmas are tagged for a particular language or double or triple tagged, e.g. the lemma for *shop(s)* in example (9), chapter 5, which facilitates transversion between Dutch and German, is probably triple tagged. The language tagging gives directions not only to the formulator to select and encode appropriate system morphemes but also to the articulator to select and encode sounds. Partial integration can be an indicator of double tagging. A lexical tag will activate particular syntax, although in some speakers the links will not be automatized so that there is considerable variation and overlap. Lexical and lexicosyntactic transference will result from double/multiple tagging. In the case of subordinate bilingual relations between closely related languages, the languages are not processed independently but conversion rules operate and they are gradually automatized.

Convergence or the relatedness of two or more languages can facilitate further transference or transversion, while a high degree of phonic/phonological integration tends to inhibit transversion. This may vary according to degree of awareness.

Each language constitutes a network. The networks are connected through items that are linked because such items (lexemes, tones) are (perceived to be) part of, or employed in, more than one language. Thus, using any item from a particular network is sufficient to activate the network (language) of which it is part or with which it is identified. There is also a secondary facilitation, where activation according to a similar procedure is further assisted by overlap in, and convergence of, grammatical structures that are the same. Transversion may be facilitated by anticipating a trigger-item or in consequence of one. (Perceived) overlaps in the lexicon and also in the prosody and syntax of the languages function as gateways to another network. In the Vietnamese and Chinese examples (see section 5.3.2), the syllable is the entity through which the overlap is perceived and the transversion occurs.

After the initial transversion, the speaker will either continue to engage in transversion (and thus separation of the codes), revert to the default mode or adapt more lexical transfers. The choice will be determined by intended meaning, context and/or identity. This choice can be adjusted throughout the processing. Both discourse factors, such as the comprehension and the interaction patterns of the interlocutor(s), and facilitation of transversion will modify the choice of code during the interaction. The affective component is also instrumental throughout the processing. Attitudes (e.g. 'I want to keep my languages apart', 'I need to use material from the other language but want to conceal this', 'I don't need to keep my languages apart') are not always very conscious but underlie the language modes which can be defined by 'separation', 'adaptation' and 'mixing' respectively as non-technical terms (see section 3.4.8, section 5.7), and what is activated and deactivated at various stages of the interaction. Some of the attitudinal decisions are shaped by the speaker's identity as, say, a Vietnamese-Australian rather than an overseas (or exile) Vietnamese. The 'separation' mode will be prominent where conversion formulae are being applied to a common set of grammatical and/or lexical rules between two or more languages and divergence is an important objective.

While transference is the result of selecting a lemma with a different language tag, transversion is facilitated later in the formulation with perceptual feedback from the internal loop – the phonological representation perceived and constructed by the speaker (Levelt et al. 1999), i.e. pre-articulatory (cf. Krashen 1982) as well as post-articulatory editing – since the feedback concerns the lexicon. This feedback tells the formulator that the facilitating item can be part of more than one language system. Feedback is made possible by the fact that active plurilinguals make plans in each of their languages. Also, frequent collocation (e.g. English NP < proper noun or common lexical item + English VP) promotes automatization. The proposed model can be modified to allow for the phonological production in one language to act as a stimulus for the production system in the other language, for instance for Dutch *smal* to provide the stimulus for English *for us* in example (14), section 5.3.1.1, referred to in section 6.3.1.2. The self-perceived item which belongs to more than one of the speaker's active languages can then perceptually activate other items from the language not currently being used, and the activation can

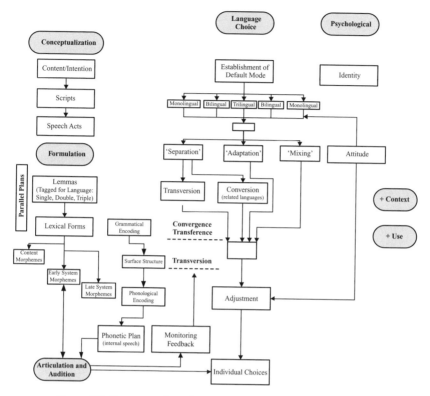

Figure 6.3 Representation of transversion in a processing model

spread up to the level of lexical concepts in the other language. This does not, however, apply to the tonal facilitation described for Vietnamese and Mandarin which I believe can be explained as syllabic feedback from the internal loop.

The collocation examples (e.g. *io parlo wog language*, example (56), section 5.4) as well as those indicating anticipational facilitation (such as *im Norden OF* Victoria, where *of* anticipates *Victoria*; example (71), section 4.4.8), show how people plan their speech ahead. They also provide evidence of chunking. The chunking is impregnated on the memory through frequent use, and sometimes also through identification with the situation in which the collocation was used. The anticipation of the head noun, in particular, facilitates transversion, making anticipational facilitation different in character from consequential facilitation. The 4M model developed by Myers-Scotton and Jake (2000, see section 3.4.1) enables us to establish a hierarchy of morphemes alongside the transference–transversion hierarchy mentioned above.

6.7   Concluding remarks

Convergence and facilitation pose a challenge to existing processing models and at the same time demonstrate the validity of aspects of some of them. They also necessitate revisions and extensions to some. Facilitation of transversion has identified the importance of feedback from the articulation to the formulation (and conceptualization) levels. Convergence at all levels demonstrates that storage and access of the two or more languages of a plurilingual cannot be separate. But both convergence and transversion have also shown the importance of the phonetic and prosodic levels in processing as a whole and their relation to the conceptual. Some of the phenomena described for plurilinguals as transversion may turn up as speech errors or style variation in monolingual processing.

A subset framework of the kind proposed by Paradis (1987), combined with his tripartite hypothesis, allowing for identical items to be linked, offers a useful neurolinguistic representation. Subordinate bilingualism in closely related languages and conversion formulae constitute a departure from the general principle that the language is chosen at the beginning of the interaction. However, not only psycholinguistic but also sociolinguistic factors determining the amount of monitoring may require a change in the default language or default 'mode' (in Grosjean's 1998, 2001 sense). While transference is the result of unclear or multiple language tagging of lemmas, transversion is further down the processing schema (see figure 6.3) because it is often the product of transference and/or convergence.

Facilitation at the lexical and prosodic levels and, in a secondary way, through syntax, provides evidence that the less active language is not completely deactivated, and perhaps also of Green's theory that plans are made simultaneously in more than one language. Facilitation entails an extension of the 1999 Levelt et al. model (which still has three components but allows for spread activation). Perceptual feedback of phonological coding makes it possible to identify particular items by phonetic and prosodic (as well as morphemic and conceptual) overlap to act as perceptual stimulus for the production of another language in transversion. Frequent occurrence of a collocation across languages makes it more likely to be used, even where one of the items is tagged (also) in another language.

This chapter has attempted to draw on our data to discuss the usefulness of various processing models or partial frameworks to interpret them. What is needed now is far more experimentation, especially on trilingual transversion and convergence.

7   Dynamics of cultural values in contact discourse

7.1   Introduction

This chapter is intended to be exploratory. Up to now, the emphasis in this monograph has been on language itself, although the role of identity and ethnicity has arisen several times, especially in chapter 2. The present chapter will focus on those aspects of language contact which most closely reflect cultural values, identity change and multiple identity, again comparing the corpora of different community languages, vintages and generations.

Particular ways of addressing people in relation to culture-specific norms of politeness may be transferred from one language to another or they may be avoided by transversion, as will be illustrated from Vietnamese. The introduction or dropping of a whole set of discourse markers constitutes a move away from communicative behaviour according to the norms of the community language. The use of some examples of modal particles will be examined in our German, Dutch and Hungarian data, making comparisons where applicable across generations and vintages and between bi- and trilinguals. Then the same will be done for some discourse markers transferred from English, which may be transversion facilitating phenomena.[1]

It is not always possible in this field to differentiate 'language' from 'culture' as a source of communicative behaviour, hence we will make use of Agar's (1994) notion of 'languaculture'.

7.2   Pragmatic transference and code-switching to express pragmatic contrasts

In this section, address illustrates how pragmatic transference can lead to interlingual convergence and code-switching can reflect dual identity, the latter being supported by diminutive use.

7.2.1   A note on politeness

Brown and Levinson's (1987) distinction between *positive* and *negative politeness* is a very important one for intercultural communication. The former is based on frankness and sincerity and the development of solidarity; the latter on restraint, modesty and respect to avoid conflicts and imposing on others. This is related to another dichotomy, *positive face*, being affirmed and encouraged, as opposed to *negative face*, being not subjected to restriction or compulsion. While all cultures generally make use of both types of politeness, one or the other may be more central to particular cultures (e.g. positive in German,[2] negative in English and especially Vietnamese), and different types of politeness may be emphasized in similar situations by different cultures. For example, *Könntest du mir einen Tee bringen?* 'Could you bring me a (cup of) tea?' based on English is more negatively polite than what would be more usual in Germany, *Bringst du mir einen Tee?* 'Are you bringing me a (cup of) tea?'

Even language shift can sometimes result from negative politeness – conflict avoidance through restraint (among other things) – in this case not speaking the community language to children in front of monolingual English speakers (including a monolingual parent), thereby limiting input in the language and sometimes creating an impression of inferiority of the language.

7.2.2   Diminutives

Wierzbicka (1985: 192) observes that code-switching patterns in Polish–English families are employed to contrast more strongly affectionate Polish attitudes to children and less emotional Anglo-Australian ones depending on the context. This is done by the use of diminutives of names (e.g. Marysieńko, cf. Mary; Klarusieńko, cf. Claire) as well as many common nouns and adjectives in parent–child discourse of parental relationship.

First generation Dutch–English and Greek–English bilinguals use diminutives, also normal in homeland varieties, as a device for integrating lexical transfers from English (section 4.5.1). They also express smallness (e.g. Dutch *fensje* 'little fence', *flokje* 'little flock', *postboxje* 'little letter-box') and an informality of discourse. They thus have both a pragmatic/cultural and a grammatical function in the preservation of the original language.

7.2.3   Address

7.2.3.1   European languages
Most European languages differentiate between a pronoun for general use (such as French *vous*, Italian *Lei*, Croatian *vy*, German *Sie* and traditionally Dutch *U*) and a pronoun of solidarity for special relationships, whether family, work, intimate or other (cf. Brown and Gilman 1960). Various contact studies in Australia covering Dutch, German, Greek and Italian in contact with English (Bettoni 1981a; Clyne 1967, 1977a; Tamis 1986) have found that second-generation Australians have a tendency to (over)generalize the

solidarity pronoun of address originally intended to denote special relationships. Hlavac (2000) recorded instances of indiscriminate alternation between *ti* and *vi* in his second-generation Croatian-Australian corpus, where the addressee remains constant, for example:

(1) a ako *ti* iđešu školu ma drugu stranu,
but if you go+3sg+INF school.to on other side

vi æete vidit da tu
you see+INF+COMP that here

'but if you go to a school on the other side, you will see that there'
(MCr 59m)

This is because community languages in an immigrant setting are usually employed within a network of family and close friends in which the pronouns Dutch *jij/jullie*, German *du/ihr*, Croatian *ti/vi*, Greek *esu/eseis* and Italian *tu/voi* would be used (or would have been used at the time). This is the context in which the languages were acquired by the second generation. Any subsequent learning of the languages in a school environment would be regarded, by most of the second generation, as artificial and is unlikely to affect the address system in local communication situations (Clyne, Fernandez, Chen and Summo-O'Connell 1997). Also, the rights and obligations set (Myers-Scotton 1993b, see above, section 2.3) pertaining to the L1 environment does not apply in Australia, thus the specialness of a friendship relationship is eroded. This is reflected in the extension of first names use, which is anecdotally far more common socially in ethnic circles in Australia than in the country of origin.

This development is confirmed in our corpus where some children and young people employ German *du* or Dutch *jij* to address a stranger older than themselves. The unmarked use of the original 'pronoun of solidarity' is extended on the basis of the unmarked use of first names in Australian English. In English-speaking countries, solidarity is based on an emphasis on secondary networks rather than on primary networks (Smolicz 1979) as in continental European countries. This change of emphasis is reflected in the use of *friend* and its community language equivalents to include acquaintance (Ger. *Freund*, Dut. *vriend*, Fr. *ami*, It. *amico*, Gk. *philos*) as well as in the widespread use of solidarity pronouns and first names.

The absence of a duality of pronouns of address in English is in itself a contributing factor. In recent years, however, changes have taken place in Europe itself. European Dutch especially has greatly extended the use of *jij*, and German speakers are employing the pronoun of solidarity and first names more rapidly and frequently than before (Clyne 1995: 131–7). However, our data was collected before these changes or from people who migrated before that time.

7.2.3.2 Vietnamese

Asian cultures and societies have a more complex and elaborate system of identifying relationships and hierarchies than western cultures and societies, relationships which need to be reflected in the address system. The modifications in Vietnamese discourse made to cope with a loosening of the social norms in Australia have been studied in Ho-Dac's (1996, 2001) research on Vietnamese–English bilinguals in Melbourne. In English, personal pronouns constitute a reference system. In Vietnamese, there is a set of lexical alternatives, including common nouns, proper nouns and personal pronouns which all represent kinship and social status. They are used for addressor, addressee and third-party reference. It is often unclear which is the appropriate term to denote the correct degree of solidarity. This is determined by the speaker's awareness of Confucianist name rectification doctrine. According to this doctrine, role terms such as *king, father* and *child* must be used in relation to the social role of interlocutors and people must behave in keeping with this (Ho-Dac 1996: 205, 211). Some pronouns such as *tao* 'I' and *mày* 'you', on the other hand, may be used to express hostility or reinforce solidarity. So to avoid communication breakdown or conflict, English pronouns are often preferred, for example:

(2)   Phỏng vấn tôi à   mà YOU muốn ME TALK ABOUT WHAT?
        interview   me PRT but you   want   me talk about what?
        'You want to interview me but what do you want me to talk about?'
        (MV 65m from Ho-Dac)

Here the possible negative connotations of *tôi* 'I' are cancelled out by the use of *you*.

In the following example, a young woman is unable to persuade her friend to lend her a book which they both need. She uses *me* to withdraw from the solidarity relation which would have been expressed in this context by *tao . . . mày*:

(3)   Cô   khó   quá thôi   khải để   ME GET IT FROM LIBRARY
        miss difficult very don't worry let me get it from library

        vậy
        FINAL+PRT

        'How difficult you are, don't worry, let me get it from the library then' (MV 66f, Ho-Dac)

On the other hand, in the following example:

(4)   YOU ALWAYS bận   a,   ME nói em   H TAKE ME THEN
        you always   busy PRT me ask younger.sibling H take me then
        'You're always busy I'll ask H to take me then' (MV 73f)

the respect and solidarity associated with *anh* 'elder brother' in Vietnamese culture, which the interlocutor was using for himself, is negated by the English transfer *you* once the brother said that he was busy that night (and therefore unable to take the mother). Thus, the code-switching can be explained by the need to negotiate the status of third parties – but an alternative interpretation could be that the speaker was unclear as to the rules. Both interpretations are possible in the following example in which the informant's father is quizzing him about an accident in which he hit another car and about the driver of the other car:

(5)   Ông ta   già chửa
        He   old   yet
        'is he old?'
        Chả HE'S ABOUT YOUR AGE DAD ổng hải bằng lái
        he he's about your age dad   he   even asked for

        con   nữa
        child's licence

        'He's about your age Dad; he even told me to show my driving licence' (MV 40m Ho Dac)

Ho-Dac points to the *chả* as an indication that the speaker does not know how to refer to the man due to the complicated address system in Vietnamese; it is thus a form of 'exploratory code-switching' (Myers-Scotton 1993b) where the parties disagree about the unmarked rights and obligations set which has normative status in the community.

7.3   Modal particles in German, Dutch and Hungarian[3]

Modal particles (MPs)[4] are uninflected words which indicate the speaker's attitude to the proposition in relation to an expectation of the interlocutor's attitude (Weydt 1969: 68; Kiefer 1988; Foolen 1993). They are common in conversation and usually integrated into a sentence without a pause, e.g:

(6)   Das schadet   *doch* nicht, wenn es deutsch ist?
        that damage+3sg MP not   when it German is
        'It doesn't hurt if it's in German, does it?' (MGWD 25f)
(7)   Es geht *ja* ganz gut aber *doch* war   nicht,
        it goes MP very well but   MP   was (it) not

        was ich wollte
        what I   want+3sg+PAST.PT

        'It works well and yet it wasn't what I wanted' (MGW 128m)

Our corpora, being based largely on interviews, are not ideal sources of MPs. Also, a full study of MPs in contact situations would necessitate a detailed analysis of the context in which they are used. However, the following comparative remarks are intended to raise some issues that are worth addressing in future research.

7.3.1   German

German MPs such as *doch, ja, wohl* and *eben*, are employed (also in non-contact situations) principally to achieve a consensus with the interlocutor by means of facts known to them (Lütten 1979) usually by appealing for agreement (Durrell 1996). In this respect they are a means of interaction management (Franck 1979) and contribute to and reflect power relations between the interlocutors. In checking for agreement, *ja* presupposes and reinforces clear evidence for the statement (König, Stark and Requardt 1990: 145; Hinrichs 1979; Durrell 1992). *Wohl* is based on a less clear presupposition, while *doch* implies less certainty or some kind of contradiction. *Eben* downtones the proposition. *Mal* may be used to downtone a potential threatening effect, in the interests of politeness, and tends to modify and reduce the action in the verb. *Denn* expresses a distancing from the interlocutor's position; it may send a downtoned signal of non-approval. Some examples:

(8)   Ich bin *ja* schon sehr lange hier?
        'I've been here a very long time, you know?' (MGPR 25f)
(9)   Ob das *eben* ist, weil ich *eben* so selten probiert habe
        'If that is just because I simply haven't tried' (MGPR 12m)
(10)   'Räumt noch wieder *mal* ein bißchen auf'
        'Have another go at doing a bit of cleaning' (MGPR 56f)
(11)   Findest du das *denn* schön?
        'You don't find that beautiful, do you?' (Astonishment)

Also confirms 'something as the logical conclusion from what has just been said' (Durrell 1996: 177) and thus sounds learned, for example:

(12)   Drei kleine Kinder, *also* die müssen Milch haben
        'Three little children, well, they have to have milk' (MGW 9f)

7.3.2   Dutch

On the whole, the Dutch system of MPs operates in a similar way to the German one. However, the most widely used MP in our corpus, *wel*, has only a weak consensus constituting function. *Wel* is an evidential (see Aikhenvald forthcoming) which expresses a positive emphasis (albeit a tentative one when combined with certain modal verbs such as *kan* 'can' and *zal* 'will'). It can denote an adversative meaning in contrast to *niet* 'not', or the affirming, evidential function. *Wel* shares some functions with German *ja* and *wohl*, but there is no exact equivalent as Dutch *wel* expresses a simple positive emphasis most of the time, for example:

(13)　　Dit is *wel* een paar jaar geleden, dat zie ik aan de autos
　　　　'This would be a few years ago – I can see that from the cars' (MD
　　　　130m 1b)

(14)　　(Explaining that he does not know many people in his district)
　　　　In Monbulk zijn er *wel*[5] veel Hollanders, maar (A) geen echte
　　　　kennissen
　　　　'In Monbulk there are certainly a lot of Dutch people but no real
　　　　acquaintances' (MD 9m 1b)

Toch[6] and *even* may have consensus imposing function, but not as strongly as their German equivalents *doch* (contrary to expectations) and *eben/mal*, in German. *Maar* can have downtoning as well as adversative and durative function (cf. Foolen 1993). Often it is combined with *alleen* and corresponds to English 'only'. *Even* generally expresses something momentary or insignificant, expressible as *This is not a big deal*, for example:

(15)　　*Even*　mijn　bril　　　　opdoen
　　　　just　 my　 spectacles　put.on+INF
　　　　'I'll just put on my glasses' (MD 17f)

A unique Dutch modal particle is *hoor* (from *horen* 'to hear'). It usually accompanies a brief statement of advice or information (mind you/you know), for example:

(16)　　Maar dan　zal　　　　　het *toch* geloof　ik　ook　niet　perfect
　　　　but　then　will+AUX　　　MP　believe　I　　also　not　perfect
　　　　Hollands　zijn,　　　*hoor*
　　　　Dutch　　be+INF　hoor (MP)
　　　　'But then it won't be perfect Dutch I don't think, you know' (MD 25f)

(17)　　Zeg maar een kleine driehonderd beleidende leden
　　　　'Let us just say: hardly three hundred committed members' (MD 77m)

All in all, power relations are not expressed as much in the use of Dutch MPs as in that of their German equivalents, as the former do not have such a strong consensus-imposing function.

7.3.3   Hungarian

MPs such as *csak* and *ugye* have a strong consensus-imposing function (Kiefer 1988), for example:

(18)   Jancsi *csak* felkel dél elött?
        'Surely Johnny will get up before noon?' (Kiefer 1988: 109)
(19)   Voltam   *ugye* Cairns környékén
        was+1sg MP   Cairns in.the.region.of
        'I was near Cairns you know' (MTG/HE 1f)

According to Kiefer (1988), *ugye* presupposes some doubt as to the validity of the proposition whereas *csak* implies that the speaker initially believed in the proposition but now doubts it. *Hát, szóval* and *tehát* all partly correspond to German *also. Szóval* implies direct evidence of its truth, *hát* that there was initial evidence to the contrary which now doesn't apply, *tehát* requires the interlocutor's agreement. *Is* (cf. German *denn*) expresses an original presupposition which there is now reason to doubt (Kiefer 1988). *De hát* has an adversative function.

(20)   *Hát* erre sincs nagyon sok   alkamam
        MP for this not   much/many opportunity+1sg+POSS
        'Well I don't have much opportunity' (H/GE 3m)
(21)   *Szóval* Sydney be   megyek
        so   Sydney ILLATIVE go+1sg+PRES
        'So I go to Sydney' (H/GE 1f)
(22)   hogy *is*   mondjam?
        how ever should.say+1sg
        'How ever should I put it?'

7.4   Modal particle use among plurilinguals

7.4.1   German

Our plurilingual data does not indicate deviation from the described MP use but there is considerable variation in MP incidence. For instance, *also* appears to be a habitual 'mannerism' in the speech of some people, and most of the instances are from a small number of informants, usually the most educated. The highest incidence (78, 71 and 62 respectively) is from three Hungarian–German–English trilinguals. This may be attributable to the existence of Hungarian MPs with similar logical functions to *also* and the fact that all three had attended school or university in a German-speaking country. The preference of certain speakers for particular MPs also extends to the use of *doch, ja* and *eben*. In the Western

Table 7.1 *Comparison of German modal particle use across corpora*

	Prewar	Western District	Wimmera	German of HGE	German of DGE
N	(50)	(27)	(33)	(36)	(36)
also	79	10	29	396	211
doch	29	29	22	25	15
ja	8	48	25	29	77
eben	7	4	5	27	10
denn	0	3	18	7	5
wohl	4	44	18	1	11
mal	7	47	12	16	24

District this is usually related to earlier intensive contact with a grandparent or more recent contact with immigrants.

The comparison between German corpora in table 7.1 shows the pattern for the most widely used MPs in our data. The table indicates a considerable level of maintenance of *ja*, *mal* and *wohl* in the Western District settlements, some presence of *ja*, *doch* and *wohl* in the Wimmera and of *ja*, *doch*, *mal* and *eben* among Hungarian–German–English trilinguals. One could speculate if the relatively lower use of MPs by the prewar German-speaking refugees might be due to pressure (and, in some cases, a desire) to behave in a 'less German' way. The Western District settlements, having been more homogeneously German than the Wimmera ones, would encourage more German communicative behaviour, and this is borne out by the occurrences of the generally common MPs. It should be noted that MPs occur especially in older women who had finished school before 1914, and those who had had some contact with recent immigrants.

7.4.2 Dutch

Wel is by far the most commonly used MP in all the generations and among both bi- and trilinguals. The adversative meaning accounts for eight of our generation 1b and second-generation examples and thirty-seven of those from the generation 1a sample (about the same number of speakers). It is to the affirming function that most of our examples belong.

A comparison of generation 1a (representative sample), 1b and second-generation data for the five most widely used MPs in our Dutch corpora (see table 7.2) indicates a gradual decrease in the use of MPs, especially *wel*. For *wel*, there is a one-third drop between generation 1a and 1b and a comparable decrease between generation 1b and the second generation. For *maar*, the big decrease in use occurs between the first and second generations. In the case of *toch*, *hoor* and *even*, there is a dramatic decrease in usage between those who arrived in Australia after junior secondary school and those who came before

Table 7.2 *Comparison of Dutch modal particle use between generations and between bi- and trilinguals*

	1a	1b	2	trilinguals
N	(60)	(30)	(29)	(36)
wel	334	100	37	305
toch	54	4	1	38
hoor	39	3	2	3
even	22	2	1	33
maar	30	28	12	95

that time, whose communicative behaviour is more predominantly Australian, and a further drop between them and the Australian-born.

The bilinguals use *even* and *toch* mainly in a non-consensus-imposing function (momentary and contradictory, respectively). Among the trilinguals, *toch* and *even*, which have equivalents in German, and *wel*, which does not, are also used relatively widely. *Maar*, predominantly in the sense of 'only', is the second most common MP among trilinguals.

Hoor is used almost exclusively by generation 1a, and hardly by trilinguals, presumably influenced by the absence of an equivalent in German.

7.4.3   Hungarian

The three MPs corresponding to German *also*, *hát*, *szovál* and *tehát* occur most in our data (total 511 times), more than consensus-constituting particles *is*, *de hát*, *ugye* and *csak* (172 times). Some speakers used one or the other logical MP very frequently – one Hungarian–German–English trilingual employing *hát* thirty-three times, another *szóval* twenty-four times (see table 7.3).

7.4.4   Comparison between the languages

Tables 7.1 and 7.2 give some indication that first-generation Dutch speakers and Dutch–German–English trilinguals are more likely to maintain the use of Dutch MPs than German–English bilinguals, and that Hungarian–German–English trilinguals tend to maintain their use of German ones. Deficiencies in the archivization of the data from our postwar German-speaking immigrants prevent their inclusion in this comparison. The largescale use of *wel* in Dutch contrasts with the far more limited use of MPs in the German corpora.

I would argue that: (a) Dutch MPs are less in conflict with Australian English cultural values in that the ones used most by our informants, especially *wel*, either do not express consensus-imposing functions or do not express them as

Table 7.3 *Hungarian modal*
particle use among trilinguals

hát	284
szóval	122
tehát	105
is	55
ugye	46
dehát	38
csak	33

strongly as the German equivalent; and (b) that the minority who do maintain Dutch are not averse to behaving in a Dutch way, especially in that the MPs express their position without affecting that of the interlocutor. The Hungarian MPs used tend also not to be consensus imposing.

7.4.4.1 Dutch and German of trilinguals
The most frequently used MP is Dutch *wel* (305 instances), followed by German *also* (211) distributed over far fewer speakers than *wel*. Dutch *toch* (42) is more prevalent than German *doch* (15) and Dutch *even* (33) than German *mal* (24). After *wel*, the most common MP is German *ja* (77), with *mal* (24) and *wohl* (11) far behind. Generally these tendencies bear no relation to the speaker's L1. It may be the non-consensus-imposing function that makes *wel* so retentive.

7.4.4.2 German and Hungarian of trilinguals
Also and its Hungarian equivalents are the MPs used most by the trilinguals, though this is due to their frequent use by certain individuals. However, only one of the three most prolific users of *also* are among the main users of the Hungarian equivalents. Similarly, the speaker who employed German MP *ja* most does not record instances of a German equivalent. Nevertheless the similar functions across languages will, I believe, reinforce their use by some speakers.

7.5   English discourse markers and their transference

7.5.1 Discourse markers

The English discourse markers (DMs) occurring in our bilingual data are co-hesive devices giving the speaker's attitude (Schiffrin 1987) or signalling intra-textual relations (Jucker and Ziv 1998). Like the MPs, they do not contribute to the propositional content of utterances in which they occur (Jucker and Ziv 1998).

Schiffrin (1987: 103) defines *well* as a response marker, often to a yes–no question, indicating that 'an upcoming contribution is not fully consonant with prior coherence options'. Schourup (1985: 16) gives its principal function as showing 'unexpressed thinking at a particular moment of utterance without displaying the thinking in detail'. *You know* has more of a consensus-constituting function, establishing that the speaker is aware of knowledge shared with the hearer (Schiffrin 1987: 102), of implications of the statement, but often in the sense that this saves giving details. *Anyway* and *anyhow* indicate a change of topic or dismissing the relevance of what has been said (Takahara 1998) and *sorry* of erasing what has been said. The literature has identified several functions of *like*, such as hedging, quotative and assuming commonality of knowledge (Romaine and Lange 1991; Tagliamonte and Hudson 1999; Holmes 1992; Macaulay 2001; Winter 2002). It signals 'loose interpretations of the speaker's beliefs' (Jucker and Ziv 1998: 155). *Sort of*, expressing approximation, is also a hedging device.

7.5.2   Transference into the community languages

The trilinguals provide the best comparable data for English as there were clear consistent topics in English within the conversation. The Dutch–German–English have espoused English DMs more than the Hungarian–German–English trilinguals. *You know* and *well* are by far the most prevalent in the Dutch–German–English, and *well* in the Hungarian–German–English trilinguals. Speakers who employ the most DMs in their English are the ones likely to transfer them into their other language(s).

The principal function of transferred DMs is hedging but it is generally consistent with those described in section 7.4.1.

Anyway is an eraser or downplayer, for example:

(23)   Dieses particular Bild   ist.. ANYWAY dies Bild   zeugt
         this   particular picture is.. anyway this picture testify+3sg

         nicht von einem sehr fruchtbaren Boden
         not   to a   very fertile   land

         'This particular picture is.. anyway this picture does not testify to very
         fertile land'
         (MGP 192m, describing a photograph of a country scene, uses *anyway*
         as a means of repair to a more literate style free from transference.)

Well has been attested in numerous community languages in Australia, such as German (Clyne 1967, 1968, 1972b), Dutch (Clyne 1977a), Italian (Bettoni 1981a), Greek (Tamis 1986), Vietnamese (Ho-Dac 1996) and Croatian (Hlavac 2000). It gives an opportunity to search for a word or expression and to express a position without any obligation, something that is useful for a person who does not feel totally at home in a new environment. It also expresses caution, modesty, restraint, or a non-committal attitude (in accordance with Anglo-Australian values), for example:

(24)   WELL je   kunt haast   zeggen, ieder kind op de
        well   you can   almost say   every child in the

        school ken ik, SORT OF
        school know I sort of

        'WELL, you can almost say, I know every child in the school SORT
        OF'
        (MGD 95m, a school principal, using *well* and *sort of* to tone down
        what might appear as an immodest statement.)

It is also used to keep the channel open for the next segment, e.g. (when asked if he/she had gone back to the country of origin):

(25)   WELL si   spera   ma WELL.. and sperava
        well   REFL hope+3sg+PRES but well   and hope+3sg+PAST

        d'andare   prima dei dei trent' anni.
        of go+INF for   some   thirty years

        'WELL there is a hope but WELL and there has been a hope of going
        for thirty years'
        (MTISE 26m discussing plans to visit Italy, a topic that causes some
        embarrassment)

as well as reflectively, for example:

(26)   (asked if he had grandchildren:)
        Well, der Sohn hat zwei Töchter
        'Well, my son has two daughters' (MGW 34m)

You know and *like* flag lexical transfers and encourage backchannelling, for example:

(27)   Kao šefica   onda to   moraš YOU KNOW expect...
        as   the boss then you have.to you know   expect...
        (MCr 52, from Hlavac 2000)

(28)   Ik denk, dat het wel dat het (A) dat het erbij YOU KNOW dat het bij
        door zal SLIPPEN
        'I think that it will slip through'
        (MD 134m, talking about the use of lexical transfers such as *beach*
        and drawing on common ground)

(29)   ...ali si   to je samo, samo znaš..   to   je samo za
         ...but be+2sg that is only   only   know+2sg that is only   for
         LIKE pretend nije to   za istinu
         LIKE pretend not   that for truth
         '...but that is only only you know..that is only for LIKE pretend that
         is not for real'
         (MCr 17, from Hlavac 2000)

You know and, to some extent, *like* express the expectation that the interlocutor
will understand what is being said and the way it is being said because of
their shared experience. These and the hedge *well* are very useful to people
in a linguistically or socially insecure situation. *Well* is more of a rationalized
hedging marker and *you know* and *like* are more solidarity oriented.

7.5.3   Comparison of corpora

The same five corpora were analyzed in relation to discourse markers as for
MPs – the speech of first-generation prewar German–English bilinguals,
second- and third-generation German–English settlement bilinguals from the
Wimmera and the Western District, first-generation postwar Dutch–English
bilinguals and their children, the German and Dutch of Dutch–German–English
trilinguals, and the German and Hungarian of Hungarian–German–English
trilinguals. For comparative purposes, this was complemented by second-
generation Croatian–English bilinguals whose parents were postwar immigrants (Hlavac 2000).

The striking aspect is the very high incidence of transference of *well* (and,
to a lesser extent, *you know*) in the German settlement data based on representative samples of twenty-seven in the Western District and thirty-three in
the Wimmera. This could be explained by the habitual use of English in the
community by the time of the interviews by speakers who are second and third
generation. The speakers from these areas are employing the DMs in both their
traditional and more specific hedging functions. DMs are prevalent in the Croatian data too, though not in the same proportion of incidence, with *you know*
and *like* leading *well*. Here too the speakers are second generation.[7] *Well* is
especially prevalent in the hedging functions among the postwar Dutch and
German-speaking immigrants, who, at the time of the data collection, were
quite recent arrivals, and were coming to terms with their bilingualism and
competition between the two systems. This was less the case with the prewar
refugees, who had largely avoided German MPs and did not use the English
DMs in their German much either. *You know* is prevalent as a hedging device
among younger Dutch–English bilinguals.

It is difficult to explain the greater use of *well* in the German data of
Hungarian–German–English trilinguals (23:6) and the slightly lower incidence

Table 7.4 *Discourse markers (excluding those in English mode)*[a]

	like	sort of	well	you know	anyway		sorry
G postwar	(200)		1	37	9	4	2
G prewar	(50)		2	6	2	1	1
WD	(27)	1	1	130	18		1
W	(33)	5	1	187	11		1
Dutch pw[b]	1a (60)	14	16	78	35[c]	?	3
	1b (30)	–	2	29	32	–	–
	2 (29)	–	3	4	2	–	–
G of HGE	(36)	1		23	–	2	9
H of HGE	(36)	1		6		2	7
Cr	(100)	41	1	25	153	2	4
D of DGE			4	15	12	1	7
G of DGE			1	11	3		

[a] Discourse markers in the Italian–Spanish–English trilingual data are restricted to *well* in example (25), two instances of *anyway* and one of *sorry* transferred into Italian and two of *anyway* transferred into Spanish. The reason for not adopting this type of communicative behaviour defies speculation. The Vietnamese–English sample contains four instances of *well* and three of *you know* in a Vietnamese context and one of *you know* in an English context.

[b] Generation 1a and 1b – sample.

[c] Twenty-two instances in the solidarizing function, thirteen in word-finding function.

of *sorry* than in the Hungarian data. Acquisition order and current use of the languages do not seem to be factors. DMs are absent in the German data from the young third generation. In the Dutch–German–English trilingual data, *well*, *you know* and *sort of* occur more in Dutch than in German. One is tempted to combine this finding with the one contrasting the Hungarian and German trilingual data and conclude that English discourse markers will find their way into discourse in closely related languages more than into less closely or unrelated languages. However, since we are dealing with open-class categories, which do not affect the typological differences, this is not very plausible. But this transference contrast in bilinguals along with the much greater incidence of transferred DMs in the Dutch–German–English than in the Hungarian–German–English trilinguals, encourages the conclusion that the underlying Hungarian–German bilingualism involving unrelated languages conditioned speakers towards a puristic tendency to diverge whereas the Dutch–German–English group, as we have seen, tends to utilize one language more as the basis for another.

The variation is largely interlocutor-based and between vintages and generations. *Well* leads the DM count with seventy-eight instances in generation 1a, twenty-nine in generation 1b and four in the second generation (in a Dutch environment). *You know* is relatively prevalent in generation 1b, to a lesser extent in generation 1a, but hardly transferred by the second generation. The latter also applies to other DMs.

Hlavac (2000: 427) shows that the *znaš/znate* 'you know' and *kao* 'like' are used almost as frequently and in the same functions as the transferred DMs in the Croatian of his second-generation informants. Sometimes alternation occurs between the Croatian and English equivalents, constituting lexico- and semanticopragmatic transference, as in the following example:

(30)   [jeə], to je ništa, um, mislim ja sam mogao, *znaš*, bit.. *kao znaš* ja sam
        to radio samo zato što sam trebao.. LIKE.. kako bi rekao..
        'Yeah, that's nothing, um, I think I could have been, you know.. like..
        you know I did that only because I had to.. like.. how can I say..' (MCr
        17m)

7.6   Comparison of modal particle and discourse marker incidence

Salmons (1990) documents the almost complete absence of German MPs in Texas German and the concomitant transference of English DMs. Goss and Salmons (2000) explore this diachronically through comparison between the speech of characters in two German-American plays dating back to 1892 and 1903 respectively. From this they deduce three stages:

  i. German MPs;
 ii. indexical code-switching introducing English DMs into German, which become 'borrowings';
iii. both systems, with German MPs dying out.

Goss and Salmons locate MPs and DMs between content and system morphemes.

Our comparison between German/Dutch MPs and DMs transferred from English does not show up groups as having necessarily abandoned the MP system and replaced the DM system over a particular time. There is a great deal of variation in the relative use of MPs and DMs due to personal style, needs and the functional specialization of the languages. However, the Dutch intergenerational comparison indicates tendencies towards a decline in the use of both (see analysis above). The one possible example of replacement is *you know* used where Dutch would normally employ *hoor*, for example:

(31)   daar zal ik geen (A) nare behoefte van hebben, *you know*
        'You won't have a bad need for that, you know' (D/G E 20f)
(32)   ik vind het ook niet leuk, *you know*
        'I don't like it either, you know' (GDE 32f)

Two of the three who used *hoor* (one GDE, one D/GE) did not record examples of *you know*.

The third was the greatest user of both.

While *well* and *also* share some aspects, (33) indicates the more reflected and deliberate logical function of *also* (cf. English *so*, *then*) and the more tentative nature of *well*:

(33)   *Well*, im öftesten in der Familie *also* immer deutsch, und englisch natürlich im öffentlichen Leben
'Well, so most frequently in the family always German, and English in public life' (H/GE 10m)

At this stage I would propose that the German and Dutch system of MPs and the Australian English system of DMs are not only structurally and functionally different but that they also reflect quite different types of communicative behaviour. As I have indicated, the German MP system provides an opportunity for consensus imposition. The Dutch MP system has this tendency too but centres around expressing one's own individual position and initiating and maintaining small-talk, in keeping with the Dutch core value of *gezelligheid* (untranslatable but corresponding to sociability).

The English DMs, on the other hand, give speakers the possibility of expressing caution, modesty and restraint, and uncertainty. Various studies on cross-cultural pragmatics have found that Germans perform speech acts in a more 'direct' way than English speakers, hedging less in oral communication, in accordance with positive politeness (see, for example, House and Kasper 1981; Kasper 1981; Blum-Kulka, House and Kasper 1989). However, Germans hedge more than English speakers in written discourse, especially academic discourse (Clyne 1993) using MPs, impersonal constructions, subjunctives and reflexives. The English DMs are useful to non-native speakers who need to hedge because of linguistic uncertainty and as instruments of identity change to a society in which it is inappropriate to show one's superiority. It must be said that English has its own means of consensus imposition – *As you know* and question tags such as *isn't it?* and *doesn't it?*

At the same time, the transference of some of the English discourse markers *you know*, *anyway*, *like* (cf. also the examples from Hlavac's Croatian data) indicates social integration and solidarity with other Australians. Items such as *anyhow*, *anyway*, *sorry* and *whatever*, which erase or marginalize what has just been said, enable the speaker to disclaim or downplay responsibility for the content of what they have just said, or more usually, the way in which they have said it. This is something that they may not be able to do so easily in their other language.

Well and *anyhow* are often employed in an English environment, even amid discourse in the other language, for example:

(34)   Well, it seems to be a guest house (MGPR 26f)

One in three to five examples in the German and Dutch corpora are in an English environment – 22.83% of the 219 examples of *well* from Western District German–English bilinguals, 27.45% of the 51 from postwar German-speaking immigrants, 52.63% of the 38 *you know* examples from the Western District and 11.5% of *well*s in generation 1a Dutch–English bilinguals.

Sometimes *well* facilitates or acts as a bridge to transversion,[8] for example:

(35)   Wenn ich mich so fühle, geh' ich 'raus in den Garten und..*well*..LOOK AFTER MY FLOWERS
        'If I feel like it, I go out in the garden and well . . . .' (MGP 105f)

(36)   Nou ik denk Parijs. *Well* . . . IT COULD BE (A) THE COLLINS STREET, BUT I'VE NEVER SEEN IT. Ik denk, dat het Parijs is.
        'Now I think Paris. Well it could be Collins Street but I've never seen it. I think it's Paris' (MD 76f, describing a picture of a Melbourne scene)

Such facilitation does not occur in the German or Hungarian data from Hungarian–German–English trilinguals. In the German and Dutch bi- and trilingual corpora and, to a lesser extent in Vietnamese, the transference of a DM can be responsible for transversion.

Thus the transference of English DMs fulfils particular needs in communicative behaviour related to cultural values, and the abandonment of the German/Dutch system indicates that another need is no longer great. Some speakers maintain both sets of functions.

7.7   Concluding remarks

In this exploratory chapter, we have considered how pragmatic features such as diminutives, forms of address, and modal particles relate to particular types of politeness, are used or abandoned or condition code-switching. Special attention is paid to the retention of modal particles in German, Dutch and Hungarian and the transference of discourse markers into German, Dutch, Hungarian and Croatian. There is evidence of a declining use of Dutch and German modal particles over generations, though Dutch *wel* especially is employed more than any German modal particle.[9] English discourse markers are transferred as hedges to express caution, modesty or insecurity. They are transferred especially by later generation groups such as second-generation Croatian–English and Dutch–English bilinguals, and second- and third-generation German–English bilinguals in former enclaves. *Well* is transferred more into Dutch than into German, more into German than into Hungarian. The abandonment of German (and to a lesser extent) of Hungarian modal particles seems to relate to their strong consensus-imposing function, a feature of positive politeness and characteristic of German and Hungarian ways of behaving. This function is weaker in Dutch modal particles, where one's position is stated more often without recourse to that of the other person(s). However, while *wel* is the most prevalent modal particle among Dutch–German–English trilinguals, altogether they use German modal particles more than Dutch ones. Perhaps this is another example of how trilinguals aim to maintain aspects of the three linguistic systems separately. Some speakers combine the culture-appropriate use of modal particles and transferred discourse markers in their community language, reflecting their multiple identity. Others have adopted the latter while dropping the former, or hardly use either. This reflects their communicative needs or their attempt to behave communicatively in an 'Australian' way.

Changes in address rules and code-switching to avoid such rules reflect the more individualistic culture and a more secondary network focus in Australia and the transference of English discourse markers a change to more negative politeness. Pragmatic transference parallels phenomena at other levels of language (cf. chapter 4), but pragmatic contrasts are also major contributing factors in indexical 'code-switching' (cf. section 3.3) and avoidance-conditioned 'code-switching'.

We have focused on a number of issues on which there is some data. The issues need to be considered in relation to a large corpus of spontaneous conversations. Other questions requiring discussion in the future include variation in turn taking between the community language(s) and English in plurilinguals, and variation in the organization of letters and oral discourse between the plurilinguals' languages. These are issues which have been discussed in other contexts (see e.g. Clyne 1994b) and which impinge on types of politeness and other cultural values.

8   Towards a synthesis

8.1   Introduction

In the preceding chapters, Australian data on and from bi- and trilinguals speaking immigrant languages in contact with English has been used as examples to explore various dynamics of language contact – of shift, convergence and transference, transversion, plurilingual processing and cultural values in contact discourse.

8.2   Data

The linguistic data analyzed is from plurilinguals speaking languages of different typologies in contact with English. This has made it possible to ascertain the effects of typological and sociolinguistic factors on particular language contact and change phenomena. For example, are the factors universal or language/culture-specific and individual? Each of the language dyads and triads gives us the opportunity to consider a different configuration of factors and issues. Each language has had a different migration and settlement history which impacts on rates of language maintenance/use and shift. Central to this monograph are the terms *transference* – the use of forms, features or structures from another language – and *transversion* – the crossing over from one language to another. The data has enabled us to focus on transference and convergence phenomena and the facilitation of transversion by overlap, transference and convergence phenomena – in a situation of rapid 'language change' (which might be attributed to 'language attrition'). The processing implications of these phenomena were also considered. The data across languages indicates three facilitation principles promoting transversion from one language to another – lexical, tonal and syntactic. Together, the convergence and facilitation phenomena give us an impression of a dynamism that defies universal constraints and underlies both inter- and intraindividual variation. The facilitation principles apply to Muysken's (2000) switching category 'congruent lexicalization' but sometimes also to his 'alternation'.

234

Language contact phenomena are exemplified in quite different ways in different community languages in contact with English, and some occur across languages (chapter 4). They can best be considered by summarizing the variation between and in the languages and groups we have been studying; see tables 8.1 and 8.2.

8.2.1   The language factor

The closely related languages German and Dutch are distant enough for the contact situation and a slightly greater shift from Dutch to effect greater morphosyntactic changes to Dutch than to German, ones which do not come to the fore in trilinguals, however. The SVO structure, rich morphological inflections and moderate distance from English of Croatian leads to one set of consequences; the SVO and isolating structure and unrelatedness of Vietnamese to another set of consequences. The fact that Vietnamese and Mandarin are tone languages provides a new opportunity for the extension of the facilitation model to prosody. The rich morphology of Hungarian places integration requirements on lexical transfers, detracting from lexical facilitation. This is very conspicuous when we compare the German and Hungarian of the same speakers. Also, these languages do not share any homophones the way German and English do. Italian and Spanish, like German and Dutch, lend themselves to subordinate bilingualism, bilateral competence and conversion rules.

In our data, illustrated in tables 8.1 and 8.2, the existing overlap between the languages, especially in the lexicon, provides a stimulus for both lexical and morphosyntactic convergence, and overlap and convergence in turn facilitate transversion. One type of convergence stimulates others. Phonetic convergence increases the likelihood of bilingual homophones in a related language; morphological correspondence and convergence lead to syntactic convergence. Even in contact between unrelated languages such as Vietnamese or Mandarin and English, tones identified with English pitch and stress can facilitate transversion. In the multiple transference of collocations, as opposed to mixed constituents, typology seems to be the most important factor and, within that, immigrant vintage and generation in Australia causes some variation, as does the tendency of the community towards anticipational facilitation of transversion (cf. Thomason and Kaufman 1988). The unusually frequent Vb + N English EL islands in Vietnamese may best be attributed to the shared word order and isolating tendencies of English and Vietnamese. This contrasts with the other languages in consideration. Some of the characteristics of German in the enclaves (e.g. phonetic convergence, case levelling) can be attributed to commonalities between the German base dialect and Australian English which were reinforced in the contact situation.

Table 8.1 *Summary comparison between language contact phenomena of different language dyads*[a]

German	Dutch	Croatian	Vietnamese
1. Some convergence.	1. Largescale convergence due to similar lexicon and common typological features with English.	1. Some case reduction tendencies.	1. Much transversion, irrespective of English proficiency.
2. Varying extent of phonetic convergence, thus important facilitators in transversion vary.	2. The incidence of bilingual homophones is increased by phonetic convergence.	2. Some facilitation of transversion, mainly by lexical transfers, but less than in German and Dutch speakers.	2. Tonal facilitation of transversion.
3. Genders are kept, though increasing (second- and third-generation) tendency towards inanimate neuter gender.	3. One gender tendency based on non-neuter.	3. Some convergence.	3. Little lexical and syntactic facilitation.
4. Plural affixes are kept but zero tendency in third generation of more recent immigrant waves.	4. One plural allomorph tendency.	4. Little collocative multiple transference of EL islands.	4. Much interclausal transversion.
5. Personal endings of verbs kept.	5. Slight tendency emerging towards zero verbal forms in second generation.	5. Relatively low language shift rate.	5. Some simple collocations constituting multiple transference of EL islands (e.g. *typical Australia*) and a few individual lexical transfers.
6. SVO overgeneralization starting in second generation.	6. SVO overgeneralization starting in first generation.		6. Where there is lexical facilitation: mainly consequential, with lexical transfers as the predominant type of trigger-word.
7. High language shift rate but not as high as Dutch. (Nineteenth-century-originated enclaves were an exception.)	7. Highest community language shift rate.		7. No need for morphological integration into isolating language.
			8. Low language shift rate.

[a] Across generations, except where otherwise indicated.

Table 8.2 *Summary comparison between language contact phenomena of different language triads*

German/Dutch/English	German/Hungarian[a]/English	Italian/Spanish/English
1. Conversion rules (and avoidance of transfers).	1. Case reduction tendency, Hungarian.	1. Some convergence between Italian and Spanish and transversion between these languages.
2. Trilingual homophones and English lexical transfers facilitate transversion.	2. More morphological integration of transfers in Hungarian, less in German.	2. Unclear separation between Italian and Spanish.
3. German's conservative influence, counterbalancing progressive influence of English on Dutch.	3. Lexical facilitation of transversion from German, not Hungarian.	3. English lexical transfers and bilingual homophones facilitate transversion but not as much as among Dutch–German–English trilinguals.
4. English discourse markers transferred more into Dutch than into German.	4. English discourse markers transferred more into German than into Hungarian.	4. Italian has medium language shift rate, South American Spanish a low shift rate, in the first generation.

All languages: Correspondence between two languages transferred to third.

[a] Fairly high language-shift rate, but not as high as Dutch and German.

Lexical transfers from English occur in all the immigrant languages studied, and it is the morphology of the recipient language – and consequently the degree of morphosyntactic integration required – that may determine if they have an impact on transversion. But there is also a speaker's choice as to whether they will employ unintegrated or integrated lexical transfers or resist them, and transversion is perhaps also a question of attitude, even beyond emblematic switching. One type of transference will facilitate another (e.g. syntactic facilitating lexical, semantic facilitating syntactic). Hence the appropriateness of a terminology putting all transference under a single umbrella.

The drift of a language (Sapir 1921; Hawkins 1986) will impact on which particular morphosyntactic changes occur in it in the contact situation and how quickly, as is indicated by comparisons between German and Dutch in contact with English. At the same time, there is, in morphosyntactic change, a preference for the 'unmarked'. A three-stage adoption of a new development in Dutch is proposed, affecting transfers from English most, then bilingual homophones and, least of all, other items. Developments latent in the heartland of the language have been shown to be accelerated in the contact situation (e.g. SVO, single definite article, generalization of one plural allomorph).

8.3   The culture factor

In our consideration of language shift (chapter 2), cultural distance and cultural core values play a significant role in the maintenance of a language for a longer but finite period. Where cultural distance is less, more rapid shift occurs. The parallel in structural change is the linguistic core values embodied in the unified typology referred to (see sections 4.4.7, 4.4.11). Where these are closely related, more convergence is likely to occur than if this is not the case. Contact-induced pragmatic change is still a relatively unexplored field. From our analysis, especially of modal particle/discourse marker use (chapter 7), it would appear that cultural core values (including types of politeness) play a more important part than linguistic typology in continuity or change, due to the strong link between pragmatics and cultural values. The retention of modal particles from the first languaculture (Agar 1994) reflects a retention of a mode of behaviour. However, pragmatic distance between the languacultures can also be a motivation for transversion if this behaviour is not considered appropriate. In the significance of the cultural factor, pragmatics and language maintenance/shift patterns show some commonalities; in both cases, identity is marked through linguistic behaviour.

8.4   Trilinguals vs. bilinguals

By and large, trilingual transversion and convergence phenomena are similar to bilingual ones but more complex. Correspondence between two languages can facilitate convergence from the third, but a typologically more conservative language (e.g. German) can reduce the effects of a typologically more progressive one (English) on the third language (e.g. Dutch). The differential distance relations put the languages in a constant tug-o'war with one another which contrasts with the unidirectional convergence more common in the bilinguals. In many of our trilinguals, competence in one language is based on a subordinate relation with a closely related one and a set of conversion rules.

The question 'Is trilingual speech like that of bilinguals in respect to transference and convergence phenomena?' needs to be answered with a guarded 'no'. Nearly all our trilinguals are first generation. Despite the challenges mentioned, in comparison with first-generation bilinguals the trilinguals, driven by clear functional delineation of the languages, metalingustic awareness and linguaphilia, tend to take more trouble to avoid certain types of convergence and transference. This is apparent from both closely related languages in contact (Dutch, German, English) and triads with related and unrelated languages in contact (Hungarian, German, English).

8.5 Generation/vintage

Each generation develops its grammar further in a particular direction, whether it is in the direction of the 'unmarked' and/or to converge with the other (another) language. In the first generation, this is most likely to be in accordance with the unified typology. Hence the SVO generalization occurs far more and faster in Dutch than in German. The refunctioning of the German neuter as an inanimate gender begins with pronouns in the second generation and extends to articles in the urban third generation of more recent immigration vintages. An emerging unmarked German accusative singular is based on the masculine accusative and reflects natural morphology (Wurzel 1989; Salmons 1994). However, sometimes a surprising new development enters into the contact situation, such as the zero plural in the urban third generation.

The examples from Dutch suggest that modal particle use decreases with generation within a common vintage and settlement pattern. Transferred discourse markers are particularly prevalent beyond the first generation irrespective of language group.

Across languages, plurilinguals with a longer period of residence in the immigration country (e.g. settlement bilinguals, prewar refugees) have developed collocations which are well established and promote anticipational facilitation of transversion. Phonetic convergence also facilitates transversion, resulting from immigration as adults (with English convergence towards Dutch) and residence over several generations (with German converging towards English). In the second generation (Dutch, German, Croatian), there is a greater tendency towards a bilingual mode based on separation of languages. Also, later generations tend to build on a change started in a previous generation, something most obvious in Dutch.

8.6   The sociolinguistic factor

A matter of sociolinguistic concern is language use. Less use of the immigrant language facilitates transference from and/or convergence towards English. Community language items may not be unavailable; they may not be preferred. Specific language use influences variation in transference/transversion behaviour. For instance, frequent collocation between English prepositions and local place names (including German ones) in English has led to a preponderance of both adverbial English EL islands in German and anticipational facilitation.

An example of how the sociolinguistic impacts on the linguistic is in variation between the settlement patterns in German, the only language for which we have such comparative data. Those lexical transfers shared by a community with dense multiplex networks (Milroy 1980) will be more highly and uniformly integrated (both morphologically and phonologically) than the transfers used by bilinguals in a more 'open/settlement' situation such as Melbourne or the ones expressing more recent innovations. Some of the characteristics of the German of the former enclaves (see table 8.3) may be attributed to sociolinguistic factors, others to linguistic ones (section 8.2.1). In both types of settlement patterns, ethnolects of the national language may take on the identity-marking functions of the community language. Closer settlement together with religious distinctiveness is a condition conducive to ethnolect maintenance.

Both individual examples and general tendencies constantly remind us of the likelihood of multiple causation. A high shift to English from Dutch coincides

Table 8.3 *German settlement patterns*

Immigrants	Enclaves
More phonologically, morphologically unintegrated lexical transfers	More phonologically/morphologically integrated lexical transfers, esp. those items used by the entire community
Semantic motivation for gender of transferred nouns	Feminine tendency in gender of a few transferred nouns used by entire community
	Some case levelling
	Phonetic convergence
	Overproportionate incidence of proper nouns as trigger-words and of anticipational facilitation (cf. postwar, with prewar immigrants in-between)

with a language with a drift towards a structure far more similar to English than to German, leading to some changes pointing towards Thomason and Kaufman's (1988) Categories 4 and 5.

Language shift to English, indicated by home language census statistics supplemented by survey information from smaller samples, is a product of many factors – the migration, premigration and postmigration experience, the relative position of language in the value systems of particular cultures, cultural distance and various individual and group factors – marriage patterns, generation/age, period of residence (a triple surrogate, see section 2.2.4), identity and cost benefits. Language shift defies a predictive model because of the multiplicity of possible factors in different combinations and because of the unpredictability of many of the sociopolitical factors.

8.7 Concluding remarks

As Muysken (2000: 15) states, a researcher's data, experience and interests exercise an influence on the models they develop. With the great expansion of research in this field, language contact studies are served by a multiplicity of models each of which captures part of the picture and contributes to the totality. I am dealing with a particular range of issues – linguistic, sociolinguistic and psycholinguistic – arising from our data. My approach has therefore been rather eclectic. In chapters 2, 4, 5 and 6, I have indicated the strengths and limitations of the models in addressing the issues arising from our data. Language contact phenomena as well as language shift often defy hard and fast linear models. For instance, our data suggests tendencies rather than constraints or universal rules. Throughout this study, it has been more useful to speak in terms of facilitation than of constraints (e.g. syntactic overlap facilitates transversion, not: different syntactic structures constrain switching). While generally in our bi- and trilingual data, there is one language which provides the grammatical frame of a clause (as in the Matrix Language Frame Model), relatedness of languages and convergence between them sometimes make it difficult to pinpoint a matrix language. Convergence is addressed in modifications to the MLF model allowing for a composite matrix language. Similarly, the models of language maintenance and shift all contribute something substantial to an understanding of the processes (see chapter 2). Of special interest are Fishman's (1991) Graded Intergenerational Disruption Scale and Smolicz's (1981) notion of the relative centrality of language in a cultural values system. However, challenges are provided by the non-linearity of the GIDS stages (especially the diglossic and the power-sharing ones) and by the rapid changes and intragroup variation in the core values.

The facilitation of transversion necessitates a modification of the Levelt et al. (1989, 1999) 'Speaking' model. My analysis and discussion support a processing model with joint storage of material from the two or more languages of the plurilingual, but with the same-language elements more closely linked, perceptual feedback from the phonological level to lemmas and the accessing of tone via initial syllables. Transversion facilitation seems to provide evidence for multiple tagging of lemmas and simultaneous planning of languages, and various contact phenomena support inhibition of the less active language.

While linguistic typology is the single most important factor in transversion and convergence in our data, cultural values and cultural – not linguistic – distance play a determining role in language shift and pragmatic change. However, an overlap between sociolinguistic (limited language use) and typological considerations suggests multiple causation of convergence and transference, e.g. in Dutch–English contact. A unified typology (Hawkins 1986) indicating drift provides a gravitation point for contact phenomena and offers a linguistic parallel to cultural core values. It is often impossible to assess if a change is externally motivated by language contact or internally motivated, and multiple causation is likely. Some latent changes are greatly accelerated by contact, especially where the languages share some unified typology. Facilitation principles work differently according to typological, sociolinguistic and individual factors.

We have also seen that language distance can be determined in many ways. For instance, while Vietnamese may be genetically unrelated to English and Italian, they are all SVO languages, which may play a role in a contact situation. On the other hand, while Dutch and German are quite closely related, they show unified contrasts in a contact situation with English, which comes out in comparisons and in the speech of trilinguals.

Language use patterns and preferred ways of using resources from more than one language will determine choice of language mode. The incidence of (unintegrated) lexical transfers will, in turn, facilitate transversion.

This monograph has been able to focus on only a small number of features of convergence, especially those prompted by the contact languages in our original corpora. The study of other languages in contact in tri- and bilinguals, for instance involving more languages of Asia (cf. for example Bisang 1998), undoubtedly raises new research issues.

Notes

1 INTRODUCTION

1. Also partly in its sequel, Jacobson (2001).
2. Space does not permit the consideration of dialect contact. Dialect–standard switching operates on the principles outlined in chapter 5 (Giesbers 1989).
3. For the purpose of this study, 'Dutch–German–English' (etc.) will include trilinguals with these languages, irrespective of acquisition order, which will be stated.
4. The data used here from Tuc Ho-Dac is a sample chosen by him because it contains examples of the phenomena under consideration.
5. There are exceptions such as Molisan-Croatian which is disappearing from its eastern Italian coastal heartland and about half its remaining speakers are in Western Australia (Clissa 2001).
6. We also have similar data from South Australia and southern New South Wales.
7. This has affected adversely the number of secondary schools teaching Greek and in turn the proficiency levels.
8. Except as a subject in mainstream schools; see below.
9. The hard line on asylum seekers taken by the Howard government re-elected in 2001 is not necessarily indicative of a position on internal multiculturalism.

2 DYNAMICS OF LANGUAGE SHIFT

1. Some of the data discussed in this chapter is treated in Clyne and Kipp (1997).
2. Logistic regression analysis was not undertaken because preliminary tests indicated that none of the correlations between the independent variables and the dependent variables achieved a value of 0.3 or above (Coakes and Steed 1997).
3. The same question was repeated in the August 2001 Census. At the time of writing, no information was available from this census. However, as parents' countries of birth were not elicited in 2001, it will not be possible to estimate second-generation language shift from the 2001 Census data.
4. The first wave of refugees from Vietnam were speakers of Chinese varieties.
5. Hirst (2001) notes an intergenerational decline in Greek-Orthodox affiliation among Greek-Australians – 90% first generation, 82% second, 45% third.
6. A similar study is in progress under the direction of Guus Extra across five European cities – Göteborg, Hamburg, Lyon, Madrid and The Hague – comparing language competence, choice, dominance, preference and vitality among young people of several language communities.

7. This formulation is based on the title of a monumental article by Fishman (1967).
8. Cf. Mufwene's (2001) founder principle.
9. Cf. Kloss – 'Pre-emigration experience with language maintenance' – examples are Greeks, Poles, Latvians, Ukrainians, Chinese.
10. While the census statistics do not permit a calculation of the shift rate, the total number of Yiddish home users in Australia was only 2,288 in Melbourne, 80.5% of the Australian total.
11. 'Xish' in Fishman's terminology refers to the mainstream and 'Yish' to the minority group.
12. While Fishman (2001) strongly emphasizes the distinction between language programs for second-language acquisition and those for identity formation and community development, there is value for ethnolinguistic vitality in the sharing of community languages within the wider community (cf. Clyne fc).
13. Internet use in community languages will be included in forthcoming research by Clyne and Kipp.
14. Languages are not given regular slots on state-run television, except for news broadcasts. However, slots are allocated on community television.
15. Smolicz and Secombe (1990) implicitly acknowledge subgroup variation in core values when they show that the Tamil language is a core value for Tamil Hindus but not for Christians. On the language–ethnicity and religion–ethnicity–language links, see Fishman's (1997: 131–68) analysis of statements in praise of the ethnic language.
16. Sorbian is a West Slavic language spoken in parts of eastern Germany.
17. This could be considered more in the methodology of future studies.

3 ON MODELS AND TERMS

1. Except where otherwise indicated, examples are in existing practical orthography (or romanization) for the appropriate language. In the code numbers for the data, M stands for Monash, the university where this project commenced, and for Melbourne, the university where it continued; Cr – Croatian; G for German; D for Dutch; H – Hungarian; I – Italian; M – Mandarin; S – Spanish; V – Vietnamese; T for trilingual; PR for prewar; P for postwar; W for Wimmera; and WD for Western District in the German data. In the German and Dutch postwar corpora, second- and later-generation informants are specifically referred to. For the trilinguals, the acquisition order is indicated, e.g. ISE = Italian, Spanish, English in that order. / denotes simultaneous acquisition of two or more languages, e.g. I/SE. For Hungarians, immigration vintage is indicated by PR (prewar), P (postwar), 56 (1956), and R (recent). G3 = third-generation corpus.
2. The highest unit projected by lexical items according to government and binding grammar. In many ways, this corresponds to a clause in traditional grammar.
3. In Australia, both lexical transference and transversion are attested in both generations and subject to substantial individual variability (see section 3.3 for terms).
4. The interconnection is more central in Johanson's (1992) model based on code-copying (section 3.4.6), inspired by Haugen's (1956) 'model' and 'replica', and Backus (1996) has also extended the scope of his analysis in this direction.

5. This may have been triggered by *hier* which is a bilingual homophone of *here* (homophonous diamorph in Haugen 1956). Myers-Scotton and Jake (2000; see below, section 3.4.1) refer to *of* as a bridge morpheme, one of the system morphemes that is processed late.
6. Note the switch back at *Schafe*.
7. Cf. 'Loanshift' in Haugen (1956).
8. 'Homeland' (after Hlavac 2000) 'comparable to monolingual' is preferred to 'Standard' since some of the speakers cannot be described as 'standard'.
9. Lemmas are abstract entries with semantic and syntactic features in the mental lexicon.
10. This means that Pandharipande's (1998) critique, for example, that the MLF model cannot cope with the transference of English nouns complete with the *-s* plural morpheme, is now superfluous.
11. Dialectal.
12. Muysken (2000) identifies separation with his 'alternation', but I would contend that 'congruent lexicalization' may also mark a transition to another language.
13. It has not been possible to calculate shift rates on the basis of the 1996 Census data because of multiple birthplace and language designations (Croatia, Yugoslavia, Croatian, 'Yugoslav', Serbo-Croatian). With the passage of time, however, respondents are increasingly opting for Croatia as well as for Croatian.

4 DYNAMICS OF CONVERGENCE AND TRANSFERENCE

1. In the data sections, glossing will be added only where it is necessary to understand the example.
2. Zuckermann (MS) has found, in the Yiddish and other influences on Israeli Hebrew, evidence for the 'principle of congruence', that the existence of a feature in more than one contributor language increases the likelihood of its persistence.
3. See chapter 6 for psycholinguistic implications of conversion.
4. For gender, see section 4.5.1.
5. Homeland Hungarian:
   egy   emeletes
   one   floor+ADJECTIVIZER
6. This informant is atypical of the trilinguals in that she has not been regularly speaking Hungarian for some years.
7. This data is derived from texts written and dictations taken by second-generation and generation 1b children.
8. Instead of dative plural.
9. Schmid (2002) reports the overgeneralization of the feminine article in her prewar refugees in the UK and US. This contrasts with the absence of gender reallocations in our refugee sample.
10. However, this is one of the features of simplification that are sanctioned in the Hungarian-language homeland community (Pléh and Bobor 2000: 127–8).
11. In German, *-s* denotes possessive in the masculine and neuter singular but not in the feminine singular.

12. This speaker is the product of nineteenth-century migration so that recent changes in the position of the verb after *weil* in its epistemic functions (Uhmann 1998) would not have affected the German base.

13. A completely grammatical sentence is not always the outcome, since some speakers do not speak English grammatically, e.g. *hoe je call dat?* 'how you call that?' from an elderly woman (MD 17f).

14. Some communities will have different attitudes towards transference from different languages (e.g. Aikhenvald 2002 on Portuguese and East Tucanoan language influence on Tariana in Amazonia).

15. This is similar to an earlier distinction between 'loanwords' and 'foreign words'.

16. In this section, language contact data from some community languages in Australia beyond our core corpus is referred to, as foreshadowed in section 3.1.

17. See also section 4.4.4.

18. It is the morphologically more integrated form that is generally the more frequent in our corpus. The unintegrated *mixed up* (cited by Muysken 2000: 174 from Clyne 1967), occurring more often than *upgemixed*, is an exception, possibly influenced by the separable prefix.

19. A multiplicity of pitch-stress patterns emerged in an acoustic analysis of a sample of forty German–English instances of lexical facilitation and the subsequent transversion from pre- and postwar immigrants and bilinguals from former enclaves.

20. Similar constructions are to be found in contact between other Indian languages such as Punjabi in contact with English (see for example Romaine 1995: 137).

21. However, one informant said *Er ist ein Onkel zu X* in German (a morpheme-for-morpheme analytic equivalent; pseudonym added). This is ungrammatical. It is possible that the construction is an older one in Australian English, not related to German, which has been retained solely or mainly in German-settled parts of Australia.

5 DYNAMICS OF TRANSVERSION

1. Cf. Facilitation by trigger-word; see section 5.3.

2. Silesian variety.

3. *What* and *wat* are, in the speaker, very nearly bilingual homophones (cf. section 5.4), hence their effect of facilitating a transversion back from English into Dutch.

4. The processing implications of such anticipations will be considered in chapter 6.

5. Cf. Pfaff (1979), see section 3.4.5.

6. In homeland Dutch, *nieuwer* should receive an *-e* inflexion.

7. Though the two are sometimes interchanged in the trilinguals, see section 4.5.

8. It should be stressed that for those whose L2 phonology is strongly influenced by L1, L2-derived lexemes in L1 will generally appear to be phonologically highly integrated.

9. Processing aspects of this will be discussed in chapter 6.

10. This speaker has been exposed at home to English *the* realized as [də] and to the same as an article of lexical transfers from English in Dutch. *Ben* is first-person singular but this may be intended as a shortened form of *bennen*, a third-person-singular form recorded in Dutch texts as early as the seventeenth century and represented in contemporary non-standard Dutch. The standard form is *zijn*.

11. Semantic transfer based on English *go* (German *fahren*).
12. Denotes high tone and ^ denotes mid tone.
13. The examples were selected before reading Muysken (2000).
14. The examples above were selected before reading Muysken (2000).
15. 'Wog' is pejorative designation for (mainly southern European and Middle Eastern) immigrants which, like here, is now sometimes employed as part of a positive self-identification.
16. Lower-case – Dutch; capitals – English; italics – Common.
17. Semantic transfer. Dutch – *dominee*; Dutch *minister* only for member of government.
18. More recently, this has been supplemented with self-taped conversations with family members or friends.
19. This is confirmed in Hulsen's (2000) research on Dutch in New Zealand.

6 DYNAMICS OF PLURILINGUAL PROCESSING

1. Tagging is also an important feature of the model of Poulisse and Bongaerts (1994).
2. I am indebted to W. J. M. Levelt for this suggestion.
3. Pauses such as *ahm* and *ah*.

7 DYNAMICS OF CULTURAL VALUES IN CONTACT DISCOURSE

1. For other aspects of how cultural values impact on variation in discourse patterns and discourse expectations, see for example Clyne (1994b), Wierzbicka (1986, 1991).
2. Austrian German, however, emphasizes negative politeness more.
3. Although the examples below are from plurilinguals, they all correspond to the use of modal particles described for monolingual speech.
4. Modal particles are a subset of discourse markers but I will refer to them only as modal particles to differentiate them from the transferred English discourse markers with quite different functions. The translations are very approximate as most MPs cannot be rendered in English.
5. German equivalent here *zwar*.
6. Sometimes combined with *wel*.
7. In Jucker and Smith's (1998) English-speaking student corpus, *like* leads *you know* and *well* in that order.
8. See also Clyne (1967: 92–4).
9. Except *also* for the Hungarian–German–English trilinguals.

References

Abandolo, Daniel Mario. 1988. *Hungarian Inflectional Morphology*. Budapest: Akadémiai Kiadó.

Adalar, Nevin and Tagliamonte, Sali. 1998. Borrowed nouns, bilingual people: the case of the 'Londraolt' in Northern Cyprus. *International Journal of Bilingualism* 2: 139–60.

Agar, Michael. 1994. *Language Shock: Understanding the Culture of Conversation*. New York: Wm. Morrow.

Aikhenvald, Alexandra. 2000. *Classifiers*. Oxford: Oxford University Press.

Aikhenvald, Alexandra. 2001. Language obsolescence: progress or decay? The emergence of new grammatical categories in 'language death'. In D. and M. Bradley (eds.), *Language Maintenance for Endangered Languages: an Active Approach*. London: Routledge Curzon, pp. 14–55.

Aikhenvald, Alexandra. 2002. *Language Contact in Amazonia*. Oxford: Oxford University Press.

Aikhenvald, Alexandra. Forthcoming. Introduction. In R. M. W. Dixon and A. Aikhenvald (eds.), *Evidentiality: A Cross-Linguistic Typology*.

Alfonzetti, Giovanna. 1998. The conversational dimension in code-switching between Italian and dialect in Sicily. In Auer (ed.), pp. 180–214.

Allan, Keith. 1984. The component functions of the high rise terminal contour in Australian declarative sentences. *Australian Journal of Linguistics* 4: 19–32.

Alvarez-Caccámo, Celso. 1998. From 'switching code' to 'code-switching': towards a reconceptualisation of communicative codes. In Auer (ed.), pp. 29–50.

Ammerlaan, Tom. 1996. 'You get a bit wobbly...' Exploring Bilingual Lexical Retrieval Processes in the Context of First Language Attrition. Copyprint 2000, Enschede (PhD, Catholic University of Nijmegen).

Andersen, Roger. 1977. The impoverished state of cross-sectional morpheme acquisition/ accuracy methodology. *Working Papers in Bilingualism* 14: 47–82.

Andersen, Roger. 1982. *Pidginization and Creolization as Language Acquisition*. Rowley, MA: Newbury House.

Annamalai, E. 1989. The language factor in code-mixing. *International Journal of the Sociology of Language* 75: 47–54.

Appel, René and Muysken, Pieter. 1987. *Language Contact and Bilingualism*. London: Edward Arnold.

Aristar, Anthony. 1999. Typology and the Saussurean dichotomy. In Polomé and Justus (eds.), pp. 409–28.

Aron, Albert W. 1930. The gender of English loanwords in colloquial American German. *Language Monographs* 7: 11–28.

Auer, Peter. 1990. A discussion paper on code alternation. In European Science Foundation, Network on Code-Switching and Language Contact, *Papers for the Workshop on Concepts, Methodology and Data, Basel,* 12–13 January 1990, pp. 68–9.

Auer, Peter (ed.). 1998. *Code-switching in Conversation: Language, Interaction and Identity.* London: Routledge.

Avermaet, Piet van and Klatter-Folmer, Jetske. 1998. The role of L2 self-assessment in language choice behaviour: Immigrant shift to Dutch in Flanders and the Netherlands. *Te Reo* 41: 137–52.

Azuma, Tamiko and Bales, Kathryn A. 1998. Memory impairments underlying language difficulties in dementia. In R. B. Gillam (ed.), *Memory and Language Impairment in Children and Adults: New Perspectives.* Gaithersburg, MD: Aspen Publishers, pp. 191–209.

Bach, Emmon. 1962. The order of elements in a transformational grammar of German. *Language* 38: 263–9.

Bach, Emmon, Brown, Colin and Marslen-Wilson, William. 1986. Crossed and nested dependencies in German and Dutch. *Language and Cognition Processes* 1: 249–62.

Backus, Ad. 1996. *Two in One: Bilingual Speech of Turkish Immigrants in the Netherlands.* Tilburg: Tilburg University Press.

Backus, Ad. 2000. Insertional code-switching in an immigrant language: 'just' borrowing or lexical reorientation? *Bilingualism, Language and Cognition* 3(2): 103–5.

Backus, Ad. 2001. The evidence from Dutch-Turkish. In Jacobson (ed.), pp. 125–54.

Bakker, Peter and Mous, Maarten (eds.). 1994. *Mixed Languages: 15 Case Studies in Language Intertwining.* Amsterdam: Institute for Functional Research into Language and Language Use (IFOTT).

Battison, Robin. 1978. *Lexical Borrowing in American Sign Language.* Silver Spring, MD: Linstock Press.

Bavin, Edith and Shopen, Tim. 1985. Warlpiri and English: languages in contact. In Clyne (ed.), pp. 81–95.

Bean, M. C. 1963. *The Development of Word Order Patterns in Old English.* London: Croom Helm.

Belazi, Heidi M., Rubin, Edward J. and Toribio, Almeida J. 1994. Code-switching and X-bar theory: the functional head constraint. *Linguistic Inquiry* 25: 221–37.

Beligan, Annemarie. 1999. Code-switching patterns in the speech of Romanian-English bilinguals. *Monash University Linguistic Papers* 2(1): 3–11.

Benor, Sarah. 2000. Loanwords in the English of modern Orthodox Jews: Yiddish or Hebrew? In S. S. Change et al. (eds.) *Proceedings of the Twenty-fifth Annual Meeting of the Berkeley Linguistics Society, 1999. Parasession on Loan Word Phenomena,* pp. 287–98.

Bentahila, Abdelali and Davies, Eileen. 1983. The syntax of Arabic-French code-switching. *Lingua* 59: 301–30.

Berckel, J. A. T. M. van. 1962. *Onderzoek woordfrequentie: resultaten, kranten.* Rapport R 642, 2. Amsterdam: Mathematisch Centrum.

Berend, Nina and Mattheier, Klaus J. (eds.). 1994. *Sprachinselforschung. Eine Gedenkschrift für Hugo Jedig.* Frankfurt am Main: Peter Lang.

Bettoni, Camilla. 1981a. *Italian in North Queensland*. Townsville: James Cook University.

Bettoni, Camilla. 1981b. Italian – maintenance or new language? *Babel* 17(2–3): 25–33.

Bettoni, Camilla. 1985. Italian language attrition: a Sydney case study. In Clyne (ed.), pp. 63–79.

Bettoni, Camilla. 1986. Italian language attrition in Sydney: the role of birth order. In C. Bettoni (ed.), *Altro Polo: Italian Abroad*. Sydney: Frederick May Foundation for Italian Studies, University of Sydney, pp. 61–85.

Bettoni, Camilla. 1991. Other community languages. In M. Clyne (ed.), *Linguistics in Australia: Trends in Research*. Canberra: Academy of the Social Sciences in Australia, pp. 75–91.

Bettoni, Camilla and Rubino, Antonia. 1996. *Emigrazione e comportamento linguistico. Un'indagine sul trilinguismo dei siciliani e dei veneti in Australia*. Np: Congedo Editore.

Bickerton, Derek. 1981. *Roots of Language*. Ann Arbor: Karomi.

Bierwisch, Manfred. 1963. *Grammatik des deutschen Verbs* (=*Studia Grammatica II*). Berlin: Akademie Verlag.

Bierwisch, Manfred. 1966. *Grammatik des deutschen Verbs*. Berlin: Akademie Verlag.

Bierwisch, Manfred and Schreuder, Robert. 1992. From concepts to lexical items. *Cognition* 42: 23–60.

Birnbaum, Henrik. 1965. Balkanslavisch und Südslavisch: zur Reichweite der Balkanismen im südslavischen Sprachraum. *Zeitschrift für Balkanologie* 3: 12–63.

Birnbaum, Henrik. 1966. On typology, affinity and Balkan linguistics. *Zbornik za filologiju i lingvistiku* 9: 17–30.

Birnbaum, Henrik. 1999. On the relationship of typology and genealogy in language classification. In Polomé and Justus (eds.), vol. 2, pp. 397–408.

Bisang, Walter. 1998. Grammaticalization and language contact construction and positions. In A. G. Ramat and P. Hopper (eds.), *Limits of Grammaticalization*. Amsterdam: Benjamins.

Bleakley, Dell. 1966. Some grammatical aspects of the German of Hatton Vale. BA (Hons.) thesis, University of Queensland.

Blum-Kulka, Shoshana, House, Juliane and Kasper, Gabriele. 1989. Investigating cross-cultural pragmatics: an introductory overview. In S. Blum-Kulka, J. House and G. Kasper (eds.), *Cross-cultural Pragmatics: Requests and Apologies*. Norwood, NJ: Ablex, pp. 1–34.

Boeschoten, Hendrik. 1998. Codeswitching, codemixing and code alternation: what a difference. In Jakobson (ed.), pp. 15–25.

Bokamba, Eyamba G. 1988. Code-mixing, language variation and linguistic theory. *Lingua* 76: 21–62.

Bolonyai, Agnes. 1998. In-between languages: language shift/maintenance in childhood bilingualism. *International Journal of Bilingualism* 2(1): 21–44.

Bolonyai, Agnes. 2000. 'Elective affinities': language contact in the abstract lexicon and its structural consequences. *International Journal of Bilingualism* 4: 81–106.

Boost, Karl. 1964. *Neue Untersuchungen zum Wesen und zur Struktur des deutschen Satzes*. Berlin: Akademie Verlag.

Boumans, L. 2000. Periphrastic verb constructions in Moroccan Arabic/Dutch codeswitching. In A. Fenyvési and K. Sandor (eds.), *Working Papers of the Bilingual Language Use Theme Group*. Szeged, pp. 67–84.

Bourdieu, P. 1982. The economics of linguistic exchanges. *Social Science Information* 16: 645–68.

Bourhis, Richard Y. 2001. Reversing language shift in Quebec. In Fishman (ed.) 2001a, pp. 101–41.

Bourhis, Richard Y., Giles, Howard and Rosenthal, Doreen. 1981. Notes on the construction of a 'subjective vitality questionnaire' for ethnolinguistic groups. *Journal of Multilingual and Multicultural Development* 2: 145–55.

Boyd, Sally. 1997. Patterns of incorporation of lexemes in language contact: language typology or sociolinguistics? In G. Guy, C. Feagin, D. Schiffrin and J. Baugh (eds.), *Towards a Social Science of Language*, volume 2: *Social Interaction and Discourse Structures*. Amsterdam: Benjamins, pp. 259–84.

Boyd, Sally, Holmen, Anne and Jørgensen, J. Norman (eds.). 1994. *Sprogbrug og sprogvalg blandt indvandrere i Norden*. Copenhagen: Center for multikulturelle studier, Danmarks Lærerhøjskole.

Broeder, Peter and Extra, Guus (eds.). 1999. *Language, Ethnicity and Education. Case Studies on Immigrant Minority Groups and Immigrant Minority Languages*. Clevedon: Multilingual Matters.

Broeder, Peter, Extra, Guus, Habraken, Miranda, Hout, Roeland van and Keurentjes, Heleen. 1993. *Taalgebruik als indicator van etniciteit*. Tilburg: Tilburg University Press.

Broersma, Mirjam. 2000. De triggertheorie voor codewisseling. De oorspronkelijke en enn aangepaste versie. MA thesis, Catholic University of Nijmegen.

Brown, R. and Gilman, A. 1960. The pronouns of power and solidarity. In T. A. Sebeok (ed.), *Style in Language*. Cambridge, MA: MIT Press, pp. 253–76.

Brown, Penelope and Levinson, Stephen. 1987. *Politeness*. Cambridge: Cambridge University Press.

Budzhak-Jones, Svitlana. 1998. Against word-internal codeswitching: evidence from Ukrainian-English bilingualism. *International Journal of Bilingualism* 2: 161–82.

Burridge, Kate. 1993. *Syntactic Change in Germanic: Aspects of Language Change in Germanic with Particular Reference to Middle Dutch*. Amsterdam: Benjamins.

Campbell, Lyle and Muntzel, Martha C. 1989. The structural consequences of language death. In Dorian (ed.), pp. 181–96.

Cavallaro, Francesco. 1997. Language Dynamics of the Italian Community in Australia. PhD thesis, Monash University.

Cenoz, Jasone. 1999. Pauses and hesitation phenomena in sociolinguistic proof. *ITL Review of Applied Linguistics* 127–8: 53–69.

Cenoz, Jasone. 2001. The effect of linguistic distance, L2 status and age on cross-linguistic influence in third language acquisition. In Cenoz, Hufeisen and Jessner (eds.), pp. 8–20.

Cenoz, Jasone and Jessner, Ulrike (eds.). 2000. *English in Europe: The Acquisition of a Third Language*. Clevedon: Multilingual Matters.

Cenoz, Jasone, Hufeisen, Britta and Jessner, Ulrike (eds.). 2001. *Cross-Linguistic Influences in Trilingualism and Third Language Acquisition*. Clevedon: Multilingual Matters.

Chen, J. Y, Chen, T. M. and Dell, G. S. 2002. Word-form encoding in Mandarin Chinese. *Journal of Memory and Language* 46(4): 751–81.

Chong-Woon, K. 1990. Code-switching in the Speech of Korean Migrants in Brisbane. PhD thesis, University of Queensland.

Clissa, John Felix. 2001. *The Fountain and the Squeezebox*. West Perth: Picton Press.

Clyne, Michael. 1967. *Transference and Triggering*. The Hague: Nijhoff.

Clyne, Michael. 1968. Transference patterns among English-German bilinguals. *ITL Review of Applied Linguistics* 2: 5–18.

Clyne, Michael. 1970a. Migrant English in Australia. In W. S. Ramson (ed.), *English Transported*. Canberra: A.N.U. Press, pp. 123–36.

Clyne, Michael. 1970b. Bilingual speech phenomena (with special reference to German–English bilinguals in Victoria). *Kivung* 4: 99–111.

Clyne, Michael. 1970c. Some aspects of the bilingual language maintenance of Australian-born children of German-speaking parents. *ITL Review of Applied Linguistics* 9: 35–47.

Clyne, Michael. 1972a. *Perspectives on Language Contact*. Melbourne: Hawthorn Press.

Clyne, Michael. 1972b. Some (German–English) language contact phenomena at the discourse level. In E. S. Firchow, K. Grimstad and N. Hasselmo (eds.), *Studies in Honor of Einar Haugen*. The Hague: Mouton, pp. 132–44.

Clyne, Michael. 1972c. Perception of code–switching by bilinguals: an experiment. *ITL Review of Applied Linguistics* 16: 45–8.

Clyne, Michael. 1975. *Forschungsbericht Sprachkontakt*. Kronberg: Scriptor.

Clyne, Michael (ed.). 1976. *Australia Talks*. (=Pacific Linguistics, Series D, No. 23) Canberra: Department of Linguistics, Research School of Pacific Studies.

Clyne, Michael. 1977a. Nieuw Hollands or double Dutch. *Dutch Studies* 3: 1–20.

Clyne, Michael. 1977b. Bilingualism of the elderly. *Talanya* 4: 45–56.

Clyne, Michael. 1977c. Multilingualism and pidginization in Australian industry. *Ethnic Studies* 1: 40–55.

Clyne, Michael. 1980a. Typology and grammatical convergence among related languages in contact. *ITL Review of Applied Linguistics* 49/50: 23–36.

Clyne, Michael. 1980b. Triggering and language processing. *Canadian Journal of Psychology* 34: 400–6.

Clyne, Michael. 1981. 'Second generation' foreigner talk in Australia. In M. Clyne (ed.), *Foreigner Talk* (=*International Journal of the Sociology of Language* 28). The Hague: Mouton, pp. 69–80.

Clyne, Michael. 1982. *Multilingual Australia*. Melbourne: River Seine (2nd edition, 1985).

Clyne, Michael (ed.). 1985. *Australia, Meeting Place of Languages* (=*Pacific Linguistics* C92). Canberra: Department of Linguistics, Research School of Pacific Studies.

Clyne, Michael. 1987. Constraints on code-switching – how universal are they? *Linguistics* 25: 739–64.

Clyne, Michael. 1991. *Community Languages: The Australian Experience*. Cambridge: Cambridge University Press.

Clyne, Michael. 1992a. Introduction. In M. Clyne (ed.), *Pluricentric Languages*. Berlin: Mouton de Gruyter, pp. 1–8.

Clyne, Michael. 1992b. Australian English in contact with other Englishes in Australia. In Rüdiger Ahrens and Heinz Antor (eds.), *Text – Culture – Reception*. Heidelberg: Winter, pp. 305–15.

Clyne, Michael. 1993. Pragmatik, Textstruktur und kulturelle Werte. In Hartmut Schröder (ed.), *Fachtextpragmatik*. Tübingen: Narr, pp. 3–18.

Clyne, Michael. 1994a. What can we learn from Sprachinseln? Some observations on 'Australian German'. In K. Mattheier and N. Berend (eds.), *Sprachinseln*. Frankfurt am Main: Peter Lang, pp. 105–22.

Clyne, Michael. 1994b. *Inter-Cultural Communication at Work*. Cambridge: Cambridge University Press.

Clyne, Michael. 1995. *The German Language in a Changing Europe*. Cambridge: Cambridge University Press.

Clyne, Michael. 1996. Sprache, Sprachbenutzer und Sprachbereich. In Goebl et al. (eds.), vol. 1(1), pp. 12–22.

Clyne, Michael. 1997a. The speech of third generation German–English bilinguals in Australia. In W. Wölck and A. de Houwer (eds.), *Recent Studies in Contact Linguistics*. Bonn: Dümmler, pp. 36–43.

Clyne, Michael. 1997b. Some of the things trilinguals do. *International Journal of Bilingualism* 1(2): 95–116.

Clyne, Michael. 1999. Australische Sprachgegenwart und österreichische Sprachgeschichte. Gemeinsamkeiten und Unterschiede. In M. Pümpel-Mader and B. Schönherr (eds.), *Sprache. Kultur. Geschichte. Sprachhistorische Studien zum Deutschen*. Innsbruck: Institut für Germanistik, pp. 395–408.

Clyne, Michael. 2000. What is it that is special about trilinguals? In A. Grotans, H. Beck and A. Schwob (eds.), *De consolatione philologicae*. Göppingen: Kümmerle, pp. 585–96.

Clyne, Michael. 2001. Can the shift from immigrant languages be reversed in Australia? In Fishman (2001a), pp. 364–390.

Clyne, Michael. Forthcoming. Towards a more language-centered view of plurilingualism. In J.-M. Dewaele and Li Wei (eds.), *Festschrift for Hugo Baetens-Beardsmore*. Clevedon: Multilingual Matters.

Clyne, Michael and Cain, Helen. 2000. Trilingualism in related languages – Dutch–German–English near and far. In G. Hirschfelder, D. Schell and A. Schrutka-Rechtenstamm (eds.), *Kulturen – Sprachen – Übergänge. Festschrift für H. L. Cox zum 65. Geburtstag*. Cologne: Böhlau, pp. 135–52.

Clyne, Michael, Eisikovits, Edina and Tollfree, Laura. 2001. Ethnic varieties of Australian English. In D. Blair (ed.), *English in Australia*. Amsterdam: Benjamins, pp. 223–38.

Clyne, Michael, Fernandez, Sue, Chen, Imogen and Summo-O'Connell, Renata. 1997. *Background Speakers*. Canberra: Language Australia.

Clyne, Michael and Kipp, Sandra. 1997. Trends and changes in home language use and shift in Australia. *Journal of Multilingual and Multicultural Development* 18: 451–73.

Clyne, Michael and Kipp, Sandra. 1998. Language concentrations in metropolitan areas. *People and Place* 6(2): 50–60.

Clyne, Michael and Kipp, Sandra. 1999. *Pluricentric Languages in an Immigrant Context: Spanish, Chinese, Arabic*. Berlin: Mouton de Gruyter.

Clyne, Michael and Mocnay, Eugenia. 1999. Zur ungarisch-deutsch-englischen Dreisprachigkeit in Australien. In K. Bührig and Y. Matras (eds.), *Sprachtheorie und sprachliches Handeln. Festschrift für Jochen Rehbein zum 60. Geburtstag*. Tübingen: Stauffenburg, pp. 159–69.

Coakes, Sheridan J. and Steed, Lyndall G. 1997. *SPSS Analysis without Analysis.* Brisbane:Wiley.

Conklin, Nancy F. and Lourie, Margaret A. 1983. *A Host of Tongues: Language Communities in the United States.* New York: Free Press.

Connor, Ulla and Kaplan, Robert B. (eds.). 1987. *Writing Across Cultures.* Reading, MA: Addison-Wesley.

Costa, Albert and Caramazza, Alfonso. 1999. Is lexical selection in bilingual speech production language-specific? *Bilingualism* 2(3): 231–43.

Coulmas, Florian. 1992. *Die Wirtschaft mit der Sprache.* Frankfurt: Suhrkamp.

Crawford, James. 2001. News from the USA Census, 2000: few surprises. *Bilingual Family Newsletter* 18: 3.

Cruz-Ferreira, Madalena. 1999. Prosodic mixing: strategies in multilingual language acquisition. *International Journal of Bilingualism* 3: 1–22.

Csernicskó, István and Fenyvési, Anna. 2000. The sociolinguistic stratification of Hungarian in Subcarpathia. *Multilingua* 19: 95–122.

Daan, Jo. 1970. Bilingualism of Dutch immigrants in the U.S.A. In V. Lange and H. Roloff (eds.), *Dichtung. Sprache. Gesellschaft. Akten des IV. Internationales Germanisten-Kongresses 1970 in Princeton*, pp. 205–13.

Dal Negro, Silvia. n.d. Mantimento, variazione e morte della lingua nel Walser di Formazza. Doctoral dissertation, Università degli Studi di Pavia.

Dalton, Lorraine, Edwards, Sandra, Farquarson, Rosaleen, Oscar, Sarah and McConvell, Patrick. 1995. Gurindji children's language and language maintenance. *International Journal of the Sociology of Language* 113: 83–98.

Dawkins, John. 1991a. *Australia's Language: The Australian Language and Literacy Policy.* Canberra: AGPS.

Dawkins, John. 1991b. *Australia's Language: The Australian Language and Literacy Policy.* Companion volume. Canberra: AGPS.

De Angelis, Gessica and Selinker, Larry. 2001. Interlanguage transfer and competing linguistic systems in the multilingual mind. In Cenoz, Hufeisen and Jessner (eds.), pp. 42–58.

De Bot, Kees. 1992. A bilingual production model: Levelt's 'speaking' model adapted. *Applied Linguistics* 13: 1–24.

De Bot, Kees. 1998. The psycholinguistics of language loss. In Extra and Verhoeven (eds.), pp. 345–61.

De Bot, Kees. 2000. Sociolinguistics and language processing mechanisms. *Sociolinguistica* 14: 74–7.

De Bot, Kees. 2001. Language use as an interface between sociolinguistic and psycholinguistic processes in language attrition and language shift. In J. Klatter-Folmer and P. van Avermaet (eds.), *Theories of maintenance and loss of minority languages.* Münster: Waxmann, 65–82.

De Bot, Kees and Clyne, Michael. 1989. Language reversion revisited, *Studies in Second Language Acquisition* 9: 167–77.

De Bot, Kees and Clyne, Michael. 1994. A 16-year longitudinal study of language attrition in Dutch immigrants in Australia. *Journal of Multicultural and Multilingual Development* 15: 17–28.

De Bot, Kees and Schreuder, Robert. 1993. Word production and the bilingual lexicon. In Robert Schreuder and Bert Weltens (eds.), *The Bilingual Lexicon.* Amsterdam: Benjamins, pp. 191–214.

De Bot, Kees and Stoessel, Sassia. 2000. In search of yesterday's words: reactivating a long forgotten language. *Applied Linguistics* 21(3): 364–88.

De Groot, Annette M.B. and Kroll, Judith F. (eds.). 1997. *Tutorials in Bilingualism: Psycholinguistic Perspectives.* Mahwah, NJ: Erlbaum.

De Rooij, J. 1987. *Variatie en Norm in de Standardtaal.* Amsterdam: Publikaties van het P. J. Meertens Instituut. Vol 7.

De Rooij, J. 1988. *Van 'hebben' naar 'zijn'.* Amsterdam: P. J. Meertens-Instituut.

De Vries, John. 1999. Foreign born language acquisition and shift. In S. Halli and L. Driedger (eds.), *Immigrant Canada: Demographic, Economic and Social Challenges.* Toronto: University of Toronto Press.

Dell, Gary. 1986. A spreading activation theory of retrieval in sentence production. *Psychological Review* 93: 283–321.

Dell, Gary. 1995. Speaking and misspeaking. In L. Gleitman and M. Liberman (eds.), *Language: An Invitation to Cognitive Science*, vol. 1 (2nd edition). Cambridge, MA: MIT Press, pp. 183–208.

Dell, Gary and Reich, Peter A. 1980. Toward a unified model of slips of the tongue. In V. Fromkin (ed.), *Errors in Linguistic Performance.* New York: Academic Press, pp. 273–86.

Dewaele, Jean-Marc. 1998. Lexical interventions: French interlanguage as L2 versus L3. *Applied Linguistics* 19(4): 471–90.

Dewaele, Jean-Marc. 2001. Activation or inhibition? The interaction of L1, L2 and L3 on the language mode continuum. In Cenoz, Hufeisen and Jessner (eds.), pp. 69–89.

Dil, Anwar (ed.). 1980. *Language and Linguistic Areas.* Stanford: Stanford University Press.

Di Sciullo, Annemarie, Muysken, Pieter and Singh, Rajendra. 1986. Code-mixing and government. *Journal of Linguistics* 22: 1–24.

Dixon, R. M. W. 1980. *The Languages of Australia.* Cambridge: Cambridge University Press.

Dixon, R. M. W. 1997. *The Rise and Fall of Languages.* Cambridge: Cambridge University Press.

Döpke, Susanne. 1992. *One parent one language – an interactional approach.* Amsterdam: Benjamins.

Donaldson, Bruce. 1981 (1987). *Dutch Reference Grammar.* 's-Gravenhage: Nijhoff.

Dorian, Nancy. 1977. The problem of the semi-speaker in language death. *International Journal of the Sociology of Language* 12: 23–32.

Dorian, Nancy. 1981. *Language Death: The Life Cycle of a Scottish Gaelic Dialect.* Philadelphia: University of Pennsylvania Press.

Dorian, Nancy (ed.). 1989. *Investigating Obsolescence. Studies in Language Contraction and Death.* Cambridge: Cambridge University Press.

Dorian, Nancy. 1994. Stylistic variation in a language restricted to private-sphere use. In D. Biber and E. Finegan (eds.), *Sociolinguistic Perspectives on Registers.* Oxford: Oxford University Press, pp. 217–32.

Dorian, Nancy. 1999. The study of language obsolescence: stages, surprises, challenges. *Languages and Linguistics* 3: 99–122.

Drach, Erich. 1937 (1963). *Grundlagen der deutschen Satzlehre.* Wiesbaden: Wissenschaftliche Buchgesellschaft.

Dufour, Robert. 1997. Sign language and bilingualism: modality implications for bilingual language representation. In de Groot and Kroll (eds.), pp. 301–30.

Duranti, Alessandro and Reynolds, Jennifer F. 2000. Phonological and cultural innovations in the speech of Samoans in Southern California. *Estudios de Sociolinguistica* 1: 93–110.

Durie, Mark. 1995. Towards an understanding of the linguistic evolution of the notion of 'X has a function Y'. In W. Abraham, T. Givón and S. Thompson (eds.), *Discourse Grammar and Typology: Papers in Honor of J. W. M. Verhaar*. Amsterdam: Benjamins, pp. 275–308.

Durović, Lubomir. 1983. The case systems in the language of diaspora children. *Slavica Lundensia* 9: 21–94.

Durrell, Martin. 1971 [1996]. *Hammer's German Grammar and Usage*. 3rd edition. London: Arnold.

Durrell, Martin. 1992. *Using German*. Cambridge: Cambridge University Press.

Duszak, Anna (ed.) 1997. *Culture and Styles of Academic Discourse*. Berlin: Mouton de Gruyter.

Ebbinghaus, Hermann. 1885. *Über das Gedächtnis*. Leipzig: Duncker und Humblot.

Edwards, John. 1992. Sociopolitical aspects of language maintenance and loss: towards a typology of minority language situations. In W. Fase, K. Jaspaert and S. Kroon (eds.), *The Maintenance and Loss of Minority languages*. Amsterdam: Benjamins, pp. 37–54.

Edwards, John. 1994. *Multilingualism*. London: Routledge.

Els, Theo van. 1985. An overview of European research on language attrition. In B. Weltens, K. de Bot and T. van Els (eds.), *Language Attrition in Progress*. Dordrecht, Holland: Foris, pp. 3–19.

Emeneau, Murray B. 1980a. India and linguistic areas. In Dil (ed.), pp. 120–65.

Emeneau, Murray B. 1965/1980b. Dravidian and Indo-Aryan: the Indian linguistic area. In Dil (ed.), pp. 167–96.

Endrody, Tibor. 1971. Prepositional Interference and Deviation in Migrant German and Migrant Hungarian. MA thesis, Monash University.

Extra, Guus. 1978. *Eerste- en tweede-taalverwerving*. Muiderberg: Coutinho.

Extra, Guus and Verhoeven, Ludo (eds.). 1993a. *Community Languages in the Netherlands*. Tilburg: Tilburg University Press.

Extra, Guus and Verhoeven, Ludo (eds.). 1993b. *Immigrant languages in Europe*. Clevedon: Multilingual Matters.

Eze, Ejike. 1998. Lending credence to a borrowing analysis: lone English-origin incorporation in Igbo discourse. *International Journal of Bilingualism* 2: 183–202.

Fenyvési, Anna. 1994. Language Contact and Language Death in an Immigrant Language: The Case of Hungarian. Unpublished MA thesis, University of Pittsburgh.

Ferguson, Charles. 1959. Diglossia, *Word* 15: 325–44.

Fishman, Joshua A. 1967. Bilingualism with or without diglossia: diglossia with or without bilingualism. *Journal of Social Issues* 23: 29–38.

Fishman, Joshua A. 1977. The social science perspective: keynote. In J. A. Fishman (ed.), *Bilingual Education: Current Perspectives*. Washington, DC: Georgetown University, pp. 1–49.

Fishman, Joshua A. 1987. Post-exilic Jewish languages and pidgins/creoles. *Multilingua* 6: 7–24.

Fishman, Joshua A. 1988. 'English only' – its ghosts, myths and dangers. *International Journal of the Sociology of Language* 74: 125–40.

Fishman, Joshua A. 1989. *Language and Ethnicity in Minority Sociolinguistic Perspective*. Clevedon: Multilingual Matters.

Fishman, Joshua A. 1991. *Reversing Language Shift*. Clevedon: Multilingual Matters.

Fishman, Joshua A. 1997. *In Praise of the Beloved Language*. Berlin: Mouton de Gruyter.

Fishman, Joshua A. (ed.). 2001a. *Can Threatened Languages Be Saved?* Clevedon: Multilingual Matters.

Fishman, Joshua A. 2001b. A decade in the life of a two-in-one language. In Fishman (ed.), pp. 74–100.

Fishman, Joshua A. 2001c. From theory to practice (and vice versa). In Fishman (ed.), pp. 451–83.

Fishman, Joshua A., Nahirny, Vladimir C., Hofman, John E. and Hayden, Robert G. (eds.). 1966. *Language Loyalty in the United States*. The Hague: Mouton.

Fishman, Joshua A., Gertner, Michael H., Lowy, Esther G. and Milán, William G. 1985. *The Rise and Fall of the Ethnic Revival*. Berlin: Mouton de Gruyter.

Fodor, Jerry A., Garrett, Merrill and Bever, Thomas G. 1968. Some syntactic determinants of sentential complexity. II – verb structure. *Perception and Psychophysics* 8: 215–21.

Foolen, Ad. 1993. De betekenis van partikels. PhD thesis, University of Nijmegen.

Franck, Dorothea. 1979. Abtönungspartikeln und Interaktionsmanagement. Tendenziöse Fragen. In Weydt (ed.), pp. 3–13.

Fuller, Janet. 2000. Morpheme types in a ML turnover. *International Journal of Bilingualism* 4: 45–58.

Fuller, Janet and Lehnert, Heike. 2000. Noun phrase structure in German-English code-switching. *International Journal of Bilingualism* 4: 399–420.

Gafaranga, Joseph. 2000. Medium repair versus other language-repair, *International Journal of Bilingualism* 4: 327–50.

Gal, Susan. 1979. *Language Shift: Social Determinants of Linguistic Change in Bilingual Austria*. New York: Academic Press.

Galbally, Frank. 1978. *Report on Post-Arrival Services and Programs for Migrants*. Canberra: AGPS.

García, Ofelia, Morin, Jose Luis and Rivera, Klaudia. 2001. How threatened is the Spanish of New York Puerto Ricans? In Fishman (ed.), pp. 44–73.

Gardner-Chloros, Penelope. 1991. *Language Selection and Switching in Strasbourg*. Oxford: Clarendon Press.

Gardner-Chloros, Penelope. 1995. Code-switching in community, regional and national repertoires: the myth of discreteness of linguistic systems. In Milroy and Muysken (eds.), pp. 68–89.

Gardner-Chloros, Penelope, Moyer, Melissa, Sebba, Mark and Hout, Roeland van. 1999. Toward standardizing and sharing bilingual data. *International Journal of Bilingualism* 3(4): 395–424.

Gass, Susan M. 1997. *Input, Interaction and the Second Language Learner*. Mahwah, NJ: Erlbaum.

Ghafar Samar, Reza and Meechan, Marjory. 1998. The Null Theory of codeswitching versus the Nonce Borrowing Hypothesis. *International Journal of Bilingualism* 2: 203–20.

Giacalone Ramat, Anna. 1983. Che cosa può offrire lo studio delle lingue in via di riduzione alle ricerche sull'acquisizione delle lingue straniere? In M. Dardano (ed.), *Parallela* (=*Akten d.2.Österr. – it. Linguistentreffens*). Tübingen: Narr, pp. 337–51.

Giacalone Ramat, Anna. 1995. Code-switching in the context of dialect/standard language relations. In Milroy and Muysken (eds.), pp. 45–68.

Giesbers, Herman. 1989. *Code-switching tussen dialect en standaardtaal*. Amsterdam: P. J. Meertens-Instituut.

Gilbert, Glenn. 1965. Dative vs. accusative in the German dialects of Texas. *Zeitschrift für Mundartforschung*. 32(3–4): 288–96.

Gilbert, Glenn. 1970. The phonology, morphology and lexicon of a German text from Fredericksburg, Texas. In Gilbert (ed.), *Texas Studies in Bilingualism*. Berlin: De Gruyter, pp. 63–105.

Giles, Howard (ed.). 1997. *Language, Ethnicity and Intergroup Relations*. London: Academic Press.

Giles, Howard, Bourhis, Richard Y. and Taylor, Donald M. 1977. Toward a theory of language in ethnic group relations. In Giles (ed.), pp. 307–48.

Giles, Howard and Powesland, Peter. 1975. *Speech Style and Social Evaluation*. London: Academic Press.

Giles, Howard, Rosenthal, Doreen and Young, Louis. 1985. Perceived ethnolinguistic vitality: the Anglo- and Greek-Australian setting. *Journal of Multilingual and Multicultural Development* 6: 253–69.

Givón, Talmy. 1971. Historical syntax and synchronic morphology: an archaeologist's fieldtrip. *Papers from the 7th regional meeting of the Chicago Linguistic Society*, pp. 394–415.

Givón, Talmy. 1976. On the VS word order in Israeli Hebrew: pragmatics and typological change. In P. Cole (ed.), *Papers in Hebrew Syntax*. Amsterdam: North Holland, pp. 153–81.

Givón, Talmy. 1979. *On Understanding Grammar*. New York: Academic Press.

Goebl, Hans, Nelde, Peter, Starý, Zdenek and Wölck, Wolfgang (eds.). 1997. *Handbook of Contact Linguistics*. Berlin: Mouton de Gruyter.

Goffman, Erving. 1981. Radio talk. In E. Goffman (ed.), *Forms of Talk*. Philadelphia: University of Pennsylvania Press, pp. 197–330.

Gold, David L. 1981. The speech and writing of Jews. In C. Ferguson and S. Heath (eds.), *Language in the USA*. Cambridge: Cambridge University Press, pp. 273–93.

Goldman-Eisler, Frieda. 1968. *Psycholinguistics*. London: Academic Press.

Gonzo, Susan and Saltarelli, Mario. 1983. Pidginization and linguistic change in emigrant languages. In R. Andersen (ed.), *Pidginization and Creolization as Language Acquisition*. Rowley: Newbury House, pp. 181–97.

Goss, Emily and Salmons, Joseph. 2000. The evolution of a bilingual discourse marking system: modal particles and English markers in German-American dialects. *International Journal of Bilingualism* 4: 469–84.

Green, David. 1986. Control, activation and resource: a framework and a model for the control of speech in bilinguals. *Brain and Language* 27: 210–23.

Green, David. 1993. Towards a model of L2 comprehension and production. In Schreuder and Weltens (eds.), *The Bilingual Lexicon*. Amsterdam: Benjamins, pp. 249–77.

Green, David. 1998. Mental control of the bilingual lexico-semantic system. *Bilingualism, Language and Cognition* 1: 67–81.

Greenberg, Joseph H. 1963. Some universals of grammar with particular reference to the order of meaningful elements. In J. Greenberg (ed.), *Universals of Language*. Cambridge, MA: MIT Press, pp. 73–113.

Grin, François. 1996. Economic approaches to language and language planning: an introduction. *International Journal of the Sociology of Language* 121: 1–16.

Grosjean, François. 1982. *Life with Two Languages*. Cambridge, MA: Harvard University Press.

Grosjean, François. 1988. Exploring the recognition of guest words in bilingual speech. *Language and Cognitive Processes* 3: 233–74.

Grosjean, François. 1995. A psycholinguistic approach to code-switching: the recognition of guest words by bilinguals. In Milroy and Muysken (eds.), pp. 259–75.

Grosjean, François. 1997. Processing mixed language. In de Groot and Kroll (eds.), pp. 225–54.

Grosjean, François. 1998. Studying bilinguals: methodological and conceptual issues. *Bilingualism, Language and Cognition* 1: 131–49.

Grosjean, François. 2001. The bilingual's language modes. In Nicol (ed.), pp. 1–22.

Gumperz, John J. 1964. Hindi-Punjabi code-switching in Delhi. *Proceedings of the 9th International Congress of Linguists*. Cambridge, MA, The Hague: Mouton, pp. 115–24.

Gumperz, John J. 1976. *The Sociolinguistic Significance of Conversational Code-Switching* (=*University of California Working Papers 46*). Berkeley: University of California.

Gumperz, John J. 1982. *Discourse Strategies*. Cambridge: Cambridge University Press.

Gumperz, John J. and Wilson, Robert. 1971. Convergence and creolization: a case from the Indo-Aryan/ Dravidian border. In D. Hymes (ed.), *Pidginization and Creolization of Languages*. Cambridge: Cambridge University Press, pp. 151–68.

Guy, Gregory and Vonwiller, Jan. 1989. The high rising tone in Australian English. In P. Collins and D. Blair (eds.), *Australian English. The Language of a New Society*. Brisbane: University of Queensland Press, pp. 21–34.

Haas, Mary. 1953. Results of the conference of anthropologists and linguists. Introduction to Chapter III. *Supplement to: International Journal of American Linguistics* 19: 42–49.

Häcki-Buhofer, Annelies and Burger, Harald. 1998. *Wie deutschschweizer Kinder Hochdeutsch lernen* (ZDL-Beiheft 98). Stuttgart: Steiner.

Haeringen, C. B. van. n.d. *Nederlands tussen Duits en Engels*. The Hague: Servire.

Haig, Geoffrey. 2001. Linguistic diffusion in present-day Anatolia: from top to bottom. In A. Aikhenvald and R. M. W. Dixon (eds.), *Areal Diffusion and Genetic Inheritance: Problems in Comparative Linguistics*. Oxford: Oxford University Press.

Håkansson, Gisela. 2001. Tense morphology and verb-second in Swedish L1 children, L2 children and children with SLI. *Bilingualism, Language and Cognition* 4: 85–99.

Halmari, Helena. 1997. *Government and Codeswitching: Explaining American Finnish*. Amsterdam: Benjamins.

Hammarberg, Bjorn. 2001. Roles of L1 and L2 in L3 production and acquisition. In Cenoz et al. (eds.), pp. 21–41.

Hansen, Marcus Lee. 1962. The third generation in America. *Commentary* 14: 492–500.

Harris, Alice C. and Campbell, Lyle. 1995. *Historical Syntax in Cross-Linguistic Perspective*. Cambridge: Cambridge University Press.

Hartung, Wolfdietrich. 1964. *Die zusammengesetzte Sätze des Deutschen* (=Studia Grammatica 4). Berlin: Akademie Verlag.

Harvey, Susan. 1974. National language usage among Dutch and Polish immigrant children. In D. Edgar (ed.), *Social Change in Australia*. Melbourne: Cheshire, pp. 131–44.

Hasselmo, Nils. 1961. American Swedish. PhD dissertation, Harvard University.

Hasselmo, Nils. 1974. *Amerikasvenska*. Lund: Esselte.

Haugen, Einar. 1953. *The Norwegian Language in America*. 2 vols. Philadelphia: University of Pennsylvania Press.

Haugen, Einar. 1956. *Bilingualism in the Americas*. Alabama: American Dialect Society.

Haugen, Einar. 1973. Bilingualism, language contact and immigrant languages in the United States. *Current Trends in Linguistics* 10: 505–91. The Hague: Mouton.

Haugen, Einar, McClure, J. Derrick and Thomson, Derick (eds). 1980. *Minority Languages Today*. Edinburgh: Edinburgh University Press.

Hawkins, John. 1986. *Comparative Typology of English and German*. London: Croom Helm.

Hebart, Theodor. 1938. *Die Vereinigte Evangelisch-Lutherischje Kirche in Australien*. North Adelaide: Lutheran Publishing House.

Heidolph, Karl Erich. 1964. Einfacher Satz und Kernsatz im Deutschen. *Acta Linguistica Hungarica* 14: 97–109.

Henzl, Vera M. 1980. American Czech: a comparative study of the linguistic modifications in immigrant and young children speech. In Sussex (ed.), pp. 33–46.

Hermans, Daan, Bongaerts, Theo, De Bot, Kees and Schreuder, Robert. 1998. Producing words in a foreign language: can speakers prevent interference from the first language? *Bilingualism, Language and Cognition* 1: 213–30.

Herwig, Anna. 2001. Plurilingual lexical organization: evidence from lexical processing in L1–L2–L3–L4 translation. In Cenoz et al. (eds.), pp. 115–137.

Hinrichs, Uwe. 1979. Partikelgebrauch und Identität am Beispiel des deutschen Ja. In Weydt (ed.), pp. 256–68.

Hirst, John. 2001. More or less diversity. In H. Irving (ed.), *The Barton Lectures: Unity and Diversity*. Sydney: NSW Centenary of Federation and ABC.

Hlavac, Jim. 1999. Phonological integration of English transfers in Croatian: evidence from the Croatian speech of second generation Croatian-Australians. *Filologija* 32: 39–73.

Hlavac, Jim. 2000. Croatian in Melbourne: lexicon, switching and morphosyntactic features in the speech of second-generation bilinguals. PhD thesis, Monash University.

Ho-Dac, Tuc. 1996. Languages in contact: Vietnamese-English code-switching in Melbourne. PhD thesis, Monash University.

Ho-Dac, Tuc. 2002. *Vietnamese-English Bilingualism. Patterns of Code-Switching*. London: Routledge Curzon.

Hoffmann, Charlotte. 2001. Towards a description of trilingual competence. *International Journal of Bilingualism* 5: 1–17.

Holmes, Janet. 1992. *An Introduction to Sociolinguistics*. London: Longman.

House, Juliane and Kasper, Gabriele. 1981. Politeness markers in English and German. In F. Coulmas (ed.), *Conversational Routine. Explorations in Standardized Communication Situations and Prepatterned Speech*. The Hague: Mouton, pp. 157–85.

Hufeisen, Britta. 1991. *Englisch als erste und Deutsch als zweite Fremdsprache.* Frankfurt: Lang.

Huffines, Marion Lois. 1989. Case usage among the Pennsylvania German sectarians and nonsectarians. In Dorian (ed.), pp. 211–26.

Hulsen, Madeleine. 2000. Language loss and language processing: three generations of Dutch migrants in New Zealand. PhD thesis, University of Nijmegen.

Hyman, Larry M. 1975. On the change from SOV to SVO: evidence from Niger-Congo. In C. N. Li (ed.), *Word Order Change.* Austin: University of Texas Press, pp. 113–47.

Isačenko, Alexander. 1965. Das syntaktische Verhältnis der Bezeichnung von Körperteilen im deutschen. *Studia Grammatica* 5: 7–27.

Jacobs, Neil. 1996. On the investigation of 1920s Vienna Jewish speech. *American Journal of Germanic Linguistics and Literatures* 8: 177–217.

Jacobson, Rodolfo (ed.). 1998. *Codeswitching Worldwide.* New York: Mouton de Gruyter.

Jacobson, Rodolfo (ed.). 2001. *Codeswitching Worldwide 2.* Berlin: Mouton de Gruyter.

Jake, Janice. 1994. Intrasentential code-switching and pronouns: on the categorial status of functional elements. *Linguistics* 32: 271–98.

Jake, Janice and Myers-Scotton, Carol. 1997. Codeswitching and compromise strategies: implications for lexical structure. *International Journal of Bilingualism* 1: 25–39.

Jake, Janice, Myers-Scotton, Carol and Gross, Steven. 2002. Making a minimalist approach to codeswitching work: adding the Matrix Language. *Bilingualism, Language and Cognition* 5: 69–91.

Jaspaert, Koen and Kroon, Sjaak. 1988. Social Determinants of Language Shift by Italians in the Netherlands and Flanders. Paper delivered at the International Workshop in the Loss and Maintenance of Minority Languages, Noordwijkerhout, August 1988.

Jescheniak, Jörg D. and Schriefers, Hebert. 1997. Lexical access in speech production: serial or cascaded processing? *Language and Cognition Processes* 12: 847–52.

Johanson, Lars. 1992. *Strukturelle Faktoren in türkischen Sprachkontakten.* Stuttgart: Steiner.

Johanson, Lars. 1999. The dynamics of code-copying in language encounters. In E. Lanza Brendemoen and E. Ryen (eds.), *Language Encounters Across Time and Space.* Oslo: Novus Press, pp. 37–62.

Jucker, Andreas and Smith, Sara W. 1998. And people just you know like 'wow': discourse markers as negotiating strategies. In Jucker and Ziv (eds.), pp.171–201.

Jucker, Andreas and Ziv, Yael (eds.). 1998. *Discourse Markers.* Amsterdam: Benjamins.

Jutronić, Dunja. 1974. The Serbo-Croatian language in Steelton, PA. *General Linguistics* 14: 15–34.

Kachru, Braj. 1978. Toward structuring code-mixing: an Indian perspective. *International Journal of the Sociology of Language* 16: 27–46.

Kachru, Braj. 1983. On mixing. In B. Kachru (ed.), *The Indianization of English.* New Delhi: Oxford University Press, pp. 193–207.

Kaminskas, Gintas. 1972. Melbourne Spanish. MA thesis, Monash University.

Kasper, Gabriele. 1981. *Pragmatische Aspekte in der Interimsprache.* Tübingen: Gunter Narr Verlag.

Kasper, Gabriele and Blum-Kulka, Shoshana (eds.). 1994. *Interlanguage Pragmatics*. Oxford: Oxford University Press.

Katsikis, Mary. 1993. Language Attitudes, Ethnicity and Language Maintenance: the Case of Second Generation Greek-Australians. BA (Hons) thesis, Department of Linguistics, Monash University.

Katsikis, Mary. 1997. The Generation Gap: an Insight into the Language and Cultural Maintenance of Third Generation Greek-Australians. MA thesis, Department of Linguistics, Monash University.

Keel, William D. 1994. Reduction and loss of case marking in the noun phrase in German-American speech islands: internal development or external interference? In Berend and Mattheier (eds.), pp. 93–104.

Keenan, Edward. 1978. Language variation and the logical structure of universal grammar. In Hans-Jakob Seiler (ed.), *Language Universals*. Tübingen: Narr, pp. 89–123.

Kenny, K. Dallas. 1996. *Language Loss and the Crisis of Cognition*. The Hague: Mouton.

Kiefer, Ferenc. 1988. Modal particles as discourse markers in questions. *Acta Linguistica Hungarica* 38: 107–25.

Kinder, John J. 1986. The verbal marking of interference in New Zealand Italian. In Bettoni (ed.), pp. 87–104.

Kipp, Sandra. 1980. German language maintenance and shift in some rural settlements. *ITL Review of Applied Linguistics* 28: 69–80.

Kipp, Sandra. 2002. German–English bilingualism in the Western District of Victoria. PhD thesis, University of Melbourne.

Kipp, Sandra, Clyne, Michael and Pauwels, Anne. 1995. *Immigration and Australia's Language Resources*. Canberra: AGPS.

Kjær, I. and Baumann-Larsen, M. 1974. De messy ting. In P. Andersen (ed.), *Festschrift til Kristian Hals*. Copenhagen: Akademisk Forlag, pp. 421–30.

Klarberg, Manfred. 1976. Identity and communication: maintenance of Hebrew, decline of Yiddish. In Clyne (ed.), pp. 89–102.

Klarberg, Manfred. 1983. The Effect of Ideology on Language Teaching. PhD thesis, Monash University.

Klatter-Folmer, Jetske. 1995. Language shift and loss in a third generation Dutch family in New Zealand. In Klatter-Folmer and Kroon (eds.), pp. 195–214.

Klatter-Folmer, Jetske and Kroon, Sjaak (eds.). 1995. *Dutch Overseas*. Tilburg: Tilburg University Press.

Klatter-Folmer, Jetske and Avermaet, Piet van (eds.). 2001. *Theories on Maintenance and Loss of Minority Languages*. Münster: Waxmann.

Klavans, Judith L. 1983. The syntax of code-switching. In L. D. King and C. A. Maley (eds.), *Selected Papers from the 13th Linguistic Symposium on Romance Languages*. Vol. 36. Amsterdam: Benjamins, pp. 213–31.

Kloss, Heinz. 1966. German American language maintenance efforts. In Fishman et al. (eds.), pp. 206–52.

Kloss, Heinz. 1969. *Research Possibilities in Group Bilingualism*. Québec: International Center for Research on Bilingualism.

König, Ekkehard, Stark, Detlef and Requardt, Susanne. 1990. *Adverbien und Partikeln: ein deutsch-englisches Wörterbuch*. Heidelberg: Groos.

Kontra, Miklós. 1990. *Fejezetek a South Bend-i Magyár Nyelvhasználatból*. Budapest: MTA Nyelvtudomanyi Intézete.

Kouzmin, Ludmilla. 1973. The Russian Language in an Australian Environment: a Descriptive Analysis of English Lexical Interference in the Speech of Bilingual Russian Migrants. PhD thesis, University of Melbourne.

Kovács, Magdolna. 2001. *Code-switching and Language Shift in Australian Finnish in Comparison with Australian Hungarian*. Äbo: Äbo University Press.

Krashen, Stephen D. 1982. *Second Language Acquisition and Second Language Learning*. Oxford: Pergamon.

Kurtböke, Petek. 1998a. A Corpus-driven Study of Turkish-English Language Contact in Australia. PhD thesis, Monash University.

Kurtböke, Petek. 1998b. Non-equivalence of delexicalized verbs in bilingual dictionaries. In Thierry Fontenelle et al. (eds.), *EURALEX '98 Proceedings*. Belgium: University of Liège, vol. 2, pp. 397–404.

Lalor, Erin and Kirsner, Kim. 2000. Cross-lingual transfer effects between English and Italian cognates and non-cognates. *International Journal of Bilingualism* 4: 385–98.

Lalor, Olga and Blanc, Michel. 1988. Language use in a bilingual Adyge-Russian community. *Journal of Multilingual and Multicultural Development* 9: 411–22.

Larmouth, Donald. 1974. Differential interference in American Finnish cases. *Language* 50: 356–66.

Lehmann, Winfred P. 1974. *Proto-Indo-European Syntax*. Austin: University of Texas Press.

Lehmann, Winfred P. 1978. *Syntactic Typology*. Austin: University of Texas Press.

Levelt, W. J. M. 1983. Monitoring and self-repair in speech. *Cognition* 14: 41–104.

Levelt, W. J. M. 1989. *Speaking*. Cambridge, MA: MIT Press.

Levelt, W. J. M., Roelofs, Ardi and Meyer, Antje S. 1999. A theory of lexical access in speech production. *Behavioural and Brain Sciences* 22: 1–75.

Li, David C. S. 2001. L2 lexis in L1: reluctance to translate out of concern for referential meaning. *Multilingua* 20: 1–26.

Li Wei. 1998a. *Three Generations, Two Languages, One Family: Language Choice and Language Shift in a Chinese Community in Britain*. Clevedon: Multilingual Matters.

Li Wei. 1998b. The 'why' and 'how' questions in the analysis of conversational code-switching. In Auer (ed.), pp. 156–79.

Lo Bianco, Joseph. 1987. *National Policy on Languages*. Canberra: AGPS.

Lo Bianco, Joseph. 2000. Policy literacy. *Language and Education* 15: 122–7.

Lockwood, W. B. 1968. *Historical German Syntax*. Oxford: Clarendon Press.

Loránd, Benko and Samu, Imre. 1972. *The Hungarian Language*. The Hague: Mouton.

LOTE Strategy Plan 1993. Melbourne: Victorian Department of Education.

Louden, Mark L. 1994. Syntactic change in multilingual speech islands. In Berend and Mattheier (eds.), pp. 73–92.

Lucas, Ceil and Valli, Clayton. 1989. Language contact in the American deaf community. In C. Lucas (ed.), *The Socio-Linguistics of the Deaf Community*. San Diego: Academic Press, pp. 11–40.

Ludwig-Wyder, Hélène. 1982. L' influence de l'anglais sur le français parlé en Australie. MA thesis, University of Melbourne.

Lütten, J. 1979. Die Rolle der Partikeln doch, eben und ja als Konsens-Konstitutiva in gesprochener Sprache. In Weydt (ed.), pp. 30–8.

Maandi, Katrin. 1989. Estonian among immigrants in Sweden. In Dorian (ed.), pp. 227–42.

Macaulay, Ronald. 2001. You're like 'Why not?' The quotative expressions of Glasgow adolescents. *Journal of Sociolinguistics* 2: 3–21.

McClelland, James and Elman, Jeffrey. 1986. The TRACE model of speech perception. *Cognitive Psychology* 18: 1–86.

McClure, Erica. 1977. Aspects of code-switching in the discourse of bilingual Mexican-American children. In M. Saville-Troike (ed.), *Linguistics and Anthropology*. Washington, DC: Georgetown University Press, pp. 93–116.

McClure, Erica. 2001. Oral and written Assyrian-English code-switching. In Jacobson (ed.), pp. 157–91.

McConvell, Patrick. 1985. Domains and code-switching among bilingual Aborigines. In Clyne (ed.), pp. 95–125.

McConvell, Patrick. 1988. MIX-IM-UP: Aboriginal code-switching, old and new. In Heller (ed.), *Code-Switching*. Berlin: Mouton de Gruyter, pp. 97–149.

McConvell, Patrick. 1991. Understanding language shift: a step towards language maintenance. In S. Romaine (ed.), *Language in Australia*. Cambridge: Cambridge University Press, pp. 143–55.

Mackey, William F. 1966. The measurement of bilingual behavior. *The Canadian Psychologist* 7a: 75–92.

McNamara, Tim J. 1987. Language and social identity: Israelis abroad. *Journal of Language and Social Psychology* 6: 215–28.

MacSwan, Jeff. 1999. *A Minimalist Approach to Intrasentential Code Switching*. New York: Garland.

MacWhinney, Barry. 1987. Applying the competition model to bilingualism. *Applied Psycholinguistics* 8: 315–27.

MacWhinney, Barry. 1992. Transfer and competition in second language learning. In Harris (ed.), *Cognitive Processing in Bilinguals*. Amsterdam: Elsevier, pp. 371–90.

MacWhinney, Barry. 1997. Second language acquisition and the competition model. In Groot and Kroll (eds.), pp. 113–42.

MacWhinney, Barry and Bates, Elizabeth (eds.). 1989. *The Cross-Linguistic Study of Sentence Processing*. Cambridge: Cambridge University Press.

Maher, Julianne. 1991. A cross-linguistic study of language contact and language attrition. In H. Seliger and R. Vado (eds.), *First Language Attrition*. Cambridge: Cambridge University Press, pp. 67–87.

Mahootian, Shahrzad. 1996. A competence model of code-switching. In J. Arnold (ed.), *Sociolinguistic Variation. Data, Theory and Analysis. Selected papers from NWAV 23 at Stanford*. Stanford: CSLI, pp. 387–400.

Mallinson, Graham and Blake, Barry. 1981. *Language Typology: Cross-Linguistic Studies in Syntax*. Amsterdam: North-Holland.

Marle, Jaap van and Smits, Caroline. 1997. Deviant patterns of lexical transfer: English-origin words in American Dutch. In Klatter-Folmer and Kroon (eds.), pp. 255–72.

Martín, Mario Daniel. 1996. Spanish Language Maintenance and Shift in Australia. PhD thesis, Australian National University, Canberra.

Martin, Nadine, Gagnon, Deborah, Schwartz, Myrna, Dell, Gary and Saffran, Eleanor. 1996. Phonological facilitation of semantic errors in normal and aphasic speakers. *Language and Cognitive Processes* 11: 257–82.

Matthews, Peter. 1997. *The Concise Oxford Dictionary of Linguistics*. Oxford: Oxford University Press.

Meechan, Marjory. 2001. Review of J. MacSwan, *A Minimalist Approach to Intrasentential Codeswitching*. *Language in Society* 30: 285–9.

Meeuwis, Michael and Blommaert, Jan. 1998. A monolectal view of code-switching: layered code-switching among Zairians in Belgium. In Auer (ed.), pp. 76–98.

Meyerstein, G. P. 1969. Interference in prepositional phrases: immigrant Slovak in America. *Lingua* 22: 63–80.

Milroy, James. 1998. Internal vs. external motivations for linguistic change. *Multilingua* 16: 311–24.

Milroy, Lesley and Muysken, Pieter (eds.). 1995. *One Speaker, Two Languages. Cross-Disciplinary Perspectives on Code-Switching*. Cambridge: Cambridge University Press.

Milroy, Lesley. 1980. *Language and Social Networks*. Oxford: Basil Blackwell.

Monheit, Dorrit. 1975. The Role of the German Ethnic School in Maintaining the German Language in Melbourne. BA (Hons.) thesis, Monash University.

Morgan, Roy. 1951. *Morgan Gallup Poll – Maintenance of Level of Immigration*. Melbourne: Morgan.

Mous, Maarten. 1994. Ma'a or Mbugu. In Bakker and Mous (eds.), pp. 175–200.

Mufwene, Salikoko. 1991. Pidgins, creoles, typology and markedness. In F. Byrne and T. Huebner (eds.), *Development and Structure of Creole Languages*. Amsterdam/Philadelphia: Benjamins, pp. 123–43.

Mufwene, Salikoko. 1994. Review of C. Myers-Scotton, *Social Motivations for Codeswitching*. *The SECOL Review* 18: 213–18.

Mufwene, Salikoko. 2001. *The Ecology of Language Evolution*. Cambridge: Cambridge University Press.

Mufwene, Salikoko and Gilman, Charles. 1987. How African is Gullah and why? *American Speech* 62: 120–39.

Mühlhäusler, Peter. 1980. Structural expansion and the process of creolization. In A. Valdman and A. Highfield (eds.), *Theoretical Orientations in Creole Studies*. New York: Academic Press, pp. 19–55.

Mühlhäusler, Peter. 1985. Patterns of contact, mixture, creation and nativization. In C. J. Bailey (ed.), *Developmental Mechanisms of Language*. Oxford: Pergamon, pp. 51–88.

Mühlhäusler, Peter. 1997. *Pidgin and Creole Linguistics*, expanded and revised edition. London: University of Westminster Press.

Müller, Max. 1862. *Lectures on the Science of Language*. 5th edition. London: Longmans, Green.

Muysken, Pieter. 1995. Code-switching and grammatical theory. In Milroy and Muysken (eds.), pp. 177–98.

Muysken, Pieter. 1997. Code-switching processes. In M. Pütz (ed.), *Language Choices*. Amsterdam: Benjamins, pp. 361–78.

Muysken, Pieter. 2000. *Bilingual Speech*. Cambridge: Cambridge University Press.

Myers-Scotton, Carol. 1992. Comparing code-switching and borrowing. *Journal of Multilingual and Multicultural Development* 13: 19–40.

Myers-Scotton, Carol. 1993a. *Duelling Languages: Grammatical Structure in Codeswitching*. New York: Oxford University Press.

Myers-Scotton, Carol. 1993b. *Social Motivations for Codeswitching: Evidence from Africa*. Oxford: Clarendon Press.

Myers-Scotton, Carol. 1997a. Codeswitching. In F. Coulmas (ed.), *The Handbook of Sociolinguistics*. Oxford: Blackwell, pp. 217–37.

Myers-Scotton, Carol. 1997b. Paperback edition of 1993a (with Afterword). New York: Oxford University Press.

Myers-Scotton, Carol. 1998a. One way to dusty death: the Matrix Language Turnover Hypothesis. In L. Grenoble and W. Whaley (eds.), *Endangered Languages*. Cambridge: Cambridge University Press, pp. 289–306.

Myers-Scotton, Carol. 1998b. A theoretical introduction to Markedness Model. In C. Myers-Scotton (ed.), *Codes and Consequences*. Oxford: Oxford University Press, pp. 18–38.

Myers-Scotton, Carol. 2000. The Matrix Language Frame Model: developments and responses. In R. Jacobson (ed.), *Codeswitching Worldwide II*. Berlin: Mouton de Gruyter.

Myers-Scotton, Carol and Jake, Janice L. 1995. Matching lemmas in a bilingual language competence and production model: evidence from intrasentential code switching. *Linguistics* 33: 981–1024.

Myers-Scotton, Carol and Jake, Janice L. 2000. Four types of morphemes: evidence from aphasia, codeswitching and second language acquisition. *Linguistics* 38: 1053–100.

Myers-Scotton, Carol and Jake, Janice L. 2001. Explaining aspects of codeswitching and their implications. In Nicol (ed.), pp. 84–118.

Nattinger, James R. and De Carrico, Jeanette S. 1992. *Lexical Phrases and Language Teaching*. Oxford: Oxford University Press.

Naumann, K. 1997. Svenska som främade språk I Schweiz. In G. Håkansson et al. (eds.), *Svenskas beskriving 22*. Lund: Studentliteratur, pp. 318–34.

Nicol, Janet (ed.). 2001. *One Mind, Two Languages: Bilingual Language Processing*. Oxford: Blackwell.

Nordenstam, Kerstin. 1979. *Norsk i svenskan*. Göteborg: Acta Universitatis Gothoburgensis.

Nortier, Jacomine M. 1990. *Code-Switching Among Young Moroccans in the Netherlands*. Dordrecht: Foris.

OMA 1989. *Issues in Multicultural Australia*. Canberra: Office of Multicultural Affairs.

Oksaar, Els. 1972. On code-switching. An analysis of bilingual norms. *Vortrag bei der dritten AILA Tagung*. Copenhagen.

Oksaar, Els (ed.). 1984. *Spracherwerb, Sprachkontakt, Sprachkonflikt*. Berlin; New York: De Gruyter.

Overbeke, Maurits van. 1972. *Introduction au problème du bilinguisme*. (Etude publiée par l'AIMAV, Association internationale pour la recherche et la diffusion des méthodes audio-visuelles et structuro-globales.) Brussels: Editions 'Labor'.

Ozolins, Uldis. 1993. *The Politics of Language in Australia*. Cambridge: Cambridge University Press.

Pandharipande, Rajeshwaie. 1998. Is genetic connection relevant in code-switching? Evidence from South Asian languages. In Jacobson (ed.), pp. 201–23.

Pandit, Ira. 1990. Grammaticality in codeswitching. In R. Jacobson (ed.), *Code-Switching as a Worldwide Phenomenon*. Berlin: Mouton de Gruyter, pp. 33–69.

Papadametre, Leo and Routoulas, Stephen. 2001. Social, political, educational, linguistic and cultural (dis-)incentives for languages education in Australia. *Journal of Multilingual and Multicultural Development* 22: 134–51.

Paradis, Michel. 1981. Neurolinguistic organization of a bilingual's two languages. In J. E. Copland and P. W. Davis (eds.), *The 7th LACUS Forum.* Columbia, SC: Hornbeam Press, pp. 486–94.

Paradis, Michel. 1987. *The Assessment of Bilingual Aphasia.* Hillsdale: Erlbaum.

Paternost, Joseph. 1976. Slovenian language on Minnesota's iron range: some sociolinguistic aspects of language maintenance and language shift. *General Linguistics* 16: 95–150.

Pauwels, Anne. 1986. *Immigrant Dialects and Language Maintenance in Australia.* Dordrecht: Foris.

Pauwels, Anne. 1995. Linguistic practices and language maintenance among bilingual women and men in Australia. *Nordlyd* 11: 21–50.

Pavlenko, Aneta. 1999/2000. New approaches to concepts in bilingual memory, *Bilingualism: Language and Cognition* 2(3): 209–30 and 3(1): 1–4.

Pawley, Andrew and Syder, Frances. 1983. Two puzzles for linguistic theory: native-like selection and native-like fluency. In J. C. Richards and R. W. Schmidt (eds.), *Language and Communication.* London: Longman, pp. 191–226.

Peñalosa, Fernando. 1980. *Chicano Sociolinguistics, a Brief Introduction.* Rowley, MA: Newbury House.

Peterson, Robert R. and Savoy, Pamela. 1998. Lexical selection and phonological encoding during language production: evidence for cascaded processing. *Journal of Experimental Psychology – Learning, Memory and Cognition* 24: 539–57.

Pfaff, Carol W. 1976. Functional and syntactic constraints on syntactic variation in code-mixing. In B. Steever et al. (eds.), *Papers from the Parasession on Diachronic Syntax.* Chicago Linguistic Society, pp. 248–59.

Pfaff, Carol W. 1979. Constraints on language mixing. *Language* 55: 291–318.

Pfaff, Carol W. 1991. Turkish in contact with German: language maintenance and loss among immigrant children in Berlin (West). *International Journal of the Sociology of Language* 90: 97–129.

Piaget, Jean. 1971. *Science of Education and the Psychology of the Child,* trans. D. Coltman. London: Longman.

Piller, Ingrid. 2001. Naturalization, language testing and its basis in ideologies of national identity and citizenship. *International Journal of Bilingualism* 5: 259–78.

Pléh, Csaba and Bodor, Péter. 2000. Linguistic superego in a normative language community and the stigmatization-hypercorrection dimension. *Multilingua* 19: 133–40.

Polomé, Edgar and Justus, Carol (eds.). 1999. *Language Change and Typological Variation: In Honor of Winfred P. Lehmann on the Occasion of his 83rd Birthday* (JIE Studies, Monograph 30). Washington, DC: Institute for the Study of Man.

Poplack, Shana. 1980. Sometimes I'll start a sentence in Spanish Y TERMINO EN ESPAÑOL: toward a typology of codeswitching. *Linguistics* 18: 581–618.

Poplack, Shana and Sankoff, David. 1988. A variationist approach to languages in contact. In U. Ammon, N. Dittmar and K. Mattheier (eds.), *Sociolinguistics.* Berlin: De Gruyter, pp. 1174–80.

Poplack, Shana and Meechan, Marjory. 1995. Patterns of language mixture: nominal structure in Wolof-French and Fongbe-French bilingual discourse. In Milroy and Muysken (eds.), pp. 199–232.

Poplack, Shana and Meechan, Marjory. 1998. Introduction: how languages fit together in codemixing. *International Journal of Bilingualism* 2(2): 127–38.

Poplack, Shana, Sankoff, David and Miller, Christopher. 1988. The social correlates and linguistic processes of lexical borrowing and assimilation. *Linguistics* 26: 47–104.

Poplack, Shana, Wheeler, Susan and Westwood, Anneli. 1989. Distinguishing language contact phenomena: evidence from Finnish-English bilingualism. In P. Lilius and M. Saari (eds.), *The Nordic Languages and Modern Linguistics 6, Proceedings of the 6th International Conference*. Helsinki, pp. 33–56.

Poulisse, Nanda. 1997. Language production in bilinguals. In de Groot and Kroll (eds.), pp. 201–24.

Poulisse, Nanda. 1999. *Slips of the Tongue*. Amsterdam: Benjamins.

Poulisse, Nanda and Bongaerts, Theo. 1994. First language use in second language production. *Applied Linguistics* 15: 36–57.

Preston, Dennis R. 1986. The case of American Polish. In D. Kastovsky and A. Szwedek (eds.), *Linguistics across Historical and Geographical Boundaries. In Honour of Jacek Fisiak on the Occasion of his Fiftieth Birthday*. Vol. 2. Berlin: Mouton de Gruyter, pp. 1015–23.

Primeau, G. 1983. *Les Hollandes à Montréal. Profil d'une communauté ethnique de Montréal*. Montréal: Conseil scolaire de l'île de Montréal.

Queen, Robin M. 2001. Bilingual intonation patterns: evidence of language change in Turkish-German bilingual children. *Language in Society* 30: 55–80.

Rayfield, Joan Rachel. 1970. *The Languages of a Bilingual Community*. The Hague: Mouton.

Riehl, Claudia M. 1998. Kontaktphänomene bei schriftlicher Textproduktion: Evidenzen für die mentale Repräsentation von Mehrsprachigkeit. Paper delivered at the Deutsche Gesellschaft für Sprache, Halle, 5 March 1998.

Riehl, Claudia M. 1999. Zur mentalen Repräsentationen der Mehrsprachigkeit. (Kolloquium, Grenzen und Grenzüberschreitungen; Halle, 2 March 1999).

Riehl, Claudia M. 2001. *Schreiben, Text und Mehrsprachigkeit*. Tübingen: Stauffenburg.

Rindler-Schjerve, Rosita. 1998. Codeswitching und Sprachkontaktforschung. *Grenzgänge* 5(9): 70–93.

Roberts, Mary C. 1999. Immigrant language maintenance in the Gujarati, Dutch and Samoan communities of Wellington. Unpublished PhD thesis, Victoria: University of Wellington.

Romaine, Suzanne. 1989. Pidgins, creoles, immigrant and dying languages. In Dorian (ed.), pp. 369–83.

Romaine, Suzanne. 1995. *Bilingualism*. Oxford: Blackwell.

Romaine, Suzanne and Lange, Deborah. 1991. The use of 'like' as a marker of reported speech and thought: a case of grammaticalisation in progress. *American Speech* 66: 227–79.

Rót, Sandor. 1985. On the national variety of Australian English. *Annales Universitatis Budapestiensis Ling*. Budapest. 16: 189–204.

Rudd, Kevin M. 1994. *Asian Languages and Australia's Economic Future*. Brisbane: Queensland Government Printer.

Rūķe-Draviņa, Velta. 1969. *Språk i kontakt*. Stockholm: Aldus/Bonniers.

Saitz, Robert Leonard. 1955. Functional Word-order in Old English Subject-Object Patterns. PhD Dissertation, University of Wisconsin.

Salmons, Joseph. 1990. Bilingual discourse marking: code switching, borrowing and convergence in some German-American dialects. *Linguistics* 28: 453–80.

Salmons, Joseph. 1994. Naturalness and morphological change in Texas German. In Berend and Mattheier (eds.), pp. 59–72.

Sankoff, David. 1998. A formal production-based explanation of the facts of code-switching. *Bilingualism: Language and Cognition* 1(1): 39–50.

Sankoff, David and Poplack, Shana. 1979. A formal grammar for code-switching. *Centro Working Papers 8*. New York: Centro de Estudios Puertorriqueños.

Sapir, Edward. 1921. *Language*. New York: Harcourt Brace.

Sasse, Hans J. 1992. Language decay and contact-induced similarities and differences. In M. Brenzinger (ed.), *Language Death*. Berlin: Mouton de Gruyter, pp. 59–80.

Savić, Jelena. 1995. Structural convergence and language change: evidence from Serbian/English code-switching. *Language in Society* 24(4): 475–93.

Schatz, Henriette. 1989. Code-switching or borrowing of English elements in the Dutch of Dutch-American immigrants. *ITL Review of Applied Linguistics* 83–4: 125–62.

Schiffrin, Deborah. 1987. *Discourse Markers*. Cambridge: Cambridge University Press.

Schmid, Monika. 2002. *First language Attrition, Use and Maintenance – the Case of German-Jews in Anglophone Countries*. Amsterdam: Benjamins.

Schmid, Stefan. 1994. *L'italiano degli spagnoli. Interlingue di immigrati nella Svizzera tedesca*. Milan: Franco Angeli.

Schmidt, Annette. 1985. *Young People's Dyirbal*. Cambridge: Cambridge University Press.

Schmitt, Elena. 2000. Overt and covert codeswitching in immigrant children from Russia. *International Journal of Bilingualism* 4: 9–28.

Schoenmakers-Klein Gunnewiek, Marian. 1998. *Taalverlies door taalcontact? Een onderzoek bij Portugese migranten*. Tilburg: Tilburg University Press.

Schourup, Lawrence. 1985. *Common Discourse Particles in English Conversation*. New York: Garland.

Schuchardt, Hugo. 1884. *Slawo-deutsches und slawo-italienisches*, edited and introduced by Dietrich Gerhardt (1971). Munich: Wilhelm Fink.

Seaman, P. David. 1972. *Modern Greek and American English in Contact*. The Hague: Mouton.

Sebba, Mark and Wootton, Tony. 1998. We, they and identity: sequential versus identity-related explanation in code-switching. In Auer (ed.), pp. 262–89.

Silva-Corvalán, Carmen. 1994. *Language Contact and Change: Spanish in Los Angeles*. Oxford: Clarendon Press; New York: Oxford University Press.

Simonini, R. C. Jr. 1956. Phonemic and analogic lapses in radio and television speech. *American Speech* 31: 252–63.

Skutnabb-Kangas, Tove and Phillipson, Robert, with Rannut, Mart. 1994. *Linguistic Human Rights*. Berlin: Mouton de Gruyter.

Smith, John-Charles. 1998. Types and tokens in language change: some evidence from Romance. In R. Hickey and S. Puppel (eds.), *Language History and Linguistic Modelling: a Festschrift for Jacek Fisiak on his 60th Birthday*. Berlin: Mouton de Gruyter, pp. 1099–111.

Smith, John-Charles. 1999. Markedness and morphosyntactic change revisited. In S. Embelton, J. Joseph and H. Niederehe (eds.), *The Emergence of the Modern Language Sciences. Studies on the transition from Historical-Comparative to Structural Linguistics in Honour of E.F.K. Koerner*, vol 2: *Methodological perspectives and applications*. Amsterdam: Benjamins, pp. 203–15.

Smolicz, Jerzy J. 1979. *Culture and Education in a Plural Society*. Canberra: Curriculum Development Centre.

Smolicz, Jerzy J. 1981. Core values and ethnic identity. *Ethnic and Racial Studies* 4: 75–90.

Smolicz, Jerzy J. and Harris, Roger McD. 1976. Ethnic language and immigrant youth. In Clyne (ed.), pp. 131–75.

Smolicz, Jerzy J. and Secombe, Margaret J. 1990. Language as a core value of culture among tertiary students of Chinese and Indian origin in Australia. *Journal of Asian Pacific Communication* 1: 229–46.

Smolicz, Jerzy J., Secombe, Margaret J. and Hunter, D. M. 2001. Family collectivism and minority languages as core values of culture among ethnic groups in Australia. *Journal of Multilingual and Multicultural Development* 22: 152–72.

Sridhar, S. N. 1978. On the function of code-mixing in Kannada. *International Journal of the Sociology of Language* 16: 109–17.

Stock, Heather. 1979. The Age Factor in Second Language Acquisition: German-speaking Postwar Migrants in South Australia. MA thesis, Monash University.

Stoffel, Hans-Peter. 1981. The morphological adaptation of loanwords from English in New Zealand Serbo-Croatian. *Wiener Slawistischer Almanach* 7: 243–52.

Stoffel, Hans-Peter. 1994. Dialect and standard language in a migrant situation: the case of New Zealand Croatian. *New Zealand Slavonic Journal* (Festschrift in honour of Patrick Waddington), 153–70.

Stolt, Birgit. 1964. *Die Sprachmischung in Luthers 'Tischreden'*. Stockholm: Almkvist and Wiksell.

Stolz, Thomas. 1987. Kreolistik und Germanistik: Niederländisch-basierte Sprachformen in Übersee. *Linguistische Berichte* 110: 283–318.

Sussex, Roland. 1982a. The phonetic interference of Australian English in Australian Polish. In Sussex (ed.), pp. 141–53.

Sussex, Roland (ed.). 1982b. *The Slavic Languages in Emigré Communities*. Carbondale/Edmonton: Linguistic Research.

Szitás, Judit. 1998. Einflüsse des Deutschen auf die Muttersprache ungarischer Immigranten in Deutschland. MA thesis, Institut für deutsche Sprache und Literatur, Universität Köln.

Tagliamonte, Sali and Hudson, Richard. 1999. 'Be like' et al. beyond America: the quotative system in British and Canadian youth. *Journal of Sociolinguistics* 3: 147–72.

Tajfel, Henri. 1974. Social identity and intergroup behaviour. *Social Science Information* 13: 65–93.

Takahara, Paul O. 1998. Functions of the English discourse marker 'anyway' and its corresponding contrastive Japanese discourse markers. In Jucker and Ziv (eds.), pp. 327–51.

Tamis, Anastasios. 1986. The State of Modern Greek as Spoken in Victoria. PhD thesis, University of Melbourne.

Tamis, Anastasios. 1988. The state of the Modern Greek language in Australia. In A. Kapardis and A. Tamis (eds.), *Greeks in Australia*. Melbourne: River Seine, pp. 67–93.

Thomason, Sarah. Forthcoming. Contact as a source of language change. In R. Janda and B. Joseph (eds.), *A Handbook of Historical Linguistics*. Oxford: Blackwell.

Thomason, Sarah and Kaufman, Terence. 1988. *Language Contact, Creolization, and Genetic Linguistics*. Berkeley: University of California Press.

Thompson, Sandra. 1978. Modern English from a typological point of view: some indication of the function of word order. *Linguistische Berichte* 54: 19–35.

Tompa, József. 1968. *Ungarische Grammatik*. The Hague: Mouton.

Trask, Robert Lawrence (ed.). 2000. *The Dictionary of Historical and Comparative Linguistics*. Edinburgh: Edinburgh University Press.

Treffers-Daller, Jeanine. 1994. *Mixing Two Languages: French-Dutch Contact in a Comparative Perspective*. Berlin: Mouton de Gruyter.

Treffers-Daller, Jeanine. 1998. Variability in code-switching styles: Turkish-German code-switching patterns. In Jacobson (ed.), pp. 177–98.

Tsokalidou, Roula. 1994. Cracking the Code – an Insight into Code-switching and Gender among Second Generation Greek-Australians. PhD thesis, Monash University.

Türker, Emel. 1998. The use of yap- in Turkish-Norwegian codeswitching. Panel paper at 9th International Conference on Turkish Linguistics, University of Oxford, 12–14 August 1998.

Turpin, Danielle. 1998. 'Le français: c'est le last frontier': the status of English-origin nouns in Acadian French. *International Journal of Bilingualism* 2: 221–33.

Uhmann, Stephen. 1998. Verbstellung in weil-Sätzen. *Zeitschrift für Sprachwissenschaft* 17: 92–139.

Valkhoff, M. F. 1972. *New light on Afrikaans and 'Malayo-Portuguese'*. Louvain: Editions Peeters Imprimerie Orientaliste.

Veltman, Calvin. 1983. *Language Shift in the United States*. Berlin: Mouton.

Vennemann, Theo. 1974. Topics, subjects and word order: from SXV to SVX via TVX. In J. Anderson and C. Jones (eds.), *Historical Linguistics*. Proceedings of 1st International Conference on Historical Linguistics, Edinburgh, 2–7 September. Amsterdam: North Holland, pp. 339–76.

Vennemann, Theo. 1975. An explanation of drift. In C. N. Li (ed.), *Word Order and Word Order change*. Austin: University of Texas Press, pp. 269–305.

Vignuzzi, Ugo. 1986. Why study Italian? In Bettoni (ed.), *Altro Polo*, pp. 171–204.

Vosse, Theo and Kempen, Gerard. 1989. A hybrid model of human sentence processing: parsing right-branching, center-embedded and cross-serial dependencies. *Proceedings of the Second International Conference on Parsing Technologies*. Cancun, Mexico.

Vũ Thanh Phuöng 1981. The Acoustic and Perceptual Nature of Tone in Vietnamese. PhD thesis, Australian National University.

Waas, Margit. 1996. *Language Attrition Downunder*. Frankfurt: Lang.

Walters, Joel. 2001. Sociopragmatic processing in bilingual production and attrition. In Klatter-Folmer and van Avermaet (eds.), pp. 83–140.

Warren, Jane. 1999. 'Wogspeak': the transformation of English in Melbourne. *Journal of Australian Studies* 62: 86–94.

Weinreich, Uriel. 1953. *Languages in Contact*. New York: Linguistic Circle of New York.

Weinreich, Uriel, Labov, William F. and Herzog, Marvin. 1968. Empirical foundations for a theory of language change. In W. P. Lehmann and Y. Malkiel (eds.), *Directions for Historical Linguistics*. Austin: University of Texas Press, pp. 95–189.

Wenskus, Otta. 1998. *Emblematischer Codewechsel und Verwandtes in der lateinischen Prosa*. Innsbruck: Universität Innsbruck.

Weydt, Harald. 1969. *Abtönungspartikeln. Die deutschen Modalwörter und ihre französischen Entsprechungen*. Bad Homburg: Gehlen.

Weydt, Harald (ed.). 1979. *Die Partikeln der deutschen Sprache*. Berlin: de Gruyter.

Wheeldon, Linda R. and Levelt, W. J. M. 1985. Monitoring the time course of phonological encoding. *Journal of Memory and Learning* 34: 311–34.

Whinnom, Keith. 1971. Linguistic hybridization and the 'special' case of pidgin and Creoles. In D. Hymes (ed.), *Pidginization and Creolization of Languages*. Cambridge: Cambridge University Press, pp. 91–116.

Whitney, William D. 1981. On mixture in language. *Transactions of the American Philological Society* 12: 5–26.

Wierzbicka, Anna. 1985. The double life of a bilingual. In R. Sussex and J. Zubrzycki (eds.), *Polish People and Culture in Australia*. Canberra: Department of Demography, ANU, pp. 187–223.

Wierzbicka, Anna. 1986. Does language reflect culture? Evidence from Australian English. *Language in Society* 15: 349–74.

Wierzbicka, Anna. 1991. *Cross-Cultural Pragmatics*. Berlin: Mouton de Gruyter.

Winter, Joanne. 2002. Discourse quotatives in Australian English: adolescents' performing voices. *Australian Journal of Linguistics* 23(1).

Winter, Joanne and Pauwels, Anne. 2000. Gender and language contact: research in the Australian context. *Journal of Multilingual and Multicultural Development* 21: 508–22.

Woods, Anya V. 2000. The Medium or the Message: Issues in Faith and Language in Ethnic Churches. PhD thesis, Monash University.

Wurzel, Wolfgang Ulrich. 1989. *Inflectional Morphology and Naturalness*. Dordrecht: Kluwer.

Yağmur, Kutlay. 1997. *First Language Attrition Among Turkish Speakers in Sydney*. Tilburg: Tilburg University Press.

Zheng, Lin. 1997. Tonal aspects of code-switching. *Monash University Linguistic Papers* 1(1): 53–63.

Zheng, Lin. 2000. Code-switching in Second Generation Chinese-Australian students. PhD thesis, Monash University.

Zipf, George K. 1948. *Human Behavior and the Principle of the Least Effort*. Cambridge, MA: Appleton Wesley.

Zubin, David and Köpcke, Klaus-Michael. 1986. Gender and folk typology: the indexical relation between grammatical and lexical categorization. In C. G.Craig (ed.), *Noun Classes and Categorization. Proceedings of a Symposium on Categorization and Noun Classification*. Amsterdam: Benjamins, pp. 139–80.

Zuckermann, Ghil'ad. MS. The Survival of Yiddish beneath Israeli.

Index of authors

Index of languages

Index of subjects